COMING TO YOUR Senses

MAKING SENSE OF THE ARTS

8th*edition*

JON D. GREEN

BYU ACADEMIC PUBLISHING

ISBN: 978-0-74093-066-9
For more information or permission to use material from this text or product contact:
BYU Academic Publishing
3991 WSC
Provo, UT 84602
Tel (801) 422–6231
Fax (801) 422–0070
academicpublishing@byu.edu

To report ideas or text corrections email us at:
textideas@byu.edu

ACKNOWLEDGMENTS

This book was born as a labor of love: love for the beauties the arts offer so freely; love for the more than twenty thousand students I have taught, whose curiosity and courage have made over thirty years of college teaching a singular sensation; love for a wife who loves me and the arts (in that order); love for children whose initial resistance to the arts has gradually given way to shameless devotion; love for all the colleagues who have held my hand, figuratively speaking, as I struggled to become a generalist in a world of specialists; love for the poorly paid army of graduate students whose suggestions have immeasurably enhanced the unity and content of this book; and love for a God who is very much alive to a world of intricate and vast symmetries against which the arts are paltry yet sublime reflections. I am also grateful to Giovanni Tata of Brigham Young University's Creative Works Division for funding this major revision of the text, as well as to the editorial services of Linda Hunter Adams and her cadre of gifted student editors: Spencer Green, John Robison, Kathryn Gille, Jacquelin Newman, and Kristi Thompson. Special appreciation goes to Kent Minson of the BYU Bookstore for his help in editing and designing this 8th edition.

CONTENTS

Preface

EDUCATION IN AMERICA

American education (K through 12) has limited its domain to the three Rs—reading, writing, and arithmetic. The arts—the fourth R—are often seen as "frills." Similarly, higher education trains the mind in the skills of logic and research. Some general education classes in college expose students to the arts, but these classes usually emphasize historical context rather than criticism and interpretation. Given the enormous power art exerts on the human psyche, it seems strange that school curricula place arts education on the sidelines. This wasn't always the case. In spite of his distrust of the arts, the Greek philosopher PLATO (ca. 428–348 or 347 B.C.) viewed music as a powerful teaching instrument, "because rhythm and harmony find their way into the inward places of the soul, on which they mightily fasten, imparting grace, and making the soul of him who is rightly educated graceful, or of him who is ill-educated ungraceful" (333).

"INTELLIGENCES"

Recent studies suggest a causal relationship between musical choices and social behavior. It is also clear that intelligence embraces a much wider range of human skills than IQ and GPA. Howard Gardner's book *Frames of Mind* identifies "multiple intelligences." In addition to verbal-linguistic and logical-mathematical, he cites the importance of musical, spatial, bodily-kinesthetic, naturalist, intra-personal, and inter-personal—a total of eight skill areas in the brain that can be pinpointed. They are all important and, like life itself, "are continuous with one another" (70). The legitimacy of multiple intelligences adds an important rationale for the interdisciplinary goals of this text.

Plato's previously mentioned claim for the educational value of musical training reveals what history missed in transferring the Greek heritage to later generations. We got *reason,* but we lost the holistic nature of Greek educational practices, the belief in the interconnectedness of all knowledge and the importance of integrating the GOOD, the TRUE, and the BEAUTIFUL into every aspect of life: music for Plato was powerful because of its ethical influence on the human soul (called the ethos of music); Pythagoras discovered that mathematical ratios could be used to create scales, which formed the basis of our own diatonic system; mathematics also figured into the proportions of Greek sculpture and architecture, often following the famous GOLDEN SECTION based on a ratio of 1.618:1, or approximately 8:5, an aesthetic ideal also found in natural forms and in the ideal human body.

RELIGION AND EDUCATION

Our Western culture has become a patchwork of often competing entities with few unifying threads to connect us to each other and to our past, partly because we have lost the spiritual base upon which this country was founded. Recent efforts at curricular reform have barely touched on the importance of religion and spirituality in the rise of this and other civilizations. This ignorance has led to lamentable miscalculations in our government's efforts to cope with the cultural revolutions in Eastern Europe and the Middle East, where religion often directly dictates political decisions. We forget that American culture itself grew out of a deeply spiritual base, from the early Puritans to the writings of Thoreau, Emerson, and William James. John Taylor Gatto, a New York teacher of the year, recently resigned from public school teaching because he felt the system undermines basic human values by replacing their importance with the "scientific vision" of the world (18). William J. Bennett has said that "the real crisis of our time is spiritual" (A5). The continuing neglect of the religious and spiritual roots of our culture by colleges and universities threatens to sever the vital link between the life of the spirit and the life of the mind in American culture.

HOLISTIC EDUCATION

This text represents a modest effort to reverse these educational trends and to rekindle in the minds and hearts of educated Americans a love for the Good, the True, and the Beautiful. Writing about the arts provides an ideal occasion for holistic education, because it engages the faculties of the whole person: the mind, the emotions, and the senses. Being required to document personal experiences with each art form brings the organizing powers of the mind to bear on the renegade impulses of the heart, in a word, to make sense of the senses. Diane Ackerman, in her book *A Natural History of the Senses,* perhaps says it best:

> The senses don't just make sense of life in bold or subtle acts of clarity, they tear reality apart into vibrant morsels and reassemble them into a meaningful pattern. . . . [They] feed shards of information to the brain like microscopic pieces of a jigsaw puzzle. . . . [T]he mind doesn't really dwell in the brain but travels the whole body on caravans of hormone and enzyme, busily making sense of the compound wonders we catalogue as touch, taste, smell, hearing, vision. (xvii, xix)

Thus, the primary objective of this text is to foster greater cultural awareness by engaging the reader in meaningful sensory contact with the major art forms of Western culture. The critical skills of looking, listening, and interpreting will last a lifetime by subtly coloring your forays into the unknown, as well as unveiling the lost delight in the familiar. And while the exercises in this text may not guarantee to everyone these rosy results, they will hopefully bring you to a new awareness of the value of the arts in enhancing the abundant life.

THE "DISEASE" OF LEARNING

Brand Blanchard defined education as "living in the presence of the best till one understands and likes it. Till the ways of feeling of fine minds become one's own. Till one catches their health by contagion" (quoted in *Great Ideas* 2). Blanchard's curious image—infecting people with the health-giving virus of great art—captures the paradox of cultural refinement: what tastes good to us may not be good for us, or the reverse, what is good for us may not taste good to us. Sometimes the best cultural fare is not that "tasty" (easily accessible) at the outset; it takes time to assimilate, but the result is often more emotionally and intellectually nutritious than what the media serves up for mass consumption. The parallels between the culinary and the cultural are both striking and commonplace: the cultured person has good taste because of selective exposure to the best his or her culture has to offer.

MAPPING THE TERRAIN

Mapping is an apt metaphor for describing the purposes of this text: it is a guidebook to an overland journey into somewhat uncharted terrain. Because we are traveling by land and not by air (a helicopter drop would ruin all the fun and much of the work), you should know at the outset some of the important road signs and intersections so you don't get lost. The text contains five sections:

I. The introductory section, LAYING THE FOUNDATIONS, is an orientation to help you see the "big picture" and to lay a foundation for preparing proper personal attitudes and expectations, so you can reach your destination (becoming a caring and informed critic of the arts).

II. The second section, AVENUES OF ACCESS, shows how our duality relates to the creative process, the aesthetic experience, aesthetic judgment, and concludes with some useful guidelines for writing about the arts.

III. The third section deals with the PERFORMING ARTS (poetry, dance, music, drama, music drama, and film).

IV. The fourth section deals with the VISUAL ARTS (painting, sculpture, and architecture).

V. The last section contains APPENDICES, aids in guiding your critical analyses, information on sources of subjects in the arts, and ways of expanding your involvement in the arts.

COMMENTARY ON THE ARTS

NOBEL PRIZE AWARD SPEECH

—*William Faulkner*

I feel that this award was not made to me as a man but to my work—a life's work in the agony and sweat of the human spirit, not for glory and least of all for profit, but to create out of the materials of the human spirit something which did not exist before. So this award is only mine in trust. It will not be difficult to find a dedication for the money part of it commensurate with the purpose and significance of its origin. But I would like to do the same with the acclaim too, by using this moment as a pinnacle from which I might be listened to by young men and women already dedicated to the same anguish and travail, among whom is already that one who will some day stand here where I am standing.

Our tragedy today is a general and universal physical fear so long sustained by now that we can even bear it. There are no longer problems of the spirit. There is only one question: When will I be blown up? Because of this, the young man or woman writing today has forgotten the problems of the human heart in conflict with itself which alone can make good writing because only that is worth writing about, worth the agony and the sweat.

He must learn them again. He must teach himself that the basest of all things is to be afraid; and, teaching himself that, forget it forever, leaving no room in his workshop for anything but the old verities and truths of the heart, the old universal truths lacking which any story is ephemeral and doomed—love and honor and pity and pride and compassion and sacrifice. Until he does so, he labors under a curse. He writes not of love but of lust, of defeats in which nobody loses anything of value, of victories without hope and, worst of all, without pity or compassion. His griefs grieve on no universal bones, leaving no scars. He writes not of the heart but of the glands.

Until he relearns these things, he will write as though he stood alone and watched the end of man. I decline to accept the end of man. It is easy enough to say that man is immortal simply because he will endure; that when the last ding-dong of doom has clanged and faded from the last worthless rock hanging tideless in the last red and dying evening, that even then there will still be one more sound: that of his *puny* inexhaustible voice, still talking. I refuse to accept this. I believe that man will not merely endure: he will prevail. He is immortal, not because he alone among creatures has an inexhaustible voice but because he has a soul, a spirit capable of compassion and sacrifice and endurance. The poet's, the writer's, duty is to write about these things. It is his privilege to help man endure by lifting his heart, by reminding him of the courage and honor and hope and pride and compassion and pity and sacrifice which have been the glory of his past. The poet's voice need not merely be the record of man, it can be one of the props, the pillars to help him endure and prevail.

WORKS CITED

Ackerman, Diane. A *Natural History of the Senses.* New York: Random House, 1990.

Bennett, William J. Quoted in *The Daily Herald* (Provo, Utah), 1 January 1994.

Gardner, Howard. *Frames of Mind: The Theory of Multiple Intelligences.* New York: Basic Books, 1983.

Gatto, John Taylor. Quoted in "Teacher attributes U.S. decline to its public school system." *Utah County Journal* 8 June 1993.

Plato. *Dialogues of Plato.* Ed. Robert M. Hutchins. *Great Books of the Western World.* 54 vols. Chicago: Encyclopaedia Britannica, 1952.

WEBSITES OF INTEREST

Howard Gardner

Additional information —
http://www.pz.harvard.edu/research/sumit.htm

Official site and additional information —
http://www.howardgardner.com/MI/mi.html

Multiple Intelligence Inventory —
http://www.ldrc.ca/projects/projects.php?id=42

William Faulkner

Audio of the speech —
http://nobelprize.org/nobel_prizes/literature/laureates/1949/faulkner-speech.html

LAYING THE FOUNDATIONS

Unit I

"Andreani." Albrecht Altdorfer.
Courtesy BYU Museum of Art.

WHAT ARE THE HUMANITIES?

Chapter 1

HISTORICAL OVERVIEW

INTRODUCTION

Anyone involved in the **humanities*** has, at one time or another, seen the blank stare that accompanies the answer to the question, "What is your field?" Many are puzzled by the discipline because it embraces so many different, yet related, fields—cultural history, philosophy, literature, the visual and performing arts, and so forth. To add to the confusion, each academic institution defines it somewhat differently, depending upon whether the curriculum reflects an emphasis on the **liberal arts** (history, philosophy, languages and literatures) or the **fine arts** (performing arts and visual arts). To penetrate this multifaceted discipline, it will be necessary to explore some possible definitions in historical context.

THE CLASSICAL DEFINITION

Our word "humanities" is related to the Latin *humanitas* or humanity, but also connotes good breeding, education, and cultural refinement. According to cultural historian Mortimer J. Adler, the humanities signifies "the general learning that should be the possession of all human beings" and is the equivalent of the Greek *pais* or *paidos,* referring to the upbringing of a child and related to the words *pedagogy* and *pediatrics* (v). The Romans used the word to refer to the legacy they inherited from Greek civilization, in particular Greek art and philosophy. Greek art reflected a rigorous allegiance to formal perfection.

***Bold terms** are defined in the Glossary (p. 245).

Our word "classic" still refers to the idealized beauty of Greek art—and their philosophy was highly rational. Our educational system, with its emphasis on intellectual training, owes a great debt to the Greeks, especially Socrates, Plato, and Aristotle.

THE MEDIEVAL DEFINITION

A fourth-century grammarian defined the humanities simply as "education and training in the good arts and disciplines," by which he meant the skills that would most likely make a person *humane.* In the Middle Ages, these were a central part of the cathedral school curriculum, consisting of seven "**Liberal Arts**:"—the *Trivium* (arts of words), namely grammar, rhetoric, and logic; and the *Quadrivium* (arts of numbers), geometry, astronomy, arithmetic, and music. We still define a "liberal arts education" as one in which a student has developed adequate communication and computational skills: how to think logically, speak persuasively, write clearly, and measure accurately.

Modern definitions of the humanities derive in large part from the *studia humanitatis* of the Italian Renaissance, which included five disciplines: grammar, rhetoric, poetry, history, and moral philosophy, comprising the "arts" of action and communication. **Art** in this general sense comes from the Latin *ars,* which simply means a technical skill. The equivalent Greek word is *techne,* which is the root of our word *technology.* Since the **Renaissance**, the humanities have come to consist of six large fields of study: religion, philosophy, art, music, literature, and history. They have often been paired as "the two cultures" that form the foundation of Western education. People usually consider themselves either "scientists" or "humanists" depending on their major focus, but all educated people must be a blend of the two in order to function successfully in today's complex world. The 1965 Act establishing the National Endowment for the Humanities (NEH) defined the humanities as "the study of languages, literature, history, and philosophy; the history, criticism, and theory of the arts; the history of law, religion, and science" (2).

A WORKING APPROACH TO THE HUMANITIES

INTERDISCIPLINARY

Because the humanities are so broadly defined, one can find humanities courses in several different areas within a college or university, including religion, fine arts, languages, philosophy, and history. While studies in fields such as art or music tend to be quite focused and oriented toward developing practical skills (how to paint or sing), humanities classes themselves are interdisciplinary, which means that their purpose is to make connections between the larger fields traditionally known as the *humanities*. A humanities class might explore how the music or architecture of eighteenth-century America reflects the religious and philosophical ideals of that time and place.

"SOPHIC" & "MANTIC"

An interesting way to look at this type of interdisciplinary approach is to consider the ancient division between the "sophic" and "mantic" sources of knowledge. **Mantic** comes from the Greek *mantis,* meaning *prophet* or *holy man* (as in praying mantis) and relates to our words *manic, mania,* and *maniac.* Thus, a mantic individual is one who relies more upon intuition and instinct than intellect. Plato thought that all inspired people, especially poets, were possessed with a kind of divine madness (*daemon*). **Sophic** derives from the Greek *sophos,* meaning *wise* and related to our words *philosophy* (love of wisdom) and *sophomore* (a wise fool). It describes a person who thinks analytically, who prefers fact over fancy. This sophic/mantic split finds curious parallels in several aspects of human experience, such as the divisions of the brain (in most people the left hemisphere is linear and logical while the right hemisphere is spatial and emotional), and the geographical orientation of the earth (the western hemisphere, the Occident, and the eastern hemisphere, the Orient). This parallel can also be seen in aca-

demic disciplines (the sciences and the humanities first articulated by C. P. Snow in *The Two Cultures*), and even in the humanities themselves (the liberal arts representing the sophic and the fine arts the mantic).

"LIBERAL" & "FINE"

In contrast to the classical "liberal" arts—literature, grammar, rhetoric, logic, geometry, astronomy, and music—the "fine" arts encompass the performing arts, the visual arts, and literature. An interdisciplinary approach to the humanities, therefore, attempts to bridge the disciplines of these two arts by drawing on the tools of the liberal arts (critical reading, thinking, and writing) in order to understand and articulate our experiences with the fine arts (the aesthetic and sensory domains). Thus, we use sophic methods to understand and articulate mantic ideas and experiences.

WHAT ARE THE AIMS OF A HOLISTIC EDUCATION?

BREADTH OR DEPTH?

Recently there has been a great deal of controversy surrounding the basic course requirements for undergraduates in universities throughout the United States. Many have been calling for a return to core courses based on the classics of Western civilization. Others (the multiculturists) are calling for just the opposite: a loosening of general education requirements because they are seen to be either racist, elitist, or chauvinistic. Nonetheless, statistics indicate that universities, in large measure, have become nothing more than vocational schools—preparing students for a specific career while largely ignoring the need to send well-rounded individuals into the work force. A humanistic or liberal arts education seeks for a balance between breadth and depth, between specialized and generalized knowledge. There are some who argue that if we all study the same things we will become alike. Lynne Cheney, former director of the NEH, protests:

> The Western tradition is a debate, though those who oppose its teaching seem to assume that it imposes consensus. What is the nature of human beings? One finds very different answers in Plato and Hobbes, or Hume and Voltaire. What is the relation of human beings to God? Milton and Nietzsche certainly do not agree. "Far from leading to a glorification of the status quo," philosopher Sidney Hook has written, " . . . the knowledge imparted by [Western civilization] courses, properly taught, is essential to understanding the world of our own experience, whether one seeks to alter or preserve it." (12, 13)

THE WESTERN TRADITION

In his book *The Closing of the American Mind*, Alan Bloom comments on the sad state of students who are no longer acquainted with the great works of Western literature:

> As the awareness that we owed almost exclusively to literary genius falters, people become more alike, for want of knowing that they can be otherwise. What poor substitutes for real diversity are the wild rainbows of dyed hair and other external differences that tell the observer nothing about what is inside. (62)

CULTURAL LITERACY

Finally, a humanistic education offers information and experience that is necessary to function well in a literate society. In *Cultural Literacy*, E. D. Hirsch argues that most Americans need not only more general information to participate fully in the life of their culture, but a *context* in which specialized terms are used. "Cultural literacy is represented not by a *prescriptive* list of books but rather by a *descriptive* list of the information actually possessed by literate Americans" (xiv). Hence, it doesn't matter what we all read, so long as we hold in common the same wealth of general knowledge. This basic idea is at the heart of Hirsch's strategy: there is a certain body of information we all need in order to communicate at all since understanding lies not in the isolated meaning of the words, but in their cultural context. We may all speak English, but we are gradually losing our shared cultural heritage, because students know little about their own culture. Learning about the humanities forges a vital link to our shared cultural heritage, the common ground that is lost when individuals are content simply to specialize in one particular field of study. Cultural literacy is a worthy goal for all human beings; it is second in importance to literacy itself.

COMMENTARY ON THE ARTS

"THE DISAPPEARANCE OF CULTURE"

—*Mortimer J. Adler*

During the last few years, my concern about the state of the higher learning in America has reached the panic stage, and my hopes for the reform of the American College and university have dwindled to the verge of despair.

The trouble is not simply that the sciences have displaced the humanities. The humanities, as currently taught and studied, are as much addicted to specialized scholarship as are the scientific departments to highly specialized research. The trouble rather is that the broadly educated generalist has become an endangered species. The ever-increasing specialization of knowledge in all fields has almost completely displaced the generalist.

In most of our colleges, the elective system reigns supreme. Its only requirement the choice of a major in one field of subject matter and a minor in another compels students to specialize before they have acquired the general cultivation that would acquaint them with the ideas and disciplines that are the components of human culture.

COLLEGES AS FARM TEAMS

When, in 1936, the late Robert M. Hutchins, president of the University of Chicago, published "The Higher Learning in America," he and I thought that the undergraduate college could be emancipated from the paralyzing clutch of the graduate and professional schools. They, like major-league baseball clubs, tend to regard the college as little more than a bush-league feeder station. We had some hopes for the establishment of a completely required curriculum. Our slender hope then was not entirely ill-founded. However much the colleges at that time needed drastic improvement, they were then in a golden age compared with the state they are in today.

In the last 40 years, the elective system has become even more chaotic in its offerings; specialization in every area of inquiry and study has grown more intense; and those who might have been disposed to become generalist teachers have been disabled by what William James called "The Ph.D. Octopus."

The slight hope possible to cherish in the 1930s has shrunk to the vanishing point today. The obstacles to the reforms required for the preservation of culture through the acculturation of the young now appear to be insuperable. The following things that would have to be done no longer seem feasible.

The acquirement of specialized scientific knowledge or of specialized scholarship in non-scientific or professional fields (the kind of knowledge that is not everybody's business) should be reserved for the graduate and professional schools. The Ph.D. should cease to be the *sine qua non* for the appointment of college teachers. Their competence should be the competence of generalists, not of specialists. The members of a college faculty should not be professors of this or that subject matter, or even members of this or that department in the graduate school. The college faculty should be completely autonomous, completely emancipated from the influence of the graduate school.

THE NEED FOR GENERALISTS

The elective system, with its majors and minors, should be abolished. Parents should send their young to college and the young should go to college not, as at present, mainly to acquire highly salable skills or to earn good livings, but solely for the purpose of becoming cultured human beings. Corporations should recognize that the most important posts they have to offer can be better filled by broadly trained generalists than by narrowly trained specialists.

None of these things is likely to happen; none can be brought about against the tide that is overwhelmingly in the opposite direction.

In the state of mind induced by these dismal considerations, I recently reread José Ortega y Gasset's *Revolt of the Masses,* first published in Spain in 1930. There, in a chapter entitled "The Barbarism of 'Specialization,'" he wrote of the scientist who "is only acquainted with one science, and even of that one only knows the small corner in which he is an active investigator." Ortega referred to such narrowly trained specialists or professionals as "learned ignoramuses,"—learned, but uncultured. As a result of an excessive specialization that is not balanced by general education, we have today, Ortega declared in 1930, more scientists, scholars, and professional men and women than ever before, but many fewer cultured human beings.

Reading that chapter sent me to a lecture Ortega gave earlier that year on "The Mission of the University." There I discovered a proposal for the reform of the university as radical as that proposed by Hutchins in 1936, but unknown to him at the time.

If I were to translate Ortega's message into terms appropriate to American institutions at present, I would render it as follows. The primary function of our institutions of higher learning, which means the function they should perform at the undergraduate level of the college, should be "to teach the ordinary student to be a cultured person."

The college should be the place where culture is transmitted by a curriculum entirely devoted to the humanistic learning of the generalist—philosophical in the sense that it deals with the basic ideas that are everybody's business. Unfortunately, philosophy today has become as specialized and technical as science. It is no longer everybody's business as it should be.

INCURABLE ILLNESS?

Anyone acquainted with the present state of American institutions of higher learning must know how much worse the situation is in 1978. The disease of specialization was accurately diagnosed by Ortega in 1930 and by Hutchins in 1936; but their prognoses did not accurately foresee that its sequelae, including the disappearance of culture from our colleges and universities and from our society, might make the malady incurable fifty years later.

The reforms they urged a half century ago no longer motivate even a sympathetic minority of academics. The evil that confronts us is not C. P. Snow's conflict between two cultures—the sciences vs. humanities—but the demise of culture itself, fragmented into an unintelligible chaos by the rampant specialization that has invaded all fields of learning. What Aristotle defined as *paideia,* the learning of the generalist that was the saving leaven in Western civilization from the Greeks until the end of the nineteenth century, no longer exists.

DISCUSSION QUESTIONS

1. Conduct your own straw poll concerning the definition of the humanities by asking several acquaintances one or both of the following two questions:

   a. What are the humanities?

   b. What should a liberal arts education accomplish?

   Note the variety of responses, even among educators. Ask several teachers in the humanities disciplines (English, history, philosophy, and so forth).

2. The root meaning of "liberal arts" is freedom. How does a liberal arts education free a person? Free from what? Freedom to do what?

3. If you were put in charge of the curriculum of a new kind of school that strove to teach "the general learning that should be the possession of all human beings," what specific courses would you place at the core?

4. Could you justify a common core of shared knowledge (in line with E. D. Hirsch's conception of "cultural literacy") to an earnest advocate of multiculturalism, who strongly believes we should replace the "classics" with works by minorities (blacks, Native Americans, Hispanics, and so forth)?

5. What is the basic difference between the liberal and fine arts? How are the humanities a bridge between the two?

6. Read the following quote from Ben Shahn's *The Shape of Content* and respond to the questions below.

   I have always believed that the character of a society is largely shaped and unified by its great creative works, that a society is molded upon its epics, and that it imagines in terms of its created things—its cathedrals, its works of art, its musical treasures, its literary and philosophic works. One might say that a public may be so unified because the highly personal experience is held in common by the many individual members of the public. The great moment at which Oedipus in his remorse tears out his eyes is a private moment— one of deepest inward emotion. And yet that emotion, produced by art, and many other such private and profound emotions, experiences, and images bound together the Greek people into a great civilization, and bound others all over the earth to them for all time to come. (39)

   a. Is it true that a society is "shaped," "unified," and "molded" by its great creative works? Explain.

   b. What are the great creative works by which our society is molded? List some.

   c. How have these works shaped and molded us, or how have they changed the way we think about and look at the world?

7. Consider the following quote from Plato's *Republic*:

   Musical training is a more potent [teaching] instrument than any other, because rhythm and harmony find their way into the inward places of the soul, on which they mightily fasten, imparting grace, and making the soul of him who is rightly educated graceful, or of him who is ill-educated ungraceful. (333)

Respond to Plato's view of the value of arts education. Can music really affect a person's ideas, feelings, behavior, or attitudes about life? Can you give some examples from your own experience? Was Darwin right when he suggested that "the loss of these [higher] tastes [may possibly be injurious] to the moral character, by enfeebling the emotional part of our nature"? Is there an ethical reason for becoming a cultured human being?

8. Consider the following quote from Leonard B. Meyer:

   The primitive seeks almost immediate gratification for his tendencies whether these be biological or musical. . . . [The mature individual is willing] to forgo immediate, and perhaps lesser, gratification for the sake of future ultimate gratification . . . [a sign] that the animal is becoming a man. (32–33)

Do you agree with Meyer's contention that the difference between art music and primitive music rests on what he calls the "speed of tendency gratification"? (32) What connection do you see between this claim and the effects of certain kinds of hard rock music on our culture and on the values and behavior of the rock culture?

WORKS CITED

Adler, Mortimer J. "The Disappearance of Culture." *Newsweek* (21 August 1978), 15.

———. *Paideia Problems and Possibilities*. New York: Macmillan, 1983.

Blanchard, Grand. *How to Get the Most from the Great Ideas*. Nashville: Carmichael and Carmichael, 1987.

Bloom, Alan. *The Closing of the American Mind*. New York: Simon and Schuster, 1987.

Cheney, Lynne. *The State of the Humanities in America*, Washington D.C.: U.S. G.P.O., 1988.

Hirsch, E. D. Jr. *Cultural Literacy: What Every American Needs to Know*. Boston: Houghton Mifflin, 1987.

Meyer, Leonard B. *Music, the Arts, and Ideas: Patterns and Predictions in Twentieth-Century Culture*. Chicago: University of Chicago Press, 1967.

National Arts and the Humanities Foundations: Joint Hearings before the Special Subcommittee on Arts and Humanities of the Committee on Labor and Public Welfare, U.S. Senate and the Special Subcommittee on Labor of the committee on Education and Labor, House of Representatives, Eighty-ninth Congress, First Session, on Bills to Establish National Foundations on the Arts and Humanities. Washington, D.C.: U.S. G.P.O., 1965.

Plato. *Republic*. Ed. Robert M. Hutchins. Vol. 7. *Great Books of the Western World*. 54 vols. Chicago: Encyclopaedia Britannica, 1952.

Shahn, Ben. *The Shape of Content*. Cambridge: Harvard University Press, 1980.

WEBSITES OF INTEREST

The Great Books, the Great Ideas, and a Lifetime of Learning, M.J. Adler — http://radicalacademy.com/adlerlowelllec.htm

Schooling Is Not Education, M.J. Adler — http://radicalacademy.com/adlerschooling.htm

Landino lecturing: woodcut title page of his Formulaio di lettre, *1492.*

THE COMMONWEALTH OF THE ARTS

Chapter 2

PURPOSES: WHY STUDY THE HUMANITIES?

WHY DOES IT MATTER?

That is a fair question to ask about this endeavor because some people see no practical use in learning about the arts. To many the arts are frills that can easily be dispensed with when school budgets are cut. This is a point of view shared by some whose profession requires intense, single-minded commitment, like coaching a prize-winning basketball team. Therefore, it was a somewhat fortuitous event that led Coach "Digger" Phelps to his personal discovery of the values of art. He seems to have viewed this as a significant turning point in his life, because he found out some things about himself and the world that he didn't know as a basketball coach, and may never have discovered had he not made a trip to Europe. Contained in Coach Phelps's brief account below are some of the major reasons why one should study the humanities.

> I had a very narrow vision of the world, and when I became a basketball coach, I guess my vision became even narrower. I lived basketball 365 days a year. When I became a basketball coach at Notre Dame, I thought I had gone to heaven. Then, in 1975, I took my first trip to Europe. It's hard to explain the impact, but all of a sudden, I saw another world. I went to museums—in Paris, London, Amsterdam—and I was overwhelmed by what I saw. I couldn't absorb all of the painters, so I fell in love with van Gogh. I studied his art. I studied his life, his struggles, his sorrows. I stopped being consumed by basketball. The change was visible. I took down the plaques and trophies in my office and I put up paintings. I switched off the hard rock music and tuned in to classical.

> I even gave up the colorful sports jackets that had become my trademark and bought three-piece suits. I still care very much about basketball. I still want to win. But there are so many other things in the world, so many things just as important, *more* important. Give me a choice now between winning the NCAA championship—for the first time in my career—and getting a van Gogh for my wall, and I'm going to have to do some very heavy thinking. (Phelps 12, emphasis added)

1. THE ARTS CAN BROADEN OUR VISION OF THE WORLD

The arts can broaden our vision of the world by letting us see into the lives of others. A painting, for example, is quite literally a window. It opens to vistas defined by the artist's unique point of view. We can learn to see how the world looks to another human being. This can also happen while reading a novel or listening to a symphony. The arts can counteract the strong tendency in our society toward specialization in the professions and exclusive rationalism in education. It is noteworthy that Coach Phelps has recently become involved in humanitarian projects, from stopping gangs and drugs in American cities to supervising a twenty-one-man Cambodian electoral team to supervise the country's first multiparty elections in twenty years. His discovery of van Gogh was a catalyst for important self-discovery and increased social awareness. Thus, a study of the humanities—philosophy, religion, literature, and art—deals in some measure with the ends of life, with possible goals of human existence.

2. THE ARTS CONNECT US WITH OTHERS AND WITH OUR OWN EMOTIONS

All human beings gain pleasure from the arts. We rejoice in another's creative expression—reading a well-crafted story or listening to a favorite piece of music. The arts can even deepen our appreciation for the human condition by bringing us into direct emotional contact with someone else's life experience. Van Gogh's self-portraits are moving visual testaments of a valiant struggle against madness and despair. The emotional impact of his art affirms the ultimate success of that struggle, at least for those of us who come after. It matters that we learn to feel deeply about another's suffering or success, because we grow most by sharing each other's burdens through communicating sympathy and understanding. The arts are particularly exacting forms of human communication.

3. THROUGH STUDY WE CAN EXPERIENCE THE ARTS MORE DEEPLY

Aristotle claimed that "to learn gives the liveliest pleasure, not only to philosophers but to men in general" (55). Viewing the arts with the critical skills of the humanities reveals deeper meanings in works. These skills involve new ways of seeing, listening, touching, and interpreting. The difference between learning about and directly experiencing could be likened to reading about oranges but never tasting one. So many accessible works of art have been created, and so many profound ideas have been explored throughout the history of the world, that we would be greatly impoverished if we had no knowledge of them.

4. ART TELLS US WHO WE ARE

Someone once noted: "Art begins by revealing the artist to you and ends by revealing you to yourself." **Aesthetic** experiences with the arts are ultimately self-reflexive. They tell us who we are and how we see the world. And the wonderful thing about the arts and humanities is that they form a bridge across time and space, like fiber-optic hook-ups to other times and places that can be piped into our own living rooms and enjoyed at our leisure. Modern technology is rapidly making all available knowledge accessible to everyone. Through his works van Gogh talks to us across time and space, as though he had strewn miniature time bombs in our path that go off when we rub against them, igniting our minds with new ideas and inflaming our feelings with compassion for his suffering.

VALUES: WHAT GOOD ARE THE HUMANITIES?

THE HUMANITIES AS A "BRIDGE"

The humanities, therefore, represent a kind of commonwealth of the arts, a cultural inheritance that celebrates our common humanity and that can greatly enhance the quality of our lives through exposure to the arts. This is why the humanities are often seen as a bridge between the past and the present, as well as a link between thinking and feeling, the psychological basis for calling humans dual creatures. Studying the humanities can help us make sense of our own experiences as they relate to universal human experience. The value of van Gogh's paintings for Coach Phelps lay in their power to broaden his vision and deepen his feelings about artistic greatness borne of human suffering. Entering the Cambodian killing fields at personal risk is a moving testimony to this broadened perspective. Everyone can have a love affair with art similar to that of Coach Phelps. All it requires is an open mind and a willingness to explore new territory. But this challenge often collides with the practical expectations of parents or the vocational demands of high school and college.

BRINGING IT ALL TOGETHER

One of the great "specialists" of the nineteenth century, Charles Darwin, recognized—perhaps too late in life—an irrevocable personal loss from overspecialization and the exclusively rationalist method of our educational system. He unwittingly gave up what Coach Phelps so ardently desired.

> Poetry of many kinds . . . gave me great pleasure, and even as a schoolboy I took intense delight in Shakespeare, especially in the historical plays. I have also said that formerly pictures gave me considerable, and music very great delight. But now for many years I cannot endure to read a line of poetry: I have tried lately to read Shakespeare, and found it so intolerably dull that it nauseated me. I have also almost lost my taste for pictures or music. . . . My mind seems to have become a kind of machine for grinding general laws out of large collections of facts, but why this should have caused the atrophy of that part of the brain alone, on which the higher tastes depend, I cannot conceive. . . . The loss of these tastes is a loss of happiness, and may possibly be injurious to the intellect, and more probably to the moral character, by enfeebling the emotional part of our nature. (81–82)

SCIENCE VS. THE HUMANITIES

In spite of Darwin's lament about the loss of these higher tastes, his great achievement was accomplished by an intense focus on one discipline (biology). The favored mode of science is to "divide and conquer," to become expert in increasingly narrower domains of knowledge, in short, to become specialists. The remarkable achievements of science over the past century or so represent the welcome fruits of this mode of rigorous inquiry. The humanities, on the other hand, have traditionally sought more general kinds of knowledge in an attempt to make creative connections between our present challenges and our past legacy. In this sense, the humanities look into the past as the sciences seek to shape the future. We need both perspectives to function as a culture, but we have arrived at a point in the early twenty-first century where generalists have become a vanishing breed.

With Robert M. Hutchins, former president of the University of Chicago, Mortimer J. Adler sought educational reforms that would avert this situation, mostly to no avail. Almost twenty-five years ago he warned that American education had become too specialized, that we had lost the primary function of undergraduate education, namely, "to teach the ordinary student to be a cultured person." As a result we face a bleak future: "The evil that confronts us is not C. P. Snow's conflict between two cultures—the sciences vs. humanities—but the demise of culture itself, fragmented into an unintelligible chaos by the rampant specialization that has invaded all fields of learning [including the humanities]" (15). Darwin's warning comes from the other side of the aisle, but it is equally sobering, because he recognized that all human faculties are interrelated, that when one is neglected, they all suffer: the intellect, the emotions, even the sense of right and wrong.

A truly "general" education invites us to develop the emotions in tandem with the intellect. This can happen only if we are willing to spend some leisure time reading, thinking, even daydreaming. People normally think of leisure time as free time, like sunbathing on the beach. Many are deceived by misleading interpretations of the Puritan work ethic. They believe that sitting around thinking is a waste of time. But the original concept of leisure involved making a calculated shift from practical pursuits—going to work, balancing the checkbook, cleaning the house, and so forth—to spiritual pursuits such as reading a good book, writing a letter, or listening to music. In other words, things that matter to human happiness are almost always ends—things worth doing for their own sakes—not means to ends, like making money. People who are active, both mentally and emotionally, are always involved in interesting activities to throw themselves into. Boredom for such a person would be unthinkable. An active mind is usually too busy to be bored. This text will draw you into experiences that are both enriching and troubling, ennobling and disorienting, but which will impart valuable knowledge, teach critical listening and looking skills, and, finally, help develop the writing skills necessary to preserve a written record of your sensory experiences.

THE REALITIES

Some who study this material will discover ideas and feelings that they never realized existed. Some experiences may not be pleasant at first, but they will likely be memorable and may eventually bring new insights into what it means to be an involved human being in a complex and contradictory world. For others the course may simply shed new light on old friends and familiar faces. Whichever the case may be, this endeavor is designed to enhance your life, to make it more than mere survival. The questions the humanities pose are not always easily answered, and you may end up with more questions than answers. This text invites you to learn to deal with ambiguities, to learn to express in words the sometimes profound experiences you will have with the arts.

COMMENTARY ON THE ARTS

"MY GRADUATION SPEECH"

—Neil Postman

Having sat through two dozen or so graduation speeches, I have naturally wondered why they are so often so bad. One reason, of course, is that the speakers are chosen for their eminence in some field, and not because they are either competent speakers or gifted writers. Another reason is that the audience is eager to be done with all ceremony so that it can proceed to some serious reveling. Thus any speech longer than, say, fifteen minutes will seem tedious, if not entirely pointless. There are other reasons as well, including the difficulty of saying something inspirational without being banal. Here I try my hand at writing a graduation speech, and not merely to discover if I can conquer the form. This is precisely what I would like to say to young people if I had their attention for a few minutes.

If you think my graduation speech is good, I hereby grant you permission to use it, without further approval from or credit to me, should you be in an appropriate situation.

Members of the faculty, parents, guests, and graduates,

have no fear. I am well aware that on a day of such high excitement, what you require, first and foremost, of any speaker is brevity. I shall not fail you in this respect. There are exactly eighty-five sentences in my speech, four of which you have just heard. It will take me about twelve minutes to speak all of them and I must tell you that such economy was not easy for me to arrange, because I have chosen as my topic the complex subject of your ancestors. Not, of course, your biological ancestors, about whom I know nothing, but your spiritual ancestors, about whom I know a little. To be specific, I want to tell you about two groups of people who lived many years ago but whose influence is still with us. They were very different from each other, representing opposite values and traditions. I think it is appropriate for you to be reminded of them on this day because, sooner than you know, you must align with the spirit of one or the spirit of the other.

The first group lived about 2,500 years ago in the place which we now call Greece, in a city they called Athens. We do not know as much about their origins as we would like. But we do know a great deal about their accomplishments. They were, for example, the first people to develop a complete alphabet, and therefore they became the first truly literate population on earth. They invented the idea of political democracy, which they practiced with a vigor that puts us to shame. They invented what we call philosophy. And they also invented what we call logic and rhetoric. They came very close to inventing what we call science, and one of them—Democritus by name—conceived of the atomic theory of matter 2,300 years before it occurred to any modern scientist. They composed and sang epic poems of unsurpassed beauty and insight. And they wrote and performed plays that, almost three millennia later, still have the power to make audiences laugh and weep. They even invented what, today, we call the Olympics, and among their values none stood higher than that in all things one should strive for excellence. They believed in reason. They believed in beauty. They believed in moderation. And they invented the word and the idea which we know today as ecology.

About two thousand years ago, the vitality of their culture declined and these people began to disappear. But not what they had created. Their imagination, art, politics, literature, and language spread all over the world so that, today, it is hardly possible to speak on any subject without repeating what some Athenian said on the matter twenty-five hundred years ago.

The second group of people lived in the place we now call Germany, and flourished about seventeen hundred years ago. We call them the Visigoths, and you may remember that your sixth- or seventh-grade teacher mentioned them. They were spectacularly good horsemen, which is about the only pleasant thing history can say of them. They were marauders—ruthless and brutal. Their language lacked subtlety and depth. Their art was crude and even grotesque. They swept down through Europe destroying everything in their path, and they overran the Roman Empire. There was nothing a Visigoth liked better than to burn a book, desecrate a building, or smash a work of art. From the Visigoths, we have no poetry, no theater, no logic, no science, no humane politics.

Like the Athenians, the Visigoths also disappeared, but not before they had ushered in the period known as the Dark Ages. It took Europe almost a thousand years to recover from the Visigoths.

Now, the point I want to make is that the Athenians and the Visigoths still survive, and they do so through us and the ways in which we conduct our lives. All around us—in this hall, in this community, in our city—there are people whose way of looking at the world reflects the way of the Athenians, and there are people whose way is the way of the Visigoths. I do not mean, of course, that our modern-day Athenians roam abstractedly through the streets reciting poetry and philosophy, or that the modern-day Visigoths are killers. I mean that to be an Athenian or a Visigoth is to organize your life around a set of values. An Athenian is an idea. And a Visigoth is an idea. Let me tell you briefly what these ideas consist of.

To be an Athenian is to hold knowledge and, especially, the quest for knowledge in high esteem. To contemplate, to reason, to experiment, to question—these are, to an Athenian, the most exalted activities a person can perform. To a Visigoth, the quest for knowledge is useless unless it can help you earn money or to gain power over other people.

To be an Athenian is to cherish language because you believe it to be humankind's most precious gift. In their use of language, Athenians strive for grace, precision, and variety. And they admire those who can achieve such skill. To a Visigoth, one word is as good as another, one sentence indistinguishable from another. A Visigoth's language aspires to nothing higher than the cliché.

To be an Athenian is to understand that the thread which holds civilized society together is thin and vulnerable; therefore, Athenians place great value on tradition, social restraint, and continuity. To an Athenian, bad manners are acts of violence against the social order. The modern Visigoth cares very little about any of this. The Visigoths think of themselves as the center of the universe. Tradition exists for their own convenience, good manners are an affectation and a burden, and history is merely what is in yesterday's paper.

To be an Athenian is to take an interest in public affairs and the improvement of public behavior. Indeed, the ancient Athenians had a word for people who did not. The word was *idiotes,* from which we get our word "idiot." A modern Visigoth is interested only in his own affairs and has no sense of the meaning of community.

And, finally, to be an Athenian is to esteem the discipline, skill, and taste that are required to produce enduring art. Therefore, in approaching a work of art, Athenians prepare their imagination through learning and experience. To a Visigoth, there is no measure of artistic excellence except popularity. What catches the fancy of the multitude is good. No other standard is respected or even acknowledged by the Visigoth.

Now, it must be obvious what all of this has to do with you. Eventually, like the rest of us, you must be on one side or the other. You must be an Athenian or a Visigoth. Of course, it is much harder to be an Athenian, for you must learn how to be one, you must work at being one, whereas we are all, in a way, natural-born Visigoths. That is why there are so many more Visigoths than Athenians. And I must tell you that you do not become an Athenian merely by attending school or accumulating academic degrees. My father-in-law was one of the most committed Athenians I have ever known, and he spent his entire adult life working as a dress cutter on Seventh Avenue in New York City. On the other hand, I know physicians, lawyers, and engineers who are Visigoths of unmistakable persuasion. And I must also tell you, as much in sorrow as in shame, that at some of our great universities, perhaps even this one, there are professors of whom we may fairly say they are closet Visigoths. And yet, you must not doubt for a moment that a school, after all, is essentially an Athenian idea. There is a direct link between the cultural achievements of Athens and what the faculty at this university is all about. I have no difficulty imagining that Plato, Aristotle, or Democritus would be quite at home in our classrooms. A Visigoth would merely scrawl obscenities on the wall.

And so, whether you were aware of it or not, the purpose of your having been at this university was to give you a glimpse of the Athenian way, to interest you in the Athenian way. We cannot know on this day how many of you will choose that way and how many will not. You are young and it is not given to us to see your future. But I will tell you this, with which I will close: I can wish for you no higher compliment than that in the future it will be reported that among your graduating class the Athenians mightily outnumbered the Visigoths.

Thank you, and congratulations.

DISCUSSION QUESTIONS

1. What parallels do you see between developing good tastes in art and food?

2. Find a color copy of one of van Gogh's self-portraits and decide why you think Coach "Digger" Phelps said: "I was overwhelmed by what I saw."

3. How do you explain the fact that van Gogh's works have commanded such enormous sums of money, even though he sold only two paintings in his lifetime? What is (should be) the basis for value in art?

4. Do you know anyone whose life was changed for the better by discovering art? Does art always improve one's life? Are all experiences with the arts positive and pleasant? Should they be? Can art be unsettling and still be good art?

5. How is it possible to lose the "higher tastes" as Darwin seems to have done? Can neglect of a "general education" cause a similar deprivation among the rest of us? Do all great achievements require such rigorous specialization and personal sacrifice?

6. What are the problems we face in trying to write about sensory experiences? Is some knowledge untranslatable from one medium to another? Isadora Duncan, the American pioneer of modern dance, once said: "If I could tell you what it [the dance] meant, there would be no point in dancing it" (Csaky 109).

WRITING EXERCISES

1. Document a personal instance in which some vivid sensory experience prompted a special insight or triggered some long-forgotten memory. Consider one of the most famous literary documentations of sense-triggered memory, the "tea-cake" episode from Marcel Proust's novel *Swann's Way:*

> [My mother] sent for one of those squat, plump little cakes called "petites madeleines," which look as though they had been moulded in the fluted valve of a scallop shell. And soon, mechanically, dispirited after a dreary day with the prospect of a depressing morrow, I raised to my lips a spoonful of the tea in which I had soaked a morsel of the cake. No sooner had the warm liquid mixed with the crumbs touched my palate than a shudder ran through me and I stopped, intent upon the extraordinary thing that was happening to me. An exquisite pleasure had invaded my

senses, something isolated, detached, with no suggestion of its origin. . . . Whence could it have come to me, this all-powerful joy? I sensed that it was connected with the taste of the tea and the cake, but that it infinitely transcended those savours, could not, indeed, be of the same nature. Whence did it come? What did it mean? How could I seize and apprehend it? (48)

2. Do you think that developing artistic skills (drawing, sculpting, writing poetry, reading musical notation, etc.) would enhance your ability to understand that medium? Why?

   What does it mean to truly know (as opposed to "knowing about") something?

   Does your method of learning in the various classes you have taken reinforce or undermine what we might call knowledge that lasts? How can you insure that you don't forget what you learn?

3. Come up with some tentative explanations as to the causes of such diametrically opposed reactions to art as "Digger" Phelps's (his discovery of art transformed his life) and Charles Darwin's (his involvement in science destroyed his former love of art). Are the arts and sciences contradictory modes of experience? In what ways do the sciences and the arts connect?

4. Agree or disagree with Alston Chase's commentary: "Students, whose role models are baseball players or rock stars, are unlikely to cherish knowledge. Those reared in the culture of instant gratification have little patience for the often laborious tasks of learning. A land wedded to wealth and entertainment is infertile soil for the flowering of wisdom" (*Salt Lake Tribune* A21).

WORKS CITED

Adler, Mortimer J. "The Disappearance of Culture." *Newsweek* 21 August 1978, 15.

Aristotle's Poetics. Trans. S. H. Butcher. New York: Hill & Wang, 1961.

Chase, Alston. "Without better education system, man will keep ruining planet." *Salt Lake Tribune* 8 October 1989: A21.

Darwin, Charles. *The Life and Letters of Charles Darwin.* Ed. Francis Darwin. New York: D. Appleton & Co., 1896.

Duncan, Isadora. Qtd. in *How Does It Feel?* Ed. Mick Csaky. New York: Harmony Books, 1979.

Phelps, Richard. "Winning Is *Not* the Only Thing." *Parade Magazine* (10 July 1983), 11–12.

Proust, Marcel. *Remembrance of Things Past.* Trans. C. K. Scott Moncrieff and Terence Kilmartin. 3 vols. New York: Random House, 1981.

WEBSITES OF INTEREST

Van Gogh Museum —
   http://www3.vangoghmuseum.nl/vgm/index.jsp

Janus.

OUR DUAL NATURE

Chapter 3

INTRODUCTION

Human beings have traditionally been defined as "dual creatures" consisting of reason and emotion. These dual tendencies that separate us from animals have given rise to a dual heritage: the sciences and the arts. We have already discovered that the humanities act as a bridge between the philosophical manifestations of human rationality, the "liberal arts," and the artistic manifestations of the urge to create, the "fine arts." In this sense, the humanities serve a valuable purpose in bringing our two natures into harmony with themselves. One simple example: writing about the arts requires the rational mind (left brain) to confront and conquer the renegade impulses of the heart (right brain).

PLATONIC MAN

This duality has been variously defined since ancient times. Plato's indictment of the arts in his *Republic* centers on their power to feed the emotions and to muddy the intellect. Technically, Plato's view of the human psyche consisted of three parts: the appetitive (the stomach), the emotional (the heart), and the rational (the brain). Nevertheless, the ideal Greek was, first and foremost, a rational creature. The reason/emotion dichotomy persisted into the Middle Ages, but was given a Christian slant by Augustine in his notion of flesh vs. spirit. In seventeenth-century France, Blaise Pascal described this tension as an

> internal war in man between reason and the passions. If he had only reason without passions . . . If he had only

> passions without reason . . . But having both, he cannot be without strife, being unable to be at peace with the one without being at war with the other. Thus he is always divided against and opposed to himself. (242)

ST. AUGUSTINE

AUGUSTINE (A.D. 354–430) was a man of the Middle Ages, caught in the middle of an all-too-human dilemma, whether to follow the enticements of the flesh or the dictates of the spirit. His *Confessions* (A.D. 397), the spiritual autobiography of one of the greatest intellects of the Western world, recounts the tensions of the divided self. We have all experienced personal variations on this universal theme.

> Many years of my life had passed by about twelve since in my nineteenth year I had read Cicero's *Hortensius,* and had been stirred to a zeal for wisdom. But although I came to despise earthly success, I put off giving time to the quest for wisdom. . . . But I was an unhappy young man, wretched as at the beginning of my adolescence when I prayed you for chastity and said: "Grant me chastity and continency, but not yet," I was afraid you might hear my prayer quickly, and that you might too rapidly heal me of the disease of lust which I preferred to satisfy rather than suppress. (Augustine 145)

MODERN MAN

Friedrich Nietzsche, in *Thus Spake Zarathustra*, puts a modern twist on our duality:

> Man is a rope, tied between beast and overman, a rope

over an abyss. . . . What is great in man is that he is a bridge and not an end. (15)

However one defines these polar tensions, human beings are drawn toward one or the other in their daily lives. Human nature and the conditions of life make these internal struggles inevitable and inescapable.

HUMAN AND CULTURAL DICHOTOMIES

It is possible to divide our two sides into categories that correspond to the division between the *liberal arts,* which represent our rational, thinking side, and the *fine arts,* which are primarily expressions of our emotional side. This, of course, is simplifying things drastically, but it gives us a jumping-off point from which we can discuss the apparent chasm that exists in both collective and individual personalities.

THE DUAL BRAIN

During the past two decades there has been growing interest in the apparent division of the human brain. The theory posits the right side (or hemisphere) of the brain as the creative, spatial, emotional side while the left side is more analytical, linear, and logical. Thus we often hear people referred to as being right-brained when they demonstrate some artistic gift and left-brained when they pursue physics or algebra. Considering the things you enjoy and the way you approach problems, are you more emotional or logical?

SOPHIC/MANTIC

Two words are often used to describe the cultural man-ifestations of these two sides of man: the Greek *sophia* (wisdom) and *mantis* (holy man). The word "sophic" is often used to describe a person who thinks analytically, who prefers fact over fancy. The "mantic" individual is one who relies more upon intuition and instinct than intellect. When we need guidance in our academic pur-suits we often seek the help of a professor, one who "pro-fesses" knowledge because of years of study and teaching. Yet sometimes we are impelled to seek a different type of guidance. Religious people, and almost all primitive peo-ples, look to a divine source for answers to profound ques-tions about the nature of the universe or the causes of human behavior. For these reasons the sophic search for wisdom is often conceived in somewhat horizontal terms (person to person), while the mantic approach is more vertically oriented (human to divine). So we see again that these two "ways of knowing" are connected and work best in tandem, somewhat like creative people who have their heads in the clouds but their feet firmly rooted in the practical matters of making things work.

THE QUINTESSENTIAL "SOPHIC" MAN

SOCRATES

SOCRATES (469–399 B.C.) is probably the greatest Western example of a sophic person. He is sometimes called the Father of Western Philosophy. Although we have no record of his having ever written anything him-self, we have many of Socrates' teachings preserved through the writings of his followers, particularly his most noted disciple, Plato. Socrates' memorable comment on everyone's ultimate responsibility to know is found in the phrase, "The unexamined life is not worth living" (45), by which he seems to argue for an intellectually probing attitude toward knowledge. His own behavior in the mar-ketplace in Athens reveals his tireless search for truth, not so much by experiment (as used in modern science), but by personal experience, a kind of wisdom borne of rea-soned thought in action.

HIS CHARACTER

Socrates had a great love of conversation. In contrast to the pre-Socratics, who were natural philosophers (inter-ested in the origin and nature of the physical world), Socrates was interested in human nature and how people view the world. For him, learning gave the greatest pleas-ure possible in life, and his devotion to the pursuit of wis-dom was uncompromising and inseparably connected to his stern moral convictions. Perhaps two of the most char-acteristic statements attributed to Socrates are:

"Give me beauty in the inward soul, and may the out-ward and inward man be one."

and

"No evil can happen to a good man, whether in life or after death."

Curiously, for someone with such a brilliant mind, Socrates was deeply conscious of his own ignorance. In the process of trying to prove the Delphic Oracle wrong in naming him the wisest man, Socrates sought one wiser than he by cross-examining those who "professed" to be wise, but these professors of wisdom withered under Socrates' probing cross-examination. Thus, Socrates sadly concluded:

I am wiser than this man: neither of us knows anything that is really worth knowing, but he thinks that he has knowledge when he has not, while I, having no knowledge, do not think that I have. I seem, at any rate, to be a little wiser than he is on this point: *I do not think that I know what I do not know.* (Plato 26, emphasis added)

THE "SOCRATIC METHOD"

For Socrates, therefore, acknowledging one's ignorance is the first step in acquiring wisdom. He firmly believed that everyone's fundamental duty was to inquire after truth. He pursued wisdom by means of a process we now call the **"Socratic method,"** which involves questioning answers more than answering questions. By asking probing questions and then questioning his students' answers, Socrates prompted others to discover the answers for themselves. He likened this process to the function of a midwife (his mother was a midwife): "I am a midwife who attends the birth of ideas." This self-directed mode of teaching and learning contrasts sharply with the passive learning typical of contemporary school systems, in which students are rewarded for successfully aping the teacher's ideas. The Socratic method assumes that the answers are already within the individual and simply have to be drawn out. In the volatile political arena of fifth-century B.C. Athens, Socrates saw himself as a gadfly, prodding the horse of state on to action and improvement.

FUNDAMENTAL VALUES

Although his radical teaching methods created a sense of insecurity in his students and got him into a lot of trouble with his peers, and even though he himself doubted much that shallower minds blindly accepted as truth, Socrates was nevertheless certain of a few fundamental values:

1. Virtue and wisdom are the greatest goods to which we can aspire.

2. Virtue creates an unshakable inner core of happiness and peace.

3. Our primary duty in life is to discourse on the *good,* the *true,* and the *beautiful.*

THE QUINTESSENTIAL "MANTIC" MAN

JESUS

As Socrates' rigorous cross-examinations make him the prime instance of the sophic mind, so the indirect spiritual mode of JESUS CHRIST makes him the perfect example of a mantic person. Socrates' rigorous ego-threatening logic can be compared to Jesus' compassionate spiritual discernment. While both men contended with their enemies in the marketplace of ideas, Socrates taught by *syllogism,* which means arguing from three propositions: two interconnected premises and a conclusion, as in "All men are mortal (major premise); kings are men (minor premise); therefore, kings are mortal (conclusion)." By contrast, Jesus' teaching method relied upon his sensitivity to human feelings (love, empathy) and the ability to imagine (hope) and trust (faith) in things that cannot be proven by fact or reason alone.

AS TEACHER

Rather than engaging his disciples in intellectual cross-examination, Christ taught by example and by means of parables (stories with a moral). It is obvious that he was not speaking to the sophic-minded when he taught the mantic "mysteries of the kingdom." For example, his encounter with Nicodemus, a "ruler of the Jews" and member of the Sanhedrin, showed the communication gap that exists between one who speaks figuratively and one who thinks literally. Nicodemus was confused by the concept of baptism as a "born again" experience. How, he wondered, can a man re-enter his mother's womb? (John 3). Christ's answer was perhaps even more vague to one who was trained in biblical interpretation:

> The wind bloweth where it listeth, and thou hearest the sound thereof, but canst not tell whence it cometh, and whither it goeth: so is every one that is born of the Spirit. (John 3:8)

THE BALANCED MIND

For people living in a technological environment, developing a mantic mentality requires a great deal of trust and self-confidence, even faith. This is where the great internal struggles of life begin, with intellect and intuition battling for control and supremacy. But the truly educated individual is at home with both. Socrates often admitted that his knowledge came from some divine, mystical source. After the Athenian court sentenced him to death, he took his friends aside to explain the meaning of what had happened.

> The prophetic guide has been constantly with me all through my life till now, opposing me even in trivial matters if I were not going to act rightly. And now you yourselves see what has happened to me—a thing which might be thought, and which is sometimes actually reckoned, the supreme evil. But the divine guide did not oppose me

when I was leaving my house in the morning, nor when I was coming up here to the court, nor at any point in my speech when I was going to say anything; though at other times it has often stopped me in the very act of speaking. . . . [Therefore] this thing that has come upon me must be a good; and those of us who think that death is an evil must needs be mistaken. (47)

Similarly, the impact of Christ on his disciples was not solely emotional or spiritual. After his resurrection, Jesus walked incognito with two of his disciples on the way to Emmaus, reasoning with them and teaching them from the scriptures "beginning at Moses . . . the things concerning himself" (Luke 24:27). After he suddenly disappeared when they recognized who he was, they responded: "Did not our heart burn within us, while he talked with us by the way, and while he opened to us the scriptures?" (Luke 24:32).

The Balanced Culture

By curious coincidence, American **culture** has been most molded by these two great traditions: Graeco-Roman philosophy and Hebrew-Christian theology. Their different worldviews represent a cultural analogue to our dual (sophic-mantic) natures. Their respective cultural artifacts (classical mythology and the Holy Bible) provide the major sources of subject matter for the arts in Western culture. Just as a person would be incomplete without a balanced commitment to the intellect and the imagination, so an education without a solid grounding in both traditions would be sadly one-sided and distorted.

COMMENTARY ON THE ARTS

Within & Without

—*Hermann Hesse*

There was once a man by the name of Frederick; he devoted himself to intellectual pursuits and had a wide range of knowledge. But not all knowledge was the same to him, nor was any thought as good as any other: he loved a certain type of thinking, and disdained and abominated the others. What he loved and revered was logic—that so admirable method—and, in general, what he called "science."

"Twice two is four," he used to say. "This I believe; and man must do his thinking on the basis of this truth."

He was not unaware, to be sure, that there were other sorts of thinking and knowledge; but they were not "science," and he held a low opinion of them. Although a freethinker, he was not intolerant of religion. Religion was founded on a tacit agreement among scientists. For several centuries their science had embraced nearly everything that existed on earth and was worth knowing, with the exception of one single province: the human soul. It had become a sort of custom, as time went on, to leave this to religion, and to tolerate its speculation on the soul, though without taking them seriously. Thus Frederick too was tolerant toward religion; but everything he recognized as superstition was profoundly odious and repugnant to him. Alien, uncultured, and retarded peoples might occupy themselves with it; in remote antiquity there might have been mystical or magical thinking; but since the birth of science and logic there was no longer any sense in making use of these outmoded and dubious tools.

So he said and so he thought; and when traces of superstition came to his attention he became angry and felt as if he had been touched by something hostile.

It angered him most of all, however, if he found such traces among his own sort, among educated men who were conversant with the principles of scientific thinking. And nothing was more painful and intolerable to him than that scandalous notion which lately he had sometimes heard expressed and discussed even by men of great culture—that absurd idea that "scientific thinking" was possibly not a supreme, timeless, eternal, foreordained, and unassailable mode of thought, but merely one of many, a transient way of thinking, not impervious to change and downfall. This irreverent, destructive, poisonous notion was abroad—even Frederick could not deny it; it had cropped up here and there as a result of the distress throughout the world brought about by war, revolution, and hunger, like a warning, like a white hand's ghostly writing on a white wall.

The more Frederick suffered from the fact that this idea existed and could so deeply distress him, the more passionately he assailed it and those whom he suspected of secretly believing in it. So far only a very few from among the truly educated had openly and frankly professed their belief in his new doctrine, a doctrine that seemed destined, should it gain in circulation and power, to destroy all spiritual values on earth and call forth chaos. Well, matters had not reached that point yet, and the scattered individuals who openly embraced the idea were still so few in number that they could be considered oddities and crotchety, peculiar fellows. But a drop of the poison, an emanation of that idea, could be perceived first on this side, then on that. Among the people and the half-educated no end of new doctrines could be found anyway, esoteric doctrines, sects, and discipleships; the world was full of them; everywhere one could scent out superstition, mysticism, spiritualistic cults, and other mysterious forces, which it was really necessary to combat, but to which science, as if from a private feeling of weakness, had for the present given free rein.

One day Frederick went to the house of one of his friends, with whom he had often studied. It so happened that he had not seen this friend for some time. While he was climbing the stairs of the house he tried to recall when and where it was that he had last been in his friend's company; but much as he could pride himself on his good memory for other things he could not remember. Because of this he fell imperceptibly into a certain vexation and ill humor, from which, as he stood before his friend's door, he was obliged forcibly to free himself.

Hardly had he greeted Erwin, his friend, when he noticed on his genial countenance a certain, as it were forbearing, smile, which it seemed to him he had never seen there before. And hardly had he seen this smile, which despite its friendliness he at once felt to be somehow mocking or hostile, when he immediately remembered what he had just been searching his memory for in vain—his last previous meeting with Erwin. He remembered that they had parted then without having quarreled, to be sure, but yet with a sense of inner discord and dissatisfaction, because Erwin, as it had seemed to him, had given far too little support to his attacks at that time on the realm of superstition.

It was strange. How could he have forgotten that entirely? And now he also knew that this was his only reason for not having sought out his friend for so long, merely this dissatisfaction, and that he had known this all the time, although he had invented for himself a host of other excuses for his repeated postponement of this visit.

Now they confronted one another; and it seemed to Frederick as if the little rift of that day had meantime tremendously widened. He felt that in this moment something was lacking between him and Erwin that had always been there before, an aura of solidarity, of spontaneous understanding—indeed, even of affection. Instead of these there was a vacuum. They greeted each other; spoke of the weather, their acquaintances, their health; and—God knows why!— with every word Frederick had the disquieting sensation that he was not quite understanding his friend, that his friend did not really know him, that his words were missing their mark, that they could find no common ground for a real conversation. Moreover Erwin still had that friendly smile on his face, which Frederick was beginning almost to hate.

During a pause in the laborious conversation Frederick looked about the studio he knew so well and saw, pinned loosely on the wall, a sheet of paper. This sight moved him strangely and awakened ancient memories; for he recalled that, long ago in their student years, this had been a habit of Erwin's, a way he sometimes chose of keeping a thinker's saying or a poet's verse fresh in his mind. He stood up and went to the wall to read the paper.

There, in Erwin's beautiful script, he read the words: "Nothing is without, nothing is within; for what is without is within."

Blanching, he stood motionless for a moment. There it was! There he stood face to face with what he feared! At another time he would have let this leaf of paper pass, would have tolerated it charitably as a whim, as a harmless foible to which anyone was entitled, perhaps as a trifling sentimentality calling for indulgence. But now it was different. He felt that these words not been set down for the sake of a fleeting poetic mood; it was not a vagary that Erwin had returned after so many years to a practice of his youth. What stood written here, as an avowal of his friend's concern at the moment, was mysticism! Erwin was unfaithful!

Slowly he turned to face him, whose smile was again radiant.

"Explain this to me!" he demanded

Erwin nodded, brimming with friendliness.

"Haven't you ever read this saying?"

"Certainly!" Frederick cried. "Of course I know it. It's mysticism, it's Gnosticism. It may be poetic, but—well, anyway, explain the saying to me, and why it's hanging on your wall!"

"Gladly," Erwin said. "The saying is a first introduction to an epistemology that I've been going into lately, and which has already brought me such happiness."

Frederick restrained his temper. He asked, "A new epistemology? Is there such a thing? And what is it called?"

"Oh," Erwin answered, "it's only new to me. It's already very old and venerable. It's called magic."

The word had been uttered. Profoundly astonished and startled by so candid a confession, Frederick, with a shudder, felt that he was confronted eye to eye with the archenemy, in the person of his friend. He did not know whether he was nearer rage or tears; the bitter feeling of irreparable loss possessed him. For a long time he remained silent.

Then, with a pretended decision in his voice, he began, "So now you want to become a magician?"

"Yes," Erwin replied unhesitatingly.

"A sort of sorcerer's apprentice, eh?"

"Certainly."

A clock could be heard ticking in the adjoining room, it was so quiet.

Then Frederick said, "This means, you know, that you are abandoning all fellowship with serious science, and hence all fellowship with me."

"I hope that is not so," Erwin answered. "But if that's the way it has to be, what else can I do?"

"What else can you do?" Frederick burst out. "Why, break, break once and for all with this childishness, this wretched and contemptible belief in magic! That's what else you can do, if you want to keep my respect."

Erwin smiled a little, although he too no longer seemed cheerful.

"You speak as if," he said so gently that through his quiet words Frederick's angry voice still seemed to be echoing about the room, "you speak as if that lay within my will, as if I had a choice, Frederick. That is not the case. I have no choice. It was not I that chose magic: magic chose me."

Frederick sighed deeply. "Then goodby," he said wearily, and stood up, without offering to shake hands.

"Not like that!" Erwin cried out. "No, you must not go from me like that. Pretend that one of us is lying on his death-bed—and that is so!—and that we must say farewell."

"But which of us, Erwin, is dying?"

"Today it is probably I, my friend. Whoever wishes to be born anew must be prepared to die." Once more Frederick went up to the sheet of paper and read the saying about within and without.

"Very well," he said finally. "You are right, it won't do any good to part in anger. I'll do what you wish; I'll pretend that one of us is dying. Before I go I want to make a last request of you."

"I'm glad," Erwin said. "Tell me, what kindness can I show you on our leavetaking?"

"I repeat my first question, and this is also my request: explain this saying to me, as well as you can."

Erwin reflected a moment and then spoke:

"Nothing is without, nothing is within. You know the religious meaning of this: God is everywhere. He is in the spirit, and also in nature. All is divine, because God is all. Formerly this was called pantheism. Then the philosophic meaning: we are used to divorcing the within from the without in our thinking, but this is not necessary. Our spirit is capable of withdrawing behind the limits we have set for it, into the beyond. Beyond the pair of antitheses of which our world consists a new and different knowledge begins. . . . But, my dear friend, I must confess to you—since my thinking has changed there are no longer any unambiguous words and sayings for me: every word has tens and hundreds of meanings. And here what you fear begins—magic."

Frederick wrinkled his brow and was about to interrupt, but Erwin looked at him disarmingly and continued, speaking more distinctly, "Let me give you an example. Take something of mine along with you, any object, and examine it a little from time to time. Soon the principle of the within and the without will reveal one of its many means to you."

He glanced about the room, took a small clay figurine from a wall shelf, and gave it to Frederick, saying:

"Take this with you as my parting gift. When this thing that I am now placing in your hands ceases to be outside of you and is within you, come to me again! But if it remains outside you, the way it is now, forever, then this parting of yours from me shall also be forever!"

Frederick wanted to say a great deal more; but Erwin took his hand, pressed it, and bade him farewell with an expression that permitted no further conversation.

Frederick left; descended the stairs (how prodigiously long ago he had climbed them!); went through the streets to his home, the little earthen figure in his hand, perplexed and sick of heart. In front of his house he stopped, shook the fist fiercely for a moment in which he was clutching the figurine, and felt a great urge to smash the ridiculous thing to the ground. He did not do so; he bit his lip and entered the house. Never before had he been so agitated, so tormented by conflicting emotions.

He looked for a place for his friend's gift, and put the figurine on top of a bookcase. For the time being it stayed there.

Occasionally, as the days went by, he looked at it, brooding on it and on its origins, and pondering the meaning that this foolish thing was to have for him. It was a small figure of a man or a god or an idol, with two faces, like the Roman god Janus, modeled rather crudely of clay and covered with a burnt and somewhat cracked glaze. The little image looked coarse and insignificant; certainly it was not Roman or Greek workmanship; more likely it was the work of some backward, primitive race in Africa or the South Seas. The two faces, which were exactly alike, bore an apathetic, indolent faintly grinning smile—it was downright ugly the way the little gnome squandered his stupid smile.

Frederick could not get used to the figure. It was totally unpleasant and offensive to him, it got in his way, it disturbed him. The very next day he took it down and put it on the stove, and a few days later moved it to a cupboard. Again and again it got in the path of his vision, as if it were forcing itself upon him; it laughed at him coldly and dull-wittedly, put on airs, demanded attention. After a few weeks he put it in the anteroom, between the photographs of Italy and the trivial little souvenirs which no one ever looked at. Now at least he saw the idol only when he was entering or leaving, and then he passed it quickly, without examining it more closely. But here too the thing still bothered him, though he did not admit this to himself.

With this shard, this two-faced monstrosity, vexation and torment had entered his life.

One day, months later, he returned from a short trip—he undertook such excursions now from time to time, as if something were driving him restlessly about; he entered his house, went through the anteroom, was greeted by the maid, and read the letters waiting for him. But he was ill at ease, as if he had forgotten something important; no book tempted him, no chair was comfortable. He began to rack his mind—what was the cause of this? Had he neglected something important? Eaten something unsettling? In reflecting it occurred to him that this disturbing feeling had come over him as he had entered the apartment. He returned to the anteroom and involuntarily his first glance sought the clay figure.

A strange fright went through him when he did not see the idol. It had disappeared. It was missing. Had it walked away on its little crockery legs? Flown away? By magic?

Frederick pulled himself together, and smiled at his nervousness. Then he began quietly to search the whole room. When he found nothing he called the maid. She came, was embarrassed, and admitted at once that she had dropped the thing while cleaning up.

"Where is it?"

It was not there any more. It had seemed so solid, that little thing; she had often had it in her hands; and yet it had shattered to a hundred little pieces and splinters, and could not be fixed. She had taken the fragments to a glazier, who had simply laughed at her; and then she had thrown them away.

Frederick dismissed the maid. He smiled. That was perfectly all right with him. He did not feel bad about the idol, God knows. The abomination was gone; now he would have peace. If only he had knocked the thing to pieces that very first day! What he had suffered in all this time! How sluggishly, strangely, craftily, evilly, satanically that idol had smiled at him! Well, now that it was gone he could admit it to himself: he had feared it, truly and sincerely feared it, this earthen god. Was it not the emblem and symbol of everything that was repugnant and intolerable to him, everything that he had recognized all along as pernicious, inimical, and worthy of suppression—an emblem of all superstitions, all darkness, all coercion of conscience and spirit? Did it not represent that ghastly power that one sometimes felt raging in the bowels of the earth, that distant earthquake, that approaching extinction of culture, that looming chaos? Had not this contemptible figure robbed him of his best friend—nay, not merely robbed, but made of the friend an enemy? Well, now the thing was gone. Vanished. Smashed to pieces. Done for. It was good so; it was much better than if he had destroyed it himself.

So he thought, or said. And he went about his affairs as before. But it was like a curse. Now, just when he had got more or less used to that ridiculous figure, just when the sight of it in its usual place on the anteroom table had gradually become a bit familiar and unimportant to him, now its absence began to torment him! Yes, he missed it every time he went through that room; all he could see there was the empty spot where it had formerly stood, and emptiness emanated from the spot and filled the room with strangeness.

Bad days and worse nights began for Frederick. He could no longer go through the anteroom without thinking of the idol with the two faces, missing it, and feeling that his thoughts were tethered to it. This became an agonizing compulsion for him. And it was not by any means simply on the occasions when he went through that room that he was gripped by his compulsion—ah, no. Just as emptiness and desolation radiated from the now empty spot on the anteroom table, so this compulsive idea radiated within him, gradually crowded all else aside, ranking and filling him with emptiness and strangeness.

Again and again he pictured the figure with utmost distinctness, just to make it clear to himself how preposterous it was to grieve its loss. He could see it in all its stupid ugliness and barbarity, with its vacuous yet crafty smile, with its two faces—indeed, as if under duress, full of hatred and with his mouth drawn awry, he found himself attempting to reproduce that smile. The question pestered him whether the two faces were really exactly alike. Had not one of them, perhaps only because of a little roughness or a crack in the glaze, had a somewhat different expression? Something quizzical? Something sphinx-like? And how peculiar the color of that glaze had been! Green, and blue, and gray, but also red, were in it—a glaze that he now kept finding often in other objects, in a window's reflection of the sun or in the mirrorings of a wet pavement.

He brooded a great deal on this glaze, at night too. It also struck him what a strange, foreign, illsounding, unfamiliar, almost malignant word "glaze" was. He analyzed the word, and once he even reversed the order of its letters. Then it read "ezalg." Now where the devil did this word get its sound from? He knew this word "ezalg," certainly he knew it; moreover, it was an unfriendly and bad word, a word with ugly and disturbing connotations. For a long while he tormented himself with this question. Finally he hit upon it: "ezalg" reminded him of a book that he had bought and read many years ago on a trip, and that had dismayed, plagued, and yet secretly fascinated him; it had been entitled *Princess Ezalka*. It was like a curse: everything connected with the figurine—the glaze, the blue, the green, the smile—signified hostility, tormenting and poisoning him. And how very peculiarly *he*, Erwin, his erstwhile friend, had smiled as he had given the idol into his hand! How very peculiarly, how very significantly, how very hostilely.

Frederick resisted manfully—and on many days not without success—the compulsive trend of his thoughts. He sensed the danger clearly: he did not want to go insane! No, it were better to die. Reason was necessary, life was not. And it occurred to him that perhaps *this* was magic, that Erwin, with the aid of that figure, had in some way enchanted him, and that he should fall as a sacrifice, as the defender of reason and science against these dismal powers. But if this were so, if he could even conceive of that as possible, then there *was* such a thing as magic, then there *was* sorcery. No, it were better to die!

A doctor recommended walks and baths; and sometimes, in search of amusement, he spent an evening at an inn. But it helped very little. He cursed Erwin; he cursed himself.

One night, as he often did now, he retired early and lay restlessly awake in bed, unable to sleep. He felt unwell and uneasy. He wanted to meditate; he wanted to find solace, wanted to speak sentences of some sort to himself, good sentences, comforting, reassuring ones, something with the straightforward serenity and lucidity of the sentence, "Twice two is four." Nothing came to mind; but, in a state almost of lightheadedness, he mumbled sounds and syllables to himself. Gradually words formed on his lips, and several times, without being sensible of its meaning, he said the same short sentence to himself, which had somehow taken form in him. He muttered it to himself, as if it might stupefy him, as if he might grope his way along it, as along a parapet, to sleep that eluded him on the narrow, narrow path that skirted the abyss.

But suddenly, when he spoke somewhat louder, the words he was mumbling penetrated his consciousness. He knew them: they were, "Yes, now you are within me!" And instantly he knew. He knew what they meant—that they referred to the clay idol and that now, in this gray night hour, he had accurately and exactly fulfilled the prophecy Erwin had made on that unearthly day, that now the figure, which he had held contemptuously in his

fingers then, was no longer outside him but within him! "For what is without is within."

Bounding up in a leap, he felt as if transfused with ice and fire. The world reeled about him, the planets stared at him insanely. He threw on some clothes, put on the light, left his house and ran in the middle of the night to Erwin's. There he saw a light burning in the studio window he knew so well; the door to the house was unlocked: everything seemed to be awaiting him. He rushed up the stairs. He walked unsteadily into Erwin's study, supported himself with trembling hands on the table. Erwin sat by the lamp, in its gentle light, contemplative, smiling.

Graciously Erwin arose. "You have come. That is good."

"Have you been expecting me?" Frederick whispered.

"I have been expecting you, as you know, from the moment you left here, taking my little gift with you. Has what I said then happened?"

"It has happened," Frederick said. "The idol is within me. I can't bear it any longer."

"Can I help you?" Erwin asked.

"I don't know. Do as you will. Tell me more of your magic. Tell me how the idol can get out of me again."

Erwin placed his hand on his friend's shoulder. He led him to an armchair and pressed him down in it. Then he spoke cordially to Frederick, smiling in an almost brotherly tone of voice:

"The idol will come out of you again. Have trust in me. Have trust in yourself. You have learned to believe in it. Now learn to love it! It is within you, but it is still dead, it is still a phantom to you. Awaken it, speak to it, question it! For it is you yourself! Do not hate it any longer, do not fear it, do not torment it—how you have tormented this poor idol, who was yet you yourself! How you have tormented yourself!"

"Is this the way to magic?" Frederick asked. He sat deep in the chair, as if he had grown older, and his voice was low.

"This is the way," Erwin replied, "and perhaps you have already taken the most difficult step. You have found by experience: the without can become the within. You have been beyond the pair of antitheses. It seemed hell to you; learn, my friend, it is heaven! For it is heaven that awaits you. Behold, this magic: to interchange the without and the within, not by compulsion, not in anguish, as you have done it, but freely, voluntarily. Summon up the past, summon up the future: both are in you! Until today you have been the slave of the within. Learn to be its master. That is magic."

NOTE: Translated by T. K. Brown, III.

DISCUSSION QUESTIONS

1. The "Delphic Oracle" was from Delphi. Where is Delphi? What is an oracle? Where do people in our day go when they want answers to questions about the future? About the weather? stock prices? demographic trends, etc.? How reliable are these sources?

2. Make a list of differences between the two terms *Sophic* and *Mantic*. Given your own personality and bent of mind, which tendency do you seem to represent most?

3. According to what you understand about the nature of Truth, which approach (mantic or sophic) can offer the most reliable handle on the way things really are? Why?

4. What did Socrates mean when he said: "No evil can happen to a good man"? Don't bad things happen to good people? And good things to bad people?

5. What is an example of the "Socratic Method" of teaching? Is it possible to teach that way anymore in a crowded contemporary classroom? Why or why not?

WORKS CITED

Augustine. *Confessions.* Trans. Henry Chadwick. Oxford University Press, 1991.

Nietzsche, Friedrich. *Thus Spake Zarathustra.* Trans. Walter Kaufmann. New York: Penguin, 1966.

Pascal, Blaise. *Pensées.* Ed. Robert M. Hutchins. 54 vols. *Great Books of the Western World.* Chicago: Encyclopaedia Britannica, 1952.

Plato. *Euthyphro, Apology, Crito, Phaedo.* Trans. F. J. Church. Indianapolis: Bobbs-Merrill, 1956.

AVENUES OF ACCESS

Unit II

"Housegirl" by Tara Green.

THE CREATIVE PROCESS:
THE ARTIST AND THE WORK
Chapter 4

INTRODUCTION

Evidence of our instinctive urge to create abounds in every era, from prehistoric times to the present. Shards of primitive pottery invariably contain fanciful designs, revealing the human need to grace an otherwise mundane object with beauty. A human hand outlined on a prehistoric cave wall in France proves humans have always possessed a creative urge: the need to leave evidence of some personal contribution behind for posterity. We can see how certain individuals have left their mark on humankind, sometimes anonymously, like the builders of the great Gothic cathedrals of Europe, and sometimes with great pomp and ceremony, like Ramses II of Egypt. We remember great **civilizations** by their artistic remains, whether architecture, music, dance, painting, or poetry.

THE NEED BEYOND REASON

Human beings seem to have a deep-seated need, not only to decorate their surroundings, but to give order to the world around them, whether by organizing the agenda for a board meeting or by spending the weekend sketching landscapes. It is easy to overlook the importance of this basic need for beauty because it is not essential to survival, only for living. In the following paragraph, Edward Hart underscores this primitive instinct by associating creativity with something as mundane as decorating a pot:

> Knowledge is its own end and beauty is its own end. When the most primitive human being added a design to the pot he had made, the design had no use. It did not make the pot either stronger or more leakproof. But it made the life of the maker richer for having conceived and executed the design; and it made the life of everyone who looked at it richer. That is the justification for the design on the pot, or for the design on a blanket or a canoe. The blanket is no warmer for the design, nor will the canoe float better; but to strip people of the means of responding to life in a distinctively human manner is to return them to a way of life indistinguishable from that of cattle. (44)

WHAT DOES IT MEAN TO CREATE?

Basically, creation involves the shaping of materials, like words, sounds, stones, movements, or colors, until they form a unity with some felt meaning. In successful art, this new whole is always greater than the sum of its parts. Virtually every civilization has a creation myth describing how the world, emerging out of chaos or nothingness, became ordered and beautiful. In this view, the act of creation endows human beings with divine status. It also endows a whole age with great significance by virtue of its artistic achievements. In his book *Civilisation*, Kenneth Clark comments on the ways in which whole cultures attempt to preserve a part of themselves for posterity. Quoting John Ruskin, Clark writes: "Great nations write their autobiographies in three manuscripts, the book of their deeds, the book of their words and the book of their art. Not one of these books can be understood unless we read the two others, but of the three the only trustworthy one is the last" (1).

The Creative Person

Creativity at its highest levels seems to involve both sides of the brain in a personal process that requires vision, inspiration, knowledge, and just plain hard work. Howard Gardner's extensive description of creativity in his recent book, *Creating Minds,* represents one of the most comprehensive definitions of the creative person since it is based on his theories of multiple intelligences. According to Gardner, the truly creative person exhibits most, if not all, of the following traits: "The creative individual is a person who regularly solves problems, fashions products, or defines new questions in a domain in a way that is initially considered novel but that ultimately becomes accepted in a particular cultural setting" (35).

While acknowledging the fact that creative people exhibit "a greater incidence of such personality traits as independence, self-confidence, unconventionality, alertness, ready access to unconscious processes, ambition, and commitment to work," Gardner cautions that "it is not clear whether people who already exhibit these characteristics become creative, or whether creative experiences endow them with these traits" (24). At any rate, creative individuals seem to have unusual capacities to become totally immersed in one task for long periods of time, and continue to work despite serious setbacks. In fact, "many of them continue to raise the ante, posing ever-greater challenges for themselves, even at the risk of sacrificing the customary rewards" (26). These creative individuals, whether artists or inventors, who impose order on the chaos around them, often do so at a high personal cost. They do not see things like everyone else and, therefore, are often rejected by the majority as being eccentric, even peculiar.

The Creative Vision

The arts beam their influence in both directions, for art is both a window through which we see into others' lives and a mirror reflecting our own personal biases and attachments. The art work can thus bind us to its maker in a symbiotic partnership: the artist taps into our common humanity (otherwise, how could a great work touch so many over such long periods of time?) and yet creates an utterly original slant on life (otherwise, how would it spark our intense interest?). Through the window of the work we see reflected in the artist's soul the burnished mirror of our own identity.

The Creative Process

We have already begun to answer the question "*why* do humans create?" but we still need to answer the question "*how* do we create?" The most exciting and exacting part of creation is the process. These rare sparks of sudden illumination are like lightning flashes in a thunderstorm: brief explosions of light preceded and followed by long stretches of darkness. Betty Edwards, a practicing artist and writer of books on creativity, has identified five distinct stages of creativity. They run parallel to the cognitive shifts she experiences while drawing. She has conceptualized them as alternating left-brain/right-brain modes of thinking.

1. The first stage (FIRST INSIGHT) involves seeing the "whole picture," a kind of puzzle with most of the pieces missing, a "vast and vague exploration" most congenial to the spatial orientation of right-brain functions (42). Often the creative act begins with something very simple, even vague. The artist will sometimes gain inspiration from an occurrence that is rather commonplace. The great Swedish filmmaker Ingmar Bergman admitted that a whole film could emerge from one loaded impulse:

   A film for me begins with something very vague—a chance remark or a bit of conversation, a hazy but agreeable event unrelated to any particular situation. It can be a few bars of music, a shaft of light across the street. . . . These are split-second impressions that disappear as quickly as they come, yet leave behind a mood—like pleasant dreams. It is a mental state, not an actual story, but one abounding in fertile associations and images. Most of all, it is a brightly colored thread sticking out of the dark sack of the unconscious. If I begin to wind up this thread, and do it carefully, a complete film will emerge. (15)

2. The creative process, however, is not a simple one. Although there may be an initial inspiration or serendipitous spark, the labor that must follow is often tortuous and drawn out. Thus, FIRST INSIGHT is followed by what Edwards calls the "SATURATION STAGE," in which the conscious mind becomes saturated with information up to the limit of its ability to contain it. This is the left-brain mode. This stage can create excruciating reactions in the creator. The following are excerpts from Gustave Flaubert's letters to his mistress, Louise Colet, during the time he was struggling to complete his great realistic novel, *Madame Bovary.*

   [January 12 or 14, 1852]: I am hideously worried, mortally depressed. My accursed Bovary is harrying me and driving me mad. . . . Ah, I am tired and discouraged! You call me Master. What a wretched Master! (309)

One year later he wrote:

[January 15, 1853]: Last week I spent five days writing one page, and I dropped everything else for it. (313)

Almost a year later:

[Friday night, 2 a.m., December 23, 1853]: . . . for I am weary of my usual snail's pace. But I fear the awakening, the disillusion that may come from the recopied pages. No matter; it is a delicious thing to write, whether well or badly—to be no longer yourself but to move in an entire universe of your own creating. (317)

Finally:

[Friday night, midnight, April 7, 1854]: I have just made a fresh copy of what I have written since New Year, or rather since the middle of February, for on my return from Paris I burned all my January work. It amounts to thirteen pages, no more, no less, thirteen pages in seven weeks. . . . What a struggle it has been! My God, what a struggle! Such drudgery! Such discouragement! (318)

3. Because thinking eventually loses its structure in the saturation phase—the puzzle pieces refuse to yield to logical analysis—a third (right-brain) stage kicks in, which Edwards calls "INCUBATION." Existing outside of conscious logic through a kind of visual logic, this mode "manipulates the gathered information in imagined visual space . . . trying for the 'best fit' (43). This incubation stage involves both expansion and reduction in the subconscious searching process. Artistic choices are dictated by intuition rather than intellect. Ezra Pound's experience writing his famous haiku, "In a Station of the Metro," illustrates how the artist rearranged his initial impulse several times before the final solution presented itself. He wrote a lengthy poem based on a single moment in the metro (the Paris subway). Yet he was not satisfied until the poem was reduced to a single sentence, and this *eighteen months* after writing the first draft. He wrote:

Three years ago in Paris I got out of a "metro" train at La Concorde, and saw suddenly a beautiful face, and then another and another, and then a beautiful child's face, and then another beautiful woman, and I tried all that day to find words for what this had meant to me, and I could not find any words that seemed to me worthy, or as lovely as that sudden emotion. . . . I wrote a thirty-line poem, and destroyed it because it was what we call work "of second intensity." Six months later I made a poem half that length; a year later I made the following hokku-like sentence:

The apparition of these faces in the crowd;
Petals, on a wet, black bough.
    (Qtd. in Condie and Lewis 231–232)

The creative process can, of course, work both ways,

by contraction and expansion. Over several months, Pound squeezed his lengthy first draft into two terse lines. Maurice Ravel, on the other hand, took a simple thirty two-bar theme and spun it out into a fifteen-minute orchestral gem called *Bolero*. Each time the passage is played it is assigned a different instrument or instruments in the orchestra, becoming gradually louder with each new entrance. The two-part melody itself never changes; the same theme is played again and again (eighteen times). *Bolero* is probably the composer's most famous work and illustrates the way the artist expands his original material to create a minor masterpiece. In even more dramatic fashion, Beethoven took a simple four-note motive and expanded it into a magnificent four-movement symphony (the Fifth). It didn't take much creativity to invent the "du-du-du dum" motive (some claim Beethoven borrowed the rhythm from a bird song in the Vienna woods), but it took real genius to spin those four notes into the fabric of a four-movement symphony.

4. The subconscious process of incubation can go on for days, weeks, months, or even years, as in the case of Pound or Ravel. But eventually everything flashes into focus in a sudden "AH-HA!" illumination, like Archimedes in his bathtub. As the resident mathematician of the tyrant Hiero of Syracuse, he was assigned the seemingly impossible task of measuring the volume of the king's crown, a gift from a subject, to determine whether it was made of pure gold. How does one measure an irregularly-shaped solid, short of pounding it into a brick? Archimedes' mind was occupied with this mathematical puzzle when, while settling into his bathtub, the solution came to him, and he exclaimed, "Eureka! I have found it!" He had come up with a right-brain solution to a left-brain problem.

5. What follows, according to Edwards, is one last stage, the left-mode "VERIFICATION," in which the artist (or scientist) tests the result to decide if it works: he / she writes the book, completes the sonata, solves the mathematical equation, or builds the machine. This final stage often involves the reactions of the reader, viewer, audience or critic.

In summary, the creative process involves five stages generally alternating between left-brain and right-brain functions:

1. FIRST INSIGHT (R-mode)

2. SATURATION (L-mode)

3. INCUBATION (R-mode)

4. "AH-HA"(R-mode)

5. VERIFICATION (L-mode)

COMMENTARY ON THE ARTS

GRAND VISIONS & TINY CLOSETS

—*Daniel Goleman, Paul Kaufman, & Michael Ray*

Our lives can be filled with creative moments, whatever we do, as long as we're flexible and open to new possibilities—willing to push beyond the routine. Consider the myriad faces of creativity:

- Groundbreaking ideas, like debt-for-land swaps that save tropical forests while helping impoverished countries, or the theory of relativity, or the concept of genetic engineering.

- The imaginative expression of caring and compassion: "meals-on-wheels" that bring food to the homebound; birthing rooms; the AIDS Quilt; Gandhi's strategy of protesting injustice with nonviolence.

- Grand visions of hope and truth that show the way to others—the Bill of Rights and the Gettysburg Address, Martin Luther King's "I have a dream" speech.

- Bright ideas that get you out of a logjam, like figuring out how to squeeze three more feet of closet space out of your bedroom, or how to pack more time into your day-to-day exercise, without giving up any of the other things you have to-or love to-do.

Whether great or small, each of these examples points to the essence of a creative act: one that is both novel and appropriate. An innovation is different from what's been done before—but that's not enough: it can't be just bizarre or eccentric. It must "work." To be creative, it must somehow be correct, useful, valuable, meaningful. The everyday expression of creativity often takes the form of trying out a new approach to a familiar dilemma. Says Dr. Teresa Amabile, a psychologist at Brandeis University, whose research is on creativity: "At work, a manager dealing with a sticky relationship between two workers can show creativity in how she handles it. She can get them to talk things over from a new perspective, or maybe bring in a third person to work with the other two, or figure out a practical way of separating them physically. It's not on the order of creativity that wins a Nobel Prize, but it is novel and it works."

CREATIVITY IS AKIN TO LEADERSHIP

However, it's not enough just to be novel and useful: an important dimension of creativity—especially the kinds of efforts that influence others and for which people become famous—is the audience. There is a crucial social dimension to the creative act.

"Being creative means you do something which is first of all unusual," says Howard Gardner, a development psychologist at Harvard University. "But it also makes enough sense, even though it's unusual, that other people take it seriously. I mean, I could talk while standing on my head, and that would be unusual, but unless I and other people found it was somehow adaptive, I couldn't be called creative for it.

"But if, say, I'd found some way to convey twice as much information in the same period of time and make you enjoy it more, that would be creative. And even if it were very unusual, it would catch on because it's an effective thing to do."

In short, how a creative effort is received makes a difference. Yet it can be argued that much of the world's creativity takes place anonymously in private moments, just for the pure pleasure of it, or for the joy of using one's talents in effective or beautiful ways. A flower arrangement in the living room, a poem in a private journal, or a cleverly constructed model boat may express creativity and never have an audience beyond the maker.

But for every act of creativity meant to have a larger impact, there needs to be an appropriate audience. In high-energy physics that audience consists of a few dozen scientific peers; in painting it might be a loose network of gallery owners, critics, and art lovers. The opinions of these audiences count far more in evaluating creativity than do the views of millions of others who have no expertise in the relevant field. Of course, that does not mean that critics are the final arbiter of a creative act. "Sophisticated" critics of the day, for instance, panned many of the greatest painters, including Monet and van Gogh.

Indeed, many of the world's most creative people have had to spend years pursuing their craft in a lonely vigil, hounded by naysayers. Virtually none of the great men and women whose creative drive has transformed the discipline in which they worked was met with acceptance at first. Most were attacked, but knew in their hearts that theirs was the right course anyway.

Creative efforts that do take hold in a given field must be persuasive to others. In the view of Professor Dean Simonton, this social dimension makes creativity akin to leadership: "A successful leader is someone who can persuade people to change their ideas or behavior. A successful creator is someone who gives other people a different way of looking at the world."

"It may be a different way of feeling about the world if it's creativity in the arts, like in poetry or painting, or a different way of understanding the world if it's in sciences," Simonton adds. "But in any case creativity is not something that's entirely within the individual—it involves reaching other people. It's a social fact, not just a psychological one. Creativity is not something that a person keeps in the closet; it comes into existence during the process of interacting with others."

BEING CREATIVE IN X

The social setting for creativity is usually one's field or domain. Says Howard Gardner, "A person isn't creative in general— you can't just say a person is 'creative.' You have to say he or she is creative in X, whether it's writing, being a teacher, or running an organization. People are creative in something."

Creativity is not a single ability that can be used by a person in any activity. According to Gardner, "Creativity isn't some kind of fluid that can ooze in any direction. The life of the mind is divided into different regions, which I call 'intelligences,' like math, language, or music. And a given person can be very original and inventive, even iconoclastically imaginative, in one of those areas without being particularly creative in any of the others."

This leads Gardner to view the creative individual as "someone who can regularly solve a problem, or can come up with something novel that becomes a valued product in a given domain." Gardner's definition of creativity is a departure from the ones found in most psychology textbooks. In those books creativity is described as some kind of global talent. Along with this view is the popular notion of handy tests that can tell people in a few minutes how creative they are.

The textbook view of creativity, says Gardner, "doesn't make any sense at all. I think you have to watch a person working for a while in a particular domain, whether it's chess, piano-playing, architecture, or trying to start a business or run a meeting. And you have to see what they do when problems come up, and how their solution is received. Then you can make your judgments about whether that person is creative or not."

"Now, the creative person," Gardner says, "has to be able to do that sort of thing regularly. It's not a flash-in-the-pan, one-time-only thing. It's a whole style of existence. People who are creative are always thinking about the domains in which they work. They're always tinkering. They're always saying, 'What makes sense here, what

doesn't make sense?' And if it doesn't make sense, 'Can I do something about it?'"

BIG C & LITTLE C

Creativity exists when key elements come together: novelty, appropriateness, and a receptive audience in its field.

That last element, the audience, applies mainly to "Big C" creativity, the glamorous achievements of geniuses. But all too many of us do not see ourselves as being very creative—because we don't have much of an audience for what we do. In fact, we focus too much on "Big C" creativity and overlook the ways each of us displays flair and imagination in our own lives.

"We've become narrow in the ways we think about creativity," observes Teresa Amabile. "We tend to think of creativity as rarefied: artists are creative, musicians are creative, so are poets and filmmakers. But the chef in her kitchen is showing creativity when she invents a variation on a recipe. A bricklayer shows creativity when he devises a new way of laying bricks, or of doing the same job with fewer materials."

Still, much of what we know about our subject comes from the study of the creative giants. Howard Gardner has studied creative geniuses working early in this century, and notes:

"The amazing thing about Albert Einstein, or Sigmund Freud, or Virginia Woolf, or Martha Graham, is that they didn't just do something new. They actually changed the field or domain in which they worked forever after. But absent an initial curiosity and passion, which every one of these people had from an early age, and absent years of commitment, when they really took dancing or painting or physics or statesmanship as far as other people had, they would never have had the kind of creative breakthrough that changes a whole field."

Gardner believes that what is true about the Big C creators holds for the rest of us. Each of us has a bent for a particular domain. "Every person has certain areas in which he or she has a special interest," says Gardner. "It could be something they do at work—the way they write memos or their craftsmanship at a factory—or the way they teach a lesson or sell something. After working for a while they can get to be pretty good—as good as anybody whom they know in their immediate world.

"Now, many people are satisfied at just being good, but I wouldn't use the word *creative* to describe this level of work."

However, there are others for whom simply being good at something is not enough—they need to be creative. "They can't get into flow when they're just doing things in a routine way," Gardner explains. "So what they do is to set small challenges for themselves, like making a meal a little differently from the way they've made it until now."

"Let's say this year you decide to plant your garden in a slightly different way. Or, if you're a teacher, you say to yourself, 'I'm sick of writing student reports this year in exactly the same old way. Instead I'm going to give the student reports earlier and allow the kids to give me some kind of feedback.'"

"None of these things is going to get you into the encyclopedia. You're not likely to change the way gardening, cooking, or teaching will be done in the future. But you are going beyond the routine and conventional, and they give you a kind of pleasure that is quite analogous to what the Big C creative individuals get."

CREATIVITY STEW

Daily life is a major arena for innovation and problem-solving—the largest but least honored realm of the creative spirit. As Freud said, two hallmarks of a healthy life are the abilities to love and to work. Each requires imagination.

"Being creative is kind of like making a stew," says Teresa Amabile. "There are three basic ingredients to creativity, just as there are three basic kinds of things a stew needs to be really good."

The essential ingredient, something like the vegetables or the meat in a stew, is expertise in a specific area: domain skills. These skills represent your basic mastery of a field. To possess these skills means that you know how to write musical notation, how to skillfully use a computer graphics program, or how to do scientific experiments.

"No one is going to do anything creative in nuclear physics unless that person knows something—and probably a great deal—about nuclear physics," Amabile observes. "In the same way an artist isn't going to be creative unless that person has the technical skills required for say, making etchings or mixing colors. The ingredients of creativity start with skill in the domain—with the expertise.

Many people have a flair for something. "Talent is the natural propensity for being able to produce great work in a particular domain," says Amabile. "For example, it's highly unlikely that, given the kind of musical training that Mozart was given, just any child could end up producing the work that Mozart produced. There was something Mozart had from the start that made it easy for him to listen to music, to understand it, and be able to produce so much, so well, at such an early age."

But without training in the skills of a domain, even the most promising talent will languish. And with proper skill development, even an average talent can become the basis for creativity.

The second ingredient in the stew is what Amabile calls "creative thinking skills": ways of approaching the world that allow you to find a novel possibility and see through to full execution. "These are like the spices and herbs you use to bring out the flavor of the basic ingredients in a stew," Amabile says. "They make the flavors unique, help the basic ingredients to blend and bring out something different."

These creative thinking skills include being able to imagine a diverse range of possibilities, being persistent in tackling a problem, and having high standards for work. "They also include the ability to turn things over in your mind, like trying to make the strange familiar and the familiar strange," Amabile adds. "Many of these skills have to do with being an independent person: being willing to take risks and having the courage to try something you've never done before."

Another variety of these skills has to do with sensing how to nurture the creative process itself, such as knowing when to let go of a problem and allow it to incubate for a while. If a person has only technical skills in a field—the first ingredient—but no creative thinking skills, the stew will turn out flat and flavorless.

Finally, the element that really cooks the creative stew is passion. The psychological term is *intrinsic motivation*, the urge to do something for the sheer pleasure of doing it rather than for any prize or compensation. The opposite kind of motivation—extrinsic—makes you do something not because you want to, but because you ought to. You do it for a reward, to please someone, or to get a good evaluation.

Creativity begins to cook when people are motivated by the pure enjoyment of what they are doing. A Nobel Prize-winning physicist, Amabile recalls, was asked what he thought made the difference between creative and uncreative scientists. He said it was whether or not their work was "a labor of love."

The most successful, groundbreaking scientists are not always the most gifted, but the ones who are impelled by a driving curiosity. To some degree a strong passion can makeup for a lack of raw talent. Passion "is like the fire underneath the soup pot," Amabile says. "It really heats everything up, blends the flavors, and makes those spices mix with the basic ingredients to produce something that tastes wonderful."

AFFINITY & PERSISTENCE

Creativity begins with an affinity for something. It's like falling in love. "The most important thing at the beginning is for an individual to feel some kind of emotional connection to something," says Howard Gardner.

Albert Einstein's fascination with physics began when he was just five, when he was ill in bed. His father brought him a present—a small magnetic compass. For hours, Einstein lay in bed, entranced by the needle that infallibly pointed the way north. When he was close to seventy, Einstein said, "This experience made a deep and lasting impression on me. Something deeply hidden had to be behind things."

Gardner believes such childhood moments are one key to understanding creative lives. "Without that initial love and emotional connection, I think that the chances of doing good creative work later on are minimal," Gardner says. "But the initial intoxication is not enough in itself. It essentially moves you to take steps to learn more about the thing that first interests you, and to discover its complexities, its difficulties, its strengths and obscurities."

From that initial love of doing something comes persistence. People who care passionately about what they are doing don't give up easily. When frustration comes, they persist. When people are resistant to their innovation, they keep going anyway. As Thomas Edison said, "Sticking to it is the genius!"

Deaf and blind, Helen Keller was cut off from the world and human contact until Anne Sullivan came along. Sullivan's creativity lay in her passion and her refusal to give up. She was willing to persist in her determination to reach Helen.

Years later, Helen Keller recalled that first moment when that persistence, love, and passion bore fruit:

"My teacher Anne Mansfield Sullivan had been with me nearly a month, and she taught me the names of a number of objects. She would put them in my hand, spell out their names with her fingers, and help me form the letters."

"But I didn't have the faintest idea of what she was doing. I do not know what I thought. I have only a tactile memory of my fingers going through those motions and changing from one position to another."

"One day she handed me a cup and spelled the word. Then she poured some liquid into the cup and spelled the letters: W-A-T-E-R."

"She says I look puzzled. I was confusing the two words, spelling cup for water and water for cup."

"Finally I became angry because Miss Sullivan kept repeating the words over and over. In despair she led me out to the ivy-covered pump house and made me hold the cup under the spout while she pumped."

"In her other hand she spelled W-A-T-E-R emphatically. I stood still, my whole body and attention fixed on the motion of her fingers. As the cool stream flowed over my hand, all at once, there was a strange stir within me, a misty consciousness, a sense of something remembered."

"It was as if I had come back to life after being dead."

CREATIVITY IS AGELESS

The potential for creativity is always present. Creativity need not wane as life goes on. "Old paint as it ages sometimes becomes transparent," wrote Lillian Hellman. "When that happens it's possible in some pictures to see the original lines. A tree will show through a woman's dress. A child makes way for a dog. And a large boat is no longer in an open sea. This is called *pentimento*, because the painter repented, changing his mind. Perhaps it would be as well to say that the old conception was replaced by a later choice. It's a way of seeing, and then seeing again."

Bill Fitzpatrick rediscovered his creativity late in life. He is proof that what we are born with is always there—that one can see and then see again. In his retirement years he took up painting, something he had loved as a young man. Now in his eighties, Fitzpatrick has won many awards for his watercolors.

"I know too many people who just sit around waiting for the undertaker," says Fitzpatrick. "I think people who are going to retire should get involved in something that's going to take their time, their effort, and their thought."

"I'm eighty, but I don't think I'm eighty—I'm sort of a stiff, hurtin' fifty. I think it's important to live like that; otherwise you're vegetating."

As a child Fitzpatrick thought he would become an artist. But then the Depression came. Like so many others, he took the best job he could find. And so, for thirty-one years he worked for Nabisco as a driver. But through it all, he would work away at his painting, finding spare moments in the long working hours. That was why he began painting watercolors: it was easy to pick up and put down. When he retired he became more serious and started entering shows.

"People say, 'If only I had the talent to draw.' They've got it, I tell them. Because once you've got the urge and you start it, it's all mechanical after that. The only thing that isn't mechanical is the creativity you use to think out your problems."

"Creativity is very important in one's life—it gives you diversity. Being creative, you try different ways of doing things. And being creative, you naturally make lots of mistakes. But if you have the courage to stay with it despite your mistakes, you'll get the answer."

"I keep going and I don't have time to think about my troubles. I'm having a ball. Once you've lost that, I think you may as well pack it in. The main thing is just don't grow up!"

Erik Erikson, the psychologist who charted the stages of personal growth over a lifetime, described the triumph of the last stage of life as a "grand generativity": a deep concern for the younger generation and for generations yet unborn. Grand generativity is a wise and creative approach to nurturing others, an affirmation of life itself in the face of death. Often, the community at large is the beneficiary of the generative older person.

Now 100 years old and blind, Mary Stoneman Douglas continues her battle to save the Florida Everglades. She began her crusade nearly half a century earlier, long before today's environmental movement, with her book *Rivers of Grass*. In 1947 she showed that the Everglades was a vast yet fragile ecosystem that was already being depleted by agricultural irrigation and encroached upon by housing developments. Educating newcomers to the state about the continuing peril to the marshlands, Mrs. Douglas founded Friends of the Everglades and is now finishing her tenth book on the subject. "There is nothing inherently wrong with a brain in your nineties," she wrote in her 1987 autobiography, *Voices of the River*. "If you keep it fed and interested, you'll find it lasts you very well."

Pablo Picasso said: "Age only matters when one is aging. Now that I have arrived at a great age, I might as well be twenty." The creative spirit, far from declining with age, may actually gain in strength and vigor as an older man or woman—squarely facing the prospect of imminent death—concentrates on what truly matters.

DISCUSSION QUESTIONS

1. Reread John Ruskin's quote (29). Is he right in insisting that art is the "only trustworthy" cultural artifact? How might (or might not) Thomas Jefferson's self-built home, "Monticello," say more about his character and cultural agenda than his speeches or journal entries? Or, for that matter, the "Declaration of Independence"?

2. Is creativity confined only to artistic endeavors? Are

scientific discoveries also the result of creative leaps of faith? Is the scientific creative process similar to Betty Edwards's five-stage paradigm?

3. If we define creativity as the act of giving order to chaos, in what way(s) can you qualify as creative without becoming a practicing artist or scientific researcher?

4. In what way does the creative act (and its product) ensure the creator's immortality? Is that a possible motive behind the creative act?

5. What does the alternating left-brain/right-brain nature of the creative process tell you about the nature of creativity? About the need for holistic education? About the value of a broader definition of human intelligence than IQs or GPA's?

WORKS CITED

Bergman, Ingmar. *Four Screenplays of Ingmar Bergman*. Trans. Lars Malmstrom and David Kushner. New York: Simon & Schuster, 1960.

Clark, Kenneth. *Civilisation*. New York: Harper & Row, 1969.

Condie, R. W., F. L. Gwynn, and A. O. Lewis. *The Case for Poetry: A Critical Anthology*. Englewood Cliffs, N J: Prentice-Hall, 1965.

Edwards, Betty. *Drawing on the Artist Within*. New York: Simon & Schuster, 1986.

Flaubert, Gustave. *Madame Bovary*. Ed. Paul de Man. New York: Norton, 1965.

Gardner, Howard. *Creating Minds*. New York: Basicbooks, 1993.

Hart, Edward L. "The Need beyond Reason." *University Education*. Provo: Brigham Young University Press, n.d. 31–42.

WEBSITES OF INTEREST

Demystifying the creative process —
http://www.productiveflourishing.com/demystifying-the-creative-process/

"The Wave." McRae Magleby, courtesy of McRae Magleby.

THE AESTHETIC EXPERIENCE

Chapter 5

THE AUDIENCE AND THE WORK

INTRODUCTION

Because the arts capture our sensory attention so compellingly, we sometimes call the experience **"aesthetic."** In fact, the artist's original creative impulse is often ignited by such an experience, either with another art or with **reality.** Thus, aesthetic experiences frame the two processes we know as the creative act and the critical response: the act of creation is prompted by an **aesthetic experience** (the artist's) and ends with another aesthetic experience (the audience's).

THE AESTHETIC STANCE

PAUL KLEE (1879–1940) was Switzerland's answer to modern art. A fine musician in his own right (he played the violin), his love for drawing and painting led him into the visual arts, but his imagination never let loose of music. Thus, you will better understand his losing himself in a reverie prompted by a passing brass band and his subsequent attempt to give the music visual (rhythmic) expression. We call this loss of a sense of time and place that attends an aesthetic experience, the **aesthetic stance.**

> Klee was once observed by one of his pupils in Dessau marching absent-mindedly, but as though under a spell, in time to the music of a passing band right down the middle of the slabs of a concrete pavement. As soon as his pupil spoke to him he broke off, alarmed and embarrassed, and in the course of the ensuing conversation about the suggestive power of the passing music and the rhythm of the slabs of concrete, Klee immediately set himself and his pupil the problem of expressing this rhythmic relationship in pictorial terms. The next day, Klee produced his solution: a rush of flowing lines set off against a hard rhythm of rectangular forms on the left-hand side. (Werner Haftmann, qtd. in Hall and Wykes 102–103)

Unless a person is either an artistic type (or crazy), it is not natural, nor is it very easy, to take the aesthetic stance, because it is frowned upon by our society ("Stop daydreaming!") or it is seen as impractical, even immature ("Grow up!"). Ironically, as was noted elsewhere, many modern artists, because they are fascinated by the uninhibited creative imaginations of children, try in their own works to recapture the unsophisticated vision of the world they had when they were young, "fresh with Eden's dew" (Thomas 268). Paul Klee's works are striking in their childlike quality. Unless we can accept this "hidden agenda," much modern art will appear trivial. Let's admit it. Artists look at the world through a different lens.

> We look up and see a coloured shape in front of us and we say—there is a chair. But what we have seen is the mere coloured shape. *Perhaps an artist might not have jumped to the notion of a chair. He might have stopped at the mere contemplation of a beautiful color and a beautiful shape.* But those of us who are not artists are very prone, especially if we are tired, to pass straight from the perception of the colored shape to the enjoyment of the chair. . . . The artist . . . [has] acquired this facility of ignoring the chair at the cost of great labor. (Whitehead, qtd. in Read 11)

THE MORE ABUNDANT LIFE

For many people, life from maturity to death is fairly mundane, only rarely touched with epiphanies. HENRY DAVID THOREAU (1817–1862) realized the dehumanizing effects of routine. In **Walden** he offered an antidote to the deadening monotony of mundane existence: "We must learn to reawaken and keep ourselves awake, not by mechanical aids, but by an infinite expectation of the dawn. . . . To affect the quality of the day, that is the highest of arts" (134). Thoreau seems to be suggesting that a person can make the very act of living an art by taking an aesthetic stance toward the world of sense experience. The fine arts can assist in this perceptual rebirth by heightening the impact of the senses on the psyche.

How do we come to this heightened awareness of the world around us, "to carve and paint the very atmosphere and medium through which we look" (134), as Thoreau said? HENRY JAMES (1845–1916) advised, "Try to be one of the people on whom nothing is lost!" (53). He seems to be saying: Don't let anything pass you by. Be open to and aware of the variety of sensory experiences in the world around you; seek out and savor the sensuous. Ironically, "one of the greatest *sensuists* of all time," according to Diane Ackerman, was "blind [and] deaf":

> Helen Keller's remaining senses were so finely attuned that when she put her hands on the radio to enjoy music, she could tell the difference between the cornets and the strings. She listened to colorful, down-home stories of life surging along the Mississippi from the lips of her friend Mark Twain. She wrote at length about the whelm of life's aromas, tastes, touches, feelings, which she explored with the voluptuousness of a courtesan. Despite her handicaps, she was more robustly alive than many people of her generation. (xviii, emphasis added)

DEFINITION

What is an "aesthetic" experience? Most simply put, it is an experience with the senses. Even though we see, hear, touch, taste, and smell every day, repeated exposure to the sights and sounds of our surroundings gradually anesthetizes us to the "sense-luscious" world we live in (Ackerman xv). Each individual lives on a different level of sensory awareness, of course, from apathetic stupor to heightened consciousness, and yet these sensory states sometimes change, depending on the activity and the surroundings, like leaving the monotony of the office and taking a vacation to the seashore or just looking at a sunset or catching the elusive scent of a flower. Georgia O'Keefe's large paintings of the convoluted interiors of flowers—her *Black Iris,* for instance—almost force a gut response to a "bee's eye" view of nature's stunning visual variety.

FRAMING THE WORLD

Natural wonders excite interest because of their beauty or sublimity, but nature changes on us; the sun sets and the flower eventually wilts and dies. The artist helps us hold on to those sublime moments by intensifying the sense experience with the elements of the **medium**. Experiencing the arts creates this kind of focus because the arts reach us primarily through the senses. They forge a link between us and the world by endowing nature with the wonder it held for us when we were children. In an almost magical manner, art "lifts the veil for the hidden beauty of the world, and makes familiar objects be as if they were not familiar" (qtd. in Stephens 13), as Shelley said, by removing things out of their conventional context and placing them on a pedestal, so to speak, for all to contemplate. Put another way, art focuses our attention on the significant things we often overlook. It accomplishes this by doing what Jerry Farber calls "framing," inviting us to take a second look (23–25).

Each major fine art has its own unique frame for riveting our attention. Painting, of course, has a literal frame. Music has the "auditory frame" of organized sound, which distinguishes it from the greater auditory range of all natural sounds. Literature reinvests words worn out by the practical requirements of everyday communication with new life by exploiting their figurative meanings and musical sounds. In fact, if you want to hear the "music" of language, listen to someone speaking a foreign tongue. Dance and drama greatly expand the natural nonverbal means of human communication (gesture, movement, facial expression) by organizing them and placing them on the stage of a theater, which is the common framing device for all the performing arts. Film's frame is the aperture of the motion picture camera projected onto the rectangular movie screen or beamed out at us from the television set, which prevents us from seeing anything outside the range of the camera's monolithic eye.

AESTHETIC DISTANCE

Framing is, of course, an artificial device that doesn't occur in the real world at all. Yet the frame suspends us between an actual and fictional reality, somewhat like standing on a threshold between two worlds, creating a tension between what is and what isn't (but could be). Hovering between these two possible options has been likened to navigating the "aesthetic distance." This means having a double consciousness: *feeling* that something is real (the action on the stage), but *knowing* it's not (the hero isn't really dead). It is an imaginary balancing act to keep both realities alive at the same time. What makes the "aesthetic stance" work has to do with what Samuel Taylor Coleridge (1772–1834) called "that willing suspension of disbelief" (169). We have to willingly cooperate with the artist's attempts to invite us into accepting as real that which is fundamentally fictional. Without this unwritten contract with the artist, we simply couldn't experience art at all.

HOW TO RECOGNIZE AN AESTHETIC EXPERIENCE WHEN IT HITS YOU

All aesthetic experiences have certain features in common. We can plumb the ruminations of many philosophers of art, beginning with Plato and ending with Virgil Aldrich and Monroe Beardsley, two contemporary "aestheticians." The following points have been distilled from their writings.

1. The aesthetic experience is one we prize for its own sake, unconnected to any practical end. It draws us into it and makes us forget where and who we are, generating a kind of compulsive focus on the thing itself.

2. The aesthetic experience engenders a sympathetic attitude toward the thing, an acceptance of objects on their own terms. With this "aesthetic stance," we tend to focus less on the content of the experience and more on the form; that is, we listen to music, not so much for what it reminds us of, but for what it reveals in the inner logic of its rhythms, melodies, and harmonies.

3. At the same time, however, we tend to get drawn into a kind of trance or reverie, becoming immersed in deep contemplation. Ideally, an aesthetic experience fully engages our intellectual, sensuous, and intuitive faculties, bringing our often-competing sophic and mantic natures together.

CONCLUSION

We are all potential artists, because we occasionally experience those rare moments of real spiritual elevation which, if we were skilled in some artistic medium, could well prompt the creation of original works of art, which could then become triggers for someone else's aesthetic experience. In the meantime, there is a glorious world of heightened intellectual and emotional intensity in the fine arts just waiting to be sampled or devoured. Francis Bacon (1561–1626) wrote, "Some books are to be tasted, oth-

ers to be swallowed, and some few to be chewed and digested" (163, spelling standardized). The refinement and enlargement of our tastes and powers of discrimination will make available to us an enormous variety of cultural fare. In matters more than food, "we are what we eat."

COMMENTARY ON THE ARTS

THREE DAYS TO SEE

—*Helen Keller*

Excerpt from Three Days to See, *by Helen Keller, published by the American Foundation for the Blind.*

All of us have read thrilling stories in which the hero had only a limited and specified time to live. Sometimes it was as long as a year; sometimes as short as twenty-four hours. But always we were interested in discovering just how the doomed man chose to spend his last days or his last hours. I speak, of course, of free men who have a choice, not condemned criminals whose sphere of activities is strictly delimited.

Such stories set us thinking, wondering what we should do under similar circumstances. What events, what experiences, what associations should we crowd into those last hours as mortal beings? What happiness should we find in reviewing the past, what regrets?

Sometimes I have thought it would be an excellent rule to live each day as if we should die tomorrow. Such an attitude would emphasize sharply the values of life. We should live each day with a gentleness, a vigor, and a keenness of appreciation which are often lost when time stretches before us in the constant panorama of more days and months and years to come. There are those, of course, who would adopt the Epicurean motto of "Eat, drink, and be merry," but most people would be chastened by the certainty of impending death.

In stories, the doomed hero is usually saved at the last minute by some stroke of fortune, but almost always his sense of values is changed. He becomes more appreciative of the meaning of life and its permanent spiritual values. It has often been noted that those who live, or have lived, in the shadow of death bring a mellow sweetness to everything they do.

Most of us, however, take life for granted. We know that one day we must die, but usually we picture that day as far in the future. When we are in buoyant health, death is all but unimaginable. We seldom think of it. The days stretch out an endless vista. So we go about our petty tasks, hardly aware of our listless attitude toward life.

The same lethargy, I am afraid, characterizes the use of all our faculties and senses. Only the deaf appreciate hearing, only the blind realize the manifold blessings that lie in sight. Particularly does this observation apply to those who have lost sight and hearing in adult life. But those who have never suffered impairment of sight or hearing seldom make the fullest use of these blessed faculties. Their eyes and ears take in all sights and sounds hazily, without concentration and with little appreciation. It is the same old story of not being grateful for what we have until we lose it, of not being conscious of health until we are ill.

I have often thought it would be a blessing if each human being were stricken blind and deaf for a few days at some time during his early adult life. Darkness would make him more appreciative of sight; silence would teach him the joys of sound.

Now and then I have tested my seeing friends to discover what they see. Recently I was visited by a very good friend who had just returned from a long walk in the woods, and I asked her what she had observed. "Nothing in particular," she replied. I might have been incredulous had I not been accustomed to such responses, for long ago I became convinced that the seeing see little.

How was it possible, I asked myself, to walk for an hour through the woods and see nothing worthy of note? I who cannot see find hundreds of things to interest me through mere touch. I feel the delicate symmetry of a leaf. I pass my hands lovingly about the smooth skin of a silver birch, or the rough shaggy bark of a pine. In spring I touch the branches of trees hopefully in search of a bud, the first sign of awakening Nature after her winter's sleep. I feel the delightful, velvety texture of a flower, and discover its remarkable convolutions, and something of the miracle of Nature is revealed to me. Occasionally, if I am fortunate, I place my hand gently on a small tree and feel the happy quiver of a bird in full song. I am delighted to have the cool waters of a brook rush through my open fingers. To me a lush carpet of pine needles or spongy grass is more welcome than the most luxurious Persian rug. To me the pageant of seasons is a thrilling and unending drama, the action of which streams through my finger tips.

At times my heart cries out with longing to see all these things. If I can get so much pleasure from mere touch, how much more beauty must be revealed by sight. Yet, those who have eyes apparently see little. The panorama of color and action which fills the world is taken for granted. It is human, perhaps, to appreciate little that which we have and to long for that which we have not, but it is a great pity that in the world of light and the gift of sight is used only as a mere convenience rather than as a means of adding fullness to life.

If I were the president of a university I should establish a compulsory course in "How to Use Your Eyes." The professor would try to show his pupils how they could add joy to their lives by really seeing what passes unnoticed before them. He would try to awake their dormant and sluggish faculties.

Perhaps I can best illustrate by imagining what I should most like to see if I were given the use of my eyes, say, for just three days. And while I am imagining, suppose you, too, set your mind to work on the problem of how you would use your own eyes if you had only three more days to see. If with the oncoming darkness of the third night you knew that the sun would never rise for you again, how would you spend those three precious intervening days? What would you most want to let your gaze rest upon.

I, naturally, should want most to see the things which have become dear to me through my years of darkness. You, too, would want to let your eyes rest long on the things that have become dear to you so that you could take the memory of them with you into the night that loomed before you.

If, by some miracle I were granted three seeing days, to be followed by a relapse into darkness, I should divide the period into three parts.

On the first day, I should want to see the people whose kindness and gentleness have made my life worth living. First I should like to gaze long upon the face of my dear teacher, Mrs. Anne Sullivan Macy, who came to me when I was a child and opened the outer world to me. I should want not merely to see the outline of her face, so that I could cherish it in my memory, but to study that face and find in it the living evidence of the sympathetic tenderness and patience with which she accomplished the difficult task of my education. I should like to see in her eyes that strength of character which has enabled her to stand firm in the face of difficulties, and that compassion for all humanity which she has revealed to me so often.

I do not know what it is to see into the heart of a friend through that "window of the soul," the eye. I can only "see" through my finger tips the outline of a face. I can detect laughter, sorrow, and many other obvious emotions. I know my friends from the feel of their faces. But I cannot really picture their personalities by touch. I know their personalities, of course, through other means, through the thoughts they express to me, through whatever of their actions are revealed to me. But I am denied that deeper understanding of them which I am sure would come through sight of them, through watching their reactions to various expressed thoughts and circumstances, through noting the immediate and fleeting reactions of their eyes and countenance.

Friends who are near to me I know well, because through the months and years they reveal themselves to me in all their phases; but of casual friends I have only an incomplete impression, an impression gained from a handclasp, from spoken words which I take from their lips with my finger tips, or which they type into the palm of my hand.

How much easier, how much more satisfying it is for you who can see to grasp quickly the essential qualities of another person by watching the subtleties of expression, the quiver of a muscle, the flutter of a hand. But does it ever occur to you to use your sight to see into the inner nature of a friend or acquaintance? Do not most of you seeing people grasp casually the outward features of a face and let it go at that?

For instance, can you describe accurately the faces of five good friends? Some of you can, but many cannot. As an experiment, I have questioned husbands of long standing about the color of their wives' eyes, and often they express embarrassed confusion and admit they do not know. And, incidentally, it is a chronic complaint of wives that their husbands do not notice new dresses, new hats, and changes in household arrangements.

The eyes of seeing persons soon become accustomed to the routine of their surroundings, and they actually see only the startling and spectacular. But even in viewing the most spectacular sights the eyes are lazy. Court records reveal every day how inaccurately "eyewitnesses" see. A given event will be "seen" in several different ways by as many witnesses. Some see more than others, but few see everything that is within the range of their vision.

Oh, the things that I should see if I had the power of sight for just three days!

The first would be a busy one. I should call to me all my dear friends and look long into their faces, imprinting upon my mind the outward evidences of the beauty that is within them. I should let my eyes rest, too, on the face of a baby, so that I could catch a vision of the eager, innocent beauty which precedes the individual's consciousness of the conflicts which life develops.

And I should like to look into the loyal, trusting eyes of my dogs—the grave, canny little Scottie, Darkie, and the stalwart, understanding Great Dane, Helga, whose warm, tender, and playful friendships are so comforting to me.

On that busy first day I should also view the small simple things of my home. I want to see the warm colors in the rugs under my feet, the pictures on the walls, the intimate trifles that transform a house into a home. My eyes would rest respectfully on the books in raised type which I have read, but they would be more eagerly interested in the printed books which seeing people can read, for during the long night of my life the books I have read and which have been read to me have built themselves a great shining lighthouse, revealing to me the deepest channels of human life and the human spirit.

In the afternoon of that first seeing day, I should take a long walk into the woods and intoxicate my eyes on the beauties of the world of Nature, trying desperately to absorb in a few hours the vast splendor which is constantly unfolding itself to those who can see. On the way home from my woodland jaunt my path would pass near a farm so that I might see the patient horses plowing the field (perhaps I should see only a tractor!) and the serene content of men living close to the soil. And I should pray for the glory of a colorful sunset.

When dusk had fallen, I should experience the double delight of being able to see by artificial light, which the genius of man has created to extend the power of his sight when Nature decrees darkness.

In the night of that first day of sight, I should not be able to sleep, so full would be my mind of the memories of the day.

The next day—the second day of sight—I should arise with the dawn and see the thrilling miracle by which night is transformed into day. I should behold with awe the magnificent panorama of light with which the sun awakens the sleeping earth.

This day I would devote to a hasty glimpse of the world, past and present. I should want to see the pageant of man's progress, the kaleidoscope of the ages. How can so much be compressed into one day? Through the museums, of course. Often I have visited the New York Museum of Natural History to touch with my hands many of the objects there exhibited, but I have longed to see with my eyes the condensed history of the earth and its inhabitants displayed there—animals and the races of men pictured in their native environment; gigantic carcasses of dinosaurs and mastodons which roamed the earth long before man appeared, with his tiny stature and powerful brain, to conquer the animal kingdom; realistic presentations of the processes of evolution in animals, in man, and in the implements which man has used to fashion for himself a secure home on this planet; and a thousand and one other aspects of natural history.

I wonder how many readers of this article have viewed this panorama of the face of living things as pictured in that inspiring museum. Many, of course, have not had the opportunity, but I am sure that many who have had the opportunity have not made use of it. There, indeed, is a place to use your eyes. You who see can spend many fruitful days there, but I, with my imaginary three days of sight, could only take a hasty glimpse and pass on.

My next stop would be the Metropolitan Museum of Art, for just as the Museum of Natural History reveals the material aspects of the world, so does the Metropolitan show the myriad facets of the human spirit. Throughout the history of humanity the urge to artistic expression has been almost as powerful as the urge for food, shelter, and procreation. And here, in the vast chambers of the Metropolitan Museum, is unfolded before me the spirit of Egypt, Greece, and Rome, as expressed in their art. I know well through my hands the sculptured gods and goddesses of the ancient Nile-land. I have felt copies of Parthenon friezes, and I have sensed the rhythmic beauty of charging Athenian warriors. Apollos and Venuses and the Winged Victory of Samothrace are friends of my finger tips. The gnarled, bearded features of Homer are dear to me, for he, too, knew blindness.

My hands have lingered upon the living marble of Roman sculpture as well as that of later generations. I have passed my hands over a plaster cast of Michelangelo's inspiring and heroic Moses; I have sensed the power of Rodin; I have been awed by the devoted spirit of Gothic wood carving. These arts which can be touched have meaning for me, but even they were meant to be seen rather than felt, and I can only guess at the beauty which remains hidden from me. I can admire the simple lines of a Greek vase, but its figured decorations are lost to me.

So on this, my second day of sight, I should try to probe into the soul of man through his art. The things I knew through touch I should now see. More splendid still, the whole magnificent world of painting would be opened to me, from the Italian Primitives, with their serene religious devotion, to the Moderns, with their feverish visions. I should took deep into the canvases of Raphael, Leonardo da Vinci, Titian, Rembrandt. I should want to feast my eyes upon the warm colors of Veronese, study the mysteries of El Greco, catch a new vision of Nature from Corot. Oh, there is so much rich meaning and beauty in the art of the ages for you who have eyes to see!

Upon my short visit to this temple of art I should not be able to review a fraction of the great world of art which is open to you. I should be able to get only a superficial impression. Artists tell me that for a deep and true appreciation of art one must educate the eye. One must learn through experience to weigh the merits of line, of composition, of form and color. If I had eyes, how happily would I embark upon so fascinating a study! Yet I am told

that, to many of you who have eyes to see, the world of art is a dark night, unexplored and unilluminated.

It would be with extreme reluctance that I should leave the Metropolitan Museum, which contains the key to beauty—a beauty so neglected. Seeing persons, however, do not need a Metropolitan to find this key to beauty. The same key lies waiting in smaller museums, and in books on the shelves of even small libraries. But naturally, in my limited time of imaginary sight, I should choose the place where the key unlocks the greatest treasures in the shortest time.

The evening of my second day of sight I should spend at a theater or at the movies. Even now I often attend theatrical performances of all sorts, but the action of the play must be spelled into my hand by a companion. But how I should like to see with my own eyes the fascinating figure of Hamlet, or the gutsy Falstaff amid colorful Elizabethan trappings! How I should like to follow each movement of the graceful Hamlet, each strut of the hearty Falstaff! And since I could see only one play, I should be confronted by a many-horned dilemma, for there are scores of plays I should want to see. You who have eyes can see any you like. How many of you, I wonder, when you gaze at a play, a movie, or any spectacle, realize and give thanks for the miracle of sight which enables you to enjoy its color, grace, and movement?

I cannot enjoy the beauty of rhythmic movement except in a sphere restricted to the touch of my hands. I can envision only dimly the grace of a Pavlova, although I know something of the delight of rhythm, for often I can sense the beat of music as it vibrates through the floor. I can well imagine that cadenced motion must be one of the most pleasing sights in the world. I have been able to gather something of this by tracing with my fingers the lines in sculptured marble; if this static grace can be so lovely, how much more acute must be the thrill of seeing grace in motion.

One of my dearest memories is of the time when Joseph Jefferson allowed me to touch his face and hands as he went through some of the gestures and speeches of his beloved Rip Van Winkle. I was able to catch thus a meager glimpse of the world of drama, and I shall never forget the delight of that moment. But, oh, how much I must miss, and how much pleasure you seeing ones can derive from watching and hearing the interplay of speech and movement in the unfolding of a dramatic performance! If I could see only one play, I should know how to picture in my mind the action of a hundred plays which I have read or had transferred to me through the medium of the manual alphabet.

So through the evening of my second imaginary day

of sight, the great figures of dramatic literature would crowd sleep from my eyes.

The following morning, I should again greet the dawn, anxious to discover new delights, for I am sure that, for those who have eyes which really see, the dawn of each day must be a perpetually new revelation of beauty.

This, according to the terms of my imagined miracle, is to be my third and last day of sight. I shall have no time to waste in regrets or longings; there is too much to see. The first day I devoted to my friends, animate and inanimate. The second revealed to me the history of man and Nature. Today I shall spend in the workaday world of the present, amid the haunts of men going about the business of life. And where can one find so many activities and conditions of men as in New York? So the city becomes my destination.

I start from my home in the quiet little suburb of Forest Hills, Long Island. Here, surrounded by green lawns, trees, and flowers, are neat little houses, happy with the voices and movements of wives and children, havens of peaceful rest for men who toil in the city. I drive across the lacy structure of steel which spans the East River, and I get a new and startling vision of the power and ingenuity of the mind of man. Busy boats chug and scurry about the river—racy speed boats, stolid, snorting tugs. If I had long days of sight ahead, I should spend many of them watching the delightful activity upon the river.

I look ahead, and before me rise the fantastic towers of New York, a city that seems to have stepped from the pages of a fairy story. What an awe-inspiring sight, these glittering spires, these vast banks of stone and steel structures such as the gods might build for themselves! This animated picture is a part of the lives of millions of people everyday. How many, I wonder, give it so much as a second glance? Very few, I fear. Their eyes are blind to this magnificent sight because it is so familiar to them.

I hurry to the top of one of those gigantic structures, the Empire State Building, for there, a short time ago, I "saw" the city below through the eyes of my secretary. I am anxious to compare my fancy with reality. I am sure I should not be disappointed in the panorama spread out before me, for to me it would be a vision of another world.

Now I begin my rounds of the city. First, I stand at a busy corner, merely looking at people, trying by sight of them to understand something of their lives. I see smiles, and I am happy. I see serious determination, and I am proud. I see suffering, and I am compassionate.

I stroll down Fifth Avenue. I throw my eyes out of focus so that I see no particular object but only a seething kaleidoscope of color. I am certain that the colors of women's dresses moving in a throng must be a gorgeous spectacle of which I should never tire. But perhaps if I had sight I should be like most other women—too interested in styles and the cut of individual dresses to give much attention to the splendid color in the mass. And I am convinced, too, that I should become an inveterate window shopper, for it must be a delight to the eye to view the myriad articles of beauty on display.

From Fifth Avenue I make a tour of the city—to Park Avenue, to the slums, to factories, to parks where children play. I take a stay-at-home trip abroad by visiting the foreign quarters. Always my eyes are open wide to all of the sights of both happiness and misery so that I may probe deep and add to my understanding of how people work and live. My heart is full of the images of people and things. My eye passes lightly over no single trifle; it strives to touch and hold closely each thing its gaze rests upon. Some sights are pleasant, filling the heart with happiness; but some are miserably pathetic. To these latter I do not shut my eyes, for they, too, are part of life. To close the eye on them is to close the heart and mind.

My third day of sight is drawing to an end. Perhaps there are many serious pursuits to which I should devote the few remaining hours, but I am afraid that on the evening of the last day I should again run away to the theater, to a hilariously funny play, so that I might appreciate the overtones of comedy in the human spirit.

At midnight my temporary respite from blindness would cease, and permanent night would close in on me again. Naturally in those three short days I should not have seen all I wanted to see. Only when darkness had again descended upon me should I realize how much I had left unseen. But my mind would be so crowded with glorious memories that I should have little time for regrets. Thereafter the touch of every object would bring a flowing memory of how that object looked.

Perhaps this short outline of how I would spend three days of sight does not agree with the program you would set for yourself if you knew that you were about to be stricken blind. I am, however, sure that if you actually faced that fate your eyes would open to things you had never seen before, storing up memories for the long night ahead. You would use your eyes as never before. Everything you saw would become dear to you. Your eyes would touch and embrace every object that came within your range of vision. Then, at last, you would really see, and a new world of beauty would open itself before you.

I who am blind can give one hint to those who see— one admonition to those who would make full use of the gift of sight: Use your eyes as if tomorrow you would be stricken blind. And the same method can be applied to other senses. Hear the music of voices, the song of a bird, the mighty strains of an orchestra, as if you would be stricken deaf tomorrow. Touch each object you want to touch as if tomorrow your tactile sense would fail. Smell the perfume of flowers, taste with relish each morsel, as if tomorrow you could never smell and taste again. Make the most of every sense; glory in all the facets of pleasure and beauty which the world reveals to you through the several means of contact with Nature Providers. But of all the senses, I am sure that sight must be the most delightful.

WRITING EXERCISES

1. Where does the word *aesthetic* come from? Check a good dictionary. Better yet, go to the best source of etymologies: the *OED (Oxford English Dictionary)*.

2. If creativity is possible in rather mundane circumstances, how can a person realize Thoreau's invitation "to affect the quality of the day," which, he says, is "the highest of the arts"? Give a couple of concrete examples from your own experience.

3. What conditions (natural and artistic) can prompt this kind of "heightened awareness"?

4. Why is a child so mesmerized by a favorite TV program? How does TV *capture* but not *liberate* the imagination?

Now that you have some notion of what an aesthetic experience involves, go out and have one. Involve yourself in an art form (film, music, poetry, painting) that you are fairly sure will draw you in. The tricky thing here is to fully give in to the experience, allowing the "willing suspension of disbelief" to occur, while still being conscious of the details of the experience, so you can remember what it was like. Be as specific and detailed in documenting your experience as possible. What was the experience like? How did you feel? What did you learn about the medium? About yourself? About the art? About life's purposes?

WORKS CITED

Ackerman, Diane. *A Natural History of the Senses.* New York: Vintage, 1990.

Bacon, Francis. *The Essays of Sir Francis Bacon.* New York: Heritage Press, 1944.

Coleridge, Samuel Taylor. *Biographica Literaria.* New York: Dutton, 1965.

Farber, Jerry. *A Field Guide to the Aesthetic Experience.* Hollywood: Foreworks, 1982.

Hall, Donald, and Pat Corrington Wykes. *Anecdotes of Modern Art.* Oxford: Oxford University Press, 1990.

James, Henry. "The Art of Fiction." In *Henry James: Literary Criticism.* New York: Literary Classics of the United States, Viking Press, 1984.

Read, Herbert. *The Philosophy of Modern Art.* New York: World Publishing, 1952.

Stephens, Meic. *A Dictionary of Literary Quotations.* London: Routledge, 1990.

Thomas, Dylan. "Notes on the Art of Poetry." Qtd. in James B. Hall and Barry Ulanov, *Modern Culture and the Arts.* 2nd ed. New York: McGraw-Hill, 1972. 267–273.

Thoreau, Henry David. *Walden and Civil Disobedience.* New York: Penguin, 1983.

WEBSITES OF INTEREST

The end of Aesthetic Experience —
http://www.jstor.org/pss/431602

Short bio of Helen Keller, learning to see —
http://gardenofpraise.com/ibdkell.htm

William Gibson Biography —
http://www.enotes.com/miracle-worker/author-biography

Nude Descending a Staircase *(1912).*
Marcel Duchamp, Philadelphia Museum of Art.

AESTHETIC JUDGMENT

THE CRITIC AND THE WORK

Chapter 6

INTRODUCTION

The goal of this chapter is to help you avoid some of the more common misjudgments about art and, more importantly, to arm you with a set of principles and expectations that will give you access to some of the great works of the past. It is useful to think of the greatest works, what some call the canon, as cryptic texts that need deciphering. Each art communicates through a special language. What is needed is a kind of Rosetta Stone to enable you to read the message. The deciphering process involves learning a new vocabulary, using a set of finely tuned perceptual skills, and willingly suspending pre-judgments and culturally acquired biases.

CONTEMPORARY CRITICAL REACTIONS TO MARCEL DUCHAMP'S 1912 "NUDE DESCENDING A STAIRCASE"

"It looks like the explosion of a shingle factory," "an assortment of half-made leather saddles," an "elevated railroad stairway in ruins after an earthquake," a "dynamited suit of Japanese armor," . . . an "orderly heap of broken violins," and an "academic painting of an artichoke," a "diagram of a shudder, and a most clever suggestion of the thing, too. The downward, slightly swerving effect is unmistakable. Moreover, it is safe to assume that the shudder is reproduced in at least 99 percent of the persons who have seen the work."

One contemporary editorialist wrote:

Crazy quilt art is not fit for children's eyes; it is nasty, lewd, immoral, indecent, obscene and scandalous. (Qtd. in Moffitt 23–27)

THE INFAMOUS "NUDE"

These critical comments were made about the most controversial modern work exhibited in the 1913 Armory Show in New York City. It was the first time the American public came face to face with the modern art styles that had developed in Europe in the first decade of the twentieth century. It appears obvious that no one, in public or private, was ready for the "shock of the new." President Theodore Roosevelt thought Duchamp's painting looked like the Navajo rug on his bathroom floor. The point of presenting this initial barrage of negative criticism is that anyone can make judgments about new, unfamiliar styles in art (or at least about styles of art that are new to the viewer). Goethe's Faust understood well the perennial human resistance to novelty:

> We are accustomed to see men disdain
> What they don't grasp;
> When it gives trouble, they profane
> Even the beautiful and the good.
>
> (486)

CRITICISM IS UNIVERSAL

In light of this scandalous event in the history of American art, it is important to realize that everyone criticizes the arts; that is, they make personal judgments about what they do and don't like. The question is, how fair and informed is the criticism? Critical reaction occurs every time someone switches the TV channel or buys a new CD, but this kind of snap judgment doesn't qualify for what we mean by informed art criticism. Most off-the-cuff critical statements made by people we might call "closet critics" are generally superficial and uninformed, primarily because the closet critics have not prepared themselves to meet the work on its own terms, or they are simply misinformed, biased, or even accidentally on target.

AMERICANS & ARTS CRITICISM

Americans in general find it more difficult than Europeans to enjoy such arts as opera or ballet, partly because our national heroes have been frontier people—like Daniel Boone or Calamity Jane—people of action who faced the challenges of frontier life and wouldn't have been caught dead going to the opera. Opera and ballet, on the other hand, grew out of the aristocratic society of Western European culture, which had created the repressive political situations our pilgrim forefathers sailed to the New World to escape. Unfortunately, since our beginnings we have tended to throw the baby out with the bath water, culturally speaking, by resisting the artistic offerings of European culture. It is easy to understand why most Americans tend to reject or dismiss as sterile the artificial atmosphere of illusion and fantasy found in most traditional operas and ballets. But there is no excuse for perpetuating cultural biases that have outlived their reason for being.

COMMON CRITICAL PITFALLS

Here are three common negative reactions to the arts and some possible correctives:

"Well, I don't know if it's any good or not, but I know what I like!"

The apparent validity of this statement is based on the belief that art judgments are personal and therefore immune from error or criticism. The admission, "I don't know if it's any good or not," contains a veiled disclaimer of responsibility due to ignorance of the subject. Such a statement ends the discussion before any light has been generated; in the long run, such a comment will likely stifle further investigation, since the speaker apparently accepts only what he or she already knows. The common statement "Beauty is in the eye of the beholder" similarly resists rejoinders. A more promising stance toward a puzzling or challenging work can be found in the late Vincent Price's modest claim: "I'm no expert, but *I like what I know.*" Our enjoyment of anything is generally related to the degree of our knowledge and exposure to it: the more we know about something, the more we are likely to be interested in it and to derive pleasure from it. Mark Twain said it best: "Folks is always down on what they ain't up on."

"My little brother could have done that!"

The problem with this statement is fairly obvious: if anyone could do it, it must not be any good. People tend to appreciate things that appear to have taken a lot of work. This reaction demonstrates a poor understanding of the artistic purpose in overcoming the limitations of the **medium** (the material the artwork is made of); one of the goals of any artist is to make the work *seem* effortless. A simple example: what kind of aesthetic pleasure could a person derive from a ballerina whose leaps appeared labored? The quickest antidote to misinformed prejudgment is to try it. In fact, the best critics usually have had some experience working in the medium they criticize, enabling them to gain an inside track on the creative challenges the artist faces.

The "my little brother" syndrome is particularly common in people's reactions to abstract art. One student decided to buy a canvas board and some oil paint to prove he could create an abstraction as good as Jackson Pollock's. At the end of the term he showed his "magnum opus" to his teacher. It was a disaster and they both knew it. Because we are conditioned to expect photographic likenesses in paintings, any work that deviates from this kind of realism tends to be judged inept by the general public. But all artists, regardless of their style, have to cope with the same basic challenges: to make the colors, lines, and forms work together harmoniously and meaningfully. Whether the result is realistic, expressionistic, or abstract has little bearing on its quality.

One further point. Some artists, especially the more modern ones (like Paul Klee, Henri Matisse, and Pablo Picasso), are actually trying to do as well as someone's kid brother. They find children's art spontaneous and true, devoid of the contrived effects some artists give their work. Picasso, while looking at some children's art, once admitted: "When I was their age, I could draw like Raphael, but it took me a lifetime to learn how to paint like them" (qtd. in Oppler 81).

"That's not art!"

This comment is the easiest to make and the hardest to explain. If we define art as anything made by an artist, then calling a work "not art" makes no more sense than calling a chef's unappetizing salad plate "not food." The best we can say is that it isn't good food. The same is true with a work of art. The only possible occasion for calling an object "not art" is in reference to natural objects like mountains or sunsets or pieces of driftwood which have some aesthetic appeal, but which were created by natural forces. Since the products of art are by definition "*artificial*" (a painting of a tree is merely an image of a tree), the artist can play the real against the illusory to great effect, forcing us to see familiar things "out of context," in short, getting us to take the "aesthetic stance" toward something in our everyday environment. Marcel Duchamp was best known and, initially, most vilified for trying to elevate common manufactured objects to the level of high art. One of his most infamous "found" works was a urinal turned upside down and placed in a museum over the title "Fountain" (1917) and signed "R. Mutt." One of the fun things about the works of many modern artists is their tongue-in-cheek wit. René Magritte's painting of a large pipe with the title (written on the canvas) *Ceci n'est pas une pipe* ("This is not a pipe!") humorously informs us that while art is not life it still has a life of its own. But both Duchamp's and Magritte's works may lose their value if their original novelty is not buttressed by skill and vision. A legitimate criticism of much modern art lies in some artists' desperate attempts at novelty for its own sake. Sometimes the search for originality is their only ticket to financial and critical success. We must not forget that artists in our century are seldom subsidized as they were in centuries past, notwithstanding occasional government grants, so they often resort to unusual, even shocking, strategies to get the public's attention.

What Is a Critic?

The word **critic** comes from the Greek *kritikos*, which means one who judges according to some criterion or standard. To become an informed critic of the arts it is helpful to consider the criteria required. The first requirement is adequate exposure. A good critic can put things into the *context* of other works in the same genre. According to E. H. Gombrich, "The term *critic* means something like *discriminator*, a person who notices differences and who makes decisions about them. A work in total isolation could be enjoyed, but it could not be criticized, because there is nothing to compare it with (41). Therefore, the more works we know, the more fine-tuned our criticism can be.

A good art critic *cares* about the subject. Otherwise why bother? The art critic's goal is clear communication, maybe even conversion. However, amateur pontificating about the arts, whether it involves telling friends about an exciting new movie or making fun of a modern art exhibit, runs the danger of gravitating toward extremes. Common reactions to an aesthetic experience run the gamut from mindless praise ("My, isn't that wonderful!") to flippant rejection ("What a piece of garbage!"). Fair-minded criticism, on the other hand, navigates a careful course between subjective involvement and objective analysis, a kind of tightrope walk across the chasm of judgment. The tightrope image is apt, since criticism is a dangerous game—we run the risk of offending our friends and being hurt by others' assessments of our own judgments.

Who's on Trial?

A story is told of a typical American tourist visiting the Louvre, the greatest art museum in the Western world. The French museum guide overheard him saying as he left, "That was a waste of time!" The guide responded, "Monsieur, this museum is not on trial. You are." In other words, what we say in front of a work of art says perhaps more about us than about the work we're judging. The other side of the issue can be illustrated by the reactions of an artist who happened through a gallery that was exhibiting some of his works. He overheard a young person say to his friend, "Can you believe that someone could ask money for such junk?" The artist was deeply hurt by this curt, insensitive reaction. Artists care about their work. This particular artist has never sold any of his paintings because they are like his children, his personal creations; therefore he can't bear to part with even one of them. All works created by an honest, skilled creator deserve our patience and respect.

Creators & Critics

Creators and critics perform different, though complementary, tasks. Yet what has been said of teachers—"Those who can, do; those who can't, teach"—applies to some critics. Tristan Bernard once said, "A critic is a virgin who wants to teach a Don Juan how to make love" (qtd. in English 44). Nevertheless, as was noted previously, the best critics have usually had some experience with the medium they criticize.

THE CHALLENGES OF A CRITIC

Clear Communication

Once a work of art grabs you, you naturally feel a desire to tell someone about it. That's the social value of arts criticism—it builds bridges of understanding between individuals through shared experiences. But the critic faces the almost impossible task of trying to articulate the inexpressible. Writers great and small lament the limitations of words to express feelings. Writing about the arts presents us with a maddening kind of task: to do justice to both the meaning of the work and the meaning to the critic. The words form the bridge between the two. A good critic clearly and convincingly articulates his or her aesthetic experience.

PROGRESSIVE EXCLUSION

A real danger in criticizing the arts lies in what might be called progressive exclusion, being ever more demanding of the medium until rarely anything pleases. To guard against this, it is wise to develop a floating scale of critical expectations. This means tailoring your level of criticism to the level of expertise possible in a particular performance. A wise teacher once said that it is unfair to gauge the quality of a doghouse by the criteria of a cathedral. A junior high assembly comes with a completely different set of aesthetic expectations than a Metropolitan Opera performance. Applied consistently, this flexible approach will enhance both the critic's credibility and the reader's acceptability.

QUESTIONS CRITICS ASK

The following six questions create a kind of prism through which we can view a work of art critically. These questions will help focus attention on important facets of the work: its type, medium, form, meaning, style, and value. Depending upon the actual work (visual or performing), you may want to read the appropriate section in Appendix I "Critical Approaches to the Arts."

I. DESCRIPTION

1. *What is it?* Here we are interested in the **genre** (type) and what could be expected from this kind of work. For example, lyric poems are too short to accommodate the development of an extended narrative. An awareness of the genre helps us have the proper expectations, that we might judge it rightly for what it is capable of achieving.

2. *What is it made of?* In other words, what is the medium (material) that makes it possible for us to experience the work: colors mixed with linseed oil, music, words, steel-reinforced concrete, and what are the medium limitations?

3. *How is it put together?* This question probes the formal properties of the work, in particular the relations between the parts and the whole. Every successful art work is "well wrought," meaning that the details have an integral connection to the complete work. This

trait is sometimes referred to as a balance between unity and variety.

II. INTERPRETATION

4. *What does it mean?* In other words, what is its expressive content? And how does the content match the form? Some poems, for example, are flawed because a sublime theme (God, truth, beauty) is poured into a sentimental mold. A good example is a poem about a loved one's death written in a sing-song metrical pattern more appropriate to a nursery rhyme than a funeral dirge.

5. *How does it mean?* This relates to matters of style— not what is communicated, but how. Style reflects the deepest strata of the artist's personality and comes out in ways even the artist is not aware of. Read more about this in Chapter 15: Form, Content, and Style in Painting.

III. EVALUATION

6. *What difference does it make?* Ultimately, we have to ask ourselves this question, whether we are switching television channels or deciding to buy a season ticket to the ballet. Our answers will often tell more about us than about the work we are criticizing.

CONCLUSION

To summarize the above discussion, consider three simple questions that could be asked about any experience with the arts. You are in good company if you ask them; they were originally posed by Goethe, the great German poet/philosopher of the eighteenth and nineteenth centuries.

1. What is the artist trying to do?

2. How well does he or she do it?

3. Was it worth doing?

If it was worth doing, the experience will fulfill the following three expectations, which are the major components of any work that "works":

1. It has *integrity* (balances unity and variety).

2. It generates *insight* (balances clarity and complexity).

3. It exhibits *inexhaustibility* (balances accessibility and profundity).

CRITICAL EXERCISES

Consider a film you like with at least a four-star rating (check a recent video movie guide for ratings). Check out the video after you have located a critical review at your local library (some of the best reviews of older films can be located in the New York Times Film Review). More popular reviews can be located in the Readers Guide, which will indicate film reviews from Newsweek, Time, etc., by year of appearance (the video jacket will usually include the year), or you can try the Web (http://www.screenit.com is a reliable source).

1. Outline the major points (positive and negative) of the critic's appraisal of the film.

2. Give your honest reactions (pro and con), supporting your opinion with evidence from the film (be specific/cite examples).

3. Add your own specific insights that the critic either missed or didn't deem important enough to mention.

4. Summarize the experience:

   What did you learn about arts criticism?

   About your own critical skills?

   About the value of taking a critical stance and supporting it?

WORKS CITED

English, John W. *Criticizing the Critics.* New York: Hastings House, 1979.

Goethe, Johann Wolfgang von. *Faust.* Trans. Walter Kaufmann. *Norton Anthology of World Masterpieces.* Ed. Maynard Mack et al. 6th ed. 2 vols. New York: Norton, 1992. 2: 464–569.

Gombrich, E. H. "A Historical Hypothesis." Ed. Thomas F. Rugh and Erin R. Silva. *History as a Tool in Critical Interpretation.* Provo, UT: Brigham Young University Press, 1978.

Moffitt, Ginger Lei. "*Nude Descending a Staircase No. 2:* From Mockery to Masterpiece." M.A. Thesis, Brigham Young University, 1990.

Oppler, Ellen C., ed. *Picasso's "Guernica."* Norton Critical Studies in Art History. New York: Norton, 1988.

WEBSITES OF INTEREST

Making sense of Marcel Duchamp — http://www.understandingduchamp.com/text.html

Photo reminiscent of Nude Descending Staircase — http://bestoflife.tumblr.com/post/65182692/artist-marcel-duchamp-walking-down-a-flight-of

Interviews with Duchamp — http://books.google.com/books?id=NVLdCWU7YfYC&printsec=frontcover&source=gbs_navlinks_s

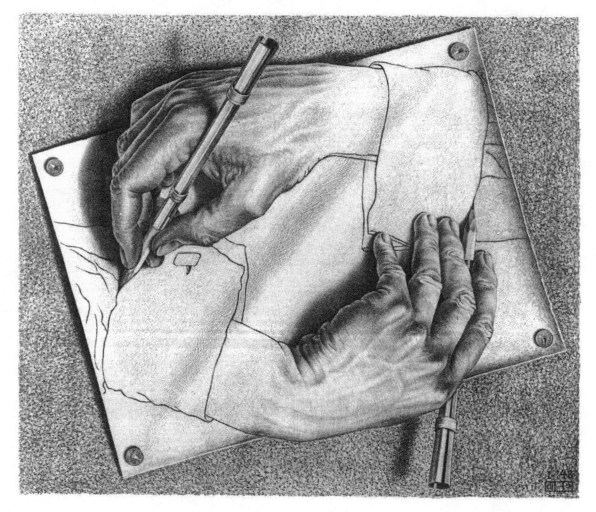

"Drawing Hands," 1948, M. C. Escher.

WRITING ABOUT THE ARTS

Chapter 7

YOU AND YOUR AUDIENCE

INTRODUCTION

The goal of this chapter is to give you a clear view of the importance of writing in the pursuit of arts appreciation and to enumerate some of the more important strategies for writing persuasively about your aesthetic experiences. As you will discover, writing is never an isolated activity. It is never easy, and good writing is never divorced from emotional attachment to a subject. This makes writing about the arts a perfect occasion for self-discovery, self-expression, self-discipline, and meaningful communication.

WHY WRITE?

THE WRITING LOOP

Plato learned an important clue to good writing from his teacher, Socrates: learning is best activated by dialogue. As a mode of learning, writing is a form of **dialectical** thinking (examining by question and answer), a kind of inner dialogue of the writer with himself. Therefore, good writing is the corollary to clear thinking.

In fact, we don't really know what we think until we read what we write. This kind of circular reasoning suggests a learning loop which looks something like the diagram below.

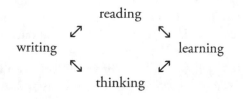

CLOCKWISE

It is possible to start anywhere on the wheel and go in any direction and make some sense of what is involved in this broader definition of writing. Indeed, it is virtually impossible to eliminate any of the elements because each one implies and draws on the other three. For example, reading naturally leads to learning and involves placing the learning into some already existing mental context, which is what thinking is all about. And thinking, even on its most superficial level, involves what actors call subtext, carrying on conversations with yourself. We could call this mental writing. The problem is that we write in our minds with disappearing ink—the silent verbalizing lasts only a minute and then gradually fades away. Ideally, we should quickly jot down our ideas before they disappear. In other words, we should write out the thinking process. This process is sometimes called "free writing," like spontaneously recording everything that comes into your mind. Every writer can tell horror stories of not taking notes and forever losing some important concept or original turn of phrase.

COUNTER-CLOCKWISE

Moving counter-clockwise, reading perceptively and actively, leads to a dialogue with the writer, prompting you to agree, modify, or take issue with the writer's ideas by writing down notes in the margins (an important part of the reading process). These notes provide convenient springboards for thinking about the issues raised; this leads to learning something new. This in turn impels you to read further in order to verify or contradict what you have learned. Eventually, your "glosses" (commentaries) on the text can supply the seeds out of which full-scale critical writing can germinate.

Whichever direction one goes on the wheel, writing should be the final step, because the written word preserves both the thinking process and what has been learned. This becomes the basis for further learning, thinking, and writing.

WHY WRITE ABOUT THE ARTS?

CREATING & CRITIQUING

"Artists cannot create art for 'the people' until people renew their capability for artistic experience. *It takes as much talent to respond to art as it does to create it*" (Highwater 17, own emphasis). Jamake Highwater's claim seems somewhat exaggerated. How many people spend as much time studying a painting, even one they like, as it took the artist to paint it? But his point makes more sense when we add the writing time necessary to fully explicate a work of art. An artwork is a kind of pivotal point between the creator, the critic, and the audience: it is the culmination of the artist's creative labors, a catalyst for the critic's professional reactions, and a trigger for the audience's aesthetic enjoyment.

THREE KINDS OF WRITING

In high school and college, students typically engage in three kinds of writing activities: (1) *reporting* (writing book reports, research papers, essay answers on exams, etc.); (2) *persuading* (writing critical reactions to issues raised in class, commenting on peer reactions, editorials to the school newspaper, etc.); and (3) *expressing* (personal statements to friends or relatives, letters home, love letters and so forth). Of all the kinds of writing typically done by students, writing about the arts is one of the most overlooked opportunities to learn to write that exist in higher education. Here are some of the more important reasons for its inclusion in the curriculum.

THE ARTS PROVIDE IDEAL OCCASIONS FOR WRITING

The popular arts (rock concerts, dances, television, and film) form the most common bond of shared experience among college students, and yet students rarely express in words what they think or how they feel about these events beyond such empty reactions as, "That concert was awesome!" or "That was so sweet!" or "That was really lame!" or "That wouldn't even entertain my dad if he was sedated!" Arts criticism is not alive and well on college campuses if these one-liners are any gauge of where we are. And yet, there are few more natural occasions for engaged writing than describing experiences with the arts, because everyone has an opinion about the movies they see, the music they listen to, or the books they read. These experiences carry definite emotional freight. Personal opinions and emotions are two of the most powerful motivators to speech and action that exist. Writing about the arts harnesses this otherwise maverick energy, giving it context and contour. To do this requires considerable discipline as well as mastery of a new vocabulary specific to each artistic species.

WRITING ABOUT THE ARTS HEALS THE SOPHIC-MANTIC SPLIT

What students soon discover when they begin to write about their aesthetic experiences is how quickly the honeymoon is over. The arts appeal directly to the senses, but it is not easy to make sense of sense experience, as anyone knows who has ever tried to write a love letter. Lovers and poets understand best how difficult it is to make words bear the full weight of one's emotions. T. S. ELIOT (1888–1965) in his long, lyrical poem *Four Quartets*, expresses his distress at the impossibility of marshaling words in the service of the poet's vision: "Words strain,/ Crack and sometimes break, under the burden,/ Under the tension, slip, slide, perish,/ Decay with imprecision, will not stay in place,/ Will not stay still" (19).

Thus, writing about the arts brings critical thinking to bear on emotional experience, bridging the two sides of our natures (left-brain/right-brain, head/heart). The traditional school curriculum emphasizes the development of intellectual skills over emotions and attitudes, and yet attitudes, more than skills, serve as primary motivators of human action. In short, few other occasions for writing require a student to verbalize an essentially nonverbal experience. In the process of learning to do this, thinking is sharpened as feelings are expressed more clearly, which in turn deepens our feelings. Writing about the arts experientially unites our two sides, the rational and the imaginative, from whence mature understanding emerges.

EXPRESSING THE INEXPRESSIBLE

The need to express the inexpressible is a constant struggle in life and in art. It is this fundamental human struggle we face in learning and writing about the arts. Pascal wrote: "The heart has its reasons, which reason does not know" (222). In other words, the heart knows things the mind does not begin to understand. As they start writing, students soon learn how limited their arts vocabulary is and yet how open-ended is the potential for creative and critical expansion of their usual nods of approval or their grunts of disdain. The arts can generate truly moving aesthetic experiences. Because aesthetic experiences, by definition, engage the primary senses of seeing and hearing, writing about the arts heightens perceptual awareness and deepens emotional and intellectual involvement in ways few other reasons for writing can accomplish.

Writing about the Arts Is Self-Reflexive

Writing brings things together and makes a personal statement that not only communicates your feelings and insights to others, but lets you know what you think and feel. Like the arts themselves, writing is both window and mirror. The best writing is both critical (public) and creative (personal). Writing about the arts provides an ideal occasion for self-discovery. In *The Critic as Artist*, OSCAR WILDE (1854–1900) speaks through his *persona* Gilbert:

> That is what the highest criticism really is, the record of one's own soul. It is more fascinating than history, as it is concerned simply with oneself. It is more delightful than philosophy, as its subject is concrete not abstract, real and not vague. It is the only civilized form of autobiography, as it deals not with the events, but with the thoughts of one's life; not with life's physical accidents of deed or circumstance, but with the spiritual moods and imaginative passions of the mind. (Qtd. in Bloom 217)

Writing Is the Road to the Real You

This text draws on many different writing strategies and exercises to release the natural tendency we all have to voice our opinions and to share our experiences with others. Everyone has opinions, and every opinion has some grain of truth, some spark of personal insight. "Everybody is original," writes Brenda Ueland, "if he tells the truth, if he speaks from himself. But it must be from his *true* self and not from the self he thinks he *should* be" (4, emphasis added). It is tempting, when we are still apprentice critics, either to adopt someone else's tastes or to slavishly follow some vaunted public authority. The power of some critics to make or break a work or a career has fostered the mistaken notion that only professional critics (the ones whose columns you read in newspapers and magazines or see on television) have a right to pontificate on artistic value. Their opinions are not necessarily unassailable, just more informed than the average person's, because they have spent more time than the rest of us in

learning their subject and craft. On the other hand, too many closet critics think that their own opinions are all that matter and that aesthetic judgment is relative and arbitrary. In spite of this great diversity of opinion, there are certain principles common to all the arts that a good critic should demonstrate, concepts which we will discuss as we deal with the sensitive issue of aesthetic judgment.

Writing Closes the Creative/Critical Loop

The very processes of creation and criticism are mirror images of each other: the artist's alternating right-brain/left-brain path from creative impulse (first insight), through labored analysis (saturation), to gestation (incubation), to discovering that the work is complete ("ah-ha"). And, finally, the reasoned clarity of the finished work (verification) finds its parallel (in reverse order) in the viewer's pathway into the work: first exposure (making sense of what is there); then having an aesthetic experience; pondering over it after the fact; then trying to put the experience into words (writing); and finally, coming to understand the work both analytically and aesthetically as the two sides of the brain finally come together in a holistic experience.

THE CREATIVE/CRITICAL LOOP

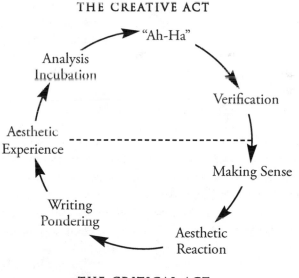

THE CREATIVE ACT

"Ah-Ha"

Analysis
Incubation

Verification

Aesthetic
Experience

Making Sense

Writing
Pondering

Aesthetic
Reaction

THE CRITICAL ACT

HOW TO WRITE ABOUT THE ARTS

Learning the Terminology

William Zinsser claims that good writing about the arts should do at least two things: teach us how to perceive (look and hear), and "give us the information we need to understand what we're looking at" and/or listening to (103–104).

The two tasks are closely related because the information largely determines the perception. Words can uncover hidden realities. For example, because Eskimos have several words for snow, their arctic environment is tagged with more verbal detail than ours; therefore, they can literally see more than we can. Art is also a language we can learn to decipher. The first step is to learn its special vocabulary and then apply that vocabulary to experiencing each art on its own terms, namely in terms of its medium (material), its elements (the various parts), and its forms (how the parts combine to make a whole). For many, learning about the arts produces the miracle of personal discovery, a breakthrough into a more ordered domain than the fleeting chaos life experience presents.

TAPPING THE METAPHORIC MIND

In *The Metaphoric Mind* Bob Samples argues that human consciousness begins as a right-brain function. The infant's first view of the world is a "blooming, buzzing confusion" because it is solely spatial and affective. The rational left-brain functions begin to form "when the private mind goes public" (24) and the child begins to attach word-labels to the unconnected fragments of its sensory experiences. But it is the maverick "metaphoric" right brain that gives form to the fragments (whether they be images or words) and makes writing vivid and interesting. The trick is to unravel the ball of thread that represents the spatial/emotional unity of the right brain into the linear, left-brain pattern of words on a page. This is what effective writing requires.

THE IMPORTANCE OF METAPHOR

Whether elevated or colloquial, writing is surely the most disciplined form of human communication. What often distinguishes interesting from pedestrian writing is **metaphor.** The Greek root of *metaphor* means, literally, "transference," or linking seemingly unlike things. A good example is Shakespeare's "Juliet is the sun" (*Romeo and Juliet* 2.2.3). Romeo could have said, "Juliet is the light of my life," or "She warms the cockles of my heart," or "My whole world revolves around Juliet." But Shakespeare's four-word metaphor says all that and more. Metaphors appealed to Aristotle because they helped readers grasp new ideas more quickly. "Now strange words simply puzzle us; ordinary words convey only what we know already; it is from metaphor that we can best get hold of something fresh" (662). Metaphors live somewhere between the profound and the pedestrian. Metaphors are memorable for Aristotle because they make "hearers *see* things" (664, emphasis added). This is the

basic reason for all writing, according to Joseph Conrad: "My task which I am trying to achieve is, by the power of the written word to make you hear, to make you feel—it is, before all, to make you *see*. That—and no more, and it is everything" (xiv, emphasis added). What good writing makes us hear, feel, and see are connections, the building blocks of all learning. Good writing is the mortar that holds the blocks together in the mind.

IMITATING GOOD WRITING

Once you have learned the basics of an art form, the best way to refine your ability to express your judgment about that form is to read the best critical writing about it. Almost without exception, the best writers are also avid readers, because reading builds a large vocabulary and supplies the mind with the memorable turns of phrase that are indispensable to good writing. Critical writers learn their craft by imitation, in both a positive and negative sense. They are drawn to approximate in their own writing the style and persuasive power of the best arts criticism they read and to shun that which confuses or disgusts them. We must do the same. Our writing goal in this course is to build vocabulary, understanding, and aesthetic sensitivity to the major fine arts by drawing upon the enriching power of metaphor, culminating in the written expression of these newly discovered aesthetic experiences. For Aristotle, the perfection of a writing style combines elevated, or metaphorical, language with clarity. "But the greatest thing by far is to be a master of metaphor. . . . [I]t is also a sign of genius, since a good metaphor implies an intuitive perception of the similarity in dissimilars" (694). The prime purpose for going through the agony of writing about the arts is to approach the ecstasy of insight that good critical writing affords. Your audience may be only yourself, but that is sufficient justification for the labor required, for it will open the door outward onto a landscape full of sublime creations and inward to a discovery of your own undiscovered greatness.

TO WHOM ARE YOU WRITING? STYLE & AUDIENCE

THE CREATIVE CHALLENGE

The only thing more intimidating than a person confronting the great unknown is a writer facing a blank sheet of paper. Edward Hart captures the creative essence of all good writing.

A person facing a blank sheet of paper faces, on a smaller scale, naturally, the same kind of problem faced by

God as he proceeded with the task of organizing our world out of chaos. And chaos is exactly the condition in our minds, no matter how crammed with information, before we begin to compose . . . and there is no greater feeling of accomplishment than that which comes from having organized chaos into the order of a well-written page. (48)

Writing not only challenges your creative instincts; it can also threaten your self-image. Craig Vetter warns the aspiring writer:

> This is your enemy: a perfectly empty sheet of paper. *Nothing* will ever happen here except what you make happen. If you are stupid, what happens will be like a signed confession of that fact. If you are unfunny, a humorless patch of words will grow here. If you lack imagination, your reader will know you immediately and forever as the slug you are. Or let me put it to you this way—and you may want to tattoo this somewhere on your bodies— BLANK PAPER IS GOD'S WAY OF TELLING US THAT IT'S NOT EASY TO BE GOD (43).

DIFFERENT STYLES

Compare the above two examples of writing about writing. How are they alike? They are both writing about the same thing—the challenge of writing. How are they different? Their styles differ dramatically. Ed Hart, professor and poet, writes in an appropriately sparse, informative style. Craig Vetter, on the other hand, is a professional writer, whose financial survival depends upon grabbing his reader by the throat. Whereas Hart maintains his professional, yet friendly distance—after quoting proverbs, he writes, "One of the best ways to get understanding is to attempt to put down on paper all that we know of a given subject" (48)—Vetter goes for the jugular: "Don't turn away, you wormy little cowards!" (43).

PURPOSE, AUDIENCE, & STYLE

This brings up three important questions about writing in general: (1) What is your purpose? (2) Who is your audience? and (3) What style will best meet the demands of both purpose and audience? Writing a humanities text, for instance, requires a shift in style to make the information more accessible and interesting to a college audience. Both of these writers are addressing college students. But while Hart's writing has the genteel touch of the academic, Vetter lowers his rhetorical sights a couple of notches to speak "your language." Which writer is better able to engage your interest? Which one do you trust more? Both grab our attention, but by different means and with quite different effects. Thus, beyond develop-

ing your own voice, which should echo the real you (not some English teacher clone), it is also useful to be able to modify the rhetorical level of that voice when addressing different audiences.

CONCLUSION

AESTHETIC PLEASURE

One humanities text begins: "The most important fact about the arts is that they give pleasure" (Britsch 1). This is a special kind of pleasure; it is aesthetic pleasure, which involves a deepening, elevating, and broadening expedition into the natural world through an imaginary restructuring of materials and situations. Ultimately, the writer's aesthetic pleasure is what distinguishes all good writing about the arts, for good arts criticism presupposes "passionate engagement" in actual works, as Robert Alter has written in *The Pleasures of Reading:* "Without a sense of deep pleasure in the experience of reading [fiction], the whole enterprise of teaching and writing . . . becomes pointless" (11). And even though the act of writing is notoriously unpleasant, if we believe the candid testimonials of countless professional writers, the product of our writing can create undeniable pleasure. As Zinsser admits, "I don't like to write, but I take great pleasure in having written—in having finally made an arrangement that has a certain inevitability like the solution to a mathematical problem. Perhaps in no other line of work is delayed gratification so delayed (34). If maturity is a measure of one's ability to forego immediate, lesser gratification, for a greater future reward, then writing is also an important key to mental and spiritual growth.

THE MIRACLE WORKER

One of the most dramatic examples of the indispensability of words in making sense of experience comes in Act III of William Gibson's *The Miracle Worker,* where Anne Sullivan drags Helen Keller down the steps to the front yard water pump to refill the pitcher Helen has just emptied onto Anne's lap. She does automatically what she has done so many times before; she spells into Helen's free palm.

> Water. W, a, t, e, r. Water. It has a—name-

> (And [then] the miracle happens. Helen drops the pitcher on the slab under the spout; it shatters. She stands transfixed. Annie freezes on the pump handle: there is a change in the sundown light, and with it a change in Helen's face, some light coming into it we have never seen there, some struggle in the depths behind it; and her lips tremble, try-

ing to remember something the muscles around them once knew, till at last it finds its way out, painfully, a baby sound buried under the debris of years of dumbness.)

Helen: Wah. Wah.

(And again, with great effort)

Wah. Wah. (118)

Helen then rushes wildly from felt object to felt object—the ground, the pump, the trellis, the bell, then her mother, her father, and finally Anne. Her dark and silent world has suddenly come alive with meaning and beauty. It is the pivotal moment of transition in her life from a little barbarian to an aspiring, maturing adult. The impact of her remarkable life was made possible by the miracle of language, first by making the world accessible to her, and then by making her unique vision accessible to the world, to us. Here is Helen's original account of her discovery of language, which, in spite of the simple elegance of her writing style, presents the dramatic breakthrough rather matter-of-factly:

> We walked down the path to the well-house, attracted by the fragrance of the honeysuckle with which it was covered. Some one was drawing water and my teacher placed my hand under the spout. As the cool stream gushed over one hand she spelled into the other the word *water*, first slowly, then rapidly. I stood still, my whole attention fixed upon the motions of her fingers. Suddenly I felt a . . . thought; and somehow the mystery of language was revealed to me. I knew then that "w-a-t-e-r" meant the wonderful cool something that was flowing over my hand. That living word awakened my soul, gave it light, hope, joy, set it free! There were barriers still, it is true, but barriers that could in time be swept away. (23–24)

THE MAGIC OF WORDS

Because we gradually learn our native tongue as young children, we forget the magic of words and how words tie us to experience, both real and imagined, such as when Helen Keller says, "suddenly I *felt a thought*." Steven Gilbar's fascinating collection *The Open Door* celebrates the discovery of reading gleaned from the personal experiences of twenty-nine famous writers. M. F. K. Fisher writes:

> I lay voluptuously on my stomach on the big bed, blissfully alone, and I felt a thrill which has never left me as I realized that the words coming magically from my lips were mine to say or not say, read or not. It was one of the peaks of my whole life. Slowly my eyes rode across the lines of print, and the New World smiled. It was mine, not

something to beg for, book in hand, from anyone who could read when I could not. The door opened, and without hesitation I walked through. (84)

WORDS AS BRIDGES

Keller's and Fisher's discovery of words harbors the central metaphor of all language: words are the bridge between the mind (our inner world) and experience (the outer world). Helen's discovery also captures the vicarious delight of all aesthetic experience: learning through the senses what others have experienced firsthand. She once said, "So I try to make the light in others' eyes my sun, the music in others' ears my symphony, the smile on others' lips my happiness." (131) For all of us who can hear and see, our senses open us up daily to knowledge that cannot be verbalized, whereas Helen's finger language was virtually the only way she could come to the visual and aural worlds we take for granted. In spite of our eyes and ears, we are all to a degree blind and deaf to the many worlds of art that surround us until we learn their special languages.

COMMENTARY ON THE ARTS

FREEWRITING

—*Peter Elbow*

The most effective way I know to improve your writing is to do freewriting exercises regularly. At least three times a week. They are sometimes called "automatic writing," "babbling," or "jabbering" exercises. The idea is simply to write for ten minutes (later on, perhaps fifteen or twenty). Don't stop for anything. Go quickly without rushing. Never stop to look back, to cross something out, to wonder how to spell something, to wonder what word or thought to use, or to think about what you are doing. If you can't think of a word or a spelling, just use a squiggle or else write, "I can't think of it." Just put down something. The easiest thing is just to put down whatever is in your mind. If you get stuck it's fine to write "I can't think what to say, I can't think what to say" as many times as you want, or repeat the last word you wrote over and over again; or anything else. The only requirement is that you never stop.

What happens to a freewriting exercise is important. It must be a piece of writing which, even if someone reads it, doesn't send any ripples back to you. It is like writing something and putting it in a bottle in the sea. The teacherless class helps your writing by providing maximum feedback. Freewritings help you by providing no feedback at all. When I assign one, I invite the writer to let me read it. But also tell him to keep it if he prefers. I read it quickly and make no comments at all and I do not speak with him about it. The main thing is that freewriting must never be evaluated in any way; in fact there must be no discussion or comment at all.

Here is an example of a fairly coherent exercise (sometimes they are very incoherent, which is fine):

> I think I'll write what's on my mind, but the only thing on my mind right now is what to write for ten minutes. I've never done this before and I'm not prepared in any way—the sky is cloudy today, how's that? now I'm afraid I won't be able to think of what to write when I get to the end of the sentence—well, here I am at the end of a sentence—here I am again, again, again, at least I'm still writing—Now I ask is there some reason to be happy that I'm still writing—ah yes! Here comes the question again—What am I getting out of this? What point is there in it? It's almost obscene to always ask but I seem to question everything that way and I was gonna say something else pertaining to that but I got so busy writing down the first part that I forgot what I was leading into. This is kind of fun oh don't stop writing—cars and trucks speeding by somewhere out the window, pens glittering across people's papers. The sky is cloudy—is it symbolic that I should be mentioning this? Huh? I dunno. Maybe I should try colors, blue, red, dirty words—wait a minute—no can't do that, orange, yellow, arm tired, green pink violent magenta lavender red brown black green—now that I can't think of any more colors—just about done—relief? maybe.

Freewriting may seem crazy but actually it makes simple sense. Think of the difference between speaking and writing. Writing has the advantage of permitting more editing. But that's its downfall too. Almost everybody interposes a massive and complicated series of editings between the time words start to be born into consciousness and when they finally come off the end of the pencil or typewriter onto the page. This is partly because schooling makes us obsessed with the "mistakes" we make in writing. Many people are constantly thinking about spelling and grammar as they try to write. I am always thinking about the awkwardness, wordiness, and general mushiness of my natural verbal product as I try to write down words.

But it's not just "mistakes" or "bad writing" we edit as we write. We also edit unacceptable thoughts and feelings, as we do in speaking. In writing there is more time to do it so the editing is heavier: when speaking, there's someone right there waiting for a reply and he'll get bored or think we're crazy if we don't come out with *something*. Most of the time in speaking, we settle for the catch-as-catch-can way in which the words tumble out. In writing, however,

there's a chance to try to get them right. But the opportunity to get them right is a terrible burden: you can work for two hours trying to get a paragraph "right" and discover it's not right at all. And then give up.

Editing, *in itself*, is not the problem. Editing is usually necessary if we want to end up with something satisfactory. The problem is that editing goes on *at the same time* as producing. The editor is, as it were, constantly looking over the shoulder of the producer and constantly fiddling with what he's doing while he's in the middle of trying to do it. No wonder the producer gets nervous, jumpy, inhibited, and finally can't be coherent. It's an unnecessary burden to try to think of words and also worry at the same time whether they're the right words.

The main thing about freewriting is that it is *nonediting*. It is an exercise in bringing together the process of producing words and putting them down on the page. Practiced regularly, it undoes the ingrained habit of editing at the same time you are trying to produce. It will make writing less blocked because words will come more easily. You will use up more paper, but chew up fewer pencils.

Next time you write, notice how often you stop yourself from writing down something you were going to write down. Or else, cross it out after it's written. "Naturally" you say, "it wasn't any good." But think for a moment about the occasions when you spoke well. Seldom was it because you first got the beginning just right. Usually it was a matter of a halting or even garbled beginning, but you kept going and your speech finally become coherent and even powerful. There is a lesson here for writing: trying to get the beginning just right is a formula for failure—and probably a secret tactic to make yourself give up writing. Make some words, whatever they are, and then grab hold of that line and reel in as hard as you can. Afterwards you can throw away lousy beginnings and make new ones. This is the quickest way to get into good writing.

The habit of compulsive, premature editing doesn't just make writing hard. It also makes writing dead. Your voice is damped out by all the interruptions, changes, and hesitations between the consciousness and the page. In your natural way of producing words there is a sound, a texture, a rhythm—a voice—which is the main source of power in your writing. I don't know how it works, but the voice is the force that will make a reader listen to you, the energy that drives the meanings through his thick skull. Maybe you don't *like* your voice; maybe people have made fun of it. But it's the only voice you've got. It's your only source of power. You better get back into it, no matter what you think of it. If you keep writing in it, it may change into something you like better. But if you abandon it, you'll likely never have a voice and never be heard.

Freewritings are vacuums. Gradually you will begin to carry over into your regular writing some of the voice, force, and connectedness that creep into those vacuums.

WRITING EXERCISE

Read the following excerpt from Richard Selzer's *Mortal Lessons: Notes on the Art of Surgery* and briefly respond to the questions that follow:

"THE EXACT LOCATION OF THE SOUL"

Someone asked me why a surgeon would write. Why, when the shelves are already too full? They sag under the deadweight of books. To add a single adverb is to risk exceeding the strength of the boards. A surgeon should abstain. A surgeon, whose fingers are more at home in the steamy gullies of the body than they are tapping the dry keys of a typewriter. A surgeon, who feels the slow slide of intestines against the back of his hand and is no more alarmed than were a family of snakes taking their comfort from such an indolent rubbing. A surgeon, who palms the human heart as though it were some captured bird.

Why should he write? Is it vanity that urges him? There is glory enough in the knife. Is it for money? One can make too much money. No. It is to search for some meaning in the ritual of surgery, which is at once murderous, painful, healing, and full of love. It is a devilish hard thing to transmit—to find, even. Perhaps if one were to cut out a heart, a lobe of the liver, a single convolution of the brain, and paste it to a page, it would speak with more eloquence than all the words of Balzac. Such a piece would need no literary style, no mass of erudition or history, but in its very shape and feel would tell all the frailty and strength, the despair and nobility of man. What? Publish a heart? A little piece of bone? Preposterous. Still I fear that is what it may require to reveal the truth that lies hidden in the body. Not all the undressing of Rabelais, Chekhov, or even William Carlos Williams have wrested it free, although God knows each one of those doctors made a heroic assault upon it.

I have come to believe that it is the flesh alone that counts. The rest is that with which we distract ourselves when we are not hungry or cold, in pain or ecstasy. In the recesses of the body I search for the philosopher's stone. I know it is there, hidden in the deepest, dampest cul-de-sac. It awaits discovery. To find it would be like the harnessing of fire. It would illuminate the world. Such a quest is not without pain. Who can gaze on so much misery and feel no hurt? Emerson has written that the poet is the only true doctor. I believe him, for the poet, lacking the impediment of speech with which the rest of us are afflicted, gazes, records, diagnoses, and prophesies. (15–16)

1. What do you make of the title in relation to Selzer's passionate attachment to the human body? Is he speaking ironically? Does he really believe the surgeon's scalpel can lay bare the human soul?

2. What do you think of Selzer's style of writing? How would you characterize it? What poetic devices does he use to grab and keep your attention? What, for example, is he saying about the human heart by comparing it to "some captured bird?"

3. What creative tensions do you detect in this kind of writing, namely, a scientist writing about medical procedures in the style of a poet? Does it work? Is that part of its appeal, exploiting the unexpected?

4. What is Selzer saying about the procedures of literary creativity and scientific scholarship (research and writing) when he says: "Perhaps if one were to cut out a heart, a lobe of the liver, a single convolution of the brain, and paste it to a page, it would speak with more eloquence than all the words of Balzac." How is this analogous to the composer, who, when asked what his piece meant, simply played it again?

5. Contrast the supreme self-confidence of Selzer's last paragraph above to Albert Camus's despair over ever arriving at a philosophical certainty about the nature of the universe (see below). Selzer delights in making metaphors about medicine; Camus despairs that we are forced to reduce the world to metaphor. Selzer is a surgeon seeking a philosophical truth in the human body; Camus is a philosopher unable to make scientific sense of the natural world.

> And here are trees and I know their gnarled surface, water and I feel its taste. These scents of grass and stars at night, certain evenings when the heart relaxes—how shall I negate this world whose power and strength I feel? Yet all the knowledge on earth will give me nothing to assure me that this world is mine. You describe it to me and you teach me to classify it. You enumerate its laws and in my thirst for knowledge I admit that they are true. You take apart its mechanism and my hope increases. At the final stage you teach me that this wondrous and multicolored universe can be reduced to the atom and that the atom

itself can be reduced to the electron. All this is good and I wait for you to continue. But you tell me of an invisible planetary system in which electrons gravitate around a nucleus. You explain this world to me with an image. I realize then that you have been reduced to poetry: I shall never know. (15)

How do the two writers differ in their attitudes toward the mysteries of the universe? How do their writing styles reflect these different attitudes? Finally, what is ironic about Selzer's confidence in the poet's prophetic gift in contrast to a modern novelist's futile struggle for certainty?

WORKS CITED

Alter, Robert. *The Pleasures of Reading: In an Ideological Age.* New York: Simon and Schuster, 1989.

Aristotle. "On Poetics." In Vol. 2, *The Works of Aristotle* Trans. W. Rhys Roberts. Vol. 9, *Great Books of the Western World.* Ed. Robert M. Hutchins. Chicago: Encyclopaedia Britannica, 1952.

———. "Rhetoric." In Vol. 2, *The Works of Aristotle.* Trans. Ingram Bywater. Vol. 9, *Great Books of the Western World.* Ed. Robert M. Hutchins. Chicago: Encyclopaedia Britannica, 1952.

Bloom, Harold. "Measuring the Canon: 'Wet Casements' and 'Tapestry.'" In *Modern Critical Views: John Ashbery* Ed. Harold Bloom. New York: Chelsea House, 1985.

Britsch, Ralph A., and Todd A. Britsch. *The Arts in Western Culture.* Englewood Cliffs, NJ: PrenticeHall, 1984.

Conrad, Joseph. *The Nigger of the "Narcissus": A Tale of the Sea.* Garden City, NJ: Doubleday, 1924.

Camus, Albert. *The Myth of Sisyphus.* Trans. Justin O'Brien. New York: Alfred A. Knopf, 1955.

Eliot, T. S. *Four Quartets.* New York: Harcourt Brace Jovanovich, 1943, 1971.

Gibson, William. *The Miracle Worker.* New York: Bantam, 1956.

Gilbar, Steven, ed. *The Open Door: When Writers First Learned to Read.* Boston: David R. Godine, 1989.

Hart, Edward L. "The Need Beyond Reason." *University Education,* Provo: Brigham Young University Press, n.d. 31–42.

Highwater, Jamake. "Imagination: The Key That Unlocks Art's Secret Language." *Christian Science Monitor* 28 June 1989: 16B–17.

Keller, Helen. *The Story of My Life.* Garden City, NY Doubleday, 1903.

Pascal, Blaise. *Pensées* Trans. W. F. Trotter. Vol. 33, *Great Books of the Western World.* Ed. Robert M. Hutchins. Chicago: Encyclopaedia Britannica, 1952.

Samples, Bob. *The Metaphoric Mind: A Celebration of Creative Consciousness.* Reading, MA.: Addison-Wesley, 1976.

Selzer, Richard. *Mortal Lessons: Notes on the Art of Surgery.* New York: Simon & Schuster, 1976.

Shakespeare, William. *Romeo and Juliet.* In Vol. 1, *Shakespeare.* Vol. 26, *Great Books of the Western World,* Ed. Robert M. Hutchins. Chicago: Encyclopaedia Britannica, 1952.

Ueland, Brenda. *If You Want to Write . . .* St. Paul: Graywolf Press, 1987.

Vetter, Craig. "Bonehead Writing." *Playboy* (August 1985), 43.

Zinsser, William. *Writing to Learn.* New York: Harper & Row, 1988.

WEBSITES OF INTEREST

Writing about the arts —
http://www.ccds.charlotte.nc.us/green/looking_and_writing_about_art.htm

Skills of Art Criticism —
http://instructional1.calstatela.edu/laa/aesthetics_2B.html

The performing arts

Unit III

DE ARTE POETICA

Logo of the Aldine Press, ca. Fifteenth Century, Venice.

INTRODUCTION TO POETRY

Chapter 8

INTRODUCTION

You may find it strange that we number poetry among the performing arts, when it is traditionally viewed as a literary art. However, since poetry presents us with virtually all the vocabulary and most of the literary forms one learns in literary theory, and because poetry grew out of an ancient oral (performing arts) tradition, we treat only this type of literature in this course. We assume (perhaps wrongly) that most students in their primary and secondary education have been exposed to more literature than any other art form. It is clear that the American school system rarely teaches students about the performing and visual arts, the very media experiences that occupy much adult leisure time (movies, plays, dances, concerts, etc.). Poetry is also easier to treat in a survey course that covers so much material and so many time-consuming activities in so short a time. We also feel a duty to preserve the love of words in our media age of the ubiquitous icon.

POETRY AS PERFORMANCE

The epic and lyric traditions since Homeric times have viewed poetry as a living performance; John Ciardi called it an expression of the "self-delighting play impulse" (6). Indeed, there is a long-standing practice of poetry actually having been performed before live audiences. The Romans gave Virgil standing ovations for public performances of his own poetry. In more recent times Dylan Thomas and Vachel Lindsay have performed their own and others' poetry. Such performances can even take on a musical dimension by virtue of the inherent metrical structure and tonal variety of spoken words. This is not to assert that all poets write with an ear toward performance. Writing poetry is a lonely and secret act. Reading poetry is also a solitary occasion, in which the actor and the audience are one and the same person.

WHAT IS A POEM?

MULTI-DIMENSIONAL LANGUAGE

The word **poetry** comes from the Greek *poieein,* which means, "to make." Thus, at its best, a poem is a well-wrought thing of words. But its effects are various. For some, like David Smith (see "Why Poetry Matters" below), poetic discovery is an eruption waiting to happen. For others, it is a sedative. The expressive power of a poem can create a holistic experience as all-embracing as a good movie. Laurence Perrine defined poetry as "a kind of multi-dimensional language . . . directed at the whole man, not just at his understanding. Poetry, to the INTELLECTUAL dimension, adds a SENSUOUS dimension, an EMOTIONAL dimension, and an IMAGINATIVE dimension." (10, own emphasis).

Because poetry is meant to stir all sides of the human experience—the mind, the senses, the emotions, and the imagination—it takes mental concentration equal to the poem's verbal dimensions to make sense of its form and content. We might call poetry freeze-dried experience. The reader's task is to reconstitute it by adding the liquid of one's own imagination and emotion. We do this by bringing to the reading of a poem an active mind, an open heart, and a familiarity with the sound and sense of words.

OUR POETIC HERITAGE

"Publishing a volume of verse," observed poet Don Marquis, "is like dropping a rose-petal down the Grand Canyon and waiting for the echo" (quoted in Lehman, 74–75). It isn't all the fault of poetry, of course. Modern society dotes on images, not words. As a consequence, poetry in our day has fallen on rather hard times, with a loyal but very small following in comparison to readers of best-selling novels, or other popular fiction. It wasn't always this way. In fact, the closer one gets to the ancient beginnings of the oral tradition in literature, the more magical and immediate the word becomes. Homer has been called the "singer of tales" because his stories could be transmitted only via the spoken or sung word, and apparently the actual delivery (voice inflections, etc.) carried as much meaning, and provided as much "musical" pleasure, as an understanding of the words themselves. Primitive religious incantations appeal for similar reasons.

THREE LANGUAGE REVOLUTIONS

Three major technological revolutions permanently changed the function of language in Western culture: the shift from an oral to a written culture (using an alphabet) in fifth-century B.C. Athens; the invention of printing in mid-sixteenth-century Germany; and, finally, the emergence of electronic media in the twentieth century (television). What has resulted is "the humiliation of the word," according to Jacques Ellul (quoted in Postman xiii). The power and prestige of the word has been significantly diminished because of the rise and omnipresence of visual forms of communication (films, videos, posters, billboards and advertising in general). Nevertheless, modern poets have continued to work their verbal magic, often drawing on extra-verbal resources like images and music.

"WORDSOUNDS"

DYLAN THOMAS (1914–1953), the twentieth-century Welsh poet whose poetry partakes of the rich sound associations of the ancient oral tradition, originally became a poet because he fell in love with nursery rhymes. What mattered was not the meanings, but "the words alone . . . the *sound* of them [which] were, to me, as the notes of bells, the sounds of musical instruments, the noises of wind, sea and rain" (267). It is not easy to come at words as this poet does, savoring "their spring-like selves, fresh from Eden's dew" (268), when "botching hacks [have] flattened them out into a colourless and insipid paste" (270). Words, for the poet, are living things, shapes of

sound that the craftsman-poet can "hew, carve, mould, coil, polish and plane . . . into patterns, sequences, sculptures, fugues of sound expressing some lyrical impulse, some spiritual doubt or conviction, some dimly realized truth" (269).

THE SENSE IN SOUNDS

THE ORIGIN OF LANGUAGE

Ancient Greek philosophers like Pythagoras, Heraclitus, and Plato subscribed to the "ding-dong" theory of language origins. As Richard Lederer puts it, "They believed that the universe is like a great bell and that every object in nature has a special 'ring.' Strike an object and out comes a word the sound of which is inherent in the thing itself" (132). This is a fascinating poetic notion, that the sounds of words are somehow connected to the objects they symbolize. English teachers burden us with a big word to define this word-sound connection, *onomatopoeia,* meaning that a word sounds like what it describes ("buzz," "hiss," "boom," etc.), and treat it as a rather trivial poetic device. But if Plato, and the rest are correct, this phenomenon reaches into the very essence of verbal communication. Consider the word for mother, or "ma" for short. This one-syllable maternal tag, according to Leonard Bernstein, must have been "one of the first proto-words ever uttered by man" (13). Many languages employ some phonetic variant of this "M" word for mother: *mater* (Latin), *mere* (French), *madre* (Spanish), *Mutter* (German), *mam* (Welsh), *mat* (Russian), *Ima* (Hebrew), *shi-ma* (Navajo), *masake* (Crow Indian), *ma* (Chinese); even in Swahili and Japanese they call her "mama." "Could it be more than mere coincidence," Lederer wonders, "that this pervasive *m* sound for words maternal is made by the pursing of lips in the manner of the suckling babe?" (132). This leads to some interesting speculation about the relationship between the sounds of language and the experiences common to all human beings.

POETIC FORMS

ORIGINAL FORMS

The first clue that you are reading a poem is the way it looks on the page. The lines are usually short, the first letter of each line is usually capitalized and the last words often **rhyme**. These are some of the characteristics we use to distinguish poems in this book from prose text. The visual form of the poem is the first thing that draws us into the poetic experience, not unlike the first impression one gets walking into a gallery of paintings: they are hung on the walls in a certain pattern.

THE THREE CLASSICAL GENRES

Our Western poetic forms began with the ancient cultures of Greece and Rome. These cultures fostered three kinds (or **genres**) of literature. The first is the **epic** (from the Greek *epos* = "word, tale, song"), which is a long, heroic, narrative poem in elevated style. The second is the **lyric,** which gets its name from a musical instrument called the lyre, since the recitation of these short, subjective poems was usually accompanied by the harp-like instrument. The last is the **dramatic** (from Greek *draein* = "to act"). The dramatic involved a narrative presented by actors impersonating characters. The evolving history of Western literature seems to follow this sequence of genres. The earliest literature grew out of the epic tradition. As cultures fostered individuality, lyric poetry prospered. And, at least in the case of Greek drama, theater in Western culture emerged from the recitation of mythic tales expressed in frenzied poems called **dithyrambs.**

TRADITIONAL FORMS

THE BALLAD

One of the simplest and most enduring forms of poetry is the **ballad.** It retains the folk song patterns of its origins—four lines of iambic verse alternating tetrameter (four-foot lines) and trimeter (three-foot lines). A nineteenth-century classic is Wordsworth's "Lucy." Here the singsong rhythms work because ballads narrate episodes from rural cultures, like southern Appalachia. More recently, popular protest songs, like "Hang Down Your Head, Tom Dooley," and popular ballad singers, like Bob Dylan and Joan Baez, have revived the ballad form. Any churchgoer is already familiar with this form, because many hymns follow this alternating tetrameter/trimeter pattern as in the text of "A Mighty Fortress Is Our God."

THE SONNET

One of the most rigorous poetic forms is the **sonnet,** a strict metrical pattern consisting of fourteen lines arranged in a particular rhyme scheme. Traditionally, there are two types: the Italian (or Petrarchan) sonnet, in which the fourteen lines are divided into two rhyming groups, an octave (*abbaabba*) and sestet (*cdecde*), to present a problem and then to resolve it; whereas the English (or Shakespearean) sonnet is divided into four sections, three quatrains and a couplet, typically rhyming *abab cdcd efef*

gg. This form lends itself to three variations on a theme with a pithy concluding couplet, as in Shakespeare's Sonnet 73 "That Time of Year."

> That time of year thou mayst in me behold
> When yellow leaves, or none, or few do hang
> Upon those boughs which shake against the cold,
> Bare ruined choirs, where late the sweet birds sang.
> In me thou see'st the twilight of such day
> As after sunset fadeth in the west;
> Which by and by black night doth take away,
> Death's second self, that seals up all in rest.
> In me thou see'st the glowing of such fire,
> That on the ashes of his youth doth lie,
> As the deathbed whereon it must expire,
> Consumed with that which it was nourished by.
> This thou perceiv'st, which makes thy love more strong,
> To love that well which thou must leave ere long.

THE ODE

A longer and more elevated form of poetry is the **ode,** an extended lyrical verse dealing with one central theme. In ancient times, odes were accompanied by music (the word comes from the Greek *oide* – "song") and appeared in Greek tragedies as poetic occasions for the **chorus** to comment on the action. The performance of the odes involved a three-part pattern: the **strophe** as the chorus moved up one side of the stage, the ANTISTROPHE as they moved down the other side, and the EPODE, as they chanted while standing in place. There are basically three types of odes in English that draw their inspiration from classical forms: the PINDARIC (with three strophes following the classical design above), as in Gray's "The Bard"; the HORATIAN (with one strophe), as in Collin's "Ode to Evening"; and the irregular (less bound by line number and rhyme scheme), as in Wordsworth's "Ode: Intimations on Immortality." One of the best-known odes in English is Keats's "Ode on a Grecian Urn," an irregular ode (containing 5 strophes), but with the conventional ten lines, written in iambic pentameter, and with a rhyme scheme that combines the Shakespearean quatrain with a Petrarchan sestet: *abab cdecde* (the last three lines depart from the pattern). The last strophe contains one of poetry's most memorable and oft-quoted lines.

> Thou still unravished bride of quietness,
> Thou foster child of silence and slow time,
> Sylvan historian, who canst thus express
> A flowery tale more sweetly than our rhyme:
> What leaf-fringed legend haunts about thy shape
> Of deities or mortals, or of both,
> In Tempe or the dales of Arcady?
> What men or gods are these? What maidens loath?

What mad pursuit? What struggle to escape?
    What pipes and timbrels? What wild ecstasy?

Heard melodies are sweet, but those unheard
    Are sweeter; therefore, ye soft pipes, play on;
Not to the sensual ear, but, more endeared,
    Pipe to the spirit ditties of no tone:
Fair youth, beneath the trees, thou canst not leave
    Thy song, nor ever can those trees be bare;
      Bold Lover, never, never canst thou kiss,
Though winning near the goal—yet, do not grieve;
      She cannot fade, though thou hast not thy bliss,
    Forever wilt thou love, and she be fair!

Ah, happy, happy boughs! That cannot shed
    Your leaves, nor ever bid the Spring adieu;
And, happy melodist, unwearied,
    Forever piping songs forever new;
More happy love! more happy, happy love!
    Forever warm and still to be enjoyed,
      Forever panting, and forever young;
All breathing human passion far above,
    That leaves a heart high-sorrowful and cloyed,
      A burning forehead, and a parching tongue.

Who are these coming to the sacrifice?
    To what green altar, O mysterious priest,
Lead'st thou that heifer lowing at the skies,
    And all her silken flanks with garlands dressed?
What little town by river or sea shore,
    Or mountain-built with peaceful citadel,
      Is emptied of this folk, this pious morn?
And, little town, thy streets forevermore
    Will silent be; and not a soul to tell
      Why thou art desolate, can e'er return.

O Attic shape! Fair attitude! With brede
    Of marble men and maidens overwrought,
With forest branches and the trodden weed;
    Thou, silent form, dost tease us out of thought,
As doth eternity: Cold Pastoral!
    When old age shall this generation waste,
      Thou shalt remain, in midst of the other woe
Than ours, a friend to man, to whom thou say'st,
"Beauty is truth, truth beauty,"—that is all
    Ye know on earth, and all ye need to know.

NON-TRADITIONAL FORMS

FREE VERSE

Of the most common non-traditional form, **free verse,**
Robert Frost once said, "I'd as soon write free verse as play
tennis with the net down" (quoted in Lehman 74–75).
And yet, since Walt Whitman wrote "Song of Myself"
(1855), a poem that was tantamount to a "declaration of
America's poetic independence," American poets like

William Carlos Williams and e. e. cummings have celebrated the poet's freedom to create new forms for new
ideas. William Carlos Williams's poem, "The Red
Wheelbarrow," brings together three vivid images in a
deceptively simple context, introduced by the urgency of
the first words: "so much depends upon." Williams'
unusual word placement owes much to the rise of
American technology in the early twentieth century, not
the least of which was the mechanical action of the typewriter, the poet's favored mode of writing. He retyped the
lines many times to get the arrangement right. Thus, for
Williams, the words on the page were comparable to paint
on a canvas, something to be manipulated for expressive
effect.

> so much depends
> upon
>
> a red wheel
> barrow
>
> glazed with rain
> water
>
> beside the white
> chickens.

Cummings, on the other hand, engaged in both typo-
graphical and syntactical, or grammatical, experimentation by rearranging the words on the page for certain
effects. He also placed words in unexpected relationships
in the sentence, such as making nouns out of verbs and
adjectives out of nouns, as in his delightful "anyone lived
in a pretty how town." "In Just—" represents one of his
most endearing and enduring mature poems. It is the first
in a group entitled *Chansons Innocents,* poems portraying
the innocence and vulnerability of childhood.

> In Just—
> spring   when the world is mud-
> luscious the little
> lame balloonman
>
> whistles   far   and wee
>
> and eddieandbill come
> running from marbles and
> piracies and it's
> spring
>
> when the world is puddle-wonderful
>
> the queer
> old balloonman whistles
> far   and   wee

and bettyandisbel come dancing

from hop-scotch and jump-rope and

it's
spring
and
   the

goat-footed

balloonMan   whistles
far
and
wee

CONCRETE POETRY

Cummings's experiments with word placement have given rise to more recent poetry in which the words function less as carriers of meaning and more as elements of construction. This is reminiscent of the visual poems one finds in the seventeenth-century poetry of George Herbert, "Easter Wings," for example, or some of Lewis Carroll's whimsical shaped poems from *Alice in Wonderland,* like the "long and sad tail of the Mouse." Twentieth-century experiments with concrete poetry bring poems close to purely visual constructs.

The technical term for such poems, *carmen figuratum,* refers to poems so written that the form of the printed words suggests the subject matter. Instead of a word sounding as it means (as in **onomatopoeia**), the poem looks as it means. Contemporary poets, such as Eugen Gomringer and Max Bense, push this visual dimension to the limit, creating "concrete" poems in which the verbal meaning is merely incidental to the shapes of the words on the page. In fact, the resulting poems are designed to be as easily understood as traffic signs. "Forsythia," is an example. The word is made into an **acronym** of telegraphic succinctness: "Forsythia Out Race Spring's Yellow Telegram Hope Insists Action," with the beginning letters strung out to suggest the spreading branches of the spring-blooming, yellow-blossomed bush.

Some of the most original works of twentieth-century art grow in the borderlands separating one discipline from another: iconic poetry, on the one hand, and narrative paintings on the other, art which includes printed words or phrases right on the canvas, like René Magritte's "Ceci n'est pas une pipe," mentioned in Chapter 6. Picasso also played with the tensions between art and reality. Such works often cause us to think, to puzzle over the nature of art and its connection to the real world. These types of mongrel works amuse and often point to deep paradoxes in human experience.

THE POWER OF FORM

In mentioning that a lyre once accompanied the lyric poem, we have noted the ancient musical roots of poetry. These roots come through in John Ciardi's theatrical definition of a poem as "a living performance, an exercise in self-delighting form" (from a lecture). What is so delightful about poetic form? In the first place, poetic form can stand alone, can delight without meaning, as in this nonsense poem:

> Big Chief Pottawattami
> Sat in the sun and said:
> Me hot am I."
> Sat in the shade and said:
> "Me cooler."
> Such is the life of an Indian ruler.

This kind of doggerel verse provides some comic relief from the mundane cares of our lives. In the second place, poetic form shapes the content—the message—by predisposing us to read it a certain way. We read free verse, for example, with less concern for the unity of sound and sense, while sonnets adhere strictly to a set **meter** and rhyme scheme. Good poems are like good people—the outward form conforms to the inner content. Otherwise there is no wholeness, no integrity. A common flaw in poetry is mismatched form and content, most often the error of amateur poets who unwittingly insert profound sentiments in a sing-song metrical pattern.

HOW DOES A POEM SOUND?

POETIC RHYTHMS

EDGAR ALLAN POE (1809–1849) made no distinction between the sound and the sense of a poem. He said that poetry is "music . . . combined with a pleasurable idea" (quoted in Perrine 152). Because both poetry and music are sound mediums, they share a common element that gives them life—rhythm—not unlike the essential rhythm of the body, the heartbeat. As musical rhythms are determined by time signatures (3/4, 4/4 time, etc.) repeated each measure, so poetic rhythms are measured by the type and number of rhythmic units (called "feet") in a line. Each foot is a pattern of stressed (´) and unstressed (˘) syllables. In English, the five standard feet are **iambic** (˘ ´), **trochaic** (´ ˘), **anapestic** (˘ ˘ ´), **dactylic** (´ ˘ ˘), and **spondaic** (´ ´). For example:

Iambic pentameter (five "iambic" feet in a line, the
English "classical" meter)

"I will not be afraid of death and bane,
Till Birnan forest come to Dunsinane."
Macbeth, (Act V, scene III, lines 59 and 60)

Trochaic tetrameter

"Peter, Peter, Pumpkin eater
had a wife and couldn't keep her."

Anapestic tetrameter

"'Twas the night before Christmas and all through
the house,
Not a creature was stirring, not even a mouse."

Dactylic trimeter

"Anyone lived in a pretty how town"

Spondaic trimeter

"Warm day, cold night, wet feet."

POETIC "TIMBRES"

Tone color (**timbre**) represents another musical element that figures prominently in the appreciation of
poetic sounds. Each vowel and consonant has its own special evocative tone: short vowels in a line of poetry create
different rhythms from long vowels, like the difference
between STACCATO and LEGATO in music, particularly if
they are linked with certain consonants. Basically, we can
divide the consonants of the alphabet into pleasant and
harsh sounds: the harsh sounds are created by a kind of
explosion, like the "plosives," *p, b, t, j,* etc.; smoother,
more pleasant sounds are created by the "fricatives," *f, v,
th,* etc.; the "sibilants," *s, z, sh,* etc.; the "liquids," *l, r,* etc.;
and the "nasals," *m, n,* etc. These sound choices in poetry
are like music: euphony (pleasant) and cacophony
(unpleasant) are similar to CONSONANCE and DISSONANCE
in music.

ROBERT HERRICK'S (1591–1674) poem "Upon Julia's
Voice" beautifully exploits the pleasant range of word
sounds to approximate the lilting quality of his lover's
voice.

> So smooth, so sweet, so silvery is thy voice,
> As, could they hear, the Damned would make no noise,
> But listen to thee (walking in thy chamber)
> Melting melodious words to Lutes of Amber.

The amorous and delicate mood of this poem draws
its effect from the soft timbres of the sibilants, liquids,
and nasals. The rhyme scheme of the two couplets is not
exact, but approximate. This is called SLANT RHYME and
creates an effect similar to a musical cadence, where the
voiced *s* in *noise* creates a more conclusive sound than the
unvoiced *c* in *voice,* and the flat *A* in *Amber* gives a lower,
more final sound than the long *a* in *chamber.* The following excerpt from Tennyson's (1809–1892) *Morte
d'Arthur* shifts from harsh onomatopoeic sounds describing his "clanking" descent from the cliffs to the lake,
where the sounds suddenly shift to fit a more serene scene.

> Dry clashed his harness in the icy caves
> And barren chasms, and all to left and right
> The bare black cliff clanged round him, as he based
> His feet on juts of slippery crag that rang
> Sharp-smitten with the dint of armed heels—
> And on a sudden, lo! the level lake,
> And the long glories of the winter moon.
> (lines 186–192, pp. 197–198)

Here there are no end rhymes. It's the final shift to mellow sounds in the last two lines that marks the moon-lit
arrival at the lake. Under the watchful eye and ear of a
great poet like Tennyson, such details are almost invisible, so seamless are the borders between sound and sense.
This marriage of music and meaning marks all good
poetry. The sounds, evocative as they may be, are never
mere decoration.

Other languages, because they contain some completely different sounds, offer a rich alternate variety of
timbres to draw upon. The concluding stanza of Detlev
von Liliencron's (1844–1909) *Die Musik Kommt* ("The
Music Is Coming") deliberately emphasizes the harsh
sounds of the German guttural *r* and *ch* sounds to create
a rather humorous effect: the martial sounds of an
approaching brass band juxtaposed with the description
of a butterfly coming around the corner (the German
word for butterfly, *Schmetterling,* creates a jarring contrast
to the thing it symbolizes, a reverse kind of onomatopoeia).

> Klingling, tschingtsching und Paukenkrach,
> Noch aus der Ferne tönt es schwach,
> Ganz leise bumbumbumbum tsching,
> Zog da ein hunter Schmetterling,
> Tschingtsching, bum, um die Ecke?
>
> (lines 31–35)

WHAT DOES A POEM MEAN?

LEARNING BY INDIRECTION

What does a poem mean? Robert Frost provided a somewhat cryptic answer to the question: "Poetry provides the one permissible way of saying one thing and meaning another." Edward Arlington Robinson added: "Poetry is language that tells us something that cannot be said" (quoted in Stevenson 1516). To the practical-minded, such double-talk smacks of downright foolishness. Most uninitiated readers of poetry get a bit impatient with the poet's beating around the bush. A common reaction is "Why doesn't he just say what he means?!?" Part of the reason lies in the fact that half the fun is in the journey, not the destination. As mentioned before, poetry is multi-dimensional language. Its purpose is not just to tell us something, but to savor the telling. As e. e. cummings might have said: more the 'how' than the 'what.' Message hunting in poetry is often maligned by poets, even those who plant messages in their poems, because of the ease with which we mistake the poetic quality for the reducible moral or content and thereby miss the pure pleasure of dwelling upon the words themselves.

Perhaps part of our uneasiness with the poet's meandering indirection comes from our desire for certainty. A Cliff Notes mentality just wants the answer. Some people also display a Puritan passion for goal-setting and thereby mistake the means for the end. But a poem is more of a road map leading us on an imaginative journey through a forest of symbols that invite us to invent a personally conceived landscape of meanings.

DENOTATIONS & CONNOTATIONS

A first step in the process of deciphering a poem is making the distinction between **denotations** (dictionary definitions) and **connotations** (the related associations). For example, "spring" *denotes* the time of year when vegetation starts anew, but it *connotes* or suggests warmth, rebirth, love, etc. People who learn a foreign language for the first time may know a word's denotations but they may not recognize its connotations. A person learning English may use the word *molest* in its denotation (to bother) and not realize it also has an especially negative connotation. Both poets and prophets prefer figurative or connotative meanings to literal or denotative meanings because they are more engaging; they invite the reader's participation in the making of meaning, rather than imposing a pre-established order on things. Notice the evocative connotations in Emily Dickinson's (1830–1886) poem "A Book":

There is no frigate like a book
To take us lands away,
Nor any coursers like a page
Of prancing poetry
(lines 1–4, p. 234)

Imagine what would be lost if she had replaced the adventurous connotations of *frigate* with *ship,* or the romantic *lands* with *miles,* or *coursers* with *horses* (Perrine 33). The poem would lose its central appeal. Who would even want to go on the journey with such pedestrian prose?

THE LITERAL & THE FIGURATIVE

The literal-minded have a particular difficulty with figurative language. The Bible is full of poetic figures. As mentioned before, when Jesus was trying to teach Nicodemus about the necessity of baptism, He said: "Except a man be born again, he cannot see the kingdom of God [and] Nicodemus saith unto him, How can a man be born when he is old? Can he enter the second time into his mother's womb, and be born?" (John 3:3–4) The truth, taught with **metaphor** and parable, eludes any strictly rational interpretation or translation. And yet we use such figurative language all the time, sometimes not even realizing it, in order to dress up our speech or to call attention to our style of language or simply to speak more interestingly. To learn some of the most common figures of speech, imagine that your roommate has just come in out of a downpour, and you say:

"Well, you're a pretty sight!" (saying the opposite of what you mean is **irony)**

"Got slightly wet, didn't you?" (saying less than you mean is **understatement)**

And your roommate replies:

"Wet? I'm drowned!" (saying more than you mean is **overstatement** or **hyperbole)**

"It's raining cats and dogs outside (making direct comparisons is **metaphor)**

. . . and my raincoat's just like a sieve!" (using "like" or "as" is **simile)** [Perrine 60]

The following are some poetic examples of figures of speech:

Irony: "Brutus is an honorable man. So are they all honorable men." —Shakespeare, *Julius Caesar,* Act I, scene ii, lines 82–83.

Understatement: "Yesterday I saw a woman flayed [skinned], and you will hardly believe how it altered her person for the worse." —Jonathan Swift

Overstatement (hyperbole): "I shall be telling this with a sigh / Somewhere ages and ages hence." —Robert Frost, "The Road Not Taken," lines 16–17.

Metaphor: "Juliet is the sun." —Shakespeare, *Romeo and Juliet*, Act II, Scene ii, line 3.

Simile: "Somewhere high up in the heaven's gorges, in the wind's blast, the stars like molting pure-white flowers in darkness fell" —Kazantzakis, *The Odyssey*, Book One, p. 9, lines 273–274.

Personification: "The yellow fog that rubs its back upon the window-panes, / The yellow smoke that rubs its muzzle on the window-panes / Licked its tongue into the corners of the evening" —T. S. Eliot, *The Love Song of J. Alfred Prufrock*, 4.

WHAT DOES A POEM VISUALIZE?

IMAGERY

An additional tool the poet uses for creating imaginative experiences with words is **imagery.** Besides providing visual prompts, words can spark direct associations to the senses—seeing, hearing, tasting, smelling, and body movement. Some of the most concentrated poetry comes in the form of Japanese HAIKU. Although the form is often lost in translation it includes three lines of five, seven, and five syllables. Haiku creates a picture designed to arouse a distinct emotion or to suggest some treasured insight. Unlike SENRYU, which also has seventeen syllables but is lighter in mood, haiku is deeply serious and highly conventional, and virtually impossible to translate. However, here are a few to give you a taste of the genre.

> When winter snows melt
> the village streets are flooded
> with laughing children.
> —Kobayashi Issa

The next haiku was found on the last page of a Japanese Kamikaze pilot's diary.

> Like cherry blossoms
> In the spring
> Let us fall
> Clean and radiant.

We begin to understand how many factors enter into the full enjoyment of a poem, how much meaning can be packed into so few words. This again shows how poetry is freeze-dried language to which we must add the liquid of our own imaginations to give it life.

TYPES OF IMAGERY

Visual: "Splintered into prisms on the rainbow walls." —Amy Lowell

Auditory: "Thy madly-whistled laughter, echoing, rumbling like an earthquake." —Walt Whitman

Taste-Smell: "Of candied apple, quince, and plum." —Keats

Touch-Motor: "a heavy sun lifts himself—is lifted—bit by bit above the edge of things," —William Carlos Williams

SUMMARY ANALYSIS: "FOUR WAYS OF LOOKING AT A POEM"

THE FOURFOLD WAY OF INTERPRETATION

At the risk of being unpoetic by saying too much, consider one final analytical exploration. One of the oldest HERMENEUTICAL approaches (from Greek *hermeneutike* = interpretive art, and connected to Hermes, the messenger god) is the fourfold way of interpreting scripture: (1) the literal, (2) the **allegorical**, (3) the moral, and (4) the **anagogical** or spiritual. For example, Jerusalem is literally a city in Palestine, allegorically it's the Christian Church, morally it's the believing soul, and anagogically it's the heavenly City of God. These levels of meaning (sometimes referred to as the **Four Senses of Interpretation**) are regularly applied to classical and medieval literature, like Virgil's *Aeneid* or Dante's *Divine Comedy*. But they also work with certain modern poems, which lend themselves to multiple levels of meaning.

> ### Tag, I.D.
>
> Bright oval on a light chain
> Last name first,
> Then Christian name
> And middle initial
> A number assigned by his master,
> A letter for his blood,
> Another for his god
> Tooth-notched
> Stainless steel coin
> For the boatman.
> —John Sterling Harris

LITERAL

On the literal level we are interested in the subject matter, the self-evident information. The title tips us off that this poem describes a seemingly simple object, an I.D. tag, the kind soldiers wear in military service. Denotatively, this poem merely describes the object: it is oval-shaped, attached to a light (ball) chain; it contains the soldier's last name, first name, and middle initial, together with his service number, his blood type, and his religious persuasion (P for Protestant, C for Catholic, J for Jew, etc.). It is not accidental to the choice of subject matter and the clinical descriptive style that the poet has been in the military and is a professor of English with a specialty in technical writing. The poem makes good sense on this level, with the possible exception of the last three lines.

ALLEGORICAL

Going a level deeper, the allegorical meaning translates abstract notions into pictures, in short, a story with an unstated moral whose meaning lies outside the narrative. The concluding two lines of this poem point us outside the narrative, but to what? The coin given to a boatman alludes to Charon, the legendary Greek who ferried dead souls to Hades across the river Styx. The ancient Greeks placed a coin in the dead person's mouth as payment for a safe journey. In a Christian context, the silver coin alludes to the original betrayal of Christ by Judas. In a capitalist society, the silver coin suggests making merchandise out of human life. By tacking on a pagan reference to a Christian poem about war, the poet may be questioning our traditional notions of war as something courageous and right (defense of family, country, etc.). By connecting the tooth-notched ID tag with this pagan ritual, the poet drives home a sobering message: war is hell and fundamentally unchristian. There are other related allusions that contribute to this **allegorical interpretation**. The word "tag" points to the final lines of a speech or play; it also suggests a ragged or tattered edge, as a worthless remnant of clothing. Its etymology derives from the Scandinavian, referring to a spike or tooth, again referring back to the tag itself, the central image in the poem.

MORAL

If allegory teaches by analogy, the moral dimension makes value judgments about the events. In wartime a soldier is a mere number, not a human being. War dehumanizes humans, making them into merchandise to be used and used up in the effort to achieve victory. If a soldier is called by a name, it's always a last name: "Jones,

hit the deck and give me 20!" His "master" is the cadre of superiors who assigns him his number and exercises complete control over the circumstances of his life and death. When his "number is up," his next of kin (his blood) receive a "letter" from the war department beginning, "We regret to inform you that . . ." The moral of the poem focuses our attention on the brutal experience of war in which traditional human values are reversed ("It's okay to kill as long as you're killing the enemy.") and treats human beings as anonymous cogs in the war machine.

ANAGOGICAL (SPIRITUAL)

The spiritual level of this poem centers around the veiled allusions to Christ in the words "Bright" and "light," "last [shall be] first," "middle" (Christ came in the middle or Meridian of time), "master" (the title given Christ by his disciples), "blood" (of the Atonement), "God," the Father of Christ, and "Stainless" (Christ the perfect being whose atonement removed the stain of sin from all humankind). These unmistakable Christian allusions point to some deep paradoxes in this poem. In the first place, Christ's redemption is paradoxical: his death brings life; his suffering releases the Christian faithful from suffering ("By his stripes we are healed"). But set in a poem about war, the Christian faces another personal paradox: How can a true Christian kill when his religion counsels him to "turn the other cheek"? to "love your enemies"? A careful reading of this poem will afflict the reader with some deep dilemmas about what it means to be patriotic, to be a practicing Christian, and to act independently of circumstances. Finally, it offers another interpretation of what it means to die for your country. Ultimately, the conclusion is left up to the reader. It's not either "Don't go to war" (or you'll get killed), or "Go to war and kill or be killed (because it's your duty), but both and more. Is giving your life for your country a redemptive act, analogous to Christ's willing sacrifice? Or is sacrifice, personal or otherwise, ultimately a pagan ritual, a mindless submission to violence and madness?

WHY POETRY MATTERS

THOUGHTS FROM THE HEART OF CAMPUS: "POETRY AS A WAY OF LIFE, NOT SUBJECT OF STUDY"

—David Smith

At the end of a psychology discussion, Professor Harold Miller read a poem called "Ideas of Order at Key West" by Wallace Stevens. It began, "She sang beyond the genius of the sea." Somewhere in the middle of the theatrical distances and bronze shadows heaped on high horizons, the bell rang. Books slapped shut and papers rattled as students began their exodus, but I could not move. He continued, "Then we, / As we beheld her striding there alone, / Knew that there never was a world for her / Except the one she sang and, singing, made." The words hung around like the smell of bread, so when the semester ended, I sold back my textbooks and found the poetry section in the bookstore. I spent most of the money on three books of poetry including *The Collected Poems of Wallace Stevens*. I reread "Ideas of Order at Key West" several times, found "Thirteen Ways of Looking at a Blackbird," lost myself in it, read "The Man with the Blue Guitar," 10 times—breathless as I read though I did not say a word out loud.

After the "shock" of hearing and reading poetry that wooed my carnal vision to sobriety, I began to rewrite my own world after the inspiration of poetry. Actually, my exposure to beautiful language had begun after two years in a Third World country made me sensitive to poverty and adversity, sending me into an emotional crash. . . . Poetry does not ignore the profound problems of life or attempt to smooth them over with simple platitudes, but it does celebrate the nobility of the human struggle. It finds in the beauty of language a way to balance the ugly and obscene.

Poetry is not a subject to study and dissect like a fetal pig; it is a way of life. Plato said "God takes away the minds of the poets and uses them for his ministers." He celebrated the mystic transformation of an audience as it listens to a beautiful verse. Poetry, then, is sacred as a way of worship. I realize that now, though it took several years to overcome my prejudice and really listen to poetry. I remember the way the world faded one day in a psychology lecture as I heard a poem read aloud. "She sang beyond the genius of the sea," and I will forever hear the echo. (Used by permission of *The Daily Universe*)

COMMENTARY ON THE ARTS

NOTES ON THE ART OF POETRY

—*Dylan Thomas*

You want to know why and how I just began to write poetry, and which poets or kinds of poetry I was first moved and influenced by. To answer the first part of this question, I should say I wanted to write poetry in the beginning because I had fallen in love with words. The first poems I knew were nursery rhymes, and before I

could read them for myself I had come to love just the words of them, the words alone. What the words stood for, symbolised, or meant, was of very secondary importance. What mattered was the *sound* of them as I heard them for the first time on the lips of the remote and incomprehensible grown-ups who seemed, for some reason, to be living in my world. And these words were, to me, as the notes of bells, the sounds of musical instruments, the noises of wind, sea, and rain, the rattle of milkcarts, the clopping of hooves on cobbles, the fingering of branches on a window pane might be to someone, deaf from birth, who has miraculously found his hearing. I did not care what the words said, overmuch, nor what happened to Jack and Jill and the Mother Goose rest of them; I cared for the shapes of sound that their names, and the words describing their actions, made in my ears; I cared for the colours the words cast on my eyes. I realise that I may be, as I think back all that way, romanticising my reactions to the simple and beautiful words of those pure poems; but that is all I can honestly remember, however much time might have falsified my memory. I fell in love—that is the only expression I can think of—at once, and am still at the mercy of words, though sometimes now, knowing a little of their behaviour very well, I think I can influence them slightly and have even learned to beat them now and then, which they appear to enjoy. I tumbled for words at once. And, when I began to read the nursery rhymes for myself, and, later, to read other verses and ballads, I knew that I had discovered the most important things, to me, that could be ever. There they were, seemingly lifeless, made only of black and white, but out of them, out of their own being, came love and terror and pity and pain and wonder and all the other vague abstractions that make our ephemeral lives dangerous, great, and bearable. Out of them came the gusts and grunts and hiccups and heehaws of the common fun of the earth; and though what the words meant was, in its own way, often deliciously funny enough, so much funnier seemed to me, at that almost forgotten time, the shape and shade and size and noise of the words as they hummed, strummed, jugged, and galloped along. That was the time of innocence; words burst upon me, unencumbered by trivial or portentous association; words were their spring-like selves, fresh with Eden's dew, as they flew out of the air. They made their own original associations as they sprang and shone. The words "Ride a cockhorse to Banbury Cross" were as haunting to me, who did not know then what a cock-horse was nor cared a damn where Banbury Cross might be, as, much later, were such lines as John Donne's "Go and catch a falling star, Get with child a mandrake root," which also I could not understand when I first read them. And as I read more and more, and it was not all verse, by any means, my love for the real life of words increased until I knew that I must live *with* them and *in* them always. I knew, in fact, that I must be a writer of words, and nothing else. The first thing was to feel and know their sound and substance; what I was going to do with those words, what use I was going to make of them, what I was going to say through them, would come later. I knew I had to know them most intimately in all their forms and moods, their ups and downs, their chops and changes, their needs and demands. (Here, I am afraid, I am beginning to talk too vaguely. I do not like writing *about* words, because then I often use bad and wrong and stale and wooly words. What I like to do is to treat words as a craftsman does his wood or stone or what-have-you, to hew, carve, mould, coil, polish, and plane them into patterns, sequences, sculptures, figures of sound expressing some lyrical impulse, some spiritual doubt or conviction, some dimly realised truth I must try to reach and realise). It was when I was very young, and just at school, that, in my father's study, before homework that was never done, I began to know one kind of writing from another, one kind of goodness, one kind of badness. My first, and greatest, liberty was that of being able to read everything and anything I cared to. I read indiscriminately, and with my eyes hanging out. I could never have dreamt that there were such goings-on in the world between the covers of books, such sandstorms and ice-blasts of words, such lashing of humbug, and humbug, too, such staggering peace, such enormous laughter, such and so many blinding bright lights breaking across the justawaking wits and splashing all over the pages in a million bits and pieces all of which were words, words, words, and each of which was alive forever in its own delight and glory and oddity and light (I must try not to make these supposedly helpful notes as confusing as my poems themselves.) I wrote endless imitations, though I never thought them to be imitations but, rather, wonderfully original things, like eggs laid by tigers. They were imitations of anything I happened to be reading at the time: Sir Thomas Browne, de Quincey, Henry Newbolt, the Ballads, Blake, Baroness Orczy, Marlowe, Chums, the Imagists, the Bible, Poe, Keats, Lawrence, Anon., and Shakespeare. A mixed lot, as you see, and randomly remembered. I tried my callow hand at almost every poetical form. How could I learn the tricks of a trade unless I tried to do them myself? I learned that the bad tricks come easily; and the good ones, which help you to say what you think you wish to say in the most meaningful, moving way, I am still learning. (But in earnest company you must call these tricks by other names, such as technical devices, prosodic experiments, etc.)

The writers, then, who influenced my earliest poems and stories were, quite simply and truthfully, all the writers I was reading at the time, and, as you see from a specimen list higher up the page, they ranged from writers of schoolboy adventure yarns to incomparable and inimitable masters like Blake. That is, when I began, bad writing had as much influence on my stuff as good. The bad influences I tried to remove and renounce bit by bit, shadow by shadow, echo by echo, through trial and error, through delight and disgust and misgiving, as I came to love words more and to hate the heavy hands that knocked them about, the thick tongues that [had] no feel for their multitudinous tastes, the dull and botching, hacks who flattened them out into a colourless and insipid paste, the pedants who made them moribund and pompous as themselves. Let me say that the things that first made me love language and want to work *in* it and *for* it were nursery rhymes and folk tales, the Scottish Ballads, a few lines of hymns, the most famous Bible stories and the rhythms of the Bible, Blake's "Songs of Innocence," and the quite incomprehensible magical majesty and nonsense of Shakespeare heard, read, and near-murdered in the first forms of my school.

You ask me, next, if it is true that three of the dominant influences on my published prose and poetry are Joyce, the Bible, and Freud. (I purposely say my 'published' prose and poetry, as in the preceding pages I have been talking about the primary influences upon my very first and forever unpublishable juvenilia.) I cannot say that I have been 'influenced' by Joyce, whom I enormously admire and whose "Ulysses," and earlier stories I have read a great deal. I think this Joyce question arose because somebody once, in print, remarked on the closeness of the title of my book of short stories, "Portrait of the Artist As a Young Dog" to Joyce's title, "Portrait of the Artist as a Young Man." As you know, the name given to innumerable portrait paintings by their artists is, "Portrait of the Artist as a Young Man"—a perfectly straightforward title. Joyce used the *painting*-title for the first time as the title of a literary work. I myself made a bit of doggish fun of the painting-title and, of course, intended no possible reference to Joyce. I do not think that Joyce has had any hand at all in my writing; certainly, his "Ulysses" has not. On the other hand, I cannot deny that the shaping of some of my "Portrait" stories might owe something to Joyce's stories in the volume "Dubliners." But then, 'Dubliners' was a pioneering work in the world of the short story, and no good story writer since can have failed, in some way, however little, to have benefited by it.

The Bible, I have referred to in attempting to answer your first questioning. Its great stories, of Noah, Jonah, Lot, Moses, Jacob, David, Solomon and a thousand more, I had, or course, known from very early youth; the great rhythms had rolled over me from the Welsh pulpits; and I read, for myself, from Job and Ecclesiastes; and the story of the New Testament is part of my life. But I have never sat down and studied the Bible, never consciously echoed its language, and am, in reality, as ignorant of it as most brought-up Christians. All of the Bible that I use in my work is remembered from childhood, and is the common property of all who were brought up in English-speaking communities. Nowhere, indeed, in all my writing, do I use any knowledge which is not commonplace to any literate person. I *have* used a few difficult words in early poems, but they are easily looked-up and were, in any case, thrown into the poems in a kind of adolescent showing-off which I hope I have now discarded.

And that leads me to the third 'dominant influence': Sigmund Freud. My only acquaintance with the theories and discoveries of Dr. Freud has been through the work of novelists who have been excited by his case-book histories, of popular newspaper scientific-potboilers who have, I imagine, vulgarized his work beyond recognition, and of a few modern poets, including Auden, who have attempted to use psychoanalytical phraseology and theory in some of their poems. I have read only one book of Freud's, "The Interpretation of Dreams," and do not recall having been influenced by it in any way. Again, no honest writer today can possibly avoid being influenced by Freud through his pioneering work into the Unconscious and by the influence of those discoveries on the scientific, philosophic, and artistic work of his contemporaries: by any means, necessarily through Freud's own writing.

To your third question—Do I deliberately utilize devices of rhyme, rhythm, and word-formation in my writing—I must, of course, answer with an immediate Yes. I am a painstaking, conscientious, involved, and devious craftsman in words, however unsuccessful the result so often appears, and to whatever wrong uses I may apply my technical paraphernalia. I use everything and anything to make my poems work and move in the direction I want them to: old tricks, new tricks, puns, portmanteau-words, paradox, allusion, paranomasia, paragram, catachresis, slang, assonantal rhymes, vowel rhymes, sprung rhythm. Every device there is in language is there to be used if you will. Poets have got to enjoy themselves sometimes, and the twisting and convolutions of words, the inventions and contrivances, are all part of the joy that is part of the painful, voluntary work.

Your next question asks whether my use of combinations of words to create something new, "in the Surrealist way," is according to a set formula or is spontaneous.

There is a confusion here, for the Surrealists' set formula was to juxtapose the unpremeditated.

Let me make it clearer if I can. The Surrealists—(that is, super-realists, or those who work *above* realism)—were a coterie of painters and writers in Paris, in the nineteen twenties, who did not believe in the conscious selection of images. To put it in another way: They were artists who were dissatisfied with both the realists—(roughly speaking, those who tried to put down in paint and words an actual representation of what they imagined to be the real world in which they lived)—and the impressionists who, roughly speaking again, were those who tried to give an impression of what they imagined to be the real world. The Surrealists wanted to dive into the subconscious mind, the mind below the conscious surface, and dig up their images from there without the aid of logic or reason, and put them down, illogically and unreasonably, in paint and words. The Surrealists affirmed that, as three quarters of the mind was submerged, it was the function of the artist to gather his material from the greatest, submerged mass of the mind rather than from that quarter of the mind which, like the tip of an iceberg, protruded from the subconscious sea. One method the Surrealists used in their poetry was to juxtapose words and images that had no rational relationship; and out of this they hoped to achieve a kind of subconscious, or dream, poetry that would be truer to the real, imaginative world of the mind, mostly submerged, than is the poetry of the conscious mind that relies upon the rational and logical relationship of ideas, objects, and images.

This is, very crudely, the credo of the Surrealists, and one with which I profoundly disagree. I do not mind from where the images of a poem are dragged up; drag them up, if you like, from the nethermost sea of the hidden self; but, before they reach paper, they must go through all the rational processes of the intellect. The Surrealists, on the other hand, put their words down together on paper exactly as they emerge from chaos; they do not shape these words or put them in order; to them, chaos is the shape and order. This seems to me to be exceedingly presumptuous; the Surrealists imagine that whatever they dredge from their subconscious selves and put down in paint or in words must essentially be of some interest or value. I deny this. One of the arts of the poet is to make comprehensible and articulate what might emerge from subconscious sources; one of the great main uses of the intellect is to select, from the amorphous mass of subconscious images those that will best further his imaginative purpose, which is to write the best poem he can.

And question five is, God help us, what is my definition of Poetry?

I myself, do not read poetry for anything but pleasure. I read only the poems I like. This means, of course, that I have to read a lot of poems I don't like before I find the ones I do, but, when I *do* find the ones I do, then all I can say is "Here they are," and read them to myself for pleasure.

Read the poems you like reading. Don't bother whether they're important, or if they'll live. What does it matter what poetry is, after all? If you want a definition of poetry, say: "Poetry's what makes me laugh or cry or yawn, what makes my toenails twinkle, what makes me want to do this or that or nothing," and let it go at that. All that matters about poetry is the enjoyment of it, however tragic it may be. All that matters is the eternal movement behind it, the vast undercurrent of human grief, folly, pretension, exaltation, or ignorance, however unlofty the intention of the poem.

You can tear a poem apart to see what makes it technically tick, and say to yourself, when the works are laid out before you, the vowels, the consonants, the rhymes and rhythms. "Yes, this is it. This is why the poem moves me so. It is because of the craftsmanship." But you're back again where you began. You're back with the mystery of having been moved by words. The best craftsmanship always leaves holes and gaps in the works of the poem so that something that is *not* in the poem can creep, crawl, flash, or thunder in.

The Joy and function of poetry is, and was, the celebration of man, which is also the celebration of God.

CREATIVE WRITING EXPERIMENT

Try creating some poetic fragments of your own. To start, consider similar sounding words that express the following meanings: *fl-* suggesting rapid movement (as the tongue darts forward to say the syllable) as in *flicker, flutter, flurry*; *sn-* suggesting something distasteful "as your nose begins to wrinkle, your nostrils flare, and your lips draw back to expose your threatening canine teeth" (Lederer 143), as in *snot, snort, snarl, sneer* the short *i* vowel in words like *little, skinny, thin, imp, shrimp*; or the *-ump* end syllable suggesting rotund masses like *rump, lump, bump, clump*, etc. No wonder Lewis Carroll named his egghead *Humpty Dumpty*. In fact, it might not be such a bad idea to begin by going back to your childhood experiences with Mother Goose Rhymes.

WRITING EXERCISES

First read Shakespeare's Sonnet 73 aloud.

> That time of year thou mayst in me behold
> When yellow leaves, or none, or few, do hang
> Upon those boughs which shake against the cold,
> Bare ruined choirs, where late the sweet birds sang.
> In me thou see'st the twilight of such day
> As after sunset fadeth in the west;
> Which by and by black night doth take away,
> Death's second self, that seals up all in rest.
> In me thou see'st the glowing of such fire,
> That on the ashes of his youth doth lie,
> As the deathbed whereon it must expire,
> Consumed with that which it was nourished by.
> This thou perceiv'st, which makes thy love more strong,
> To love that well which thou must leave ere long.

Scan the poem by

1. Charting its rhyme scheme.

2. Determining its metrical patterns (kind and number of feet per line).

3. Discovering unusual sound elements (alliteration, onomatopoeia, etc.),

Then thoroughly answer the following questions:

1. What limitations does the sonnet form impose on the content? Or, put another way, how does the poet manipulate the form to say more than the words alone could express?

2. What does the imagery of the first quatrain ("bare ruined choirs, where late the sweet birds sang") suggest about the relationship between nature and man-made monuments, like cathedrals?

3. What is the poem about? (What is the theme? What is Shakespeare talking about here?)

4. What different metaphors does the poet use (incidentally, a different one for each quatrain) to underscore the implications of the theme? And even more importantly, what relationship does the sequence of the metaphors (year, day, hour) have to the meaning of the poem as expressed in the concluding couplet?

READING

Grooming

The poem stands on its firm
legs. Its claws are filed, brush
and curry-comb have worked
with the hissing groom to polish
its smooth pelt. All morning, hair
by hair, I've plucked away each small
excess; remains no trace of
barbering, and all feels natural.
It is conditioned to walk, turn
to the frailest leash, swing
without effort into ecstatic
hunting. Now I am cleaning
the teeth in its lion jaws
with an old brush. I'll set it
wild on the running street, aimed
at the hamstring, the soft throat.
             —Leslie Norris

When I Heard the Learn'd Astronomer

When I heard the learn'd astronomer,
When the proofs, the figures, were ranged in columns
     before me,
When I was shown the charts and diagrams, to add,
     divide, and measure them,
When I sitting heard the astronomer where he lectured
     with much applause in the lecture-room,
How soon unaccountable I became tired and sick,
Till rising and gliding out I wander'd off by myself,
In the mystical moist night-air, and from time to time,
Look'd up in perfect silence at the stars
             —Walt Whitman

Because I Could Not Stop for Death

Because I could not stop for Death—
He kindly stopped for me—
The carriage held but just Ourselves—
And Immortality.

We slowly drove—He knew no haste
And I had put away
My labor and my leisure too.
For His Civility—

We passed the School, where Children strove
At Recess—in the Ring—
We passed the Fields of Gazing Grain—
We passed the Setting Sun—

Or rather—He passed Us—

The Dews drew quivering and chill—
For only Gossamer, my Gown—
My Tippet—only Tulle—

We paused before a House that seemed
A Swelling of the Ground—
The Roof was scarcely visible—
The Cornice—in the Ground—

Since then—'tis Centuries—and yet
Feels shorter than the Day
I first surmised the Horses' Heads
Were towards Eternity—
             —Emily Dickinson

A SAMPLER OF GREAT READING

I. LIGHTER READING

Isaac Asimov, *Foundation Trilogy*

Ray Bradbury, *Dandelion Wine*

Willa Cather, *Paul's Case*

Ernest Hemingway, *The Old Man and the Sea*

Carson McCullers, *A Member of the Wedding*

Robert Pirsig, *Zen and the Art of Motorcycle Maintenance*

Edgar Allen Poe, *Fall of the House of Usher*

John Steinbeck, *The Pearl*

Henry David Thoreau, *Walden*

Mark Twain, *Huckleberry Finn*

II. HEAVIER READING

James Agee, *A Death in the Family*

Aristotle, *Poetics*

St. Augustine, *Confessions*

Samuel Beckett , *Waiting for Godot*

Boccaccio, *The Decameron*

Castiglione, *The Courtier*

Willa Cather, *My Antonia*

Miguel de Cervantes, *Don Quixote*

Geoffrey Chaucer, *Canterbury Tales*

Charles Dickens, *Great Expectations*

T. S. Eliot, *Four Quartets*

William Faulkner, *Dry September*

Sigmund Freud, *On the Interpretation of Dreams*

Homer, *Iliad, Odyssey*

Eugene Ionesco, *The Bald Soprano*

James Joyce, *Dubliners*

Franz Kafka, *The Metamorphosis*

Thomas Mann, *Death in Venice*

Arthur Miller, *Death of a Salesman*

Machiavelli, *The Prince*

Herman Melville, *Moby Dick*

Molière, *Le Bourgeois Gentilhomme* ("The Bourgeois Gentleman")

Montaigne, *Essays*

Pascal, *Dialogues*

Luigi Pirandello, *Six Characters in Search of an Author*

Plato, *Dialogues*

William Shakespeare, *Sonnets, Romeo and Juliet, Taming of the Shrew*

Sigrid Undset, *Kristen Lavransdatter*

Virgil, *Aeneid*

Voltaire, *Candide*

Tennessee Williams, *A Streetcar Named Desire*

Thomas Wolfe, *Look Homeward, Angel*

III. Heaviest Reading

Anton Chekhov, *Three Sisters*

Dante, *Divine Comedy*

Fyodor Dostoevski, *Crime and Punishment, The Brothers Karamazov*

William Faulkner, *The Sound and the Fury*

Gustave Flaubert, *Madame Bovary*

Johann Wolfgang von Goethe, *Faust I*

Henrik Ibsen, *The Wild Duck, A Doll's House*

Joseph Conrad, *Heart of Darkness*

James Joyce, *Ulysses*

Franz Kafka, *The Castle*

Thomas Mann, *The Magic Mountain, Dr. Faustus*

William Shakespeare, *Hamlet, Othello, King Lear*

Sophocles, *Oedipus Rex*

Leo Tolstoy, *Anna Karenina, War and Peace*

Virginia Wolfe, *To the Lighthouse*

IV. Odds & Ends

A memorable Biography: William Gibson, *A Mass for the Dead.*

A superb collection of short stories: Flannery O'Conner, *A Good Man Is Hard to Find* or *The Collected Stories of Eudora Welty.*

Cultural Periodicals you should take time to browse in sometime (soon): *Horizon, The New Yorker, The World and I, The American Scholar, Critical Inquiry,* among many others.

WORKS CITED

Bernstein, Leonard. *The Unanswered Question.* Cambridge, MA. Harvard University Press, 1976.

Ciardi, John. *How Does a Poem Mean.* Boston: Houghton Mifflin, 1975.

Dickinson, Emily. *Poems of Emily Dickinson.* Norwalk, CT: Easton Press, 1980.

Eliot, T.S. *The Complete Poems and Plays: 1909–1950,* Orlando: Harcourt, Brace Jovanovich, 1980.

Hall, James B., and Barry Ulanov. *Modern Culture and the Arts.* New York: McGraw-Hill, 1972.

Harris, John Sterling. *Barbed Wire.* Provo, UT: Brigham Young University Press, 1974.

Issa, Kobayashi. *The Dumpling Field.* Trans. Lucien Stryk. Athens: Swallow Press, Ohio University, 1991.

Kazantzakis, Nikos. *The Odyssey: A Modern Sequel.* Trans. by Kimon Friar. New York: Simon & Schuster, 1969.

Lederer, Richard. *Crazy English.* New York: Pocket Books, 1989.

Lehman, David. *Newsweek* (21 March 1988), 74F–74H.

Perrine, Laurence. *Sound and Sense: An Introduction to Poetry.* 6th ed. New York: Harcourt Brace Jovanovich, 1982.

Postman, Neil. *Conscientious Objections.* New York: Vintage, 1988.

Smith, David. "Poetry as a Way of Life." *Daily Universe,* Brigham Young University.

Stevenson, Burton Egbert, ed. *The Home Book of Quotations, Classical and Modern.* New York: Dodd, Mead, & Co., 1967.

Tennyson, Lord Alfred. *Poems.* London: The Scholar Press, 1976.

Williams, William Carlos. *The Collected Earlier Poems.* Norfolk: James Laughlin, 1951.

WEBSITES OF INTEREST

Vendler, Helen. *Poems, Poets, Poetry: An Introduction and Anthology.*

Luminarium: Anthology of English Literature — http://www.luminarium.org/

Bio/intro to great American poets — http://www.americanpoems.com/

Pleasure of Poetry — http://books.google.com/books?id=y9UfDmUgUmoC&printsec=frontcover&source=gbs_navlinks_s

Shakespeare's sonnet 73 — http://www.shakespeare-online.com/sonnets/73.html

Courtesy Brigham Young University.

INTRODUCTION TO DANCE

Chapter 9

INTRODUCTION

We move from poetry to **dance**, two primary means of human expression—poetry because it forms the basis of our instinct for storytelling, and dance because it is the one art form that needs no exterior support. Its instrument is the human body itself. And whereas poetry in our day plays only a minimal role in engaging people in aesthetic experiences, dance draws young and old alike into social interaction. In primitive cultures, dance played a central role in religious expression. Today it functions primarily as entertainment. But it is one of the few arts that has retained its importance in human experience across time.

WHAT IS DANCE?

EMOTIONAL FEVER CHART

Dance movement is the fever chart of human emotions molded by time, space, and energy. Because dance requires only a moving body to exist, it has sometimes been called the "mother of the arts," the primal medium for creative human expression. The natural impulse to move rhythmically is built into the living processes of the body itself: our life forces pulsate in regular patterns, like the trochaic beat of a healthy heart (*thump*-thump *thump*-thump), or the tension-release of breathing, or the fall-recovery sequence of walking, etc. This may be why dance came first among the arts. But the question of its priority among the fine arts is less important than its potential for artistic expression and creative expansion. Perhaps the closest thing to the magic of dance movement can be

found in a group of small children moving spontaneously to their favorite music. In these moments of youthful exhilaration, children reveal the inherent emotionalism of all dance. As Araminta Little once said: "Dance is a quicksilver experience . . . changing, amorphous . . . much like a child—a human changeling suspended between being and nonbeing" (8). In fact, it would be impossible for children not to move to music. Yet their flailing arms and erratic jumps are not yet dance per se. Dance starts when the movements become organized according to the choreographer's vision and the performer's skill level. Dance takes on many forms, from Native American rain dances to the abstract, unaccompanied movements of the modern dance pioneer, Merce Cunningham. The variety and purposes of dance are virtually endless.

A BRIEF HISTORY

PRIMITIVE ORIGINS

The dance historian Curt Sachs wrote that "music and poetry exist in time; painting and architecture in space. But dance lives at once in time and space. The creator and the thing created, the artist and the work are still one and the same thing" (3). From the beginning of history, people have moved instinctively to music with their built-in instrument, the body. Tribal cultures have even felt in rhythmic bodily movements some magical tie to the cosmos—thus the religious importance of fertility dances, rain dances, etc. By curious coincidence, the circular patterns of movement in the macrocosm (planets revolving around the sun) parallel the movements of subatomic particles (electrons encircling the nucleus in an atom) and provide a compelling association with the earliest dances of which we have any visual record: the ring dance.

DANCE AS RITUAL

We know from **cave paintings** that ancient peoples, sometimes costumed as animals, danced in ritualistic ways, as certain primitive tribes still do today. Egyptian tomb paintings depict religious dancing connected to funeral processions patterned on the legend of Isis and Osiris. Also portrayed are exuberant, acrobatic secular entertainments associated with those rites. This dual nature of dance—ennobling and intoxicating—was evident in Greek culture also. Plato noted: "Movement of the body may be called dancing, and includes two kinds; one of the nobler figures, imitating the honorable, the other of the more ignoble figures, imitating the mean" (*Laws* VII 814). Havelock Ellis defines the duality of dance more specifically. The art of dancing represents "the supreme manifestation of physical life [love], but also the supreme symbol of spiritual life [religion]" (238). Thus, dance binds humans to their god, to their world, and to each other.

FROM RITUAL TO PERFORMANCE

It is important to realize that we don't fully understand the role of dance in primitive societies. Dance is no longer central to our religious life. We are used to viewing dance as mere entertainment, whereas primal people didn't separate the performance from life. "So the specialness of the 'artist,' as understood in the Western world, and the individuality which has become dominant in the white world's view of artistic expressiveness are alien to tribal peoples, for whom ritual is the pervasive mode of communication and the exclusive form of public expression" (Highwater 19). **Ethnic dances** became codified into culture-specific forms over time, as in the ceremonial dances of Cambodia and India, or the Noh play of Japan, a highly abstract kind of "god-dance" consisting of noble posturing, dancing, chanting, and acting. Early folk dances probably developed out of the most persistent of the primitive ritual dances. In the beginning there was little difference between ethnic and folk dance, but **folk dance** eventually branched off as participation (social) dance, while ethnic dances became entertainment performances (spectacle). It is only when the cohesive social values of a people disappear that the arts take on a separate function and importance. That process occurred in Western culture with the shift from ancient tribal rituals to conventionalized Christian religious ceremonies and, finally, to the self-serving spectacles presided over by Renaissance princes, the nucleus of a major dance form, namely ballet.

FROM BALLET TO MODERN

Although in the Middle Ages the church banned dancing as a low form of bodily pleasure, a variety of entertainers—jugglers, acrobats, conjurers, minstrels, and dancers—were familiar at medieval fairs and marketplaces. It wasn't until the Renaissance, however, that public dance spectacles and dancing masters emerged to form the basis for what we know today as **ballet.** DOMENICO DA PIACENZA, author of the earliest extant dance instruction book, viewed dancing as a synthesis of movement, space, and music. During the fifteenth-century Italian Renaissance, LORENZO DE MEDICI (the "Magnificent") (1449–1492) established Florence as a cultural capital of Europe and staged great pageants both in and out of doors. These spectacular court dance displays, called *balletti* (from Italian *ballare,* "to dance"), became a regular feature of important events, like royal weddings, state banquets, etc. For example, the marriage of the Duke of Milan to a Spanish princess was celebrated in 1489 with a lavish "dinner ballet," complete with danced interludes between courses, called entries (*entrées*). A special dance for each course was chosen from classical mythology: the fish entree was brought in by attendants who then performed a ballet about the sea gods; Hebe or Bacchus would bring in the drinks, Pamona, the fruit, etc. In 1494, KING CHARLES VIII (1470–1498) of France marched into Italy and claimed the throne of Naples. He was so impressed and delighted by the balletti given in his honor, that he imported Italian dancing masters and musicians back to France. Lorenzo's descendent, CATHERINE DE MEDICI (1519–1589), became queen of France in 1547 and greatly accelerated the establishment of ballet as a national art form in France. When Catherine's grandson, Louis XIV (1638–1715), came to power, he was already a dancer himself and founded the first state-sponsored Royal Academy of Dance in 1661—one of the many reasons why ballet terms are in French. The Academy consisted of thirteen dancing masters who set about codifying all the court dances (*ballets de cours*), positions, arm movements, steps, etc. Until almost the end of the seventeenth century, only men danced in theaters. MADEMOISELLE LA FONTAINE (1655–1738) may be regarded as the first true **ballerina.** She took the principal female role in Lully's *Le Triomphe de l'amour* in 1681. Thus, Louis established the principle of royal or state patronage of dancing, later copied by many countries, most notably Russia in the nineteenth and early twentieth centuries.

LES BALLETS RUSSES

The one performance in all ballet history that most dancers wish they could have seen occurred in Paris on the evening of May 29, 1909. It was the European debut of *Les Ballets Russes,* the birth of a new era in ballet, inspired and carried out by SERGEY PAVLOVICH DIAGHILEV (1871–1929), the famous Russian impresario. No one has ever assembled a finer roster of dancers, some of whom became legends in their own lifetimes. The leading *danseur* (male dancer) was VASLAV NIJINSKY (1890–1950), possessor of an incredible elevation (ability to leap), a magnetic stage personality, and an acting ability to match his fabulous dance technique. Heading the list of ballerinas was ANNA PAVLOVA (1882–1931), one of the legendary prima ballerinas of all time, whose fragile loveliness and memorable interpretations helped her achieve a popularity hitherto unheard of in the world of ballet.

STRAVINSKY & BALANCHINE

One significant musical sidelight of Diaghilev's impact on Western Europe came in the person of a young unknown Russian composer named IGOR STRAVINSKY (1882–1971), who was commissioned to write ballet scores for *Les Ballets Russes.* From his pen came three incredible early twentieth-century scores: *Firebird, Petrushka,* and *Rite of Spring.* Another luminary from *Les Ballets Russes* who had an incomparable impact on American ballet was GEORGE BALANCHINE (1904–1983). Lincoln Kirstein invited the young Russian dancer/choreographer to New York to establish the School of American Ballet in 1934 (later changed to the New York City Ballet in 1948). By his death in 1983, Balanchine had become a legend in his own time, creating a distinctive American style of ballet, freer in its forms as a result of the influence of American dance (tap, jazz, modern, etc.).

MODERN DANCE

One of the chief founders of **modern dance** was ISADORA DUNCAN (1878–1927), an American dancer from San Francisco whose early exposure to ballet was decidedly negative. She wrote in her autobiography, *My Life*: "When the [ballet] teacher told me to stand on my toes I asked him why, and when he replied 'Because it is beautiful,' I said that it was ugly and against nature, and after the third lesson I left his class, never to return" (21). A typically "liberated" woman, a free thinker, and daring dance innovator, Isadora left ballet for the freedom of interpreting music in looser flowing costumes and with more spontaneous, expressive movements. She became

both the scandal (she was wont to dance bare-footed and bare-breasted in front of admiring audiences) and the delight of Europe during the first two decades of the twentieth century.

MARTHA GRAHAM

The other major American figure responsible for the emergence of modern styles was MARTHA GRAHAM (1895–1991), the "grande dame" of modern dance. Her legendary discipline places her style somewhere between the rigorous demands of ballet and the expressive freedom of modern dance. In all her works, there is a psychological truth, as she draws many of her timeless themes from the conflicts found in ancient Greek myths. Dance for her was a kind of fever chart, "a graph of the heart," she once said. She regularly associated dance with the other arts, particularly poetry. One of her most famous early pieces was *Appalachian Spring* (1944), danced to the music of Aaron Copland. Copland's theme was borrowed from an old Shaker melody with the simple poetic text: "'Tis the gift to be simple / 'Tis the gift to be free / 'Tis the gift to come down / Where we ought to be." Martha Graham believed that dance was the loftiest, most beautiful of the arts, because it represented the essential movements of life itself. MARTHA GRAHAM, DORIS HUMPHREY (1895–1958), and CHARLES WEIDMAN (1901–1975) all began their careers at the Denishawn School founded by RUTH ST. DENIS (1879–1968) and TED ("PAPA") SHAWN (1891–1971), who became dance partners in 1914. Their school was the first institutional dance theater in America (Coe 129). Shawn was fond of quoting six words from Ouspenski: "Art is the communication of ecstacy" (Rogosin 9).

BALLET & MODERN MERGE

A typically American blend of ballet and modern dance emerged in the dancing styles and choreography of two Russian defectors, RUDOLF NUREYEV and MIKHAIL BARYSHNIKOV, both of whom brought a masculine respectability to ballet and also, because of their incredible skill and charisma, achieved a kind of superstar quality that made them nearly as recognizable to the general public as any rock or movie star. It is refreshing to discover that Baryshnikov has taken modern dance lessons to expand his dance vocabulary. The results of this cross over can be seen in the film *White Nights* (1985), where he pairs up with tap dancer GREGORY HINES in some stunning dance sequences combining ballet, modern, and tap, the latter being one of America's unique contributions to the art of dance.

MODERN CONTEMPORARY

Some other major figures in more recent modern dance innovations include the following. PAUL TAYLOR, along with Martha Graham, artfully combines the best of ballet and modern. His best works span a range from classical ballet to the **avant garde.** His style is characterized by humor and a sense of the macabre. His *Epic* (1957) was an almost motionless dance performed to telephone time signals. ALWIN NIKOLAIS boasts that he is an artistic eclectic, seeking "a polygamy of motion, shape, color, and sound (qtd. in Anderson 424). He is a kind of one-man show: he choreographs the dances, composes the music, and designs the scenery, costumes, and lighting. His works are "abstract mixed-media pieces of dazzling complexity" (Anderson 425). MERCE CUNNINGHAM is perhaps best known for his collaborations with the composer John Cage, where chance (indeterminacy) governs the movements expressing some of the unpredictability of life itself. TWYLA THARP is doing some of the most innovative recent modern choreography. Her dances are another "hybrid mixture of ballet discipline and modern freedom, but in an even wider sense than Martha Graham or Paul Taylor. Her iconoclastic style draws inspiration from pop dance forms (jazz, tap, and social dance) making her tight discipline seem wholly improvised. One of her most memorably American "pop" creations is *Eight Jelly Rolls,* eight dances set to the music of Jazz great JELLY ROLL MORTON. Her dances greatly appeal to both dance experts and the common man, because she bridges high and popular art so convincingly, as can be seen in her popular *Push Comes to Shove,* a delightful mix of classical ballet and vaudeville.

WHAT TO LOOK FOR IN BALLET

INTRODUCTION

Because ballet was first formalized in the royal courts of France, French became its official language. Ballet exercises, steps, body positions, and movement directions all use French terminology. But the style of ballet dancing varies with time and place. The court ballets performed at Louis XIV's court at Versailles in the seventeenth and early eighteenth centuries set the basic patterns for classical ballet. When performed outside, however, they looked more like military counter-marches than dance, because the performers wore heavy costumes and sometimes rode on horses (our word *carousel* comes from this French custom). Nineteenth-century Romantic ballets were more a matter of story-telling and mimed gesturing than twentieth-century ballets, which became more athletic and abstract. One can even perceive differences among different national companies today: the French remain more classical, emphasizing charm and elegance; the Russians strive for physical strength and technical perfection; the British style is less flamboyant and more serene; and the emerging American style is a blend of French, Italian, and Russian influences (Balanchine, after all, was trained in Russia), but tends to be freer in style, influenced perhaps by the wider expressive range of modern dance.

TECHNIQUES

Ballet training requires years of rigorous discipline and immense physical stamina. Edward Villella, Balanchine's former lead dancer at the New York City Ballet, once claimed that "it takes more strength to get through a six-minute **pas de deux** than to get through four rounds of boxing" (quoted in Treaster 29). He had been a welterweight boxing champion in college. Strange as it may seem, the Institute of Sports Medicine in New York says that ballet is second only to football in the severity of its physical requirements, making it a notch tougher than hockey. To accomplish graceful movements under such physical stress requires great physical control and mental concentration. There are three essential preparatory stages before a ballet dancer can begin to train properly: ALIGNMENT, TURNOUT, and EXTENSION.

ALIGNMENT

Alignment essentially means good posture; that is, the various body parts—head, shoulders, arms, ribs, hips, legs, and feet—are all in correct relative position to one another. Any departure from the balanced posture will strain muscles and ligaments and cause undue friction on the joints. If one segment of the body is out of line, all others will be affected. For example, if the ballerina's body isn't absolutely straight, she will spin off point when doing

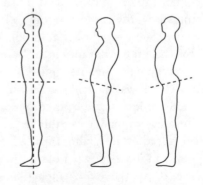

a **pirouette**, much like what happens when trying to drive a car with a bent drive shaft.

TURNOUT

Turnout refers specifically to the rotation of the legs from the hips. Most people stand and walk with their legs roughly parallel with little or no turnout. But ballet requires that the dancer develop the ability to rotate the leg from the hip (not the knee) socket, and a series of positions have been established that facilitate this type of turnout. Historically, complete turnout developed slowly—by 1700 the angle of turnout was 90 degrees; by 1800 it was 180 degrees, the turnout required of today's professional ballet dancers.

EXTENSION

Extension means that the dancer's limbs are trained to create the longest, most lyrical line possible. This accentuates the vertical line of the body and allows the hands and feet to become expressive extensions of the arms and legs. This is particularly important for the ballerina, who must learn to dance on point, on her toes. To do this, she wears special shoes that have a padded, extended toe. By training her ankles to extend forward, she can stand on her toes, thereby extending the length of her whole body. Dancing on point also allows her to navigate complex movements in more graceful ways, like doing a PIROUETTE, or holding a precarious position, such as an ATTITUDE or an ARABESQUE. Because it is difficult to maintain balance on point, she often needs a male dancer

for support. One of the most elegant parts of a ballet is the *pas de deux,* a duet between the male dancer and the ballerina, where the elegance and grace of her movements are complemented by the power and nobility of his.

REPRESENTATIVE BALLET STEPS

INTRODUCTION

There are many different ballet steps that provide the vocabulary for the ballet **choreographer** (literally, designer of dance). Following are schematic drawings of seven commonly used steps in ballet. When you see a ballet performance, you will get more out of it if you can begin to "read" the movements and respond to the technical

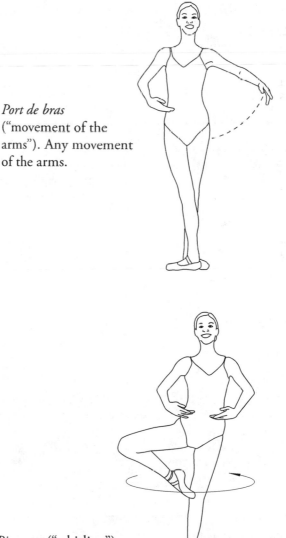

Port de bras ("movement of the arms"). Any movement of the arms.

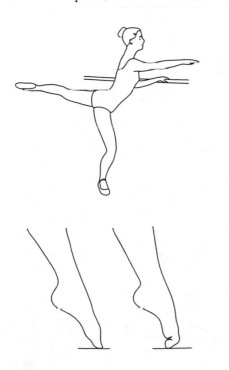

Pirouette ("whirling"). A complete turn of the body on one foot.

Jeté ("To throw"). A transfer of weight from one foot to the other.

Attitude croisée derriere ("to the back").

Attitude ("Posture"). A posture created by Carlo Blasis, who based it on the statue of Mercury by Giovanni da Bologna. The body is supported on one leg with the other raised and bent.

Attitude croisée devant ("to the front").

Cabriole ("leap, caper"). A step or elevation. The working leg is followed by the other leg, which beats against it, sending it higher. The landing is made on the lower leg.

Arabesque ("Arabian," Moorish in style"). The body is supported on one leg with the other leg raised in back, making the longest possible line. Shown left to right: First *arabesque*, second *arabesque*, and third *arabesque*.

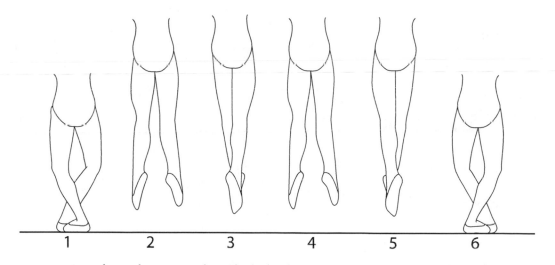

Entrechat. A leap upward in which the dancer repeatedly crosses his feet. The number of crossovers identifies the type. Shown above is an *entrechat six.*

expertise of the dancers. In spite of the formulas required to dance ballet, the best dancers can execute these set movements with stunning virtuosity and deep emotional expressiveness.

WHAT TO LOOK FOR IN MODERN DANCE

INTRODUCTION

A pivotal moment in the separation of ballet from modern dance came in the early life of the American pioneer of modern dance Isadora Duncan. She started her first school of dance when she was six years old. Her mother came home one day and found that she had collected half a dozen children from the neighborhood and

was teaching them to wave their arms. Her mother sent her to a famous ballet teacher in San Francisco, but, Isadora said, "his lessons did not please me [because they were] ugly and against nature. . . . I dreamed a different dance" (21).

ISADORA DUNCAN

The new dance Isadora Duncan dreamed of was one unfettered by convention and formulas, one free to express emotions directly and spontaneously. John Martin, the pioneering dance critic of the *New York Times*, described ballet as "spectacular dance" and modern dance as "expressional dance" (Terry 91), each with distinctly different purposes. Ironically, most modern dance designers returned to ancient themes for their inspiration: Isadora

Duncan to classical Greece; Martha Graham to Greek tragedy and early American culture; Ruth St. Denis to ancient Egypt and the Orient. Originally, the press and the public were often disoriented or disgusted by the new dances, partly because there was no clear story line and partly because the dancers often broke social conventions by dancing in bare feet, bare legs, and bare midriff. In addition, modern dancers didn't use the set vocabulary of ballet. In the spirit of Picasso's counsel to paint each object (tree, animal, person) in a style to fit that object, modern dancers viewed each dance as an invitation to reinvent the vocabulary of movement to fit the purpose of that specific dance. While the ballet focused on the spine, modern dance followed Isadora Duncan's discovery of the solar plexus as the center ("soul") of all movement.

BALLET VS. MODERN

A simple way to recognize the fundamental distinction between ballet and modern dance is to consider the force of gravity on the human body. In all dance, gravity is the one constant; it is the force against which all dances must work. The grace of the ballet dancer is a direct result of the discipline necessary to defy gravity. The exhilaration of seeing Baryshnikov execute a *grand jeté* comes from an awareness of how difficult it is to make a **virtuoso** maneuver seem effortless and graceful. Grace is the quality Balanchine saw as the key to the beauty of ballet. But whereas ballet works *against* gravity, modern dancers often work *with* it, exploring its expressive effects on a falling body. Doris Humphrey, Ruth St. Denis's protégée, stood in front of a mirror and experimented with falling off-balance, trying to discover how far she could tilt without crashing to the floor. The excitement of dance grew out of the audience reaction to a body precariously poised on an arc between upright and horizontal. Whether the public understood her principle of "fall and recovery" wasn't important, as long as viewers could respond to the dance feats which evolved from this principle (Terry 85).

A USEFUL APPROACH TO MODERN DANCE CRITICISM

CATHY BLACK'S ADVICE TO THE FIRST-TIME VIEWER OF MODERN DANCE

1. *Preconceptions:* Modern dance is eclectic, personal, and often abstract. Don't go with any preconceived expectations of what the dance should be like. Think of yourself as an empty cup waiting to be filled. Don't expect any meaning in the narrative sense of the word. Go to experience the dance, not necessarily to understand it. Do you ever ask a bird to explain its song?

2. *Judgment:* Only judge after the performance, not before, and never during. There are many levels of perception in dance—visual, musical, dramatic, kinetic, even philosophical—not all of which can be found in every dance. Apply the levels that match the purpose and style of the dance in question. The kinetic is most often central to modern dance and transcends intellectual analysis. As John Martin argues, "The dance is the expression . . . of concepts which transcend the individual's power to express by rational and intellectual means" (84).

3. *Postconceptions:* Promise that before you make your final judgment, you periodically immerse yourself in several modern dance concerts, because modern dances are harder to get into than ballet or folk or ballroom. It takes time for the soft focus to crystallize. Modern dance choreographers are anxious to "speak" to members of the audience by inviting them to plug their own life experiences into the interpretation of the dance. Seeing dancers rolling across the floor is an invitation to remember what it was like to roll down a grassy slope when you were a child. (Personal communication with C. Black, summer 1993).

CRITICAL OBSERVATIONS ABOUT BALLET & MODERN DANCE

CHOREOGRAPHER GEORGE BALANCHINE'S *APOLLO*

Balanchine, even after his death, remains the most formidable figure in American ballet. His New York City Ballet, with a huge Ford Foundation grant, became the showplace for a new kind of ballet, which veteran British dance critic, Arnold Haskell, described as "visual music" (Terry 33). By playing with the interrelations of dance gesture and musical sound, Balanchine initiated an aesthetic revolution in the three hundred-year-old history of classical dance, minimizing story, sets, and elaborate costumes, and replacing them with pure choreography that mirrored the style and rhythm of great music. His masterpiece *Apollo* (1928), choreographed to Stravinsky's music, was the turning point in Balanchine's career. It is now one of the most difficult and coveted roles in a male dancer's repertoire.

I have gradually learned that movements and gestures, like tones in music and shades in painting, have certain family relations and, as groups, have their own laws. The more conscious an artist is, the more he comes to understand these laws and to respond to them. I have tried to develop my choreography inside the framework that such relations suggest.

To achieve unity, one must avoid separating elements similar in mood and essence. In spite of the fact that movements may have different names, they may nevertheless belong with each other because of their inner relationship. Only one's artistic feeling and experience can decide on their similarity. (Balanchine, qtd. in Sorell, *Faces* 95)

A DANCER'S REACTION TO BALANCHINE'S *APOLLO*: EDWARD VILLELLA

Edward Villella was the former lead dancer with the New York City Ballet while under Balanchine and later was the director of the Miami City Ballet. His masculinity has helped to dispel the impression that male ballet dancers are effeminate. He grew up as the block bully in an Italian working-class family in Queens, where he had to defend his study of ballet with his fists. He witnessed, first hand, the golden age of American ballet:

An amazing era in which George Balanchine single-handedly transformed the art. I watched him do it. I was part of it all. He showed me what he wanted me to do in such ballets as Apollo and Bugaku by demonstrating the choreography. I imitated his movements and was able to grasp the roles. I often felt he was not only the greatest choreographer I'd ever seen but also the greatest dancer. (10)

My reaction [to Balanchine's invitation to tackle the role] was pure terror. I believe that *Apollo* is the ultimate challenge for a dancer, and I was terrified that I wouldn't be able to get my body in condition so that I could even attempt it. . . . It combines bravura technique and attack with pure neoclassical lyricism. It's a series of sophisticated dances as opposed to bursts of bravura. A flexible strength is necessary to execute these steps and gestures and link them smoothly. Linkage, a smooth, pure line, is important in ballet. As Balanchine said in a program note to accompany the ballet, *Apollo's* about eliminating. It's about elongation. It's clear, open. . . . The role can't be done working from tension. (145)

TWO CRITICAL REACTIONS TO BALANCHINE'S *APOLLO*

EDWIN DENBY (OCTOBER 23, 1945)

Apollo is about poetry, poetry in the sense of a brilliant, sensuous, daring, and powerful activity of our nature [the

birth and maturing of a god]. . . . What you see onstage is strangely simple and clear. It begins modestly with effects derived from pantomime, a hint of birth pangs, a crying baby, a man dancing with a lute, and it becomes progressively a more and more directly classic dance ballet, the melodious lines and lyric or forceful climaxes of which are effects of dance continuity, dance rhythm, and dance architecture. And it leaves at the end, despite its innumerable, incidental inventions, a sense of bold, open, effortless, and limpid grandeur. Nothing has looked unnatural, any more than anything in Mozart sounds unnatural. But you feel happily the nobility that the human spirit is capable of by nature. (329–330)

DEBORAH JOWITT (MAY 21, 1979)

What Baryshnikov presents us with is not so much the young reckless Apollo becoming mature—and without the birth scene, why would we suppose this anyhow?—but Dionysus becoming Apollo. He seems in the process to be molding and channeling his own wild pleasure in dancing as much as he is harnessing the Muses. In his solo, when he brushes one leg across himself to the side and swings both arms in the opposite direction, he emphasizes neither the jazzy asymmetry nor the archaic two-dimensionality of the step, but shows with fierce zest how one part of the body is pulling against another. With the Muses, he is tender shepherd and straining horse tamer and companion; he gives us the sense that he is learning his own nature through the course of the dance (25).

MODERN DANCE CHOREOGRAPHER MARTHA GRAHAM'S *APPALACHIAN SPRING*

Martha Graham's choreographic style stands midway between the rigors of ballet and the free expression of modern dance. "Freedom to a dancer means only one thing—discipline," she once said (Croce 52), which captures the essential paradox of dance as described by one of Balanchine's star male dancers, Edward Villella: "Total control and total freedom." Almost single-handedly, Martha Graham carved for herself an indispensable niche in the American dance landscape that has greatly expanded the vocabulary of modern dance. She believed that the dancer's movements should reflect the spirit of the country in which the dance takes root. In her attempts to liberate the American soul from the "prison of Puritanism," she created dances which evoked images of early America with what Walter Sorell calls "an astounding economy of gesture" (*The Dance through the Ages* 195). Her technique is characterized by internal tensions that express themselves in angular, percussive movements of the limbs and the exaggerated contraction and release of the torso. One of her most characteristic creations was *Appalachian Spring* (1944), the story of America's simple beginning seen through the eyes of a young bride and her husband, set to the music of Aaron Copland.

Each art has an instrument and a medium. The instrument of the dance is the human body; the medium is movement. The body has always been to me a thrilling wonder, a dynamo of energy, exciting, courageous, powerful; a delicately balanced logic and proportion. It has not been my aim to evolve or discover a new method of dance training, but rather to dance significantly. To dance significantly means "through the medium of discipline and by means of a sensitive strong instrument, to bring into focus unhackneyed movement: a human being."

I did not want to be a tree, a flower, or a wave. In a dancer's body, we as audience must see *ourselves*, not the imitated behavior of everyday actions, not the phenomena of nature, not exotic creatures from another planet, but something of the miracle that is a human being, motivated, disciplined, concentrated. (44–45)

TWO CRITICAL REACTIONS TO *APPALACHIAN SPRING*:

Martha Graham

Appalachian Spring is essentially a dance of place. You choose a place . . . part of the house goes up . . . you dedicate. The questing spirit is there, and the sense of establishing roots. . . . If you have ever seen spring come, the first shimmer of one of those willow trees in the light, or when you have seen the ground break for the first moment—it is that moment that I hoped would come out of the words "Appalachian Spring." (qtd. in Coe 144–145)

Robert Coe

Rich with nostalgia, *Appalachian Spring* never condescends to the values it seeks to affirm; rather it seems to make visible the eloquence of inarticulate emotion, to make heard the silence of a uniquely American feeling. The dance summons the daring self-sufficiency and pride of an older America: Graham places the dancers in curious isolation from one another, interconnected, as Marcia Siegel has suggested, only "by means of their common ceremonies, myths, and aspirations." Beneath the joyous surface of the work, sustaining its dramatic power, seethes a hell-fired terror: The dance takes its title from a line in "The Dancer," part of Hart Crane's poem, "The Bridge," which tells the story of a newly married Indian brave captured by an enemy tribe and put to death at the stake, merging himself with his tormenters' ecstasy as they dance around his burning body. The Graham dancer must experience a similar symbolic immolation—and yet, ironically,

the pioneers in *Appalachian Spring* conquer fear and isolation through open innocence, creating an enduring vision of American pioneer times with special significance during the hardships of World War II. (146)

OTHER DANCE STYLES

INTRODUCTION

Most dance histories focus on ballet and modern because these two styles of dance have most occupied the creative energies of choreographers in the past. But Walter Terry lists a third style of dance that dramatically differs from the two traditional "art" styles: jazz dance, which embraces the tap dance virtuosity of Fred Astaire, the remarkably subtle body language of Bob Fosse, the acclaimed choreography of Jerome Robbins, and the ice dance elegance of Olympic gold-medalist John Curry, who argues that skating and ballet share the same quality of movement (Saal 125). A recent derivative of jazz dance is aerobics, sometimes called "aerobicize" or "jazzercize" (Williamson 10). From this diverse list, it is clear that the line separating high from popular culture is very thin and perhaps unnecessarily rigid. We will conclude this discussion of dance by focusing on two important popular dances which have become major exhibition styles: FOLK DANCE, whose roots can be traced back to dance's ethnic origins; and BALLROOM DANCE, which grew from social dance styles in the U.S., Europe, and Latin America.

FOLK DANCE

Folk dances are, by definition, dances reflecting the values of the "folk," the people of a certain geographical locale. Originally they were primitive man's attempts to favorably influence supernatural forces for human interests (Armstrong 5–6). Later they served to express the characteristic temperament and environment of each unique culture. In some countries, particularly in Eastern Europe and the Middle East, they are still a vital part of community life. The Israelis have made the Hora (an ancient round dance for mixed couples) the basis for many of their folk dances, of which the most famous is the *Hava Nagila* ("Come let us be merry") (Buckman 222). In many Western countries, folk dances have been artificially re-created to be performed on stage. Sometimes the impulse to preserve a dying culture lies behind efforts to preserve and perform a country's native dances. The popularity of folk dancing may even reflect an attempt to counter the dehumanizing effects of an over-industrialized society. Two countries which have most successfully translated their folk dances into theatrical forms are Russia and Poland, with the Yugoslavians and Bulgarians trailing close behind. Igor Moiseyev, whose dance company exhibits great technical skill in portraying Ukrainian culture, once explained his basic approach to folk dance:

> If we analyze the movement of the dance of any nation we find that, in its basis, each system of folk dance possesses only a limited number of different movements, the movements upon which is based the entire system of dance we call root movements. If we know a number of fundamental movements, a number of the roots of which the language of dance is composed, and are familiar with the laws of connected movements, our own fantasy will make it possible to add a number of new movements . . . in the same system." (Qtd. in Sorell 87)

BASIC FORMATIONS

Given the ancient preference for ring dances, it is instructive that, of the nine basic folk dance formations, seven are variations on the circle (Jensen 18–19). The circle is symbolic of the sun or wheel of life and suggests eternity (it has no beginning or end). Other important symbolic dance formations are the square (symbol of man and woman as complementary opposites), the diamond or lozenge (symbol of re-birth), the "V" shape (representing bull's horns), and the triangle (sacred symbol of the Earth Mother goddess) (Armstrong 8–9).

Folk dancing is a significant cultural and artistic phenomenon. There are numerous annual folk dance festivals held throughout the world. These intercultural exchanges have made folk dance a kind of international language through which different cultures can communicate with each other. There are many such U.S. festivals held each year. Some of the more recognized are the Murfreesboro Festival in Tennessee, the Folkmoot Festival in North Carolina, the Rexburg Festival in Idaho, and the Springville Folkfest in Utah.

Here are some of the more common root movements, associated with different countries, to look for when attending a folk dance performance:

ENGLAND

The *Morris Dance* is a very old dance consisting of a number of variations around a common theme of regeneration (imitating a fertility symbol like a horse, bull, or unicorn) and traditionally danced only by men of a certain social status. The name "Morris" probably comes from the word *Moorish* and involves leaping, stamping, and making phallic gestures. It was originally associated with the Maypole (a phallic symbol of the green tree of regeneration).

SCOTLAND

The *Highland Fling* involves dancing on one leg while "flinging" the other. Another popular Scottish folk dance is the "Schottische," where a double circle of couples moves with a Schottische step (step-hop pattern).

GERMANY AND AUSTRIA

The *Schuplattler* from Bavaria and the Tirol is a wild wooing dance, where the man claps his hands, slaps his thigh, and yells to attract the girl's attention. The *Ländler* from the Austrian Alps is a direct descendent of the medieval man stamping out the rhythm as he turns the girl's face close to his.

SPAIN

The *Jota*, from Aragon, is an energetic couple dance in 3/4 time with a placed kick from a bent knee, usually performed to the accompaniment of castanets. The *Fandango* (which means "go and dance"), a couple dance in 6/8 time, is the ancient prototype of all Spanish dances. It begins slowly and works up to an intense climax of frenzied spinning movements. The *Flamenco,* which is perhaps the most familiar Spanish folk dance, really isn't a particular dance at all but an improvised style of flamboyant heel-stamping with many regional variations. It is a couple dance in which the man plays the matador and the woman is the cape.

ITALY

Because Italy didn't become a unified country until 1870, there are no modern Italian folk dances, but the *Tarantella* captures some of the flavor of the Italian character. A courting dance, its constant movements and rapid turns were supposed to help in working the tarantula's poison out of the system.

GREECE

Unlike Italy, Greek folk dances trace their ancestry to ancient times. One of the best-known descendants is the *Kalamatianos,* in which the group is led by a singing dancer who waves a handkerchief and performs solo jumps and turns. The *Misirlou,* based on the Greek *Kritikos,* originated among the Greek-Americans. Its simple Grapevine/two-step sequence has many variations.

UKRAINE

The *Hopak* is the national dance of the Ukraine and poses one of the greatest challenges to the folk dancer. Every step used in this dance can be found in numerous Russian dance styles (*pas de basque,* Russian polka, *prysiadkas,* buzz-step turns, lunge steps, etc.).

LITHUANIA

The *Kalvalis* (meaning "little smith) originated in Lithuania in the middle of the nineteenth century. The hand-clapping in the refrain represents the hammer striking the anvil.

PHILIPPINES

The *Tinikling* dramatizes the story of the long-legged tinikling bird as it runs through the weeds and rice paddies. The natives try to catch the bird by hitting its legs with long bamboo poles. The dancers represent the bird and their ankles occasionally get caught between the poles.

KOREA

The *Fan Dance* represents a beautiful movement of a flower blooming as a circle of female dancers with fans moves to small, specified foot patterns.

UNITED STATES

Country Dances were imported to America by immigrant settlers from Europe. They were originally labeled "contry" or "contra" (contrary) dances because of the opposing lines the dancers moved in. The "Virginia Reel" is typical: the "top couple" breaks off, performs a figure, and moves down one place. These "contra" dances were important precursors to the modern square dance.

Square Dances came to the U.S. during the War of 1812 (from British contredanses and French quadrilles). The Americans changed the style of music and added the caller. "Calling" helped the dancers know the order of the figures and enabled the caller to create a dance by juggling the order. The calls are familiar to most people—promenade (walk), allemande left, grand chain, etc.,—and create an interesting design of interweaving couples. Square dancing appealed to the American desire to level European social hierarchies.

Round Dances were originally those partner dances that the church criticized as being too intimate: the waltz, polka, schottische, and varsovienne. Gradually, American round dancing combined the rhythms and steps of the waltz and other ballroom favorites with the square dance to add variety (Buckman 233).

WHAT TO LOOK FOR IN FOLK DANCE

1. *Rhythm:* How well do the dancers express with their bodies the basic rhythmic patterns of the folk music? This involves keeping time with the beat and expressing in body language the quality of the beat (percussive, lyrical, etc.). The more closely you can feel the basic meters (2/4, 3/4, 4/4, 6/8), the easier you will be able to detect the groupings of rhythmic patterns (usually in multiples of four: 4, 8, 16, 32, etc.). Folk dancing differs from social and square dancing in that the sequence of dance steps is fixed (Jensen 10).

2. *Styling:* Styling involves two levels of performance: (1) the dancers' appearance on stage (posture, carriage, etc.) and (2) the more subtle sense of nationality behind each dance. Pay attention to the country and its cultural identity as revealed in the style of the music and costuming. Some of the more common types of costumes: dirndls and lederhosen for the Alpine countries; the elaborately embroidered dresses and tightly fitting pants of Hungary; the simple matching of blue and white costumes of Israel; the long sequined skirts, ornamented jackets, and large hats of Mexico; the kilts from Scotland; and baggy pants and colorful streamers of the Ukraine.

3. *Body Control:* Basically, body control involves physical stamina and mental concentration. This is particularly important for the male dancer, who occasionally must execute very difficult, even acrobatic maneuvers, as in the Russian *prysiadka* and "coffee-grinder."

BALLROOM DANCE

In the Middle Ages there was little difference between social dance and folk dance. To get a feel for the cultural environment that spawned social dance proper, look at some of Pieter Brueghel's scenes of peasant life in sixteenth-century Flanders. His *Peasant Dance* (ca. 1568) captures the frivolity and gluttony that characterized a Netherlandish *kermis* (church fair), as strangely indifferent couples high-step on the village green. Their mismatched dance positions suggest a jolly free-for-all. Sometime near the birth of ballet in the Renaissance courts of Europe, the lusty folk dances of the peasants were transformed into the mannered dances of the kingly courts. The dancing moved from the town square into the royal ballroom and finally onto the stage. It was from these courtly social dances that ballet was formed in seventeenth-century France. The aristocratic taste of the French court held sway in cultural as well as dance matters until after the French Revolution.

DANCE & CULTURAL REVOLUTIONS

Probably no dance style in history has been more closely tied to the prevailing cultural revolutions than social dance. In the eighteenth century, the Industrial Revolution urbanized European culture and the French Revolution wiped out the French aristocracy, as well as its dance. Short bobs replaced powdered wigs and dark coats replaced colored silks. But George Washington still opened his inaugural ball with his favorite dance, the minuet. By 1815, however, the waltz had precipitated a dance revolution. As the spirit of naturalism invaded social dance, men held their partners in closed position, their bodies actually touching (although the rule was to keep one foot apart). By the "Gay 90s," the two-step had been added to the waltz as well as assorted country dances, like rounds, jigs, reels, and squares (Ellfeldt 105).

THE COTILLION

The nineteenth-century cotillion, a group mixer that provided a pleasant way to get acquainted, gave way to freer, more individual, kinds of dance positions and formations. Exhibition ballroom dancing emerged from the social dance revolution of the early twentieth century, as dancers moved out of the exclusive clubs into public establishments, where people of all classes could perform. This dance revolution was, again, an outgrowth of a larger cultural revolution taking place in the United States: industrialization created a culturally diverse urban population; the increased leisure that followed rising prosperity attracted the middle class to new mass entertainments such as vaudeville, films, and the cabaret; technological advances, such as the automobile and telephone, allowed increased intimacy between the sexes; the women's suffrage movement encouraged women to pursue leisure activities outside the home, like attending afternoon tea dances, popular between 1910 and 1915 (Malnig 2).

EXHIBITION BALLROOM

Three important influences on the popularity of exhibition **ballroom dance** were (1) the rise of cabaret (café dancing and singing) society in large cities; (2) the emergence of vaudeville (theatrical variety shows), which reached hundreds of cities and towns across the country; and (3) the popularity of ballroom dancing in musical theater.

THE CABARET

The **cabaret** brought ballroom dance out of private homes and small meeting places into a more public setting, uniting men and women of different social and economic classes, while at the same time providing an arena to popularize exhibition ballroom teams.

VAUDEVILLE

Vaudeville cleaned up its act and began appealing to a large middle-class population. Many ballroom teams actually began as struggling vaudeville performers. Comedian George Burns, for example, got his start as a ballroom dancer. His brief foray into ballroom dancing was invaluable for his career as a professional performer (Malnig 54).

MUSICALS

The Hollywood musicals of the 30s and 40s featured some of history's greatest dancing pairs: Irene and Vernon Castle were originally cabaret stars who made it big in musical theater (the 1914 production of *Watch Your Step* was one of the first musicals to glorify the contemporary ballroom dance craze); Fred Astaire and Ginger Rogers starred in a series of movie musicals and rewrote the book on exhibition ballroom dance by popularizing new dances (the Carioca and the Continental, for example) and greatly expanding the vocabulary of ballroom dancing. Fred Astaire was more than a ballroom dancer; "he was a virtuosic performer who fused tap, ballet, and ballroom to create a highly personal style" (Malnig 124).

BALLROOM COMPETITIONS

Ballroom dance competitions began in the 1930s and fueled what Julie Malnig has called "The Contemporary Renaissance" of ballroom dancing in the 1980s (137ff.). Hundreds of competitions are now held each year. The competition is tough; often only six finalists are chosen from fifty or more entries.

BALLROOM DANCE STYLES

INTERNATIONAL LATIN

Cha-cha: Another Cuban import requiring Latin motion, it became popular in the mid-1950s among young and old alike, partly because it is relatively easy to execute. Its name is supposed to have come from the hissing sound made by the heelless slippers worn by Cuban women. One contemporary critic considers it to be "a curious combination of sexy come-on and staid standoffishness" (Buckman 200), perhaps because of the crossover and half-chase steps, which alternates close and open position. RHYTHM: the triple mambo in duple meter (rest-2–3-4 and 1). STEP: forward-back-step-close-step.

Samba: Originally a group dance first performed by African slaves in Brazil, it became a couple dance when it arrived in the U.S. during the 1939 New York World's Fair and was popularized by Carmen Miranda in the movies (you remember, the Latin dancer with fruit-laden headgear). It has virtually become the national dance of Brazil. Everyone dances it in the streets of Rio during Carnival. A jazzed-up version of the samba, the Bossa Nova, was popular during the early 1960s. Its characteristic movement is a bounding and dropping action. RHYTHM: uses a chassé rhythm (quick-and-split-1-and-2) to counts 1-and-2–3-and-4. STEP: forward-back and side, with the upper torso leaning back on forward steps and forward on back steps.

Rumba: The most famous of the Latin American dances to gain popularity in North America and Europe, the rumba arrived in the U.S. from Cuba in the late 1920s and immediately became popular after being performed in film by George Raft and Carole Lombard. It combined African and Caribbean rhythms in a dance which was originally highly erotic. It requires a special style of dancing called "Latin Motion," which is achieved by moving the hips in opposition to the foot in motion. RHYTHM: duple meter (2/4 or 4/4). STEP: forward-back-side, back-forward-side.

Paso Doble: This dance originated in Spain, although it is said to have entered Europe through the influence of Louis XIV, who saw a bullfight and wanted a dance to capture its rhythm and excitement. The key to performing this dance is affecting a matador look, lifting the upper torso and proceeding almost march-like around the floor (the man is the matador; the woman is the cape). In competitions it usually ends with a flamenco flourish. It first gained popularity in Europe and the U.S. in the 1930s. RHYTHM: duple meter (fast 4/4) intermittently interrupted by a fanfare. STEP: walk step.

Jive: A child of the jukebox era of the 1950s, jive is like American triple swing or jitterbug (Lindy), but tighter and with slightly different step patterns. RHYTHM: fast 4/4 but with 6-beat step pattern: 1-and-1–2 3-and-a-4 back-step. An interesting side-note: Obviously inspired by Steven Spielberg's blockbuster film *Jurassic Park,* composer-pianist Irving Fields has written "Dance of the Dinosaurs," a piano composition played over the taped sounds of instruments imitating adult and baby dinosaurs clumping about. He is looking for a recording company to immortalize his Jurassic jive.

INTERNATIONAL STANDARD

Waltz: The waltz originated in Germany in the eighteenth century, although it had its roots in folk dancing. Its swinging turns required the dancers to hold on to each other for balance, which got the dancers into trouble for dancing "chest to breast." A German book proving that "the waltz is a main source of the weakness of the body and mind of our generation" was popular as late as 1799 (Buckman 124). Its proper execution requires the dancers to glide around the floor in a lyrical rising/falling motion. RHYTHM: the only exhibition ballroom dance in 3/4 time (1–2–3 1–2–3). The VIENNESE WALTZ is performed at a faster tempo with more turns and fewer steps.

Tango: The tango is unique as an example of "cultural colonization" (Buckman 17 1). It apparently originated in the "tangano," a dance peculiar to the African slaves sent to Haiti and Cuba in the eighteenth century and combined with the rhythms of the *habañera* ("Havana Dance") of nineteenth-century Cuba, then taken to Argentina by migrating blacks, to mingle with the *milonga,* a popular dance in the slums of Buenos Aires. When it arrived in Europe in the early twentieth century, its steamy eroticism had to be tamed. The modern tango bears little resemblance to the originals. It is now a staccato dance performed with great control, "one in which partners truly move as one. To a ballroom purist, a well-executed tango is as satisfying as is a flawless downhill run to an Alpine skier" (Dow 71). RHYTHM: slow-quick-quick alternating with long pauses and stylized body positions.

Foxtrot: A perfect dance to demonstrate ragtime music, the foxtrot derives its name from Harry Fox, a vaudeville star who executed a trotting dance to ragtime in the Ziegfeld Follies of 1914. Since the Roaring 20s, the foxtrot has become America's fundamental ballroom dance form. Its original jerky movements have been smoothed out over time. RHYTHM: basic 4/4 time with emphasis on the first and third beats. STEP: slow-quick-quick slow-quick-quick.

Quickstep: As the foxtrot proper got slower and slower, another dance was born, which is essentially a fast foxtrot, the quickstep, a dance that could be performed at a fair speed but with smooth "walking" movements. The required rise and fall in the quickstep is performed on the ball of the foot, the knees alternating flexed and straightened. RHYTHM: even 4/4 time in a quick tempo. STEP: slow and quicksteps together in any order; invites improvisation.

AMERICAN STYLE

American style ballroom dancing is a grab bag of International, Latin, and Modern, but the American style tends to be freer (more laid back) than its European counterparts. It also includes additional dances, like the mambo, two-step, polka, and swing. The MAMBO comes from Cuba and is characterized by a beat in every bar on which the dancer takes no step, somewhat like a fast cha-cha without the cha-cha rhythm. Its steps are embellished with kicks and body wiggles. The TWO-STEP requires a smooth ball-change to either side in 2/4 rhythm. The SWING is similar to the Jive but requires different footwork.

The WEST COAST SWING has a basic four-beat syncopated rhythm, but with a six-count step pattern (so the dance is often out of sync with the beat). The couple moves on a track, toward and away from each other.

WHAT TO LOOK FOR IN BALLROOM DANCE

In the highly competitive world of ballroom dance competition, performances are judged on four general criteria: (1) timing and rhythm; (2) hip movement and head control; (3) accuracy of footwork; and (4) level of difficulty But there are also specific expectations for each division.

BALLROOM (STANDARD):

1. Posture
2. Body carriage

3. Dance position (elbows high, shoulder relaxed)
4. Clean, precise footwork
5. Quality of movement (flowing, uninterrupted line)

LATIN:

1. Posture
2. Body carriage
3. Latin (hip) Motion (in rumba, cha-cha, and mambo)
4. Clean, precise footwork
5. Correct interpretation of different Latin rhythms

THREE DANCE COORDINATES

THE PHYSICAL COORDINATE

Here is a simple final formula to keep in mind when viewing any dance performance. It charts three elemental tensions that create excitement in dance. The first we might call the PHYSICAL COORDINATE. The tension generated here is the one we have just been talking about: weight vs. weightlessness, centered on the vertical axis of the backbone as the dancer strives to overcome the downward pull of gravity. Ballet seems especially appropriate to this coordinate because ballet training emphasizes vertical extension. The result is a grace of movement seldom equaled in other styles of dancing.

THE PSYCHOLOGICAL COORDINATE

The second could be called the PSYCHOLOGICAL COORDINATE because the most elemental manifestation of its tension is breathing in and breathing out (inspiration and expiration). Margaret H'Doubler contends that all movement, no matter how complex, is built upon this instinctive expansion and contraction of the body when breathing. Because the central movement of breathing occurs in the solar plexus (the diaphragm), modern dance seems most fitted for exploiting the expressive potential of this coordinate. Notice how modern dance movements seem to expand from this center in undulating extensions.

THE SOCIAL COORDINATE

The third coordinate goes beyond the dancer's body and establishes relationships between two or more bodies moving in space: the SOCIAL COORDINATE. This tension involves the dynamics of attraction and repulsion, which is perhaps most evident in the **pas de deux** between the male dancer and the ballerina, as in *Romeo and Juliet* (music by Prokofiev). The space between the lovers is electric with desire as they move together, in stark contrast to the scenes where Juliet dances with Paris (her parents' pick). Her dislike for him is almost palpable. The social coordinate plays a major role in responding to folk and ballroom dance styles because the performances consist almost exclusively of ensembles,

SUMMARY & RECENT DEVELOPMENTS

Dance in the latter part of the twentieth century seems to have pursued a direction similar to music, a movement away from the traditional and accessible toward the more abstract and experimental. The mid-century collaborations between the **avant garde** composer John Cage and Merce Cunningham set the parameters of this trend. (The fact that Cage was a student of Arnold Schönberg and Cunningham was a student of Martha Graham establishes the line of influence from the early pioneers of modernism in both arts). This collaboration produced some of the most innovative mixed media performances of the century, combining dance, mime, poetry, music, slide projections, and even moving pictures. But what set them apart from their predecessors was their attraction to the seemingly chance occurrences of real life. Cunningham's choreography departed dramatically from Martha Graham's story-telling dance style and her use of the body to express psychological states by means of contractions out of the solar plexis and back. As Cage treated natural sounds (traffic noises at Hollywood and Vine, for example), as musical to him as orchestral sounds, so Cunningham considered all body movements, such as running, jumping, and falling, as equally important to dance. For this reason, his performance pieces often seem disjointed and sporadic, much like a Pollock painting or a Cage composition. Lucinda Childs takes Cunningham's gestural style to its logical conclusion in her choreography for Philip Glass's opera *Einstein on the Beach* (1976). It obeys Cunningham's credo of pure movement by reducing body motions to patterns that are geometric, recurrent, and—for some critics—unspeakably boring" (*Fiero*, VI, 133–134).

COMMENTARY ON THE ARTS

MOVEMENT IS LIFE

—*Isadora Duncan*

Study the movement of the earth, the movement of plants and trees, of animals, the movement of winds and waves—and then study the movements of a child. You will find that the movement of all natural things works within harmonious expression. And this is true in the first years of a child's life; but very soon the movement is imposed from without by wrong theories of education, and the child soon loses its natural spontaneous life, and its power of expressing that in movement.

I notice that a baby of three or four coming to my school is responsive to the exaltation of beautiful music, whereas a child of eight or nine is already under the influence of a conventional and mechanical movement, in which it will remain and suffer its entire life, until advancing age brings on paralysis of bodily expression.

When asked for the pedagogic program of my school, I reply: "Let us first teach little children to breathe, to vibrate, to feel, and to become one with the general harmony and movement of nature. Let us first produce a beautiful human being, a dancing child." Nietzsche has said that he cannot believe in a god that cannot dance. He has also said, "Let the day be considered lost on which we have not danced."

But he did not mean the execution of pirouettes. He meant the exaltation of life in movement. The harmony of music exists equally with the harmony of movement in nature.

Man has not invented the harmony of music. It is one of the underlying principles of life. Neither could the harmony of movement be invented: it is essential to draw one's conception of it from Nature herself, and to seek the rhythm of human movement from the rhythm of water in motion, from the blowing of the winds on the world, in all the earth's movements, in the motions of animals, fish, birds, reptiles, and even in primitive man, whose body still moved in harmony with nature.

With the first conception of a conscience, many became self-conscious, lost the natural movements of the body; today in the light of intelligence gained through years of civilization, it is essential that he consciously seek what he has unconsciously lost.

All the movements of the earth follow the lines of wave motion. Both sound and light travel in waves. The motion of water, wind, trees and plants progresses in waves. The flight of a bird and the movements of all animals follow lines like undulating waves.

If then one seeks a point of physical beginning for the

movement of the human body, there is a clue in the undulating motion of the wave. It is one of the elemental facts of nature, and out of such elementals the child, the dancer, absorbs something basic to dancing.

The human being too is a source. Dancing expresses in a different language, different from nature, the beauty of the body; and the body grows more beautiful with dancing. All the conscious art of mankind has grown out of the discovery of the natural beauty of the human body. Men tried to reproduce it in sand or on a wall, and painting thus was born. From our understanding of the harmonies and proportions of the members of the body sprang architecture. From the wish to glorify the body sculpture was created.

The beauty of the human form is not chance. One cannot change it by dress. The Chinese women deformed their feet with tiny shoes; women of the time of Louis XIV deformed their bodies with corsets; but the ideal of the human body must forever remain the same. The Venus of Milo stands on her pedestal in the Louvre for an ideal; women pass before her, hurt and deformed by the dress of ridiculous fashions; she remains forever the same, for she is beauty, life, truth.

It is because the human form is not and cannot be at the mercy of fashion or the taste of an epoch that the beauty of woman is eternal. It is the guide of human evolution toward the goal of the human race, toward the ideal of the future which dreams of becoming God.

The architect, the sculptor, the painter, the musician, the poet, all understand how the idealization of the human form and the consciousness of its divinity are at the root of all art created by man. A single artist has lost this divinity, an artist who above all should be the first to desire it—the dancer.

Dancing, indeed, through a long era lacked all sense of elemental natural movement. It tried to afford the sense of gravity overcome—a denial of nature. Its movements were not living, flowing, undulating, giving rise inevitably to other movements. All freedom and spontaneity were lost in a maze of intricate artifice. The dancer had to be dressed up artificially to be in keeping with its unnatural character.

Then when I opened the door to nature again, revealing a different kind of dance, some people explained it all by saying, "See, it is natural dancing." But with its freedom, its accordance with natural movement, there was always design too—even in nature you find sure, even rigid design. "Natural" dancing should mean only that the dance never goes against nature, not that anything is left to chance.

Nature must be the source of all art, and dance must make use of nature's forces in harmony and rhythm, but the dancer's movement will always be separate from any movement in nature.

NOTE: Probably 1909.

WRITING EXERCISES

1. In the following quote, Havelock Ellis creates a dual parentage by pairing dance and architecture as the two primary and essential arts from whence all the other arts sprang:

   > The art of dancing stands at the source of all the arts that express themselves first in the human person. The art of building, or architecture, is the beginning of all the arts that lie outside the person; and in the end they unite. Music, acting, poetry proceed in the one mighty stream; sculpture, painting, all the arts of design, in the other. There is no primary art outside these two arts, for their origin is far earlier than man himself; and dancing came first. (138)

   What do you think of his claims? How might they be true? Why would dance and building come first? What would be some of the reasons? How might his claims be untrue? How do dance and architecture unite "in the end?" What do "music, acting, poetry" have in common?

2. Even though you probably haven't seen a performance of Balanchine's *Apollo* (live or recorded), critical descriptive and prescriptive reactions provide a general outline of what it might look like. Which one of the two critics quoted in the text (Denby or Jowitt) more evocatively recalls the essential imagery and movements of this famous dance solo? Justify your choice by describing the poetic devices the critic employs to engage the reader's interest. This brings up an important point concerning writing about the arts: the best critics delve into the essence of the work quite quickly and then, often poetically, elaborate on that central image: Denby focuses on birth imagery; Jowitt on maturation imagery (growing from a Dionysian to an Apollonian figure).

   As you read critics' columns in newspapers or magazines, pay attention to how they present the strengths and weaknesses of the works they review. It will demonstrate how you can see more and write better about your aesthetic experiences.

3. Go to your local video store and check out *American Ballet Theater at the Met* and view Martina van Hammel and Patrick Bissel's *Pas de Deux*. See how many of the ballet steps illustrated in the text you can

identify. You won't often see better dancing anywhere than on this taped program.

4. To gain a better appreciation for the discipline required to dance ballet, try executing some of the dance steps illustrated in the text. Good dancers make it look effortless, but you will readily discover how difficult it really is. Just be careful and don't wreck your back or knees. You should warm up first.

5. Edward Villella, former lead *danseur* with George Balanchine's New York City Ballet, once observed that the paradox of dance involves "total freedom and total control." What do you think he meant by that statement? Does this paradox relate to other areas of your life? Which? How?

6. If you've ever seen *A Chorus Line* (on Broadway or in the movie with Michael Douglas) you know professional dancers have to dance—it's in their blood. Read the following quotation from Merce Cunningham which appears on an unevenly typewritten paragraph in his book of notes, entitled *Changes:*

> You have to love dancing to stick to it. It gives you nothing back, no manuscripts to store away, no painting to show on walls and maybe hang in museums, no poems to be printed and sold, nothing but that fleeting moment when you feel alive. It is not for unsteady souls. (Qtd. in Jowitt 32)

Have you ever wondered why people would give their lives to dancing professionally when the pay is so erratic, the pain often so unbearable, and the future so short (a professional dancer is usually "over the hill" by 40). List some conceivable reasons why dance is so compelling. Talk to a dancer to round out your list.

WORKS CITED

Anderson, Jack. "The Modern Dance." *The Dance Anthology.* Ed. Cobbett Steinberg. New York: New American Library, n.d.

Armstrong, Lucile. *A Window on Folk Dance.* Huddersfield, West Yorkshire, England: Springfield Books, 1985.

Buckman, Peter. *Let's Dance.* New York: Penguin, 1978.

Coe, Robert. *Dance in America.* New York: E. P. Dutton, 1985.

Castro, Donald S. *The Argentine Tango as Social History 1880–1955.* Lewiston: Edwin Mellen Press, 1991.

Copeland, Roger, and Marshall Cohen. *What Is Dance?* New York: Oxford University Press, 1983.

Croce, Arlene. *Afterimages.* New York: Knopf, 1978.

Denby, Edwin. *Dance Writings.* Ed. Robert Cornfield and William Mackay. New York: Knopf, 1986.

Dow, Allen. *The Official Guide to Latin Dancing.* Secaucus, NJ: Chartwell Books, 1980.

Duncan, Isadora. *My Life.* New York: Liveright, 1955.

Ellfeldt, Lois. *Dance, from Magic to Art.* Dubuque, IA: W. C. Brown Co., 1976.

Ellis, Havelock. *The Dance of Life.* In Cobbett Steinberg, *The Dance Anthology.* New York: New American Library, 1980.

Fiero, Gloria. *The Humanistic Tradition.* 3rd ed. New York: McGraw-Hill, 1998.

Graham, Martha. "A Modern Dancer's Primer for Action." In *The Dance Anthology.* Ed. Cobbett Steinberg. New York: New American Library, 1980.

Highwater, Jamake. *Dance: Rituals of Experience.* Pennington, NJ: Princeton Book Company, 1992.

Jensen, Mary Bee, and Clayne R. Jensen. *Folk Dancing.* Prove, UT: Brigham Young University Press, 1973.

Jowitt, Deborah. *The Dance in Mind.* Boston: David R. Godine, 1985.

Little, Araminta. "The Meaning of Dance for Young Children." In *Dance Dynamics.* Washington D.C.: National Dance Association, 1978.

Malnig, Julie. *Dancing Till Dawn: A Century of Exhibition Ballroom Dance.* New York: Greenwood Press, 1992.

Martin, John. *The Modern Dance.* New York: Dance Horizons, 1933; rpt. 1972.

Plato, *Laws.* Ed. Robert M. Hutchins. 54 vols. *Great Books of the Western World.* Chicago: Encyclopaedia Britannica, 1952.

Rogosin, Elinor. *The Dance Makers: Conversations with American Choreographers.* New York: Walker, 1980.

Saal, Hubert. "Ballet on Ice." *Newsweek* (4 December 1978).

Sachs, Curt. *World History of the Dance.* Trans. Bessie Schoenberg. New York: Norton, 1937.

Sorell, Walter, ed. *The Dance Has Many Faces.* New York: a capella books, 1992.

The Dance through the Ages. New York: Grosser & Dunlap, 1967.

Terry, Walter. *How to Look at Dance.* New York: William Morrow and Company, 1982.

Treaster, Joseph B. "Ballet: The Agony behind the Ecstacy." *Family Health* (October 1978): 28–31.

Villella, Edward. *Prodigal Son: Dancing for Balanchine in a World of Pain and Magic.* New York: Simon & Schuster, 1992.

Williamson, Liz. *Jazz Dance.* New York: Sterling Publishing Company, 1983.

WEBSITES OF INTEREST

http://www.paballet.org/outreach/steps.aspx

Evolution of Ballet —
    http://books.google.com/books?id=a9Ht2zcHc6wC&prin
    tsec=frontcover&source=gbs_navlinks_s

Examples of Dance

Foxtrot —
    http://www.youtube.com/watch?v=_T89R1gUuuk

Waltz —
    http://www.youtube.com/
    watch?v=9-yIRGHPGPM&feature=related

German Folk Dance —
    http://www.youtube.com/
    watch?v=s0q1uqEB84k&feature=related

Ballet —
    http://www.youtube.com/
    watch?v=DBeUxXSNiFc&feature=related

Modern —t
    http://www.youtube.com/watch?v=uL1rB0GPIhI

Tango —
    http://www.youtube.com/watch?v=ZQFkS2xtnrA

Isadora Duncan video, poor quality —
    http://www.youtube.com/
    watch?v=L3oKiO0-u0U&feature=related

Appalachian Spring —
    http://www.youtube.com/watch?v=aEvcP-vXk4M

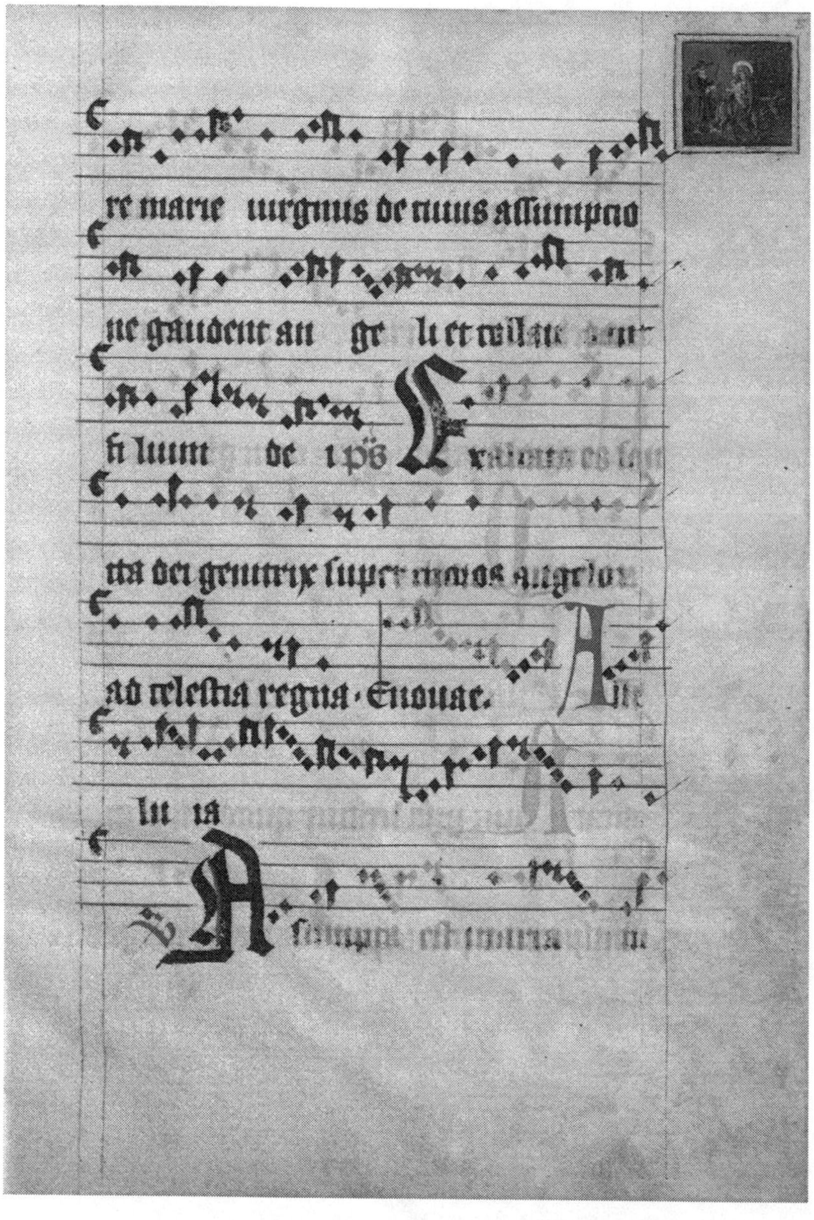

Fourteenth-century manuscript, BYU Archives

INTRODUCTION TO MUSIC

Chapter 10

INTRODUCTION

Given its presence in all cultures, music has often been called the universal language. This is not entirely true. Music is universally accessible within one general culture, like tonal music in the West. But non-Western cultures have sounds the Western ear has a hard time enduring, the singing style of Peking Opera, for example, or listening to more than a few minutes of certain non-Western timbres (like the Japanese Hichiriki). What people probably mean by "universal language" is this: music can be more readily assimilated and experienced than learning a foreign language. The statement also suggests that we can come closer to the essence of different cultures by learning to understand their music.

In comparison to some of the other arts, music draws us in and moves us more directly and forcibly because it bypasses the censor of the brain. Reading a poem or attending a drama requires some mental engagement to figure out what's going on. Music, on the other hand, hits us directly and elicits an immediate reaction. For this and other reasons, music has played a large role in all cultures, whether evoking cosmic truths, as in the chants of Tibetan monasteries, or entertaining masses of youths at a rock concert.

The great irony of teaching music appreciation is this: it is the one art form which people have been most exposed to (except perhaps architecture), and yet it is the one art which seems most difficult to get a mental handle on. This chapter has been designed to offer as clear an introduction to this important art form as possible. The details of notation and vocabulary found in conventional music texts have been greatly reduced; you should learn well what is given here and begin to apply it in your own music listening.

WHAT IS MUSIC?

PRIMITIVE PEOPLES

The answer to this question varies, depending upon the time frame the question refers to. For primitive peoples, as for children, song preceded speech. Babies coo before they can talk. Originally, music was probably indistinguishable from language—the sounds of love, fear, anger, joy—and indispensable in man's early attempts to mimic natural sounds: "Nature gave [man] his first musical instruments" (Mann 13).

THE ANCIENT GREEKS

For the ancient Greeks, music was defined in philosophical and cultural terms, as any "harmonious" activity related to the Muses. Our word *music* comes from the Greek word for muse: (*musa*), more specifically from *mousike techne,* the art (technique) of the Muses, namely activities connected to the creative domains of the nine daughters of Zeus and Mnemosyne (goddess of memory)—Clio (history), Urania (astronomy), Melpomene (tragedy), Thalia (comedy), Terpsichore (dance), Calliope (epic poetry), Erato (love poetry), Euterpe (lyric poetry), and Polyhymnia (songs of the gods). Even though music later became associated with Polyhymnia, the Greeks defined music in a much broader way than we do today.

THE HEBREWS

The Hebrews of the Exodus viewed music in a religious context, as a paean to their god for saving them from their enemies: "And Miriam the prophetess, the sister of Aaron, took a timbrel [tambourine] in her hand; and all the women went out after her with timbrels and with dances. And Miriam answered them, Sing ye to the Lord, for he hath triumphed gloriously; the horse and his rider hath he thrown into the sea" (Exodus 15:20–21). Interestingly, some medieval writers believed that the word *music* derived from the Egyptian word *moys* (water), construing from this a connection with Moses (whose name indeed may be derived from *moys*) (*Harvard Dictionary of Music* 548).

MEDIEVAL, RENAISSANCE, & MODERN

The medieval mind refined the Greek definition of music, dividing music into three levels embracing the "harmony of the world:" *musica mundana* (harmony of the universe); *musica humana* (harmony of the human body and soul), and *musica instrumentalis* (actual musical sound). Since the **Renaissance,** which revived the mathematical basis of music and connected it to the other arts, in particular, architecture, music has been defined primarily in terms of audible patterns of sound produced by vibrating bodies (instruments or the human voice). Only recently has MODERN MUSIC expanded the definition to include disorganized sound (noise) as a legitimate province of musical sound, in particular, in the **aleatory** experiments of John Cage (1912–1992). Because of modern recording devices, more people listen to music than ever before in the history of the world (Storr xi). Technology has not only redefined the musical experience; it has greatly magnified its impact.

HOW & WHY DOES MUSIC AFFECT US?

It is a perennial mystery exactly how mere sound can penetrate the soul and make one person so revere the works of another. A touching example is Schubert's reverence for Mozart:

> All my life I shall remember this fine, clear, lovely day. I shall hear softly as from a distance, the magic strains of Mozart's music. . . . In the dark places of this life they point to that clear-shining and distant future in which our whole hope lies. O Mozart, immortal Mozart, how many, how infinitely many inspiring suggestions of a finer, better life have you left in our souls! (Qtd. in Holmes 100)

"Is it not strange that sheeps' guts should hale souls out of men's bodies?" Benedick asks in Shakespeare's *Much Ado About Nothing*. The paradox of music lies in its being grounded in the vibration of purely physical materials (sheep gut, horse hair, and dead wood), obeying the strictest rules of mathematics and physics, and yet evoking such sublime responses in the listener. As Claude Levi-Strauss observed, "Music is the only language with the contradictory attributes of being at once intelligible and untranslatable" (qtd. in Storr xi). In spite of the mystery and paradox, some illuminating answers have been formulated over time.

BEGINNINGS

In the absence of documentation, it is impossible to determine the purpose or impact of music on prehistoric peoples. But it has been fairly well established that "all music is an expression of physical movement, every theme and phrase a reflection of some bodily gesture" (Mann 16). But to our ancient ancestors, these rhythms were religious and magical—for us they are often merely mathematical and physical.

THE CLASSICAL AGE

For the ancient Greeks the impact of music was therapeutic (it refined the soul), educational, and political. Plato said that "when modes of music change, the fundamental laws of the State always change with them" (*Republic* IV, qtd. in *Great Treasury* 1054). Aristotle proposed the use of music "for intellectual enjoyment in leisure." He goes on: "Even in mere melodies there is an imitation of character. . . . Some of them make men sad and grave . . . others enfeeble the mind . . . another, again, produces a moderate and settled temper. . . . Enough has been said to show that music has a power of forming the character, and should therefore be introduced into the education of the young" (*Politics* 1338, 1339, qtd. in *Great Treasury* 1054–55).

THE MIDDLE AGES

Medieval music served two unequal masters, the church and the secular world. Secular tunes, both bawdy and refining (in the troubadour tradition), gave expression to the life experiences of the common people, but church music played on the religious emotions by setting a mood of deep meditation. The ethereal effects of **Gregorian Chant** were perfect musical counterparts of the monastic life.

SINCE THE RENAISSANCE

Sir Thomas Browne voiced the Renaissance rediscovery of music as Pythagorean proportion when he wrote: "For there is a musick where ever there is a harmony, order or proportion; and thus far we may maintain the musick of the Spheares" (*Religio Medici*, 11, 9, qtd. in *Great Treasury* 1057). And Congreve revived the Greek belief in the therapeutic power of music "to soothe a savage breast, To soften rocks, or bend a knotted oak" (*The Mourning Bride*, I, i, qtd. in *Great Treasury* 1057), a conclusion as mystifying as Darwin's perplexity in the face of music's utter uselessness in the process of natural selection (and, therefore, the most mysterious of the arts) and Schopenhauer's awe that its indefiniteness best points us to the Absolute: "[Music] does not express a particular and definite joy, sorrow, anguish, horror, delight, or mood of peace, but joy, sorrow, anguish, horror, delight, peace of mind themselves" (*The World as Will and Idea*, Vol. I, 52, qtd. in *Great Treasury* 1958).

CONTEMPORARY VIEWS

As we arrive at the present, studies of the effects of music on the human psyche naturally become more connected to psychology and physiology. Susanne K. Langer connects feelings to music by means of form (*Gestalt*): "Because the forms of feeling are much more congruent with musical forms than with the forms of language, music can reveal the nature of feelings with a detail and truth that language cannot approach (199). One of the best recent studies of the psychological and biological significance of music is Anthony Storr's *Music and the Mind*. He argues that, of all the arts, music has the closest link to the human body; its rhythms are analogues to "breathing, walking, the heartbeat and sexual intercourse" (33). And yet music's real significance lies in its power to order our lives. He concludes that, while not an official belief system, music is "a way of ordering human experience" (187).

MEDIUMS OF MUSIC

ALL SOUND CAN BE MUSIC

One of the strangest sounds I ever heard was in Tibet. I was permitted to enter the temple of one of the Lamaist monasteries which was famous for an immense drum in front of the central altar. The moment I entered the monastery I was conscious of a deep agitated sound that seemed to be coming from a great distance and yet was within the temple. Never in my life had I heard such a mysterious and complex sound. In addition to the central altar, this temple has an enclosed altar on each side. I asked permission to go into these enclosures, and there I found monks seated Lama fashion on the ground, chanting to themselves from ancient books. Each one was chanting in a different key and singing a different chant, but they were all singing with deep voice and extremely softly, so that the temple was filled with a kind of agitated murmur. This was not music in the ordinary sense, but it was one of the most fascinating sounds I have ever heard, with all the rhythms of the chants crossing each other like the mazes of a labyrinth. (Stokowski 48)

INTRODUCTION

The stuff of which music is made is sound produced by some vibrating body. Normally we distinguish between noise (disorganized sound) and music (organized sound), although in our century the avant-garde composer JOHN CAGE (1912–1992) reveled in the great variety of noises and silences surrounding us every day. "There is no noise, only sound," he often said, and his compositions prove it. In his 1962 work *0'0"*, he chopped up vegetables, put them in a blender and drank the juice. Probably his most provocative composition was *4'33"* (1952) which consisted of a performer sitting at a piano for four minutes and 33 seconds and then leaving the stage. Nevertheless, for purposes of this text, we will define medium in music as organized sound and silence.

Although wind and string instruments have been known for nearly five thousand years, the earliest musical instruments are clappers (percussion instruments) found by archaeologists in ancient Egypt. It is possible that singing accompanied their rhythmic beat, but the use of pitch may have been quite limited.

THE PHYSICS OF MUSICAL SOUND

Any sustained tone, whether sung or played, creates a complex of audible events. Imagine plucking a taut string. If you could slow down the back-and-forth movement you would notice a couple of things. First, the whole string moves at a certain regular speed (the "concert A" to which an orchestra tunes vibrates at 440 cycles per second). This is called the FREQUENCY, which determines the PITCH. The string also moves in a certain arc from side to side. This is called the AMPLITUDE, which determines the loudness of the sound, its **dynamics.** Finally, there are small vibration arcs along the length of the string, producing what are called OVERTONES or "harmonics," which determine the **timbre,** or "tone color," of a sound. In the nineteenth century, Hermann von Helmholtz found a way to measure these secondary vibrations. The first five different overtones naturally create a pentatonic scale (five tones), common in the music of the Orient and in folk songs in the West (like playing only on the black keys). One of the mysteries of music grows out of the realization that its emotional power is grounded in the precise laws of the physics of sound and the theories of mathematics first formulated by the ancient Greeks (the Pythagoreans).

THE EVOLUTION OF MUSICAL INSTRUMENTS

Just as the kind of material used to sculpt a statue determines to some degree its impact, stone as opposed to wood, for example, so the expanding range of sound possibilities of musical instruments has broadened the composer's options and increased the sound impact of the symphony orchestra. Mozart's music sounds different from Wagner's in large measure because valve systems for brass instruments were perfected in the nineteenth century, greatly increasing the dynamic range of the romantic orchestra.

Think of the wide array of different timbres (tone colors) in the symphony orchestra as a giant artist's palette. The composer's gift is to spin out the different colors in their infinite variety of tonal ranges and combinations into a musical fabric in time and space. WALT DISNEY (1907–1966) tried to create a visual analogue to this marvelous box of musical colors in *Fantasia* (1940), with varying degrees of success. Disney conducted a similar experiment with Prokofiev's visual musical narrative, *Peter and the Wolf*, where each animal was associated with a different instrument: Peter with the string orchestra, his grandfather with the bassoon, the cat with the clarinet, the duck with the oboe, the bird with the flute, and the wolf with the low brass. Sometimes it is appropriate to make these kinds of visual or narrative associations, as in PROGRAM MUSIC (descriptive music that has a "program"), but generally timbre creates the tonal background for the other instruments.

INSTRUMENTS OF THE ORCHESTRA

SOUND PRODUCTION

To fully appreciate the composer's sensitive ear and the kaleidoscope of colorful sounds that make up a symphonic work, it is helpful to become aware of the special quality of sound associated with each instrument of the orchestra. The four families of orchestral instruments are grouped according to the similarity of their sounds. This similarity reflects how the sound is produced. To produce musical sound, instruments need three things: a VIBRATOR, a RESONATOR, and a PITCH REGULATOR. The STRING CHOIR produces sound by drawing a bow over a string (the vibrator) and being amplified through its taut wooden body (the resonator). The performer's left fingers determine the pitch by lengthening and shortening the string (pitch regulator). The WOODWIND CHOIR produce their sounds by blowing through a reed (the vibrator) into a wooden or

Percussion · Timpani · Trumpets · French horns · Trombones · Tuba · Double basses · Harps · Clarinets · Bassoons · Violas · Piano · Flutes · Oboes · Second violins · Cellos · First violins · Conductor

metal tube (the resonator) and using keys to control the length of air (the pitch regulator). The BRASS CHOIR makes sound by vibrating the lips in a cupped mouthpiece, pushing the sound through a conical metal tubing, and using valves, or, in the case of the trombone, a sliding mechanism, to produce the different pitches. The unique timbre of each section of the orchestra, as well as each instrument in that section, is a product of the kind of

material that is vibrating and resonating. The PERCUSSION SECTION generates the rhythmic pulse in orchestral music and generally doesn't have pitch, with the exception of the tympani (kettle drums), harp, chimes, marimba, glockenspiel, xylophone, and piano. In addition to the percussion instruments illustrated below, there are also the whip, tambourine, and castanets.

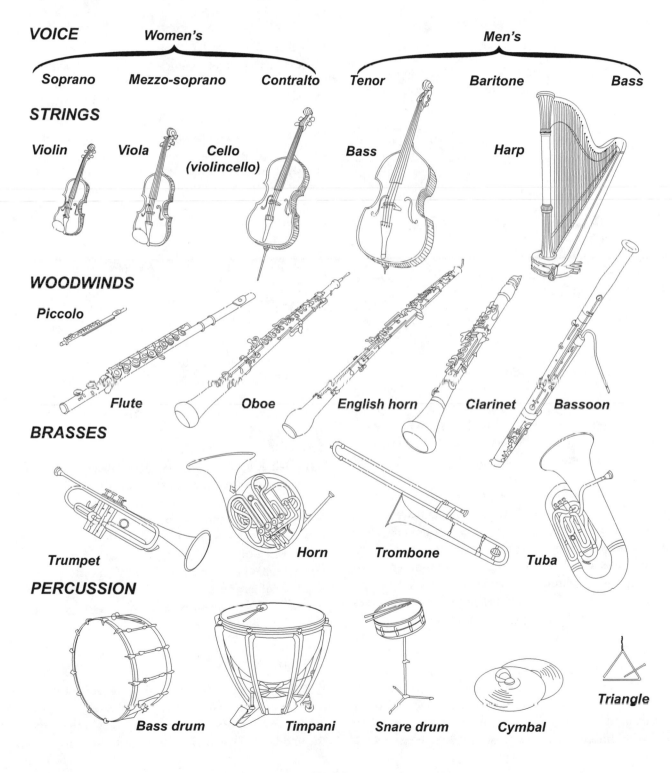

VOICE

Women's — Soprano, Mezzo-soprano, Contralto
Men's — Tenor, Baritone, Bass

STRINGS
Violin, Viola, Cello (violincello), Bass, Harp

WOODWINDS
Piccolo, Flute, Oboe, English horn, Clarinet, Bassoon

BRASSES
Trumpet, Horn, Trombone, Tuba

PERCUSSION
Bass drum, Timpani, Snare drum, Cymbal, Triangle

THE THREE "CHOIRS"

Because the strings, woodwinds, and brasses produce scalar pitches and play in ranges roughly corresponding to the human voice (soprano, alto, tenor, and bass), they are sometimes called orchestral "choirs." Dividing up each section this way will help you remember instrumental timbres and ranges. For example, the strings are divided into soprano (violin), alto (viola), tenor (cello), and bass (string bass).

THE SYMPHONY ORCHESTRA

When you attend your next concert, learn to recognize the appearance and characteristic sound of each group of instruments in the orchestra and remember where they are usually placed. It's amazing how much more the ear hears when the eye can see what's going on. Notice the conductor's gestural cues to the instrumentalists, for example. Conducting is a kind of gestural dancing.

HOW TO LISTEN TO MUSIC: THE ELEMENTS

INTRODUCTION: FORMALISTS VS. EXPRESSIONISTS

Music is undoubtedly the best-loved and least understood of all the arts. In light of this fact, and the hemispheric specialization of the brain, it is useful for you to know that critical appreciation of music requires both the right and left lobes, since, as we have already discovered, music is both highly mathematical and deeply emotional. Since analysis is a left-brain function, studying the elements and structure of music will not normally produce the kind of emotional high that listening to your favorite music will. But, as in the creative process itself, the more left-brain information and insights one gleans from studying an art form, the deeper the potential appreciation and emotional involvement. Among music critics are at least two contrasting approaches to musical interpretation: the FORMALISTS, who limit any discussion of musical meaning to its technical features (thematic development, harmonic progression, modulations, orchestration, tempo changes, etc.); and the EXPRESSIONISTS, those who wax eloquent on the effects music has on the listener. Both extremes are self-limiting. Our goal is to bring informed analysis to bear on deepening the musical experience without getting lost in theoretical technicalities that are mainly of academic interest. Anthony Storr assures us that "an untrained listener who loves music does not simply immerse himself in a sea of treacle. . . . He is also acutely aware of repetition, change of key, and resolution. . . . [A] listener does not have to be a trained musician to recognize that Haydn is a master of surprise" (78). The goal of this section is to bring you to this level of informed musical listening.

COPLAND'S 3 LEVELS OF MUSICAL LISTENING

One of America's greatest composers, AARON COPLAND (1900–1990), was also a master teacher and an engaging writer. In his book *What to Listen For in Music,* he outlines three planes or levels of musical listening: (1) the SENSUOUS, listening to sounds; (2) the EXPRESSIVE, reacting to the extra-musical associations music evokes; and (3) the SHEERLY MUSICAL, attending to music on its own terms. It is the last, the "sheerly musical" level, which requires an understanding of the six musical elements: rhythm, melody, harmony, timbre (tone color), tempo, and dynamics. Most listeners are unaware of this third plane. It is the purpose of this section of the course to help you understand what to listen for in "sheerly musical" terms (9–19).

THE ELEMENTS OF MUSIC

1. RHYTHM

Most historians agree that if music started anywhere, it started with a rhythmic beat (indeed, our very bodies are rhythmical—we live all our lives with the trochaic beating of the heart: *lub*-dub, *lub*-dub). Thus, **rhythm** represents the accent patterns in music (sometimes recognizable apart from the melody itself). Meter is a means of measuring rhythm by organizing its accent patterns into irreducible ordered groupings called "measures" (divided by vertical lines into bars with equal numbers of beats). For example, the **time signature** tells us the kind of beat pattern the piece has: 3/4 time tells us that there are 3 beats per measure and a quarter note gets one beat. Other popular time signatures are 2/4, 4/4, and 6/8. Syncopation results when the composer disrupts our normal expectations of where the accent patterns fall (normally on the first beat of a measure: ONE-two-ONE-two, or ONE-two-three-ONE-two-three, etc.) to create a shock effect, like in jazz: one-TWO-three-FOUR.

2. MELODY

The **melody** can be seen as the "subject" of music. It is the "horizontal" aspect and, not unlike a dramatic plot, grows to a climax as it moves from its beginning through the middle to the end. The unique arrangement of musical tones is chosen from certain organized successions of sounds called **scales** (the distance from one tone or tones to the next in a scale, up or down, is called an INTERVAL).

Scales

There are at least five scale systems that are used in music, although only two (major and minor) figure prominently in Western music. Major and minor scales are sometimes called MODES because they originate in the eight modes (scale systems) of medieval and ancient Greek music. Each mode created a different mood.

The MAJOR scale sounds "major" because of its unique patterns of whole and half tones [experiment with this by playing the white keys of a piano beginning with middle C to the C an octave higher—notice that the order of whole and half steps is: W-W-1/2-W-W-W-1/2]. This scale creates a stable, generally positive mood, in contrast to the darker, stranger sound of the minor.

The MINOR scale sounds "minor" because, by lowering the third, sixth, and seventh steps of the major scale (and sometimes raising the seventh step), the sequence of whole and half tones is altered (W-1/2-W-W-1/2-W-W) creating a more somber, mysterious mood than the major scale. The key to recognizing its strange tonality is to listen for the "lowered third."

The CHROMATIC scale (often associated with Richard Wagner's music) is made up of successions of only half steps, like playing all the black and white keys of the piano in succession, up or down. It creates greater tonal ambiguity and allows more gradual resolutions of harmonic tensions.

The WHOLE-TONE scale (associated with Debussy's musical Impressionism) is made up of successions of only whole steps (C D E F♯ G♯ A♯ C, for example). Because of the "tritone" (augmented 4th from C to F♯), this scale undercuts the "diatonic" system, creating tonal and harmonic ambiguity.

The PENTATONIC scale (often associated with Oriental music) is made up of only five tones, like playing only the black keys on the piano keyboard ("Peter, Peter, Pumpkin Eater"). Many traditional American folk tunes are pentatonic, like "Barbara Allen."

3. HARMONY

Sometimes referred to as the "vertical" aspect of music, **harmony** is created by playing two or more notes together (three tones, a TRIAD, or more played together is called a CHORD; if played in sequence, it is called an ARPEGGIO).

The earliest kind of music (and most contemporary primitive music) had no harmony at all, but only melody

buttressed by simple rhythms. In fact, some medieval music, **Gregorian Chant,** for example, didn't even have any clear rhythm, but only melodies (and not very singable ones at that). Music without harmony is called **monophony,** one of the three discernible **textures** of music (along with polyphony and homophony). The other two are based on harmony, the simultaneous sounding of more than one tone. The earliest kind of harmony was **polyphony** or **counterpoint** (literally note against note) in which (1) a single melody was played at different times (like in rounds, "Row, Row, Row, Your Boat," for instance), or (2) two different melodies played simultaneously. The most complex kinds of polyphony or counterpoint are fugues, in which four or five or more melodic lines move in contrast to each other "contrapuntally." J. S. Bach was the past master of this texture. The third kind of musical texture is what we call **homophony,** in which chordal structures are built over a clearly defined bass line and underneath a clear melodic line. You hear this texture most today, because it is the prevailing musical texture of most popular songs as well as the hymns you sing in church. To remember the differences among these three textures think of the following: monophony is like singing in the shower (one single melodic line, sung as solo or in unison); polyphony is like singing a round around the campfire; and homophony is like singing in the church choir.

Emotional Response

More than any other musical element, with the possible exception of melody, harmony creates our emotional responses to music. Its power to evoke feelings is rooted in the attraction (gravitational pull) some tones of the scale have to the beginning tone (the first step of the scale, the TONIC or "home base"). The strongest pull is experienced by the 4th, 5th, and 7th steps of the scale. When these same steps, together with some additional filler tones, are transferred from the melody into the bass line, they form the foundation of chords and intensify the gravitational pull back to home base (the TONIC). For example, a CADENCE (the chords played at the end of a musical phrase which lead you back to the tonic) is usually based on the chordal sequence, IV-V-I, like the concluding chords of most hymns.

4. TIMBRE

Timbre (pronounced "tamber") is a musical term used to describe the characteristic quality of sound produced by a voice or instrument. The quality of the sound will be influenced by many factors: the material from which an instrument is made, the size and shape of an instrument or vocal mechanism, and the way in which an instrument or voice is used. Timbre lends itself best to Copland's first level of musical listening—the "sensuous"—and is probably the most useful place to start fine-tuning your musical-appreciation ear.

5. TEMPO

Tempo comes from the Italian word for time and refers to the speed at which a piece of music is played. An interesting philosophical question emerges when one begins to think about speed in music: What determines our designation of fast and slow? Faster than what? Slower than what? Allowing for individual variations, there exists in the mind a sense of "normal" speed which has been "clocked" at about 70 beats per minute, approximately the rate of the normal heartbeat or the speed at which most people walk. In music, this speed is referred to as *tempo guisto* ("just tempo"). Anything noticeably faster or slower than this creates tension. Thus, in musical terms, "man is the measure of all things" (Protagoras). Some relatively common tempos in music are: *largo* (very slow), *adagio* (slow), *andante* (moderately slow), *allegro* (moderately fast), *presto* (very fast). The following Italian adjectives are often used with tempo markings: *molto* (very), *più* (more), *meno* (less), *poco* (a little), and *ma non troppo* (but not too much). Different movements in symphonies are often designated by their tempo markings. The first movement of Beethoven's Fifth Symphony, for example, is marked *Allegro con brio* ("fast with vigor").

6. DYNAMICS

Dynamics refers to the sound intensity of music (its loudness and softness), identified in music by the letter *f* (for **forte** = loud) and *p* (for **piano** = soft), *pp* = *pianissimo* (very soft) and *ff* = *fortissimo* (very loud). Our most popular modern keyboard instrument, the "piano" was originally called the *pianoforte* ("soft-loud" thing), because it was able to play loud and soft by employing a felt-tipped hammer in contrast to its predecessor, the harpsichord, which created sound by means of a plectrum which plucked the string, restricting it to one dynamic level.

Ravel's **Bolero**

As with the other elements, the development of contrast in dynamic level is very important in music. The famous *Bolero* by MAURICE RAVEL (1875–1937), for example, would sound like a simple exercise in repetition were it not for the slow and steady increase in dynamic level and changes in orchestration (*timbre*). Such building up of volume is called *crescendo* (abbreviated *cresc.*), and is indicated on a musical score by the mark < . The opposite, a *decrescendo*, creates a gradual softening effect. Also called the *diminuendo* (*dim.*), this effect is indicated by the mark > . A well-loved symphony that virtually dies away at the close is Tchaikovsky's Symphony No. 6 (the "Pathétique"). It was much criticized when first performed because at that time symphonies were expected to come to a loud and dramatic close.

ORCHESTRAL FORMS IN MUSIC

INTRODUCTION

Analyzing music is not much different than dissecting frogs: you need to cut it up into parts to figure out what makes it tick. But it is clear that no one listens to music this way. We experience music holistically. While listening we are aware of all the musical events at once. So now our task is to separate music into its parts. To do this requires that we attend to something called musical form. It is easier to understand form by referring first to the visual arts, because their forms are constantly before us in one spatial framework. Instead of having one rectangular frame surrounding the whole painting, in music there are many smaller frames, or perhaps we should call them brackets, which separate the sequences of sound events. One thing that makes perceiving musical form more difficult is the fact that it moves in time and requires an alert audio memory. To see a painting like you listen to music would require sitting in a dark room and having someone trace (left to right, top to bottom) the various parts of a painting with a pen light. To get the whole picture you would have to retain in memory all the lines and colors you had seen and then assemble the complete picture in your mind. Luckily, we instinctively respond to musical rhythms, melodic lines, and tone colors. Now we simply need to bring these into our critical awareness.

DISCOVERING SIMPLE SONG FORMS: BINARY & TERNARY FORMS

Basically, music is organized on the principles of repetition and contrast: some parts are alike, some are different, and some are alike with a difference. All good music invites the listener to discover these similarities and differences. We are drawn to our favorite musical pieces because of the melodies and, to a lesser extent, the rhythms and harmonies.

To begin with the simplest musical pieces, popular songs, we find two basic forms: two-part (AB or **binary**) and three-part (**ABA** or **ternary**). The letters simply indicate the different parts of the melody.

ABA forms give a greater sense of completion and wholeness, like going on a journey and ending up back home again. "Home on the Range" is an example of the typical "popular song" form (notice that the A section is repeated in the second line with basically the same tune but with different words):

A: O give me a home, where the buffalo roam, where the deer and the antelope play;

A: Where seldom is heard, a discouraging word, and the skies are not cloudy all day;

B: Home, home, on the range, where the deer and the antelope play;

A: Where seldom is heard, a discouraging word, and the skies are not cloudy all day.

Most popular songs follow this form, although many extend it to include several different verses of text, but with virtually the same melodic sequence, so it ends up looking something like this: A B A B A B A.

HOW TO RECOGNIZE SIMPLE MUSICAL FORMS

A simple way to accomplish this is to practice mapping a piece you are familiar with. William Thomson in *Music for Listeners* likens this process to charting the "terrain" of a musical landscape, following the hills and valleys (rise and fall of the melody) and outlining the borders separating one section from the next. A hypothetical mapping might look something like this (31–33):

Stage 1: Listen carefully with as little note-taking as possible; then think back over the composition at the end, taking notes on basic features.

Stage 2: Listen to the main parts, where the melody (theme) changes (indicate with capital letters AB, etc.) and determine the relative time durations (long, short, etc.).

Stage 3: Add interesting details to each section: draw on your own descriptions ("peaceful," "jumpy theme," "placid moonlight setting," "wild confusion," etc., as well as some of the musical terms you have learned; *crescendo*—becomes louder; *decrescendo*—becomes softer; *ritardando*—becomes slower; *accelerando*—becomes faster; *timbre*—different instruments and combinations enter or alternate (strings, woodwinds, brass, etc.).

Stage 4: Realign your map with successive listenings for greater precision.

ORCHESTRAL FORMS

INTRODUCTION

One of the most popular expansions of the ABA form in music is the RONDO. Here the main theme alternates with other themes called EPISODES, providing contrast and continuity; the rondo always begins and ends with the A theme. Schematically, it looks something like this: A B A C A B A, where the A section functions as a recurring refrain throughout the piece. Richard Strauss's *Til Eulenspiegel* is a modified rondo, as is Mussorgsky's *Pictures at an Exhibition,* where the walking theme functions as the A refrain.

THEME AND VARIATIONS

THEME AND VARIATIONS is an important musical form based on the principle of variation, modification of a given melody, generally a simple theme, repeated over and over, each time embellished in a different manner, so that it becomes essentially a demonstration of how many ways there are to say the same thing. Variations usually progress either by contrast or by increasing elaboration or both. The schema looks something like this: A A1 A2 A3 A4, etc. Variations can occur as independent compositions, like Bach's "Goldberg" variations or Beethoven's "Diabelli" variations, or as movements in sonatas and symphonies. Beethoven's "Apassionata" piano sonata or Haydn's "Surprise" Symphony are notable examples. One of the most charming instances of this form is Mozart's piano piece entitled *Variations on a Theme: "Ah, vous dirai-je, Maman,"* more familiar to us as "Twinkle, Twinkle, Little Star." The fourth movement of Schubert's "Trout" quintet is a theme and variations, as is Brahms's orchestral piece *Variations on a Theme by Haydn.*

THE CONCERTO

The CONCERTO (from *concertare* = to contend) is a musical form based on the principal of contrast. Originally it involved "competing" groups of instruments, as in the Baroque CONCERTO GROSSO, where a small group, known as the *concertina,* played against a larger group, known as the *ripieno* ("full"), and ended with the whole ensemble playing together. Bach's six Brandenburg Concertos (1721) and Vivaldi's *Four Seasons*

(1725) are outstanding examples of this early concerto form. The later solo concerto rose to prominence during the Romantic Age (nineteenth century), sparked by the rise of the solo **virtuoso**. The most popular solo concertos were written for the violin and piano. The form is essentially that of the classical sonata, except that the concerto has only three movements instead of the symphony's usual four. Some of the most popular VIOLIN CONCERTOS are by Beethoven (D major), Mendelssohn (E minor), Brahms (D major), Tchaikovsky (D major), and Bruch (G minor). Some of the greatest PIANO CONCERTOS are by Mozart (D minor, A major, C major), Beethoven (Emperor), Schumann (A minor), Brahms (D minor, B-flat major), Chopin (E minor, F minor), Grieg (A minor), Tchaikovsky (B-flat minor), and Rachmaninoff (Second in C minor).

THE SUITE

The SUITE was originally a collection of dances, all binary and all in the same key. Today a suite is a collection of separate orchestra pieces which have been put together because of some unity of idea, not necessarily musical. Some of the more common dance sections are prelude or overture, minuet, gavotte, allemande, courante, sarabande, and gigue. The modern orchestral suite often has little connection with the earlier (Baroque) suites of J. S. Bach, for example, being simply a collection of programmatic compositions divided into movements, such as Tchaikovsky's *Nutcracker Suite* (composed specifically for ballet), or Ferde Grofé's *Grand Canyon Suite* (composed for the concert stage).

THE SONATA ALLEGRO (FIRST MOVEMENT) FORM

INTRODUCTION

With this brief introduction, we are prepared to tackle the larger, more complex, yet similar symphonic forms that make up the repertoire of the great symphony orchestras. The most popular classical form of all is the **Sonata-**

Allegro form, sometimes called the **"First Movement" form,** because it has been used for the first movements of symphonies ever since Haydn. In the late **Renaissance** and **Baroque** eras, SONATA simply meant any extended musical form for one or more "sounding" instruments (from *sonar* = to sound), to distinguish it from the **cantata** (*cantar* = to sing), and the keyboard TOCCATA (from *toccare* = to touch). Later the sonata took on a more general meaning as a piece in different mediums in three or four movements and in different though related keys. Beethoven wrote many piano sonatas whose forms and movements correspond quite closely to the forms of his nine symphonies. A SYMPHONY is a large musical composition for orchestra, having four movements, each in a contrasting tempo, form, and key. Notice that the principle of REPETITION AND CONTRAST is at work in the large picture as well as within the melodies and larger sections of the movements themselves.

EXPOSITION, DEVELOPMENT, & RECAPITULATION

The **Sonata-Allegro** or **First Movement form** is a basic ABA form consisting of three major divisions—the **exposition**, the **development**, and the **recapitulation**—followed by a concluding passage, the **coda** (Italian for "tail") falling outside the basic structure of the composition, and added in order to heighten the sense of finality. The **exposition** "exposes" usually two themes in contrasting keys and moods. The second section, called the **development**, "develops" fragments of the main themes in various ways in order to create a special feeling of dynamic growth and dramatic conflict. The basic procedure is based on the "motival technique," working with short melodic motives derived by chopping up the two themes introduced in the exposition. There is considerable modulation (shifting to different keys) and "dialogues" between different sections of the orchestra, particularly between the strings and the woodwinds. The recapitulation is essentially a restatement of the exposition (although now the second theme remains in the home key). The movement closes with the coda. All in all, this form follows the general curve profile of any dramatic

MOVEMENT	MOOD	FORM	TEMPO
1st movement	Dramatic	Sonata-allegro	Allegro
2nd movement	Lyrical	Theme & Variations	Andante
3rd movement	Dance-like	Minuet & Trio	Allegretto Scherzo
4th movement	Dramatic	Sonata-allegro	Theme & Variations

work, perhaps because of its capacity for creating dramatic contrast and formal unity.

SMALLER PIANO FORMS

Prelude: The term "prelude" originally referred to a piece meant to be played before something else, but the word is less definite now. It can also mean a piece played separately. (The preludes of Chopin are independent compositions.)

Impromptu: A piece of music which has connotations of spontaneity and rather slight organization. (Chopin's popular *Fantasie Impromptu* is a good example.)

Nocturne: A piece of music which is supposed to suggest the atmosphere of night. (Chopin wrote many of these for the piano.)

Etude: This is a technical study, usually of great difficulty.

VOCAL FORMS

INTRODUCTION

The human voice is the most unique instrument there is, the one most capable of producing a great range of variations in tone quality. Despite an orchestra's great variety of tone color, it cannot compete with the special timbre of a **chorus** or choir, partly because the human voice produces its sounds by the vibration and sympathetic resonance of living tissue and bone. For this reason, the spirit and character of the performer may be more an embedded part of the sound than when performing on a musical instrument. A chorus may often perform with piano, organ, or even full orchestra accompaniment, but it also frequently performs with no accompaniment at all, referred to as *a cappella* (meaning "as in the chapel"). Here are some of the most important forms of choral music:

Motet: The most popular form of vocal music from the thirteenth through the seventeenth centuries was the **motet.** This form (from the French word *mot,* meaning "word) emphasized the text and, though it was often written in Latin, it came to use the vernacular or everyday language, especially French but later German, and sometimes even a hybrid combination, with each voice or group of voices singing a different text, often in different languages. It was originally an unaccompanied, polyphonic, religious composition, but later motets (after 1600) added instruments and often contained amorous texts.

Madrigal: The favorite musical pastime in Italy during the Renaissance was the singing of **madrigals**. Unlike the sacred motets, madrigals were secular songs performed by four or five voices in imitative style (polyphony) but often interspersed with homophonic passages. The text was sung in the vernacular and often based on love lyrics. Sometimes the mood was light and idyllic, sometimes sad and sentimental. You can usually tell a madrigal by the "Fa la la" refrains.

Oratorio: A much longer form than the motet or madrigal, the seventeenth-century **oratorio** was a musical setting for solo voices, chorus and orchestra of an extended story (usually religious) performed in a concert hall or church. Like opera, oratorios contain **arias** and **recitatives**, though the choral parts are much more dominant in the oratorio than in opera. Unlike opera, an oratorio is performed without scenery, costumes, or physical action. The most famous of all oratorios is Handel's *Messiah* (1742).

Cantata: Essentially a "little oratorio," the **cantata** contains basically the same elements you would find in an oratorio (choral sections, solos, recitatives, etc.). Although it is based mostly on religious texts, it can be secular, but its wider appeal is its brevity (lasts between twenty and forty minutes) and thus appears more frequently in churches for Christmas and Easter programs and also occasionally finds its way into the concert hall as well.

Passion: A passion is similar in its parts to the cantata and oratorio, except it is a musical setting of the story of the Crucifixion as told by one of the four Evangelists. The most notable example of this form is J. S. Bach's *St. Matthew Passion* (1729).

Mass: The mass is the central service of the Roman Catholic Church. It represents the commemoration of the Eucharist—Christ's sacrifice on the cross. The musical portions fall into two basic types, the ORDINARY and the PROPER.

I. The ORDINARY (consisting of unchanging texts):

1. *Kyrie Eleison* ("Lord have mercy upon us")

2. *Gloria* ("Glory be to God on high")

3. *Credo or Creed* ("I believe in one God," etc.)

4. *Sanctus* ("Holy, holy, holy")

5. *Agnus Dei* ("O Lamb of God, that takest away the sins of the world")

II. The PROPER (consisting of texts that vary according to the religious emphasis of a particular day or feast):

1. Introit

2. Gradual

3. Offertory

4. Other prayers

Since sections of the Proper were generally sung only once a year—when it was "proper"—composers gradually came to focus more on the Ordinary and eventually developed its five parts into a **Mass** form utilized as a purely musical structure separate from any practical uses by the Church. In fact, since the time of J. S. Bach, most masses—such as those by Mozart, Beethoven, Brahms, Berlioz, etc.—are far too elaborate and long to be used in the Catholic liturgy and are generally performed in the concert hall, or, even when in cathedrals, performed nevertheless as a concert rather than as a religious service.

Requiem: From the Latin *requies,* to rest, a requiem is a mass for the dead—omitting the more joyful and exuberant Gloria and Credo sections and adding other texts appropriate to the situation. One of the most appealing concert requiems is Fauré's *Requiem.*

SUMMARY AND RECENT DEVELOPMENTS

The foundations of modern music were laid by ARNOLD SCHÖNBERG (1854–1951) and IGOR STRAVINSKY (1882–1971). Stravinsky's great success as the composer for Diaghilev's *Ballet Russe,* with such ballets as *The Firebird* and *The Rite of Spring,* set the stage for his experiments with bitonality, composing one piece in two separate but simultaneous keys. His ballet *Petruschka* is famous for the "Petruschka chord," two simple major triads played a minor second apart, creating a jolting dissonance. Schönberg's Twelve-Tone System, on the other hand, emancipated dissonance by doing away with the need for traditional tonal centers (**tonality**), giving each tone of the chromatic scale equal time in the piece of music. A "tone row" of twelve tones in a certain order became the unifying force behind this new music (**atonality**). By the middle of the twentieth century, composers like Milton Babbitt in the U.S., Karlheinz Stockhausen in Germany, and Pierre Boulez in France were experimenting with ways of extending Schönberg's Twelve-Tone System to include a series of durations (rhythmic values), dynamic levels, or even tone colors, to serve as a unify-

ing idea. A movement called **serialism** grew out of this effort to order a musical piece around a series of different treatments of musical elements. It was a small step from these serialist innovations to the **minimalist music** of Steve Reich and Philip Glass, whose compositions are characterized by the repetition of short melodies over a steady, mesmerizing rhythmic pulse. Perhaps the most known instance of this music is Phillip Glass's background music to Godfrey Reggio's art films, such as *Koyaanisqatsi* (Hopi for "life out of balance"). John Cage's **aleatory** (chance) music is a perfect **counterpoint** to this totally organized kind of modern music. His compositions are clever collages of natural sounds placed together by chance happenings, like six radios arbitrarily tuned to different stations. His most known piece is *4'33,"* in which a performer sits at a piano for four minutes and thirty-three seconds. The "music" produced in each performance consists of the ambient sounds that happen to occur during that slice of time: breathing, coughing, shuffling feet, or the sounds outside the hall. It's hard to imagine where modern musical innovations can go from these seeming dead ends. Time will tell.

COMMENTARIES ON THE ARTS

HOW WE LISTEN TO MUSIC

—*Aaron Copland*

We all listen to music according to our separate capacities. But, for the sake of analysis, the whole listening process may become clearer if we break it up into its component parts, so to speak. In a certain sense we all listen to music on three separate planes. For lack of a better terminology one might name these (1) the sensuous plane, (2) the expressive plane, (3) the sheerly musical plane. The only advantage to be gained from mechanically splitting up the listening process into these hypothetical planes is the clearer view to be had of the way in which we listen.

The simplest way of listening to music is to listen for the sheer pleasure of the musical sound itself. That is the sensuous plane. It is the plane on which we hear music without thinking, without considering it in any way. One turns on the radio while doing something else and absentmindedly bathes in the sound. A kind of brainless but attractive state of mind is engendered by the mere sound appeal of the music.

You may be sitting in a room reading this book. Imagine one note struck on the piano. Immediately that one note is enough to change the atmosphere of the room—proving that the sound element in music is a powerful and mysterious agent, which it would be foolish to deride or belittle.

The surprising thing is that many people who consider themselves qualified music lovers abuse that plane in listening. They go to concerts in order to lose themselves. They use music as a consolation or an escape. They enter an ideal world where one doesn't have to think of the realities of everyday life. Of course they aren't thinking about the music either. Music allows them to leave it, and they go off to a place to dream, dreaming because of and apropos of the music yet never quite listening to it.

Yes, the sound appeal of music is a potent and primitive force, but you must not allow it to usurp a disproportionate share of your interest. The sensuous plane is an important one in music, a very important one, but it does not constitute the whole story.

There is no need to digress further on the sensuous plane. Its appeal to every normal human being is self-evident. There is, however, such a thing as becoming more sensitive to the different kinds of sound stuff as used by various composers. For all composers do not use that sound stuff in the same way. Don't get the idea that the value of music is commensurate with its sensuous appeal or that the loveliest sounding music is made by the greatest composer. If that were so, Ravel would be a greater creator than Beethoven. The point is that the sound element varies with each composer, that his usage of sound forms an integral part of his style and must be taken into account when listening. The reader can see, therefore, that a more conscious approach is valuable even on this primary plane of music listening.

The second plane on which music exists is what I have called the expressive one. Here, immediately, we tread on controversial ground. Composers have a way of shying away from any discussion of music's expressive side. Did not Stravinsky himself proclaim that his music was an "object," a "thing," with a life of its own, and with no other meaning than its own purely musical existence? This intransigent attitude of Stravinsky's may be due to the fact that so many people have tried to read different meanings into so many pieces. Heaven knows it is difficult enough to say precisely what it is that a piece of music means, to say it definitely, to say it finally so that everyone is satisfied with your explanation. But that should not lead one to the other extreme of denying to music the right to be "expressive."

My own belief is that all music has an expressive power, some more and some less, but that all music has a certain meaning behind the notes and that that meaning behind the notes constitutes, after all, what the piece is saying, what the piece is about. This whole problem can be stated quite simply by asking, "Is there a meaning to music?" My answer to that would be, "Yes." And "Can you state in so many words what the meaning is?" My answer to that would be, "No." Therein lies the difficulty.

Simple-minded souls will never be satisfied with the answer to the second of these questions. They always want music to have a meaning, and the more concrete it is the better they like it. The more the music reminds them of a train, a storm, a funeral, or any other familiar conception the more expressive it appears to be to them. This popular idea of music's meaning—stimulated and abetted by the usual run of musical commentator—should be discouraged wherever and whenever it is met. One timid lady once confessed to me that she suspected something seriously lacking in her appreciation of music because of her inability to connect it with anything definite. That is getting the whole thing backward, of course.

Still, the question remains, How close should the intelligent music lover wish to come to pinning a definite meaning to any particular work? No closer than a general concept, I should say. Music expresses, at different moments, serenity or exuberance, regret or triumph, fury or delight. It expresses each of these moods, and many others, in a numberless variety of subtle shadings and differences. It may even express a state of meaning for which there exists no adequate word in any language. In that case, musicians often like to say that it has only a purely musical meaning. They sometimes go farther and say that all music has only a purely musical meaning. What they really mean is that no appropriate word can be found to express the music's meaning and that, even if it could, they do not feel the need of finding it.

But whatever the professional musician may hold, most musical novices still search for specific words with which to pin down their musical reactions. That is why they always find Tchaikovsky easier to "understand" than Beethoven. In the first place, it is easier to pin a meaning-word on a Tchaikovsky piece than on a Beethoven one. Much easier. Moreover, with the Russian composer, every time you come back to a piece of his it almost always says the same thing to you, whereas with Beethoven it is often quite difficult to put your finger right on what he is saying. And any musician will tell you that that is why Beethoven is the greater composer—because music which always says the same thing to you will necessarily soon become dull music, but music whose meaning is slightly different with each hearing has a greater chance of remaining alive.

Listen, if you can, to the forty-eight fugue themes of Bach's *Well Tempered Clavichord*. Listen to each theme, one after another. You will soon realize that each theme mirrors a different world of feeling. You will also soon realize that the more beautiful a theme seems to you the harder it is to find any word that will describe it to your complete satisfaction. Yes, you will certainly know whether it is a gay theme or a sad one. You will be able, in other words, in your own mind, to draw a frame of emotional feeling around your theme. Now study the sad one a little closer. Try to pin down the exact quality of its sadness. Is it pessimistically sad; is it fatefully sad or smilingly sad?

Let us propose that you are fortunate and can describe to your own satisfaction in so many words the exact meaning of your chosen theme. There is still no guarantee that anyone else will be satisfied. Nor need they be. The important thing is that each one feel for himself the specific expressive quality of a theme or, similarly, an entire piece of music. And if it is a great work of art, don't expect it to mean exactly the same thing to you each time you return to it.

Themes or pieces need not express only one emotion, of course. Take such a theme as the first main one of the *Ninth Symphony,* for example. it is clearly made up of different elements. It does not say only one thing. Yet anyone hearing it immediately gets a feeling of strength, a feeling of power. It isn't a power that comes simply because the theme is played loudly. It is a power inherent in the theme itself. The extraordinary strength and vigor of the theme results in the listener's receiving an impression that a forceful statement has been made. But one should never try to boil it down to "the fateful hammer of life," etc. That is where the trouble begins. The musician, in his exasperation, says it means nothing but the notes themselves, whereas the nonprofessional is only too anxious to hang on to any explanation that gives him the illusion of getting closer to the music's meaning.

Now, perhaps, the reader will know better what I mean when I say that my music does have an expressive meaning but that we cannot say in so many words what that meaning is.

The third plane on which music exists is the sheerly musical plane. Besides the pleasurable sound of music and the expressive feeling that it gives off, music does exist in terms of the notes themselves and of their manipulation. Most listeners are not sufficiently conscious of this third plane.

Professional musicians, on the other hand, are, if anything, too conscious of the mere notes themselves. They often fall into the error of becoming so engrossed with their arpeggios and staccatos that they forget the deeper aspects of the music they are performing. But from the layman's standpoint, it is not so much a matter of getting

over bad habits on the sheerly musical plane as of increasing one's awareness of what is going on, in so far as the notes are concerned.

When the man in the street listens to the "notes themselves" with any degree of concentration, he is most likely to make some mention of the melody. Either he hears a pretty melody or he does not, and he generally lets it go at that. Rhythm is likely to gain his attention next, particularly if it seems exciting. But harmony and tone color are generally taken for granted, if they are thought of consciously at all. As for music's having a definite form of some kind, that idea seems never to have occurred to him.

It is very important for all of us to become more alive to music on its sheerly musical plane. After all, an actual musical material is being used. The intelligent listener must be prepared to increase his awareness of the musical material and what happens to it. He must hear the melodies, the rhythms, the harmonies, the tone of colors in a more conscious fashion. But above all he must, in order to follow the line of the composer's thought, know something of the principles of musical form. Listening to all of these elements is listening on the sheerly musical plane.

Let me repeat that I have split up mechanically the three separate planes on which we listen merely for the sake of greater clarity. Actually, we never listen on one or the other of these planes. What we do is correlate them—listening in all three ways at the same time. It takes no mental effort, for we do it instinctively.

Perhaps an analogy with what happens to us when we visit the theater will make this instinctive correlation clearer. In the theater, you are aware of the actors and actresses, costumes and sets, sounds and movement. All these give one the sense that the theater is a pleasant place to be in. They constitute the sensuous plane in our theatrical reactions.

The expressive plane in the theater would be derived from the feeling that you get from what is happening on the stage. You are moved to pity, excitement, or gaiety. It is this general feeling, generated aside from the particular words being spoken, a certain emotional something which exists on the stage, that is analogous to the expressive quality in music.

The plot and plot developments is equivalent to our sheerly musical plane. The playwright creates and develops a character in just the same way that a composer creates and develops a theme. According to the degree of your awareness of the way in which the artist in either field handles his material will you become a more intelligent listener.

It is easy enough to see that the theatergoer never is

conscious of any of these elements separately. He is aware of them all at the same time. The same is true of music listening. We simultaneously and without thinking listen on all three planes.

In a sense, the ideal listener is both inside and outside the music at the same moment, judging it and enjoying it, wishing it would go one way and watching it go another—almost like the composer at the moment he composes it; because in order to write this music, the composer must also be inside and outside his music, carried away by it and yet coldly critical of it. A subjective and objective attitude is implied in both creating and listening to music.

What the reader should strive for, then, is a more active kind of listening. Whether you listen to Mozart or Duke Ellington, you can deepen your understanding of music only by being a more conscious and aware listener—not someone who is just listening but someone who is listening for something.

DISCUSSION QUESTIONS

1. Explore the role music plays in your own life. What kind of music moves you most? Can you define what it is about the music that excites or moves you? Is it the melody, the rhythm (beat), the performance, the lyrics? If your musical preferences are primarily popular, listen to a piece you don't think you'd like very much and try to figure out what it is about the piece that makes it appealing to others and why it doesn't appeal to you.

2. After reading Aaron Copland's essay "How We Listen to Music."

   a. Decide which level you normally listen on and why.

   b. Explain what Copland means by "musical meaning."

   c. Draw the analogy with theatre: what are the theatrical analogies of going to a concert?

   d. Interpret Copland's point when he writes: "In a sense, the ideal listener is both inside and outside the music at the same moment. . . ."

3. Just for fun, listen to the natural sounds around you and become more aware of the rich variety of tonal differences. This practice will help you to better distinguish instrumental sounds in a symphony orchestra.

LISTENING EXERCISES

1. Listen carefully to Ravel's popular *Bolero* (available on many different recordings). The piece begins with a flute solo and then progresses to larger and more complex instrumental combinations to the end of the piece. Following the sequence of instruments and ensembles playing will help you become more sensitive to the unique sounds of each instrument and group. Describe the unique timbre of each of the solos and ensembles to better get a feel for the differences in instrumental tone colors. They appear in the piece in the following order:

flute

clarinet

bassoon

E-flat clarinet

oboe d'amour

flute/trumpet

tenor sax

soprano sax

piccolo/french horn/celeste

high woodwinds

trombone

woodwinds

add first violins

add more woodwinds

second violins and trumpets

rest of strings

full orchestra

As you listen, notice that of the six musical elements (rhythm, melody, harmony, tempo, timbre, and dynamics) only the timbres and dynamics change throughout. This is unusual, and makes this piece unique. Also be aware of the emotional tensions created by the contrast of a changing dynamics and an unchanging tempo. What is the reason for this tension? And what is the conductor's role in heightening this tension?

A SAMPLER OF CLASSICAL MUSIC

I. LIGHT LISTENING

Albinoni, Adagio for Strings and Organ in G Minor

J. S. Bach, Little Fugue in G Minor, Air for G String

Samuel Barber, Adagio for Strings

Benjamin Britten, *Young Person's Guide to the Orchestra*

Chopin, Etudes (especially E Minor, Op. 10, No. 3)

Aaron Copland, *Fanfare for the Common Man*

Debussy, *Prelude to the Afternoon of a Faun*

George Gershwin, *Rhapsody in Blue, An American in Paris*

Grieg, *Peer Gynt Suite*

Ferde Grofé, *Grand Canyon Suite*

Pachelbel, Canon in D Major

Prokofiev, *Peter and the Wolf,* Classical Symphony

Ravel, *Bolero, Pavanne for a Dead Princess*

Respighi, *Fountains of Rome*

Saint-Saëns, *Carnival of the Animals* (especially *Le Cygne*)

Erik Satie, *Gymnopédies* (I–III)

Schönberg, *Verklärte Nacht* (*Transfigured Night*)

Smetana, *Die Moldau*

Tchaikovsky, *Nutcracker, Swan Lake, Romeo and Juliet*

II. HEAVIER LISTENING

J. S. Bach, Brandenburg Concertos (6)

Beethoven, Symphony No. 3 in E-Flat Major, Op. 55 (Eroica); Symphony No. 5 in C Minor, Op. 67; Symphony No. 6 in F Major, Op. 68 (Pastoral)

Berlioz, *Symphonie Fantastique*

Leonard Bernstein, *Chichester Psalms, Mass*

Max Bruch, Concerto for Violin and Orchestra No. 1 in G Minor, Op. 26

Chopin, Piano Concerto No. 1 in E Minor, Op. 11

Aaron Copland, *Appalachian Spring*

De Falla, *Nights in the Gardens of Spain* (for Piano and Orchestra)

Dvořák, Symphony No. 9 in E Minor, Op. 95 (New World)

Fauré, *Pavanne, Requiem*

Gershwin, Concerto in F

Grieg, Concerto for Piano and Orchestra in A Minor, Op. 16

Handel, *Water Music*

Haydn, Symphony No. 94 in G Minor (Surprise)

Gustave Holst, *The Planets*

Charles Ives, Symphony No. 3 (Town Meeting)

Lalo, *Symphonie Espagnole, for Violin and Orchestra, Op. 21*

Mendelssohn, *Incidental Music for A Midsummer Night's Dream*

Mozart, Concerto for Piano and Orchestra No. 21 in C Major (K. 476); Symphony No. 40 in G Minor (K. 550)

Mussorgsky, *Pictures at an Exhibition* (orchestrated by Ravel)

Carl Orff, *Carmina Burana*

Prokofiev, *Romeo and Juliet* (ballet)

Rachmaninoff, Concerto for Piano and Orchestra No. 2 in C Minor, Op. 18; Rhapsody on a Theme of Paganini, Op. 43

Rimsky-Korsakoff, *Scheherazade, Symphonic Suite,* Op. 35

Saint-Saëns, Symphony No. 3 in C Minor, Op. 78 (Organ)

Schubert, Symphony No. 8 in B Minor (Unfinished)

Richard Strauss, *Til Eulenspiegel's Merry Pranks, Op. 28*

Stravinsky, *The Firebird, Petrushka*

Tchaikovsky, Concerto for Piano and Orchestra, No. 1 in B-Flat Minor, Op. 23; Concerto for Violin and Orchestra in D Major, Op. 35

Ralph Vaughan Williams, *Fantasia on Greensleeves*

Vivaldi, *The Four Seasons,* Op. 8

Wagner, *Prelude to Die Meistersinger*

III. HEAVIEST LISTENING

J. S. Bach, *St. Matthew Passion,* Mass in B Minor

Bartok, Concerto for Orchestra

Beethoven, Symphony No. 9 in D Minor, Op. 125 (Ode to Joy)

Brahms, Symphony No. 4 in E Minor, Op. 98

Handel, *Messiah*

Mahler, Symphony No. 2 in C Minor (Resurrection)

Mozart, Requiem

Rachmaninoff, Symphony No. 2 in E Minor, Op. 27

Schönberg, Concerto for Orchestra

Stravinsky, *Rite of Spring*

Tchaikovsky, Symphony No. 6 in B Minor, Op. 74 (Pathétique)

Wagner, *Prelude and Love Death (Liebestod)* from *Tristan und Isolde*

WORKS CITED

Copland, Aaron. *What to Listen For in Music.* Rev. ed. New York: McGraw-Hill, 1957.

Downes, Edward. *The New York Philharmonic Guide to the Symphony.* New York: Walker and Company, 1976.

Great Treasury of Western Thought. Ed. Mortimer J. Adler and Charles van Doren. New York: R. R. Bowker Company, 1977.

Harvard Dictionary of Music. 2nd ed. Cambridge, MA: Belknap Press of Harvard University Press, 1969.

Holmes, John L. *Composers on Composers.* New York: McGraw-Hill, 1976.

Hutchings, Arthur. *Mozart: The Man, The Musician.* London: Thames and Hudson, 1976.

Kamian, Roger. *Music: An Appreciation.* New York: Schirmer, 1988.

Langer, Susanne K. *Philosophy in a New Key.* New York: New American Library, 1951.

Levy, Kenneth. *Music: A Listener's Introduction.* New York: Harper & Row, 1983.

Ludwig van Beethoven. Ed. Joseph Schmidt-Georg and Hans Schmidt. Hamburg: Deutsche Grammophon Gesellschaft, 1974.

Mann, William. *James Gallway's Music in Time.* New York: Harry N. Abrams, 1982.

Menuhin, Yehudi. *Theme and Variations.* New York: Stein and Day, 1972.

Stanley Sadie's Music Guide: An Introduction. Ed. Stanley Sadie. Englewood Cliffs, NJ: Prentice-Hall, 1986.

Stokowski, Leopold. *Music for All of Us.* New York: Simon & Schuster, 1943.

Storr, Anthony. *Music and the Mind.* New York: The Free Press, 1992.

Thomson, William. *Music for Listeners.* Englewood Cliffs, NJ: Prentice-Hall, 1978.

WEBSITES OF INTEREST

Websites for basic music elements and music history
http://www.nmsu.edu/~muzinc/nutsbolts981.htm
http://w3.rz-berlin.mpg.de/cmp/classmus.html
http://library.thinkquest.org/22673/
http://www.learner.org/resources/series105.html

What to listen for in music, Aaron Copland —
http://books.google.com/books?id=dsyPycO3GfgC&printsec=frontcover&source=gbs_navlinks_s

Tabernacle Choir, arr. by Mack Wilberg —
http://www.youtube.com/watch?v=t_9_uQiMmyQ

Mozart Clarinet concerto, London Symphony Orchestra —
http://www.youtube.com/watch?v=Wg1pWZauSFw

Graphic by Aubrey Beardsley, courtesy of Brigham Young University.

INTRODUCTION TO DRAMA

Chapter 11

A HUMAN NEED

The urge to act out a story is as compelling as the perennial fascination with "once upon a time." Children engage in both with equal abandon and delight. Our ancestors engaged in remarkably similar pastimes. But of the three classical literary genres—epic, lyric, and drama—the last is probably the most recent, partly because it contains aspects of the other two: its subjects are frequently drawn from the heroic legends of the Homeric epics, and its choral odes bespeak the dramatist's personalized commentary on the action. Its invention in ancient Greece set the stage for the great achievements and masters of drama that followed: Roman farces, medieval mystery plays, Shakespeare, Molière, Ibsen, Chekhov, and the modernists—Brecht, Pirandello, Pinter, Tennessee Williams, and Tom Stoppard, to mention only a few. In fact, the preeminence of **plot** and character development in the vast majority of twentieth-century film, theater, and television productions indicates the enormous debt we owe to the Greek theatrical tradition.

Technological advances in the modern media (film and television) have been both a boon and a bust for theatre. The media has greatly expanded the reach of drama beyond the limited audiences that could be accommodated in one theater at one time in the past, but the power of film to rivet attention and control audience response has largely displaced theater as the primary medium of our century. Nevertheless, theatre still retains a small but strong following and it still offers a type of experience that cannot be duplicated on the screen. There is an immediacy to live theatre because it exists in the present. The closeness to the action is greatly enhanced by the fact that actors and audiences must collaborate to make the dramatic illusion work (Coleridge said that the audience must "willingly suspend disbelief"), thereby producing intense emotional release (Aristotle called it "**catharsis**"). Thus, the potential for emotional and intellectual involvement is perhaps greater in live theatre because the audience must work harder. When you give more, you get more.

WHENCE DRAMA?

A play in a book is only the shadow of a play and not even a clear shadow of it. . . . The printed script of a play is hardly more than an architect's blueprint of a house not yet built or [a house] built and destroyed. The color, the grace and levitation, the structural pattern in motion, the quick interplay of live beings, suspended like fitful lightning in a cloud, these things are the play, not words on paper nor thoughts and ideas of an author.

—Tennessee Williams (Qtd. in Cohen 23)

A LIVING PERFORMANCE

Ritual performances preceded the alphabet and the printing press, but it is easy to forget the fact and to mistake the words on the page for the action on the stage. The difference is not unlike the contrast between musical notation and music. The notes are merely symbols of sounds, but it is the actual music that moves us. So with drama. The proof of its power lies in the live performance. But where did the performance originate? As with other ancient art forms, like dance, painting, and architecture, drama grew out of religious ritual. The shift from ritual to drama is shrouded in mystery, but in the Western world it occurred at least by 538 B.C. when Pisistratus ordered the first Athenian competition for tragedy (Burdick 8). The move from ritual involvement as participant to public spectacle as spectator may have been prompted by a basic human instinct to dress up a story. The Homeric legends provided the mythic foundations of Greek society by narrating its heroic past. It is probably not coincidental that Greek plays treated many of these ancient legends, and since they were narrated orally by a bard (singer), it was a relatively small step from telling the story to impersonating the hero. This often happens when parents get carried away while reading a story, letting voice inflections and gestures dramatize a favorite tale.

PLAY AS "PLAY"

Tennessee Williams was right. The real power of the play resides in the action, not the words that merely direct the action. The emergence of spectators separated the action from the audience, creating an air of dramatic illusion—it is only "play-like." The idea of playing also connects theatre to sports events. The Dionysian theatrical contests and the Olympian sports contests were two important cultural events of ancient Greece. And yet, Greek theatre was more than just a game, because the stories acted out drew on fundamental mythic patterns in Greek culture and were tied directly to Dionysian ritual. Passages in Aristotle's *Poetics* link the origins of tragedy to a choral chant known as the **dithyramb**, a frenzied poem sung in honor of Dionysus and accompanied by music and dancing. It can still be seen in the choral odes in classical Greek tragedies. The very configurations of the ancient Greek theatre reveal its ritualistic origins: the circular "orchestra" where the "chorus" chanted and danced represents a physical remnant of circular dancing around an altar.

GREEK ORIGINS

Greek drama proper began when the leader of the chorus stepped out from the group and began impersonating the hero instead of merely reciting his deeds. This crucial act has been attributed to Thespis (flourished around 543 B.C.), who is also credited with inventing the mask, which enabled one person to portray a number of different characters. With multiple actors came dialogue, the basic means of dramatizing conflict. Once there were actors, a stage, and an audience, the words and actions could come alive. The actor's challenge was to make the action credible; the audience's task was to willingly suspend its disbelief, as Coleridge wrote. These were two "courageous acts of imagination" (Boorstin 207) and set the stage for the centuries of Western drama that followed.

THREE GREAT AGES OF DRAMA

CLASSICAL (GREEK)

It was either Thespis or his successor Phrynichus who invented the dramatic form we know as tragedy by distinguishing one performer from the rest of the chorus, thereby creating dialogue. Tragedy is the greatest form of theatre in the Western world, comparable in complexity and profundity to Japanese Noh drama or even the symphonic form in music. The word **tragedy** is somehow connected to the performance of dithyrambs in honor of the god Dionysus, since its etymology derives from two Greek words: *tragos* (goat, the sacrificial animal) and *aeidein* (to sing or chant), making the Greek word for tragedy, *tragoidia*. Aristotle's *Poetics* defines tragedy as "an imitation of an action that is serious, complete, and of a certain magnitude" (61). By carefully analyzing the six elements (plot, character, thought, diction, song, and spectacle), Aristotle established a critical base for all subsequent commentary on theatre. By establishing *catharsis* (the purgation of pity and fear) as one of the chief aims of tragedy, he elevated tragedy to the status of supreme theatrical genre and defined the nature of the dramatic experience for centuries to come.

Greek Conventions

In practice, Greek theatre consisted of a number of conventions quite unfamiliar to our theatrical tradition. Their dramas were performed in large amphitheaters holding between 15,000 and 17,000 spectators. The chorus chanted, sang, and danced on the circular "orchestra" (from *orcheisthai,* "to dance"). It provided the crucial link between the spectators and the spectacle, representing in turn the voice of the community, the personal commentary of the playwright, and the reactions of the townspeople in the play. Two or three main actors could play several roles by putting on different masks, wearing colorful costumes and stilted shoes. There was no changeable scenery, only a large wooden structure, called the *skene* on the other side of the orchestra, opposite the audience, which functioned as both palace and changing room. Dramatic performances were a principal part of the Dionysia, a six-day celebration honoring the god Dionysus that took place in late March. Attendance at the plays was mandatory for all citizens. They arrived at sunup and sat through a tetralogy (three tragedies and a satyr play) before dark. While modern renditions of ancient Greek plays may seem restrained and moralistic, it should be remembered that Greek theatre was a passionately social affair, involving loud music, vigorous dancing, and sometimes obscene spectacles in their satyr plays, which provided comic relief to the tragedies that preceded them.

Tragedy vs. Comedy

In plumbing the roots of Greek drama, it is easy to overlook the other part of the Dionysian sacrificial ritual, namely, the fertility rite. This rite, called the Comus, also involved singing and dancing (from *komos* "to revel" and *aeidein* "to sing"), but celebrated the life impulse (sex) as tragedy focused on suffering and death. Unfortunately, the Greeks developed their tragedies to a higher form than their comedies, due perhaps to the bias we find in Aristotle: comedy is the imitation of characters "of a lower type [consisting] in some defect or ugliness" (59).

Nevertheless, the Greeks recognized the importance of comic relief by adding a satyr play at the end of each tragic trilogy. The differences in basic feeling between tragedy and comedy dictate their different forms and effects: tragedy views life up close, with emotional involvement, while comedy views life at a distance, with intellectual detachment; the tragic plot, governed by Fate, follows a linear causal chain of events leading to inevitable destruction, while comic plots are typically episodic and circular, leading to ultimate victory over the circumstances of chance (Fortune). While there are basically only two types of tragedy—high tragedy (of character) and low tragedy (of situation), sometimes called melodrama—comedy gave birth to a variety of offspring: high comedy (of character), satire (comedy of ideas), and low comedy or farce (of situation), with its slapstick variants. The word "slapstick" derives from an important sixteenth-century Italian comic tradition, the *commedia dell'arte,* in which stock characters (such as Colombina and Arlecchino) improvised clownish business from a written plot. Arlecchino's "slapstick" was a wooden sword with a hinged flap that made an exaggerated clap when striking Pantalone's behind. The English "Punch and Judy" puppet shows follow this Italian line of comedy.

The "Big Four"

From the invention of the tragic form by Thespis, it took only a century for tragedy to blossom into a golden age of theater, presided over by its three greatest ancient practitioners, AESCHYLUS (525–456 B.C.), SOPHOCLES (ca. 496–406 B.C.), and EURIPIDES (ca. 484–406 B.C.). The fourth luminary, ARISTOPHANES (ca. 450–ca. 388 B.C.), was a writer of comedies.

Thousands of tragedies, comedies, and satyr plays were written in ancient Greece. We know the names of hundreds, but only forty-three remain in complete form. Of these, Sophocles' *Oedipus Tyrannos* (425 B.C.) is the best known and, according to Aristotle, the greatest. He based his theory of tragedy in the *Poetics* on this play because of its complex plot and compelling characterization of the hero, Oedipus, King of Thebes. Plot and character were the two most important elements of drama for Aristotle. Comparing plot to line and character to color in a painting, he notes: "The most beautiful colors, laid on confusedly, will not give as much pleasure as the chalk outline of a portrait" (63). In other words the plot provides the dramatic outline of the story (the structure) while the characters flesh out the human dilemma. Aristotle proved his point of the supremacy of plot by demonstrating that even a brief synopsis of the key events creates a cathartic response.

Oedipus

The plot of *Oedipus Tyrannos* reads like a modern detective story, with the following exceptions: the Greek audience already knew the ending (they were familiar with the Oedipus legend); and the hero (detective) turns out to be the culprit, creating a tragic reversal and recognition, two vital elements in Aristotle's definition of a complex plot structure. At the beginning of the play, Oedipus seeks the murderer of his predecessor, King Laius, but discovers during the course of the play that it is he himself; and worse, that the former king was his own father and the widow he has married is his own mother. His gradual recognition of this terrible truth about himself drives the rising action in the play. His painful awareness is all the more poignant because the pieces of evidence seem at first to dispel his growing suspicions of his own guilt: Jocasta assures him a band of robbers (not one individual) killed the king at the crossroads; the messenger from Corinth brought the happy news that the king of Corinth had died (only to add that this king was not Oedipus' real father). In spite of his desperate attempts to escape the prophecy that he would kill his father and marry his mother, Oedipus falls into the trap and unwittingly commits the two most heinous sins conceivable to the Greeks, patricide and incest. His wife-mother, Jocasta, commits suicide. Oedipus blinds himself and is exiled from Thebes. In contrast to the graphic realism of the modern media, the Greeks used the convention of the messenger to report the actual blinding. The messenger's dramatic oral delivery, together with Oedipus' appearance with bloodied eye-sockets, ignites the imagination in ways more vivid than could be achieved by the graphic realism of modern film.

Catharsis

The pattern of the plot creates **catharsis** (the purgation of pity and fear): pity because of Oedipus' "unmerited misfortune"; fear because of the terrible suffering of someone like ourselves. As tragic "protagonist," Oedipus makes a terrible mistake (*hamartia*) when he succumbs to sudden anger and kills an old man at a crossroads. This mistake is sometimes called a tragic flaw (in Greek heroes the most common flaw is *hubris* or pride), although, ironically in the case of Oedipus, the defining part of Oedipus' character is a thirst to know (the Greek verb to know, *oida,* is part of his name). This deeply embedded Greek desire for knowledge becomes the hero's ultimate undoing: Oedipus' pursuit of self-knowledge (the Greek motto was "Know thyself") leads to self-destruction. For Edith Hamilton, the essence of tragedy resides in the power of human beings to face terrible adversity with dignity: "It is by our power to suffer, above all, that we are of more value than the sparrows" (Hamilton 233). Greek drama plumbed the depths of what it means to survive as a human being in an inscrutable universe. The repercussions of its mythical themes have resonated throughout Western culture ever since.

RENAISSANCE (ELIZABETHAN)

In the *Symposium* Socrates predicted that tragedy and comedy would one day be realized and reconciled by the same genius. The Elizabethan Age found that genius in WILLIAM SHAKESPEARE (1564–1616), one of the few men in history whose greatness matched the age that spawned him.

The Globe: Its Trappings

Attending Shakespeare's Globe Theatre in London was a much different experience from observing the performance of a Greek tragedy in Athens, although in both, high-born characters acted out deeply tragic scenarios. The most obvious physical difference was size. The whole Globe could have easily fit into the circular orchestra of the Greek theater (both were approximately 80 feet in diameter). Elizabethan actors didn't wear masks, and since the audience was much closer, the acting (voice inflections, facial expressions, gestures) and staging took on

greater importance. But since women were not allowed on stage, all female parts were played by young boys, a convention we might find difficult to accept today. And since Shakespeare's language carried so much of the meaning (his 21,000-word vocabulary greatly increased his capacity for both precise description and poetic ambiguity), there was little need for elaborate set design. In *Macbeth,* Birnam Wood was merely suggested by a plant placed downstage. The action took place on a raised thrust stage with a trap door for the grave scene in *Hamlet* and beneath a canopy painted with stars to suggest the sky or heaven. The back of the stage abutted the tiring house (used for dressing rooms to attire the actors) which contained a curtained area (decorated with a black curtain for tragedy and a multicolored one for comedy) and crowned by a small turret with a flag and trumpeter to announce the day's performance. Because the octagonal center of the Globe was open to the sky, all performances were staged during the day, usually between 2 and 5 p.m.

Oedipus vs. Othello

The distinctions between Sophocles and Shakespeare's dramas are evident by comparing *Oedipus* with *Othello.* Both plays treat the fate of fundamentally good men who are afflicted with a tragic flaw: Oedipus suffers from an impetuous nature; Othello is afflicted with the green-eyed monster of jealousy. Both protagonists are leaders who wield great power and whose compulsion to know leads to terrible consequences when their illusions are destroyed. But whereas Oedipus struggled against the realities of an outside force, Othello succumbed to an inner affliction. In this sense, Shakespeare elevates character above plot and man above the gods as central issues in his plays. In comparison to the moral gravity of Greek tragedy, Shakespeare deftly inserted humorous elements into his tragedies to provide comic relief and to intensify the tragic scenes by contrast. In both tragedy and comedy, it is the nature of the balance between the strengths and weaknesses of the characters and the deserved or undeserved nature of the catastrophe that determines whether the result is tragic or comic. With minor editing of character and situation, for example, tragic Othello becomes comic Othello:

> A not-too-intelligent Moor, by means of boastful tales of his military exploits, induces a well-born Venetian girl to elope with him. They are sent by a tolerant Doge to Cyprus, where the Moor's ensign, "honest" Iago, understandably vexed at being passed over for promotion in favor of an inexperienced young dandy, plays a practical joke on the Moor. He convinces him, on the flimsiest of evidence, that his wife has cuckolded him with the dandy. Enraged—and not troubling to check the facts—the Moor strangles

his innocent wife. With the exception of the ending, which may go a bit too far for some tastes, we have here the rudimentary outline of a comedy—a comedy in the manner of Machiavelli or Aretino, perhaps—vicious, but unmistakably comic. Othello ceases to be a tragic hero and becomes the classic dupe. (Soule 40)

Probably no playwright in history peopled the world's stage with such a menagerie of original personalities, from flawed heroes to noble vagrants, than William Shakespeare of Stratford-upon-Avon. In his plays, humans struggle against other humans or their own human nature, not against Fate or the gods.

MODERN

As varied and memorable as are the great ages of the past, probably no previous period of theatrical activity has been more varied, experimental, controversial, or socially influential than the past hundred years of modern theatre. Modern theatre exhibits the effects of the great revolutions that have occurred since the Renaissance: the Copernican Revolution of the sixteenth century, the intellectual revolutions of the seventeenth and eighteenth centuries, the political and biological revolutions of the eighteenth and nineteenth century, and the social and psychological revolutions of the twentieth century. The reactions of modern playwrights to these dramatic shifts in human perspective have taken modern theatre in at least three stylistic directions: the realist/naturalist plays of Ibsen, Strindberg, Chekhov, Shaw, Tennessee Williams, and Arthur Miller; the symbolic/existentialist plays of Maeterlinck, Eliot, Pirandello, Ionesco, Beckett, and Pinter; and the expressionist/epic theater of Buechner, Wedekind, Kokoshka, Brecht, and O'Neill.

The Modern Worldview

When reading or seeing Willy Loman in Arthur Miller's *Death of a Salesman* (1949), for example, it is clear that great changes have occurred in our worldview since the time of Sophocles and Shakespeare. Scientific and technological advances have greatly enhanced the quality of modern life, but they have also fostered a rampant materialism, hastening the demise of religion as a viable force in explaining the human condition. Copernicus placed the earth in orbit around the sun, displacing us from the center of the universe. Darwin took away the legitimacy of a religious explanation for man and the origin of the universe. Freud displaced human will with subconscious drives to explain human behavior. Willy Loman is heir to these major shifts in human perspective. He is not a man of means. He is a lowly salesman (his name is

symbolic of his social status). The democratization of the masses has created the tragedy of the common man, but a man devoid of the self-assurance of past heroes, due in part to the dehumanizing effects of the theory of evolution, Freudian psychoanalysis, the death of God, and the Industrial Revolution, which have tended to make modern man feel like a mere cog in a machine.

Willy's Tragedy

ARTHUR MILLER (1915–2005) takes issue with Aristotle's major premises. He argues that the common man is as apt a subject for tragedy as kings were because all human beings share similar emotional situations regardless of social station. He posits new criteria for the tragic hero: "So long as the hero may be said to have alternatives of a magnitude to have materially changed the course of his life, it seems to me that in this respect at least, he cannot be debarred from the heroic role" (32). For Miller, the tragic feeling is evoked when the character will lay down his life to preserve his personal dignity. Thus, the tragic flaw is really nothing but the character's refusal to remain passive in the face of a challenge to his dignity. From the individual's personal onslaught against the threatening cosmos comes the terror and fear that is classically associated with tragedy.

Willy Loman shares much with the tragic heroes of the past, particularly Oedipus, for both are heroes of great plays who seek answers to the same question: "Who am I?" Oedipus is destroyed by pursuing the answer to its grim end; Willy never finds the answer, and that is his undoing. In his final act of self-delusion, he commits suicide for the $20,000 insurance money he can leave to his son. Like Oedipus' blind prophet, Teiresias, Biff tries to get Willy to see within, but Willy can't bear the revelation.

Arthur Miller, of all modern playwrights, has succeeded in building a mythical framework around the dilemma of modern man, comparable to the great legends of the past, by creating a mythical hero of the American Dream, Willy the Salesman, the modern Everyman. But Miller sees a significant difference in the two heroes.

Had Oedipus, for instance, been more conscious and more aware of the forces at work upon him he must surely have said that he was not really to blame for having cohabited with his mother since neither he nor anyone else knew she was his mother. He must surely decide to divorce her, provide for their children, firmly resolve to investigate the family background of his next wife, and thus deprive us of a very fine play and the name for a famous neurosis. But he is conscious only up to a point, the point at which guilt begins. Now he is inconsolable and must tear out his eyes. What is tragic about this? Why is it not even ridiculous? How can we respect a man who goes to such extremities over something he could in no way help or prevent? The answer, I think, is not that we respect the man, but that we respect the Law he has so completely broken, wittingly or not, for it is that Law which, we believe, defines us as men. The confusion of some criticism viewing *Death of a Salesman* in this regard is that they do not see that Willy Loman has broken a law without whose protection life is insupportable if not incomprehensible to him and to many others; it is the law which says that a failure in society and in business has no right to live. (35)

AN APPROACH TO ANALYZING DRAMA

INTRODUCTION

Reading a drama is not the same as experiencing its performance on the stage or screen. The best approach is to read it first, then see it. By only reading the play, the immediate impact of the live performance (the acting, scenery, costumes), as well as the director's unique interpretation, is eliminated. Simply viewing the performance prevents a full understanding of the literary substance of the play (the symbolism, the word play, the thematic development, etc.). In this sense, drama is an amphibious genre like music: it exists on both page and stage. Only by attending to both realms can we arrive at its full meaning. Actually, there are two meanings to plays, as reflected in these two statements: "I understand its meaning" indicates a literary comprehension; "It means something to me" reveals an emotional reaction. Engaging both the head and the heart is necessary for the play to come alive in someone's life.

FIRST READING: FIRST IMPRESSIONS

It is a good idea to read through the play as quickly as possible, to get the overall impression. Don't worry about the stage directions, but focus on the dialogue and character relationships. Try to identify the central conflict, the overall structure of the plot, and the direction of the character development. At this stage you might want to take brief notes on plot sequence and relationships among the main characters (you should end up with two kinds of diagrams: a "play-by-play" account of the scenes and acts and a clustering pattern of circled names with verbal links). At the end of this first reading you should:

1. *Have a sense of the plays historical milieu,* by having read an introduction to the playwright and his time (this is commonly found in the forward to most popular editions of great plays).

2. *Be able to list what actually happens,* but be careful to distinguish between the STORY (the chronological sequence of events) and the action or PLOT (which may break up the story in different ways, with flashbacks, for example).

3. *Determine the central conflict.* Drama can't exist without conflict. This can be found quite easily by looking for the lines of tension between the protagonist and antagonist. On what point or issue do their differences hinge? How are the differences resolved in the end?

SECOND READING: CONSCIOUS ANALYSIS

Once you know the general pattern of the play, its character relationships and how they express the central conflict, you can go back and begin looking at the text as you would any good piece of literature, discovering the more complex meanings hidden behind the dialogue and action. Look carefully at the following elements of the play: plot, character, setting and literary devices.

PLOT

The PLOT can be viewed as the spine of the play along which the action travels, gradually unfolding the meaning by creating an arch of rising action, climax, and conclusion. Any well-wrought play will follow some compelling sequence of events. Notice how the play is divided into acts and scenes and how loosely or tightly they are related and whether there are repeated patterns or events in adjacent scenes and in different acts. Look for the emergence of the central conflict, which can be formulated into a dramatic question. Most classical dramas adhere to the following sequence:

1. *Exposition:* introducing characters and clarifying setting (time and place).

2. *Inciting Moment:* the point where the dramatic question emerges.

3. *Complication:* tracing the rising action, the "thickening" of the plot.

4. *Crisis:* "point of no return," where the action moves forward to the end.

5. *Climax:* high point of the action, when the dramatic question is answered.

6. *Dénouement:* falling action, the final "unraveling" of the plot's strands.

CHARACTER

Even though there may be as many as ten or fifteen different characters in a play (Shakespeare's usually contain between fifteen and twenty; modern plays have less), normally only three to five are central to the plot development. Pay particular attention to the speeches delivered by these major figures in the play, especially the soliloquies of the protagonist, for they most clearly reveal the inner struggles—what's going on in the character's mind. An **aside** is also a means of discovering inner feelings, except this convention has the actor directly addressing the audience.

SETTING

The setting of the play offers clues to time, place, and, combined with the dialogue, a sense of the kind of world the play embraces. To a certain degree, the setting governs our reactions to the action. It may be familiar or unfamiliar to us. If the latter, we will have to work harder to suspend our disbelief and will need to become familiar with the historical context.

LITERARY DEVICES

As with any literary work, drama communicates by means of literary devices. Modern plays are more prosaic and tend to employ colloquial speech patterns, but classical drama, like Shakespeare, often resorts to poetry when the action becomes particularly emotional. But beyond specific poetic devices, look for repeated motifs or symbols which act as thematic threads of meaning that tie the sequence of events together and amplify the meaning of the whole.

ATTENDING THE PERFORMANCE

Once you have done your homework (above), attending the performance can be an exhilarating experience because you are ready for action, you know what to expect, and your critical energies are focused on what's important. Unless you are a professional drama critic, dramatic judgment doesn't involve weighing the merits of the play itself. What we're interested in is how effectively the director, actors, set designer, et al., "realize" the playwright's written dramatic vision on stage.

WHAT TO LOOK FOR IN A PERFORMANCE

Staging

Be aware of the stage arrangement. Modern theaters are usually either proscenium (where we look through the stage frame to the action), or theater-in-the-round (where the audience surrounds the action). We experience the action somewhat differently in each one. The proscenium arch functions as a "fourth wall" for the actor and a "peephole" for the audience. The actors play like we're not there, and we play like they can't see us. In this sense, the audience plays the role of voyeur, or hidden camera and, therefore, experiences less direct interaction with the action on stage, although all public performances require some collaboration between actors and audience for the magic to work. Theater-in-the-round places the audience in direct proximity to the action, creating a more immediate sense of involvement, but detracting somewhat from the dramatic illusion, because the rest of the audience is also clearly visible. A blurring of the distinctions between these two stagings has come as a result of proscenium performances being staged without curtains. An important question to ask yourself: why did the director choose a particular stage arrangement?

Acting

Consider the competence and credibility of the acting. Good acting is convincing. We shouldn't have to work hard at believing that the person is the character. The Greek word for actor is *hypocrites,* one who plays a role. But the playing must be believable and competent. The aesthetic involvement is quickly compromised if an actor forgets a line or stumbles over a phrase. These are inexcusable lapses in a professional production. And now that you know the play, from your reading and analysis, consider the interpretation of the character by the actors and the director. Directors usually play a large role in the actors' development of the character. Were the casting choices well made? Do the lovers seem physically and visually well matched?

Mise-en-scène

Notice the *mise-en-scène,* the physical surroundings, the visual milieu (the stage sets, lighting, and costuming). Are they consistent with the tone and time of the play? Do they call attention to themselves? (i.e., are they obvious?). Are the sets and costumes integrated in style and color relationships? Or if the action is placed in a contemporary setting, as in some modern adaptations of

Shakespeare's plays, does it work? And does it still work with the actors speaking Elizabethan English?

CONCLUSION

Each performance, of course, must be judged on its own merits. The most memorable and gripping theatrical experiences come from convincing acting, sound directing, and appropriate stage design coupled with the audience's adequate preparation. It is a delicate balance. Any flaw can easily derail the show and destroy the dramatic illusion. Successful theatre is truly a collaborative enterprise, involving the technical skills of professionals and the interpretive ability of informed audiences.

A TEST CASE FOR DRAMATIC ANALYSIS: SHAKESPEARE'S *ROMEO & JULIET*

FIRST READING: HISTORICAL MILIEU

One of Shakespeare's most famous plays, *Romeo and Juliet* (1599) is possibly his first tragedy and, therefore, is seldom ranked with his late great tragedies—*Hamlet* (1600), *Othello* (1604), *King Lear* (1605), and *Macbeth* (1606)—although its popularity has persisted, due in part to Shakespeare's unique capacity to individualize universal human experience. The man who wrote this play knew what it felt like to be in love.

PLOT: SUMMARY

The plot tells the tragic tale of youthful passion in conflict with familial duty. Young Romeo, pride of the Montague household of "fair Verona," first meets Juliet, a Capulet, at a masked ball. They fall in love before either realizes their families are sworn enemies. They swear a vow of undying love and are secretly married by Friar Lawrence. In a confrontation between Romeo's friend, Mercutio and Juliet's cousin, Tybalt, Tybalt mortally wounds Mercutio. In reprisal, Romeo kills Tybalt and is banished to Mantua. Juliet, in despair at the prospect of being forced to marry Paris, her parents' choice, conspires with Friar Lawrence to drink an herbal potion that renders her seemingly dead. The plan backfires when the message doesn't reach Romeo before he hears about Juliet's "death." He returns to her crypt to take his life at her side. Juliet awakens just after Romeo dies and kills herself with his dagger. The two families reconcile their hate at the cost of their lost loves: "For never was a story of more woe / Than this of Juliet and her Romeo" (V, iii. 309–310).

CENTRAL CONFLICT

The central conflict in this play revolves around the long-standing feud between the Montagues and the Capulets as it collides with the sudden passion the two lovers feel for each other. But the more poignant manifestation of the conflict is seen in the lovers' own divided loyalties: they must choose between their two loves—family and each other.

SECOND READING: CONSCIOUS ANALYSIS

This play has the conventional five acts of Shakespeare's tragedies. The Bard deftly patterns the plot to create both dramatic flow within each act and dramatic intensity by juxtaposition between acts. Act I begins with a brawl in the marketplace, a public display of the families' hate for each other and ends with Romeo and Juliet falling in love. Act II begins with their love vows at the balcony and ends with their secret marriage. Act III begins with Mercutio's and Tybalt's deaths and ends with Romeo's exile. Act IV begins with Friar Lawrence's secret solution to Juliet's dilemma and ends with her public "death." Act V begins with Romeo's return to the tomb and ends with the lover's suicides.

COMIC INTERLUDES

The repeated pattern of each act reveals a shift from hate to love, from jest to dead earnestness, from appearance to reality. Shakespeare is a master of creating dramatic heightening by contrast. He places Mercutio's ribald ridiculing of Romeo's love immediately before the balcony scene in Act II. He plays off the Nurse's *comic* evasions of Juliet's anxious questions about Romeo's intentions in Act II scene v, against the Nurse's tragic evasions in Act III scene ii, when she has to tell Juliet that Romeo (now her husband) has killed Tybalt (her cousin) and is banished.

RISING ACTION

The rising action through Act V reveals another pattern, the skewed curve of the plot. Shakespeare masterfully places the brawl (outward manifestation of the feud) at the beginning of the play to EXPOSE the two warring factions and to introduce the main characters to the audience within the first five minutes of the play. By the end of Act I we have arrived at the INCITING MOMENT when the conflict becomes clear to the protagonists. Upon discovering their family connections, Romeo laments: "Is she a Capulet? O dear account, my life is my foe's debt"

(I.v.117–118). And Juliet: "Prodigious birth of love it is to me, That I must love a loathed enemy" (I.v.140–141). The COMPLICATION occurs at the end of Act II when the two marry, a church-anointed bond that puts the two lovers on a collision course with their families and fate.

CRISIS, CLIMAX, & DÉNOUEMENT

The CRISIS (the point of no return) results from Romeo's killing of Tybalt and his subsequent banishment. Romeo and Juliet's love cannot endure the forced separation at the end of Act III. So Friar Lawrence's solution, planned and carried out in Act IV, leads, by a fateful mix-up, to the CLIMAX of their deaths in Act V. Shakespeare drives home the tragic futility of it all by placing Romeo's hoped-for discovery of what's going on so close to Juliet's awakening. If she had only awakened three minutes earlier! If Friar Lawrence had only been able to make it to Mantua on time! The DÉNOUEMENT resolves the final moments of the play as Prince Escalus pronounces his judgment on the two families and reiterates the nature of the conflict that is now resolved at such a tragic cost: "Capulet! Montague! See what a scourge is laid upon your hate, That heaven finds means to kill your joys with love" (V.iii.291–293).

CHARACTER: FOUR LEVELS OF LOVE

The secondary CHARACTERS of this play hold our interest only as they highlight the poignant predicament of Romeo and Juliet. It is the lovers who compel our attention throughout the play, and Shakespeare has placed in their mouths his most eloquent and moving statements about love. He leads us to their amorous exchange at the end of Act I by stages, from the lowest kind of physical attraction (LUST) as expressed in the obscene punning between Sampson and Gregory in scene i, through the INFATUATION of love-sick Romeo for Rosaline later in scene i, to the MARRIAGE relationship arranged by Ser Capulet between Paris and Juliet in scene ii. Shakespeare has set us up for their discovery of TRUE LOVE at the ball.

THE LANGUAGE OF LOVE

As this adolescent romance blossoms into religious devotion, we sense a growth in their two characters. Romeo's infatuation for Rosaline appears all-consuming to those around him—"Love is a smoke raised with the fume of sighs" (I.i.196)—but it is only a prelude to the passion he feels for Juliet: "My life were better ended by their hate, Than death prorogued, wanting of thy love" (II.ii.77–78). Juliet's love for Romeo is couched in touchingly tentative

phrases, until she is sure his errand is honorable: "O gentle Romeo, If thou dost love, pronounce it faithfully. Or if thou thinkest I am too quickly won, I'll frown and be perverse, and say thee nay, So thou wilt woo; but else not for the world. In truth fair Montague I am too fond (II.ii.93–98). This fragile fourteen-year-old girl takes on tragic stature in Act III when she implores the Nurse to consider her terrible dilemma, torn between obedience to parents and love for husband and in mortal danger of accidental death by drinking the potion: "Alack, alack, that heaven should practise stratagems Upon so soft a subject as myself" (III.v.211–212).

SETTING

Shakespeare's habit of drawing on historical events and royal characters for his dramatic subjects makes his choice of a non-aristocratic pair for tragic treatment quite unusual, if not revolutionary (maybe even anticipating Miller's elevation of the common man). However, the story itself was not that original. There are many legendary precedents of true love thwarted by fate: the classical tale of Hero and Leander, the medieval legend of Tristan and Yseult. Shakespeare's immediate inspiration was a long and rather dull poem by Arthur Brooke, based on Boiastuau's French adaptation of an earlier Italian novel by Masuccio. That Shakespeare places the action in Italy (Verona) invites association with a far-off, romantic clime, but, more importantly, gives greater credence to the family feud, since warring factions between families was commonplace during the late Middle Ages and early Renaissance. Dante's exile from Florence was the direct result of his being on the wrong side of the struggles between two strong political factions, a situation that originally began with a family feud.

SYMBOLS, MOTIFS, FIGURES OF SPEECH

All good literature provides ample terrain for dislodging golden nuggets of thought. Shakespeare's plays provide particularly rich veins to mine due to his native poetic gift and his remarkable command of the King's English. Shakespeare's plays offer something for everyone: action and ribald humor for the common person; thematic complexity for the thinking person; and eloquence and formal perfection for the lettered and cultured. In this he was a master of rhetorical devices in delineating changing moods and contrasting meanings. We are reminded of Jonson's "Speak, that I may see thee" (qtd. by Kermode in Evans 1198). Notice how deftly he shifts gears from common speech to oratory as he moves from the street scenes to the ball and from coarse humor to intimate expressions of love: the obscene punning in Act I, scene 1—"Draw thy tool"—the oxymoronic expressions of Romeo's love for Rosaline—"O heavy lightness, serious vanity"—the holy imagery and sonnet form in which Romeo and Juliet's avowals of love are couched—

> If I profane with my unworthiest hand
> This holy shrine, the gentle sin is this,
> My lips two blushing pilgrims ready stand
> To smooth that rough touch with a tender kiss.
> (I.v.95–98)

The association of their love with religious devotion, drawn from the rich lore of medieval romance (chivalry), pervades their intimate exchanges and gives Romeo his name (from Rome, the site of Christian pilgrimages): Romeo's first outburst in the garden is "Call me but love, and I'll be new baptized" (hinting at the central issue of names in the play); Juliet's reaction to Romeo's sworn oath is "Do not swear at all. Or if thou wilt, swear by thy gracious self, Which is the god of my idolatry, And I'll believe thee" (II.ii.113–116). Of course, one of literature's most famous metaphors is Romeo's first reaction to seeing Juliet on the balcony: "But soft, what light through yonder window breaks? It is the East, and Juliet is the sun" (II.ii.2–3). Finally, Shakespeare resorts to "monosyllabic plainness" (Kermode in Evans 1057) as the two struggle to preserve their love in the face of an impossible predicament. Romeo's last words are: "Thy drugs are quick. Thus with a kiss I die." Juliet's last words: "O happy dagger! This is thy sheath; there rust, and let me die" (V.iii.120, 169–170).

WOMB/TOMB

One of the most powerful motivic threads that tie the scenes and acts of this play together is introduced at the end of Act I when Juliet says to the Nurse: "Go ask his name—if he be married, My grave is like to be my wedding-bed" (I.v.134–135). This "love-death" motif pervades the play from beginning to end and functions almost like a musical theme and variations. Notice how it changes character in the following instances: Romeo to Friar Lawrence in Act II scene vi—"Then love-devouring death do what he dare, It is enough I may but call her mine"; Juliet lamenting to the Nurse in Act III scene ii—"But I a maid die maiden-widowed, Come cords, come nurse, I'll to my wedding-bed, and death, not Romeo, take my maidenhead"; Lady Capulet to her husband in Act III scene v—"I would the fool were married to her grave;" Juliet to her mother at the prospect of having to marry Paris in the same scene—"Delay this marriage for a month, a week, Or if you do not, make the bridal bed

In that dim monument where Tybalt lies"; Capulet to his wife in Act IV scene v—"Death lies on her like an untimely frost Upon the sweetest flower of all the field"; and, finally, in Act V scene iii, the most gruesome image of all, spoken by Romeo as he breaks through the door of the crypt—"Thou detestable maw, thou womb of death, Gorged with the dearest morsel of the earth, Thus I enforce thy rotten jaws to open, And in despite I'll cram thee with more food."

The conclusion is the climax of the play and a high-point in Shakespeare's manipulation of contrast to dramatize difference. What more paradoxical tension than to align the womb (the source of life) with the tomb (the monument of death)? In one charged image, Shakespeare realizes Socrates' vision of the reconciliation of comedy (life) and tragedy (death).

SUMMARY & RECENT DEVELOPMENTS

Technically, modern theatre began in the late nineteenth century with the realist plays of Henrik Ibsen (*A Dolls' House*), August Strindberg (*Miss Julie*), and Anton Chekhov (*The Seagull*). But since World War II, there has been an explosion of experimentation in new, sometimes nonrealistic, avant-garde directions. One important outgrowth of nineteenth-century **realism** is what has been called "American Selective Realism," in which the playwright heightens certain details of action, scenery, and dialogue while omitting others, exemplified in plays such as Tennessee Williams's *A Streetcar Named Desire* (1947) in which Marlon Brando made his dramatic debut with *Gone with the Wind* star Vivian Leigh, the pathetic story of the personal disillusionment of sex-starved Blanch du Bois, or Arthur Miller's *Death of a Salesman* (1949), the tragedy of a common traveling salesman, or Edward Albee's *Who's Afraid of Virginia Woolf* (1962), a lacerating profile of a failed marriage (Elizabeth Taylor won her second Oscar in the 1966 filmed version with Richard Burton). European plays related to this American movement are works by England's "Angry Young Men," which dealt with class conflict and political disillusionment, such as John Osborne's *Look Back in Anger* (1956), whose character, Jimmy Porter, gave vehement voice to the rage of the English working class, or the German documentary dramas of the 1960s, like Peter Weiss's *The Investigation* (1965), about war crime trials of Nazi guards at a concentration camp. But the most visceral theatrical reactions to the horrors generated by World War II (nuclear annihilation and the holocaust) are manifest in THEATER OF THE ABSURD, which takes its cues from existentialist philosophy's belief that there is no meaning in human existence; all is futile. Samuel Beckett's *Waiting for Godot,* perhaps the most famous and lasting of these enigmatic dramas, traces the cyclical plot of four characters who spend their entire time onstage waiting for nothing to happen. Two significant developments of the 1960s and 1970s were happenings, unstructured events that were staged in the real world (on a street corner or at a bus stop), and multimedia events, the merging of theater with other arts, like dance, film, and television. A current form of the latter, that combines theater, dance, and media, is called performance art. Peter Brook's theater innovations represent more recent developments which have been called "Postwar Eclectics," in which the director incorporates nonrealistic techniques into more traditional, commercial theater. A good example of this is Brooks's scaled-down version of the opera *Carmen* at the Met staged inside an arena on a dirt floor (Wilson/Goldfarb 336–337).

possible—but merely as a useful categorization that describes our field of primary interest.

Let us now take a closer look at our definition. It makes six crucial assertions:

1. Theater is work.

2. Theater is artistic work.

3. In theater, actors impersonate characters.

4. Theater is performance.

5. Theater is live performance.

6. Theater involves a scripted play.

What do we mean by these assertions? What do they tell us about the nature of theater, or, more importantly, the *necessity* of theater? These are the questions that underlie the opening chapter of our investigation into this complex and rewarding subject.

COMMENTARY ON THE ARTS

WHAT IS THE THEATER?

—Robert Cohen

What *is* the theater, this art that excites such imagination across so many climes and cultures?

The word derives from *theatron,* the Greek word for "seeing-place," which was coined to describe the semicircular hillside benches that seated the audience during ancient Greek dramatic performances. We still use the word "theater" to refer to a structure where performances take place, but we also use it to describe the events themselves.

In its various usages "the theater" today may refer to a culture's entire dramatic literary heritage, or it might encompass only plays, or it might refer as well to mime shows, musical extravaganzas, minstrel entertainments, cabaret revues, acted-out storytellings, even puppet shows. By extension, the word is occasionally broadened to include motion pictures and radio and television productions. Metaphorically, "theater" has even been applied to political boundaries and military operations (the "Pacific Theater" and the "European Theater" of World War II).

For the purposes of this book, we shall consider "the theater" as simply *that body of artistic work in which actors impersonate characters in a live (that is, not filmed) performance of a scripted play.* This definition is not to be taken as a final pronouncement on the true meaning of the word—should such a thing even be thought

Work

The "work" of the theater is indeed hard work. An original play—as distinct from a revival—usually takes about one year to produce, and often five years or more from conception to actual presentation. Rehearsal alone accounts for a minimum of four weeks, and for most effective productions it goes on a good deal longer. The labors of theater artists in the final weeks before an opening are legendary: the ninety-hour week becomes a commonplace, expenditures of money and spirit are intense, and even the unions relax their regulations to allow for an almost unbridled invasion of the hours the ordinary world spends sleeping, eating, and unwinding. The theater enterprise may involve hundreds of people in scores of different efforts—many more backstage than onstage—and the mobilization and coordination of these efforts is in itself a giant task. So when we think of the "work" embodied in the plays of Shakespeare, for example, or of Neil Simon, we must think of work in the sense of physical toil as well as in the loftier sense of *oeuvre,* by which the French designate the sum of an artist's creative endeavor.

The work of the theater is generally divisible into a number of crafts:

acting, in which actors perform the roles of characters in a play;

designing, in which designers map out the visual and audio elements of a production, including the scenery, properties, costumes and wigs, make-up, lighting, sound concepts, programs, advertising, and general ambience of the premises;

building, in which carpenters, costumers, wig-makers, electricians, make-up artists, recording and sound engineers, painters, and a host of other specially designated craftsmen translate the design into reality by constructing and finishing in detail the "hardware" of a show; and

running, in which technicians execute in proper sequence, and with carefully rehearsed timing, the light and sound cues, the shifting of scenery, the placement and return of properties, and the assignment, laundering, repair, and changes of costumes.

Also involved are a number of managerial functions:

producing, which includes securing all necessary personnel, space, and financing, supervising all production and promotion efforts, fielding all legal matters, and distributing all proceeds derived from receipts;

directing, which includes controlling and developing the artistic product and providing it with a unified vision, coordinating all its components, and supervising all rehearsals;

stage managing, which includes the responsibility for "running" a play production in all its complexity in performance after performance; and

house managing, which includes the responsibility for admitting, seating, and providing for the general comfort of the audience.

And finally, there is playwriting, which is in a class by itself. It is the one craft of the theater that is usually executed away from the theater building and its associated shops—that may indeed take place continents and centuries away from the production it inspires.

Of course the work of the theater need not be apportioned precisely as we have indicated above. In any production, some people will perform more than one kind of work; for example, many of the "builders" will also be "runners." Moreover, many a play has been produced with the actors directing themselves, or the director handling production duties, or the dialogue improvised by the actors and director. On occasion most if not all of the craft and managerial functions have been performed by the same person: Aeschylus, for one, not only wrote, directed, and designed his Greek tragedies; he probably also performed the leading parts. But although there is nothing inevitable or necessary about the allocation of craft functions of the theater's work, the functions themselves have remained fairly constant over the theater's history. In virtually every era we can look back and see the same sorts of work going on—and the same kinds of efforts being expended—as we see in the work of the theater today, be it professional or amateur, American or European, commercial or academic. Later on in this book we shall take a closer look at these various craft and managerial functions which go into the creation of a theatrical event.

Theater is also work in the sense that it is not "play." This is a more subtle distinction than we might at once imagine. First, of course, recall that we ordinarily use the word "play" in describing the main product of theater work. This is not merely a peculiarity of the English tongue, for we find that the French *jeu,* the German *Spiel,* and the Latin *ludus* all share the double meaning of the English "play," referring both to plays and playing in the theatrical sense, and to sports activities, or games. This association points to a relationship that is fundamental to the understanding of theater: theater *is* a kind of game, and it is useful for us to see how and why this is so.

The theater and games have a shared history. Both were developed to a high level of sophistication in Greek festivals: the Dionysian festivals for theater and the Olympian festivals for sport were the two great cultural events of ancient Greece at which the legendary Greek competition for excellence was most profoundly engaged. The Romans merged sports and theater in their circuses, where the two were performed side by side and in competition with each other. In much the same fashion, the Elizabethan Londoners built playhouses to accommodate both dramatic productions and animal-baiting spectacles somewhat akin to the modern bullfight; the stage that was set up for the plays was simply removed for "play." Today, sports and dramatic quasi-theater dominate the television fare which absorbs so much leisure time not only in America but in most of the Western world. Moreover, professional athletes and entertainers are among the foremost celebrities of the modern age—and many a retired sports hero has found a second career in acting. Thus it is not extraordinary that sports and the theater still share in the compound use of the word "play."

For the individual, a link between games and theater is formed early in life, in "child's play," which usually manifests both game-like and drama-like aspects. The game of hide-and-seek, for example, is a playful competition between children that can be repeated over and over, a harmless but engrossing activity involving counting, hiding, searching, and at last the triumph of finding. It is also an acting out of one of childhood's greatest fears—the fear of separation from the parent, or "separation anxiety," as psychologists term it. Hide-and-seek affords the child a way of dealing with that fear by confronting it over and over "in play" until it loses much of its potency. Play is *often* grounded in serious concerns, and through play the individual gradually develops means of coping with life's challenges and uncertainties.

Drama and sports are different but related adult forms of the same "play." One of the aspects of adult play—in both its forms—is that it attracts a tremendous amateur following; as child's play is engaged in without prompting or reward, so adult sports and theater commonly yield no remuneration beyond sheer personal satisfaction. Both sports and theatricals offer splendid opportunities for intense physical involvement, competition, self-expression, and emotional engagement—and all within limits set by precise and sensible rules. What is more, both can generate an audience because the energies and passions they project are rarely expressed so openly in daily life beyond the playgrounds of childhood. It is little wonder that persons who spend a lifetime in the theater or in athletics are often regarded as child-like—or, more pejoratively, as immature and irresponsible for their "playing" evokes myriad memories of youth.

But the theater must finally be distinguished from child's play, and from sports as well, because theater is by its nature a calculated act from beginning to end. Unlike adult games, which are open-ended, every theater performance has a preordained conclusion. The Yankees may not win the World Series this year, but Hamlet definitely will die in the fifth act. The *work* of the theater, indeed, consists in keeping Hamlet alive up to that point— brilliantly alive to make of that foreordained end a profoundly moving, ennobling, even surprising climax to the whole experience.

We might say, finally, that *theater is the art of making play into work; specifically, into a work of art.* It is exhilarating work, to be sure, and it usually inspires and invigorates the energies and imaginations of all who participate; it transcends more prosaic forms of labor as song transcends grunts and groans. But it is work: that is its challenge, and the great accomplishments of the theater are always attended by prodigious effort.

> The stage is an institution combining amusement with instruction, rest with exertion, where no faculty of the mind is overstrained, no pleasure enjoyed at the cost of the whole. When melancholy gnaws the heart, when trouble poisons our solitude, when we are disgusted with the world and a thousand worries oppress us, or when our energies are destroyed by overexercise, the stage revives us, we dream of another sphere, we recover ourselves, our torpid nature is roused by noble passions, our blood circulates more healthily. The unhappy man forgets his tears in weeping for another. The happy man is calmed, the secure made provident. Effeminate natures are steeled, savages made man, and, as the supreme triumph of nature, men of all ranks, zones, and conditions, emancipated from the chains of conventionality and fashion, fraternize here in a universal sympathy, forget the world, and come nearer to their heavenly destination. The individual shares in the general ecstasy, and his breast has now only space for an emotion: he is a *man.*

—Friedrich von Schiller

WORKS CITED

Aristotle. *Poetics*. Trans. S. H. Butcher. New York: Hill and Wang, 1961.

Boorstin, Daniel J. *The Creators*. New York: Random House, 1992.

Burdick, Jacques. *Theater*. New York: Newsweek, 1974.

Evans, G. Blakemore et al., eds. *The Riverside Shakespeare*. New York: Houghton Mifflin, 1974.

Hamilton, Edith. *The Greek Way*. New York: Norton, 1942.

Miller, Arthur. "Introduction" to *Collected Plays*. New York: Viking, 1957.

Soule, Donald. "Comedy, Irony, and a Sense of Comprehension." *Humanities Association Review* 13 (1962–1963): 37–54.

Williams, Tennessee. In Robert Cohen, *Theatre*. Palo Alto, CA: Mayfield, 1981.

Wilson, Edwin, and Alvin Goldfarb. *Theater: The Lively Art*. 3rd ed. New York: McGraw-Hill, 1999.

WEBSITES OF INTEREST

Western Drama Through the Ages —
http://books.google.com/books?id=F8s_VTNuqU4C&printsec=frontcover&source=gbs_navlinks_s

Othello's final speech —
http://www.youtube.com/watch?v=epW6H6UlfcE

Death of a Salesman scene —
http://www.youtube.com/watch?v=UnTqlxajQ5Q

Photo from the Brigham Young University musical production of The Gondoliers.

INTRODUCTION TO MUSIC DRAMA

Chapter 12

INTRODUCTION

Most Americans don't see much use for opera. To our practical bent, opera seems impossibly pretentious and emotionally overwrought. To our sports mentality, opera goers seem culturally elitist and musically out in left field. Who could possibly derive aesthetic pleasure from watching an overweight older woman singing high notes that could crack a crystal goblet at twenty paces? The answer is: most Europeans. Where did we get off, since we are heirs to much of Western Europe's cultural traditions? Part of the answer lies in our early dismissal of the high culture surrounding the politically suppressive systems we sailed to America to escape. Part of the answer is that we still retain a kind of frontier (macho) mentality, particularly among the working classes who instinctively prefer popular culture to high culture. However, among most Americans, there is an ironic twist to all this opera bashing: the one experience that seems to have converted most students to an interest in the fine arts is contemporary **musicals**, many of which have been imported from Europe, like *Cats, Les Misérables,* or *Phantom of the Opera.* What most people don't realize is that these modern musicals are a uniquely American invention and very close to classical opera: the drama is all sung; there are elaborate sets and costumes; the singers navigate loud and high vocal ranges; the plots are convoluted and complex; the situations cover a wide range of emotions. The point is simply this: music drama (whether opera or musical) affords one of the most powerful means of expressing deep emotion in an elaborate dramatic setting. It is worth your time, effort, and money to see if it speaks to you.

WHENCE OPERA?

Origins

Opera started fifty thousand years ago with people making noises as they came out of their caves. And out of those noises came Verdi and Puccini and Wagner. There was a noise for fear, for love, for happiness and for anger. That was one-note, atonal opera, and that's where it began. At that point it was a natural human expression, and that turned into song. And, at some later time, that process became codified, constructed, and turned into art. (Brook 169)

One way to view opera is to see it as an artistic expression of some major nonverbal ways human beings communicate with each other: expanded voice inflection becomes song; organized gesture becomes acting; visual cues become elaborate set design, etc.

Definition

But historically, opera is just under four hundred years old. The word OPERA is the plural form of the Latin word *opus,* which simply means "work." Sometimes you see it linked to the title of a musical composition, like "opus 24" (the 24th work of that composer). Opera is a combined art form made up of at least three different arts: MUSIC, DRAMA, and VISUAL SPECTACLE. In the eyes of some, its very complexity destroys its credibility. That issue you will have to decide for yourself by keeping an open mind (and ear).

HISTORICAL ORIGINS

The precariousness of its birth at the turn of the seventeenth century in Italy didn't augur well for opera's claim to legitimacy as a "pure" art form, since it was virtually invented by mistake. A group of late Renaissance intellectuals living in Florence organized themselves into what they called the "Florentine Camerata." One of their objectives was to effect a revival of ancient Greek drama. From their limited knowledge of this theatrical tradition—they knew it involved highly declamatory speaking, singing, chanting, dancing, and costuming—they set about to exhume a dead relic (the authentic conventions of Greek drama), but in the process they gave birth to a new art form, opera. Aside from its multimedia character, the most characteristic feature of this new mongrel form was its declamatory singing style. This new style of singing grew out of the theory of one of the leading members of the camerata, VINCENZO GALILEI (the famous astronomer's father). He claimed to have rediscovered the nature of ancient Greek solo song, which he called *monody,* but which has since been referred to as *recitative,* an accompanied vocal declamation halfway between speaking and singing. Vincenzo claimed that for every phrase of poetry there was one unique melodic and rhythmic pattern that perfectly expressed it. His idea grew out of the fact that the emotional dimension of spoken language is carried by voice inflection (the rise and fall of the speaking voice). He argued that the correct way to set vocal works was to use a solo melody which would merely enhance the natural speech inflections of a good orator. This device made it not only possible, but inevitable, that music drama would be entirely sung, which it still is even today, in its "grand opera" form.

OPERA SERIA

It is appropriate that opera was born in the Baroque age, the age of theatricality and excess, as an outgrowth of lavish court entertainments. CLAUDIO MONTEVERDI (1567–1643) composed the first true, full-length opera, *Orfeo* (1607), and thereby helped to create *opera seria* (serious opera). Its plot, like most early operas, was based on Greek **myth**, in this case the legend of Orpheus and Euridice. Monteverdi capitalized on Galilei's theories by effecting a blend between dramatic logic and musical expression, although his successors let the virtuosity of the singers take over. By century's end opera had declined into poorly dramatized vocal pyrotechnics. CHRISTOPH WILLIBALD GLUCK (1715–1787) revived the waning power of serious opera by replacing its sawdust characters with more monumental tragic types reminiscent of ancient Greek drama. He sought to make music subordinate to the claims of drama. By the early 1700s, opera had become the craze in London, and GEORGE FREDERICK HANDEL (1685–1759), a transplant from Germany, was riding the crest of this wave by composing many operas in the Italian style.

OPERA BUFFA

Then, in 1728, JOHN GAY (1685–1732) wrote *The Beggar's Opera* as a satire on Italian opera. Its phenomenal success marked a shift in public taste away from grand opera in England and led Handel into oratorio writing (he wrote *Messiah* in 1742). This lampoon of *opera seria* also gave rise to another type of opera, ***opera buffa,*** whose witty descendants have delighted audiences ever since: England's comic opera tradition with Gilbert and Sullivan; Austria's unforgettable operettas by Franz Lehár, Johann Strauss, et al.; and America's own home-grown music drama variety, *musical comedy,* with the widely popular works from the Gershwins (George and Ira), Cole Porter, Rodgers and Hammerstein, Lerner and Loewe, Leonard Bernstein, Stephen Sondheim, and more recently, Andrew Lloyd Webber in England and Boublil and Schönberg in France.

WOLFGANG AMADEUS MOZART (1756–1791) was the first of the German-speaking composers to write opera. His *Marriage of Figaro* (1786), based on a political satire, is pure comedy. Mozart's operas, however, stand somewhere between the serious and the comic, for his last major work, *Don Giovanni* (1787), begins humorously and ends tragically. It deals with an insatiable lover who wins the hearts of all the ladies but perishes because he fails to recognize the boundaries of humanity. Mozart's forte as an opera composer resided in his ability to compose music that was expressive of each character.

NINETEENTH-CENTURY OPERA: WAGNER'S "GESAMTKUNSTWERK"

Grand opera became "grand" (French for large) with a vengeance in the nineteenth century with the grandiose works of the great romantic composers of Germany and Italy. RICHARD WAGNER (1813–1883) refused to call his stage works operas and instead called them *Musikdramen* because of his theory that music and drama should join together like "a lover's kiss." He could bring off this kind of unity because he was his own librettist (he wrote the music and the words). In addition, he developed the notion of ***leitmotif,*** a musical motive (fragment), a kind of "musical word," which became attached to a person, idea, feeling, or object in his operas and which could greatly enhance the emotional associations in the drama, besides providing an effective means of unifying the music and the action.

VERDI'S "OPERA VERISMO"

In the latter half of the nineteenth century, two great Italian composers, GIUSEPPE VERDI (1813–1901) and GIACOMO PUCCINI (1858–1924), began to write operas in a more realistic, less fanciful style. Although earlier operas had drawn inspiration mainly from myths, Verdi's *La Traviata* (1853) treated contemporary situations peopled by characters dressed as those sitting in the audience, and allowed violent acts to be shown on stage. This new kind of realistic opera is sometimes called *opera verismo.* Some of the most memorable successors of *La Traviata* are Leoncavallo's *I Pagliacci* (1892) and Puccini's *Madama Butterfly* (1900). These great nineteenth-century operas continue to be the mainstay of the major opera houses around the world, in spite of the fact that operas are still being written, even rock operas, like *Tommy* by The Who.

SUMMARY & RECENT DEVELOPMENTS

In spite of the wide popularity of the standard nineteenth-century repertoire, operas are still being written and a few find their way to the stage, such as *Salome* (1905) by Richard Strauss, a dark opera about female hysteria and strange sexuality, or Gian-Carlo Menotti's *The Medium* (1946), about conjuring up the spirits of departed relatives, or *The Consul* (1950), about the Iron Curtain countries. More recently, operas have drawn their inspiration from current events, like John Adams's *Death of Klinghofer,* about black nationalism, or Anthony Davis's *X,* about gay rights.

Opera is perhaps unique among the major art forms in its conservative attitude toward change as we move into the twenty-first century. While its history is often viewed as a subcategory of music history, it has been slower to embrace the radical changes modern music has undergone. This may be due in part to the staying power of the grand opera of the eighteenth and nineteenth centuries in the repertoire of the major opera houses of Europe. Nevertheless, important modernist composers like Arnold Schönberg (1874–1951) and his foremost student, Alban Berg (1885–1935), have written major operas in the new musical style of atonality, employing a new vocal delivery called *Sprechstimme* (a kind of gliding through the pitches, creating ghostly effects). This musical style is ideal for the psychological subjects of Berg's two most powerful operas, *Wozzeck* (1921), and *Lulu* (1935), about a par-

tially insane soldier and a sexually repressed woman, respectively. These Freudian works have reached large audiences, but it wasn't until the 1951 television premiere of Gian-Carlo Menotti's *Amahl and the Night Visitors* that opera audiences grew geometrically. Opera's appeal has grown dramatically since the first "Three Tenors Concert" was broadcast from the Baths of Caracalla in Rome in 1990. But mainstream modern opera has remained beyond the accessibility of most theater-goers because of its extreme innovations. Philip Glass's first opera, *Einstein on the Beach* (1976), was hailed as a revolutionary theatrical event: it has no **arias,** no recitative, no plot, and no characters in any real sense, yet it is opera because it involves music and text within a theatrical structure. It also creates a new relationship with the audience by an almost Brechtian subversion of the audience's emotional immersion in the action, a very anti-opera development.

MUSICALS: THE COMMON MAN'S OPERA

INTRODUCTION

In trying to define the uniquely American genre of the musical, Leonard Bernstein once wrote: "The glittering world of musical theater is an enormous field that includes everything from your nephew's high-school pageant to [Wagner's] *Götterdämmerung*" (152). He helps us discover the nature of musicals by placing them somewhere on a continuum between Variety Show and Wagnerian Music Drama with the following chart:

Variety Show (Music Hall, Vaudeville, etc.)

Revue (e.g., *Ziegfeld Follies*)

Operetta (e.g., *Naughty Marietta*)

Comic Opera (e.g., *H.M.S. Pinafore*)

Opera Buffa (e.g., *Barber of Seville*)

Opera Comique (e.g., *Carmen*)

Opera Verismo (e.g., *I Pagliacci*)

Grand Opera (e.g., *Aida*)

Wagnerian Music Drama (e.g., *Das Rheingold*)

American Musical Comedy belongs somewhere between the two poles of Bernstein's list. Unlike variety shows and Broadway revues, musicals have fleshed-out characters within a clear plot structure, and yet retain the media mix one expects in a variety show: singing, dancing, comic routines, etc. Unlike opera, musical comedies don't exhibit continuous singing in elevated opera recitative, but they do contain sophisticated music and sometimes grand spectacle (think of *My Fair Lady* or *The Phantom of the Opera*).

THE AMERICAN MUSICAL

In general, the requirements for **musicals** include the following: a typically American theme; down-to-earth characters (in contrast to the aristocratic milieu of European operetta); songs that are integrated into the plot; words written in the American vernacular (verbally, in colloquial American dialects; musically, in the black American musical style, namely **jazz** and its many variants); and "plot-dancing," originally created by Agnes DeMille for Rodgers and Hammerstein's *Oklahoma* (1943). With Rodgers and Hammerstein's *South Pacific* (1949), Bernstein sees a return of the musical to its operatic roots in the double soliloquy at the beginning. Bernstein's text was written for an October 1956 telecast. The very next year Bernstein himself, along with Stephen Sondheim and Arthur Laurents, made musical history by completing *West Side Story*, which took the "comedy" out of American musicals and made them vehicles for tragedies. Since then there has been an even more dramatic turn toward opera with recent European musicals (mainly from England) which are all sung. The two major differences between these musicals of the 80s and 90s and opera are that musicals contain music written in the pop style (not traditional or avant garde) and that they are delivered in "belt" rather than in classical operatic singing style. But at times even these distinctions break down. Linda Ronstadt seems equally at home singing pop tunes, the *Pirates of Penzance*, or *La Bohème*.

THE CHALLENGES

One of the great difficulties in approaching musical theater has to do with the fact that it is a mixed medium, like opera. Not simply music, not exclusively drama, musical theater combines both, along with dance, to create an art form that is, at its best, much greater than any of its parts. The second difficulty is that it requires a greater "willing suspension of disbelief" than a play or film. The addition of musical numbers causes the production to be much less realistic than spoken drama because it does not imitate life (people don't go around singing to each other). There are basically three types of musicals, each requiring a progressively greater degree of audience collaboration and suspension of disbelief. Almost any musical will fit into one of these categories: show musicals, fairy tale musicals, and folk musicals, or some combination.

THREE TYPES

SHOW MUSICALS were the earliest kind of musical, containing songs that were not a necessary part of the story line. In fact, the narrative usually served simply as a vehicle to get from one unrelated musical number to the next. The plot always depended upon some type of show within a show. Cole Porter's *Kiss Me Kate*, or *Cabaret*, a hit musical from the 70s, are good examples of show musicals.

FAIRYTALE MUSICALS, unlike show musicals, attempt to integrate musical numbers into the story line and dialogue; however, the plot is grounded in some fantastic setting, a world of make-believe. And because the story is fantastic, it does not seem unreasonable that the characters in such a world should sing and dance. *Brigadoon, Annie, Camelot,* and *Into the Woods* fit well into this category.

FOLK MUSICALS take a story line from a seemingly realistic situation and combine it with musical numbers. This combination of realism with occasional outbursts of song defines the folk musical and distinguishes it from both show musicals and fairy tale musicals. Things that cannot be said in dialogue are expressed in song; therefore, the musical number serves as a kind of modern-day soliloquy. In other words, the songs do not serve so much to further the story line as they do to allow the characters to pour out their feelings, thus allowing the audience a chance to learn of their private thoughts and emotions. *West Side Story* is an obvious example of the folk musicals as well as *Show Boat* and *Oklahoma*. One can easily compare the balcony scene in Shakespeare's *Romeo and Juliet* with Tony and Maria's love song in *West Side Story*.

CONTEMPORARY MUSICAL THEATER

The history of American musical theater is filled with the names of the great popular composers in American history: Victor Herbert, Jerome Kern, George and Ira Gershwin, Irving Berlin, Cole Porter, Lerner and Loewe, and Rodgers and Hammerstein. During the past three decades two composers have distinguished themselves as the most important and prolific composers for the Broadway stage: Andrew Lloyd Webber from England and Stephen Sondheim from America.

THE ENGLISH MUSICAL

ANDREW LLOYD WEBBER achieved a rare feat in 1989 when he had three musicals playing on Broadway at the same time. These three shows—*Cats, Starlight Express,* and *Phantom of the Opera*—were all imports from

London's West End, where they had established their reputations before coming to New York. With the average cost of staging a musical in the range of six million dollars, it is understandable why a producer does not want to present a show until it has an established track record. *Phantom of the Opera* had a pre-sell of over eleven million dollars in tickets before it even opened on Broadway; people actually bought tickets over a year in advance. In collaboration with lyricist Tim Rice, Webber wrote several other musicals in the 1970s, such as *Jesus Christ Superstar* and *Joseph and the Amazing Technicolor Dreamcoat.* A recent success, *Sunset Boulevard,* won the Tony for Best Musical in 1995.

THE "SONDHEIM SYNDROME"

On this side of the Atlantic the most important Broadway composer began his career as Bernstein's lyricist for the 1957 production of *West Side Story.* STEPHEN SONDHEIM was only twenty six years old when he worked on that show. In the years since, he has written many shows, as both composer and lyricist, such as A *Funny Thing Happened on the Way to the Forum* (1962), *A Little Night Music* (1973), and the Pulitzer-prize-winning *Sunday in the Park with George* (1984). Sondheim's longest running show to date is *Into the Woods,* a pastiche of fairy tales that played from 1987 until 1989. While Webber has traditionally been a great success at the box office, Sondheim has been a bigger hit with the critics. Sondheim's plots and music are somewhat more complex and difficult to follow than Webber's. It might be said that Webber writes for the common people and Sondheim writes for the thinking person. Sondheim's themes and story lines are meant to be thought about and mulled over, not simply enjoyed for a few brief hours in the theater. *Sweeny Todd,* for example, tells the story of a barber who kills his clients as a form of revenge on the town that wronged him many years earlier. The twist in the plot comes when the woman who lives downstairs begins to use the corpses in her meat pie business. *Sunday in the Park with George* is a fictionalized account of the life of Pointillist painter, George Seurat, yet many feel that it is actually an autobiographical sketch of the life of Sondheim himself.

SUMMARY & RECENT DEVELOPMENTS

The golden era of American book musicals (musicals that tell a story) is generally considered to be the time between *Oklahoma* (1943) and *Fiddler on the Roof* (1964). Since 1965, several trends come into focus. After the anti-

establishment musical *Hair* (1967), which had no actual story line, fewer and fewer book musicals were written. In their place arose the conceptual musicals of Stephen Sondheim, which placed more emphasis on the lyrics than on the music and dance, like *Company* (1970) and *Follies* (1971). Another trend in musicals of the 1970s and 1980s is the rise of the choreographer as director, best seen in Michael Bennett's stunningly successful A *Chorus Line,* but also noteworthy are Gower Champion's *Hello Dolly!* (1964) and *42nd Street* (1980), Bob Fosse's *Sweet Charity* (1966) and *Pippen* (1972), and Tommy Tune's *Grand Hotel* (1989) and *The Will Rogers Follies* (1991). Still another direction taken by musicals in the last three decades of the twentieth century was the emergence of British musicals and their importation to the U.S., most notably a rash of blockbusters by Andrew Lloyd Webber, beginning with *Jesus Christ Superstar* (1971) and including *Evita* (1979), *Cats* (1982), *The Phantom of the Opera* (1987), and *Sunset Blvd.* (1993). The year of the *Phantom* (1987) brought perhaps the greatest success story of all, Schönberg and Bloubil's world sensation, *Les Misérables,* based on the Victor Hugo novel. As the stage spectacle in these recent successes has grown ever grander, so the costs have risen astronomically, which may explain the recent trend toward revivals of earlier musicals, such as *Showboat* and *Oklahoma,* and animated films made into musicals, like Disney's *Beauty and the Beast.* New musicals began appearing on Broadway during the mid-1990s, like the huge success of Jonathan Larsen's *Rent,* an adaptation of *La Bohème,* involving rock, jazz, Latin, and operatic styles of music. It seems that this American original still has some life left in it.

DISCUSSION QUESTIONS

1. People of all ages have been exposed to American musical comedy. The variety is large enough that nearly everyone has a favorite. Few Americans, however, are opera buffs, and yet, musicals are becoming more and more "operatic:" the drama is heavy, even tragic; the sets are pyrotechnical extravaganzas; all the dialogue is sung, etc. List some of the reasons why *Les Misérables* is a sell-out and *La Traviata* only draws the cultural elites. Why does opera seem to be an elitist medium in America, while it appeals to a broad population in Europe? On the other hand, how do you explain Luciano Pavarotti's incredible popularity among all classes of people? In 1990, the only musicians who sold more recordings than he were Elton John and Madonna (Remnick 37).

2. If you've seen *Cats, Les Misérables,* or *The Phantom of the Opera,* or some other contemporary musical, describe and explain the moment of highest emotional intensity in the performance. Was the music sung or played? In your opinion, which is potentially more dramatic? Why?

3. The noted English composer Ralph Vaughan Williams often observed that voice inflection lies at the root of all song, that *how* we say something means as much or more than *what* we say. Think about this in terms of your own experience. Does it seem true? Does music (defined as "any expressive sound") figure in all communication? Write a short essay on this, tying your points to actual experiences you have had.

> I was once at an open-air service in the Isle of Skye, where a sermon was being preached in Gaelic. . . . At first the preacher spoke in a rather monotonous voice—a sort of sing-song—as he had to raise his voice a good deal to make himself heard. But as he became more and more excited over his discourse his speaking gradually changed to a sort of irregular chanting on four distinct musical tones. Here, then, you have the rough beginnings of song—excited speech gradually becoming distinct musical tone. (Qtd. in Kennedy 31)

WORKS CITED

Bernstein, Leonard. *The Joy of Music.* New York: Simon & Schuster, 1959.

Brook, Peter. *The Shifting Point: Theatre, Film, Opera 1946–1987.* New York: HarperCollins, 1987.

Kennedy, Michael. *The Works of Ralph Vaughan Williams.* London: Oxford University Press, 1964.

Remnick, David. "The Last Italian Tenor." *New Yorker* 21 June 1993, 36–45.

WEBSITES OF INTEREST

Brief History of Opera —

http://artsedge.kennedy-center.org/content/2374/2374_aida_operahistory.pdf

Phantom of Opera —

http://www.youtube.com/watch?v=oZDcSrODALQ

History of the Musical —

http://www.scaruffi.com/history/musical.html

Humphrey Bogart and Ingrid Bergman in Casablanca, *courtesy of BYU Library.*

INTRODUCTION TO FILM

Chapter **13**

INTRODUCTION

From film's birth in the last decade of the nineteenth century, it was virtually guaranteed that film would be the artistic medium of the twentieth century, given its machine technology, its almost universal reach, and its emotional impact. Speaking of its awesome cultural influence, Erwin Panofsky once wrote:

> If all the serious lyrical poets, composers, painters and sculptors were forced by law to stop their activities, a rather small fraction of the general public would become aware of the fact and a still smaller fraction would seriously regret it. If the same thing were to happen with the movies the social consequences would be catastrophic. (357)

What is remarkable about this quote is that it was made in 1935, before the advent of public television broadcasting. Of all the performing arts we have studied so far, **cinema** is the last. It is also the youngest and clearly enjoys the broadest exposure if we include the worldwide spread of television. In fact virtually all of the other performing arts have greatly broadened their audiences as a result of television coverage, especially via PBS stations.

In spite of the fact that film and television produce images in a different way (film, originally, by running a celluloid strip through a projector; television by beaming an image through a cathode-ray tube), both manipulate the raw visual material in virtually the same way, by using conventional film techniques (see below). Therefore, for purposes of learning about the general motion picture medium and its criticism, we will focus on film in this chapter. However, the perceptual impact and audience involvement is subtly but significantly different in the two mediums: the small 27-to 35-inch television screen is normally viewed in a lighted room at rather close proximity, while the film image is projected onto a large screen in a darkened movie theater; the television program usually lasts no longer than thirty to sixty minutes and is frequently interrupted by commercials, while films last much longer (two to three hours) and sustain their narrative flow without interruption.

FILM AS "TOTAL ART"

THE TWENTIETH-CENTURY "GESAMTKUNSTWERK"

Cinema has been called "total art" because it involves photography, music, literature, drama, the visual arts, and sometimes even dance. It is also a huge collaboration requiring the professional skills of artists in many different fields; thus the final work is really a compilation and fusion of many talents. The untrained viewer sometimes sees a film as something that just happens, unaware of the extent of human intervention, seeing it only as something recorded mechanically by an anonymous movie camera, or as a mirror of real life. Such a viewer is usually aware of the actors (that's often what gets the audience there in the first place), yet entirely overlooks the work of the cinematographer, the **director,** and the **editor,** to say nothing of the crews who work on set design, costuming, make-up, matting, background music, sound effects, etc. When attending your next film, notice the army of experts listed in the credits. Realize that a clearer understanding of their contributions will greatly enhance your appreciation of a film's meaning and quality.

PROS

As a twentieth-century art form, film has certain advantages over most other arts. It not only reaches the widest audience of any of the arts, but many experts claim that no artistic medium yet created has quite the power to move us as deeply as the medium of moving images linked to a sound track enhanced by music. One might argue that music can move us even more deeply than a visual image, but when the two are combined—and are given a lifelike dimension through the movement—then the greater impact seems indisputable. Panofsky rather prophetically anticipated the unique effect of cinema long before modern special effects by noting that film combines the "dynamization of space" and "spatialization of time" (359). In other words, moving pictures virtually telescope the dynamic flow of the time arts into the graphic immediacy of the space arts, giving birth to a new kind of "super art."

CONS

Film's disadvantages are primarily its transient quality and its susceptibility to commercialization. A book can be reread and music can be listened to over and over again, but a movie is an elusive medium (mere flickering light), notwithstanding the plethora of video and DVD rentals, which allow people to control the flow of time and focus on specific scenes for analysis. The more recent DVD technology will eventually make it possible for much more careful analysis of a film than at present. Until that time, technical and symbolic subtleties of a really good film are often lost on viewers untrained to catch them as they pass by. The commercial aspect can also be very detrimental to the integrity of cinema. Filmmakers are often forced into unwanted compromises, their artistic decisions dictated by the demands of the box office to recoup the enormous costs required to produce and market a film. In addition, the seductive power of huge profits can sidetrack artists of otherwise reliable aesthetic integrity.

MILESTONES IN FILM HISTORY

1600 B.C.: Egyptians may have experimented with pictures and motion, ostensibly by carving still pictures of their gods in slightly different positions and then, like the "Little Big Books," riding past the columns, training their eyes on the passing images that appeared to come alive.

Fifteenth-Sixteenth Centuries: Alberti and Da Vinci's experiments with the *camera obscura* (lit. dark chamber), in which an image was projected through a small aperture in a darkened enclosure onto the opposite wall.

1824: Peter Mark Roget's discovery of "persistence of vision," a phenomenon of the eye that makes still pictures seem like real motion because an image on the retina remains briefly visible ("persists") after its actual disappearance.

1839: Louis-Jacques-Mandé Daguerre showed the Paris Academy of Science his successful photographic process that yielded a clear picture on a silvered copper plate, producing the original photographs called "Daguerreotype."

1869: The development of Celluloid, trademark for the transparent cellulose derivative used as a base for film stock, was as an important break-through for the projection of film onto large screens.

28 December 1895: The "birth of cinema" as we know it, when the Lumière brothers in France first projected a moving picture on a screen to a paying audience. Their invention, the Cinématographe, was a combination camera-projector with a patented claw for moving the film forward to create the illusion of movement.

23 April 1896: First public display of Edison's Kinetoscope (Edison's answer to the Lumières' Cinématographe) in a program of short films accompanying a vaudeville show in New York. The program consisted of twelve short subjects and, according to Ephraim Katz, "marked the birth in America of a new form of art and a great new industry" (405). The Lumière brothers are considered the founders of the realist tradition of cinema. By 1908 there were five thousand movie houses in the U.S.

1897: Georges Méliès built the first European film studio at Montreuil, France, and began making films indoors with artificial lighting.

1902: Méliès's *A Trip to the Moon* considered one of the first fantasy films, in contrast to the Lumière brothers' realistic "newsreel" films.

1903: Edwin S. Porter's *The Great Train Robbery,* the first full-length (12-minute) "epic" narrative film with a cast of 40, effectively exploited cinematic innovations like tracking and editing. It ended with the famous scene of a bandit firing a pistol directly at the audience. *The Great Train Robbery* remains one of the most important milestones in screen history" (Katz 1093).

1906: The first animated cartoon: J. Stuart Blackton's *Humorous Phases of Funny Faces.*

1915: D. W. Griffith's *The Birth of a Nation,* perhaps the single most important film in the development of cinema as a major art form, had an enormous impact on the future of cinema as a legitimate artistic "grammar." He pioneered the use of epic cinematography, close-ups, editing, and cross-cutting techniques.

1925: Some consider Sergei Eisenstein's *Battleship Potemkin* the best edited film of all time. Although the story line is fragmented, Eisenstein's genius created unforgettable images of military tyranny and astonishingly inventive rhythmic editing, called montage, in the "Odessa Steps" sequence.

1927: The first full-length, popular sound film, *The Jazz Singer,* opened with Al Jolson's singing and his now famous (and prophetic) one-liner: "You ain't heard nothin' yet!"

1935: The first feature film made with Technicolor's three-strip camera and three-color printing technique was Rouben Mamoulian's *Becky Sharp.*

1939: The two film classics, *Gone with the Wind* and *The Wizard of Oz,* were produced in the same year and directed by Victor Fleming: the latter experimented with contrasting black and white and color in the Kansas-to-Oz transition; the former set an industry standard for color films with an epic sweep and started the liberalization of the film code with Clark Gable's "Frankly, my dear, I don't give a damn" scene with Scarlet O'Hara.

1940: The year of the first American television network broadcast, marking the beginning of the decline of major studio control of the film medium.

1941: The completion of Orson Welles's masterpiece, *Citizen Kane,* one of the most influential films ever made and, by some judgments, the greatest. It remains a masterwork in its original soundtrack with the deep-focus camera work of Gregg Toland, consisting of stark images and dramatic back lighting, and its creative editing by Robert Wise, who later directed *West Side Story* and *The Sound of Music.*

1948: U.S. v. Paramount anti-trust case, resulting in the end of the studio monopolies.

1951: Color televisions first appear in the U.S.

1952: First 3-D movies.

1953: The debut of Cinemascope and the wide-screen format.

1967: Establishment of the MPAA rating system in the U.S.

1970: Emergence of the Video Industry.

1975: First national Cable Network (HBO).

1977: *Star Wars* released, quietly becoming one of the highest grossing films.

1978: Siskel and Ebert appear on first PBS film review show.

1981: *MTV* launched.

1991: Apple introduces Quicktime digital audio/video technology.

1994: Digital Satellite System (DSS) begins direct-to-home broadcasting in U.S.

1995: *Toy Story* is the first fully computer animated feature film.

1997: DVD video players begin selling in the U.S.

THE PROCESS

THE PEDESTAL

The art of the cinema rests firmly on a square pedestal mounted, so to speak, on four legs: script, **cinematography**, editing, and directing (which includes the quality of the acting). A film stands or falls on the stability of these four legs.

SCREENWRITER

According to Lee R. Bobker, the relationship between a film script and the finished film is unique. In a stage play, for example, the words the playwright puts on paper govern the primary message and overall quality of the play, despite any particular performance of it. But in cinema, the original script may change considerably during the shooting of the raw footage. Bobker explains that "it undergoes many reworkings by people other than the scriptwriter—notably by the director, and to a lesser degree by the editor and the cameraman" (13). In addition, because film is so visually compelling, the film image is completely integrated with the expressive content of the spoken word to the extent that neither can fully exist alone. One reads plays all the time with great interest and pleasure. However, no one but a film historian enjoys reading a screenplay, because too much of the meaning is tied to the moving image. Nevertheless, a poorly written script can irreparably damage an otherwise promising film. In fact, you can often spot a poor script because it usually calls attention to itself.

CINEMATOGRAPHER

Compared to the stage, the key element in the creation of the film image is the filmmaker's ability to control the eye of the audience. The cameraman must draw us into the action and engage both our thoughts and our emotional reactions. The images within the film frame must convey the meaning of the action but also be visually interesting, like a painting. Zeffirelli's *Romeo and Juliet* (1968), for example, contains many still frames worthy of a Renaissance painting in color and composition. The best cinematographers are "artists of the moving image." Controlling the camera (what we see) also means creating a point of view, much like a novelist establishing point of view. In film, the cinematographer must determine both what the viewer sees and how the viewer perceives the reality of what he or she sees. In general, the moving camera renders cinematic space "fluid." Because the camera and the action within the camera frame moves, it "moves" us, it engages our emotions by kinetic involvement in the action.

EDITOR

If the motion picture camera creates fluid space, editing creates fluid time by cutting up and rearranging the raw footage into a series of images that not only tell a story, but create a kind of dynamic rhythm analogous to music. The great early silent filmmakers of the Twenties, the American, D. W. Griffith, and the Russians, Pudovkin and Eisenstein, helped create the original film language by discovering **montage**, the "fluid integration of the camera's total range of shots, from extreme close-up to distant panorama, so as to produce the most coherent narrative sequence, the most systematic meaning, the most effective rhythmic pattern" (Mast and Cohen 71–72). But editing does more than create a rhythmic ebb and flow of images. It enables the filmmaker to control our sense of time passing. To make it seem longer for a person to walk from the front door to the street, for example, the **editor** cuts from the person moving across the porch to some other scene, returning to the person at the same point as the previous shot. To speed up the action, the editor cuts back to the person at a much farther point than real time would have allowed. In this way, time for the filmmaker

becomes as malleable as clay in the hands of a sculptor, and as expressive. Finally, editing contributes directly to the deeper meaning of a film sequence, as Pudovkin and Eisenstein discovered. In their attempts to apply a Marxist **dialectical** pattern to their editing, they discovered that a single image, a man smiling, for example, conveys a different meaning, depending upon what image follows: if a sunset, the smile conveys love of nature; if a table piled with food, hungry anticipation; if a child, parental love; if a hurt child, sadism; if a scantily clad woman, lust, etc. Thus, editing creates significant levels of meaning by connecting significant shots in sequence.

DIRECTOR

Finally, the one person most responsible for the tone and style of a film is the **director**, simply because the director usually has the greatest input and control over the whole process from beginning to end. In fact, the director's work usually precedes that of the writer. Each director has a distinctive style, almost as distinctive as one's signature, but infinitely more difficult to pin down. And once a director establishes a style, it is sometimes difficult to get the public or the critics to go along with a shift to a new direction. Note the problem Steven Spielberg had with his impressive foray into the world of mature films. In *The Color Purple* (1985) everyone expected him to stay with films conceived more from a child's point of view. Or consider the unique rendering of danger and intrigue found in the films of Alfred Hitchcock. There is more to his style than creating dangerous situations where you least expect them, just as there is more to David Lean's style than panoramic shots of deserts and jungles. As you become more sensitive to a director's style, look for his or her treatment of the following: (1) choice of subject matter; (2) the quality of the script; (3) choice of leading actors and the credibility of their performances (the film director, like the stage director, often functions as traffic controller and interpreter); (4) the pace, cadence, and rhythm of the editing and, finally, (5) any other distinctive choices made in any of the many other cogs in the film machine, including background sounds, musical or natural.

CINEMATIC TERMS & TECHNIQUES

There are many techniques which can enhance a film and aid in putting over the intentions of its makers; however, these same techniques, if not used artistically, can draw attention to themselves and become mere gimmicks. The film becomes art when it exhibits integrity, artistic and otherwise, everything contributing subtly to the organic whole. As you read through these techniques and realize that you've seen these in operation for years and just didn't know they had a name, begin to determine what affect each one has on you, the viewer, and why the filmmaker chose to use that particular technique. This alone can greatly enhance your perceptive viewing habits. Soon you will begin to detect the inner workings of the director's mind.

FILM ELEMENTS

Frame: (1) Each still photograph in the series that makes up a strip of film; and (2) the rectangle itself within which the film appears.

Shot: What is recorded by a single operation of the camera (from the command "lights, camera, action!" to "cut!").

Scene: A group of shots with continuous action.

Sequence: A group of scenes forming a self-contained unit.

VARIOUS SHOTS

Establishing shot: Generally a long shot that shows the audience the overall location of the film before moving in on the action.

Long shot: A shot filmed from a distance, showing a broad view of the scene. It is used to "objectify" the action, where the director exercises less control over audience response.

Close-up: A shot filmed up close, showing only a limited view of the scene (only the face, for example). It draws the audience into the action to more directly identify with the action. An extreme close-up generally includes only the actor's eyes or mouth.

Low-angle shot: A shot in which the subject is photographed from below. This makes the subject appear larger than life (typical of Westerns), to "heroicize" the main character.

High-angle shot: A shot taken from above the action. It provides a bird's-eye view, tending to make the characters seem small and vulnerable.

Point-of-view shot: (also called Subjective or Reaction shot): A shot which shows the scene from the point of view of a character (often abbreviated **POV**). Effective in getting the viewer into the skin of the character.

Tracking shot: (also called Trucking or Dolly shot): Generally a **tracking shot** is any shot in which the camera moves from one point to another, either sideways, in or out. The camera can be mounted on a set of wheels that move on tracks or on a rubber-tired dolly or "truck" or it can be hand-held. Also called **Travel shot.** [*Note:* Sometimes one can mistake a travel shot for a zoom if it is moving toward or away from the action.]

VARIOUS CUTS

A **cut** is defined as selecting and joining two shots with a splice. Also, in the finished film, a cut refers to any instantaneous change from one frame to another.

Straight cut: A **straight cut** is a straightforward, unobtrusive joining of two shots or scenes.

Jump cut: A **jump cut** is a sudden jump forward or backward in space or time which has no apparent logical reason. Nothing else in the camera angle or scene has changed.

Match cut: A **match cut** connects two adjacent shots by means of matching similar physical shapes or layouts which appear in each of the two shots, creating a visual (and/or logical) link between them.

Cross cut: A **cross cut** is a common technique (especially in adventure or chase films) of alternating scenes from two or more lines of action occurring simultaneously in different places.

TRANSITIONAL TECHNIQUES

Dissolve: A transition between two shots in which the first image gradually disappears while the second image gradually appears. For a moment the two images blend. This momentary blending is called SUPERIMPOSITION, in which one image is super-imposed over another, like double exposure.

Fade: Another transitional technique that might be defined as a **dissolve** that fades into a blank screen (fade-out) or gradually appears from a blank screen (fade-in). A **cross fade** is a combination of a fade-out and fade-in. Here we see the end of one scene fade out into a blank screen, then quickly fade in again to a new scene. This is usually used to indicate the passage of time or distance.

Wipe: A **wipe** is a transition between shots in which a line passes across the screen in any direction, eliminating the first image as it passes through the frame and replacing it with the next image.

Iris: Iris is a transition between shots in which a circle begins from a single point in the center of the screen and expands to fill the entire screen. It may work in both directions (in or out).

SPECIAL CAMERA TECHNIQUES

Pan: This is movement of the camera from left to right or right to left around the imaginary vertical axis that runs through the camera from top to bottom. A swish pan (or "zip pan") is rapid panning, causing a blurred, disorienting sensation.

Tilt: This is where the camera tilts up or down, rotating around the horizontal axis that runs from left to right through the camera head.

Zoom: This is a shot using a lens whose focal length is adjusted during the shot, either in or out (far to near or near to far). **Zooms** are sometimes used in place of tracking shots, but the differences between the two are significant.

Rack or *Follow focus:* **Rack focus** involves shifting the focus (close or distant) during a shot to direct the viewer's attention from one subject to another as it moves away from or toward the camera. Don't mistake this for a zoom, in which the image stays in focus throughout.

Telephoto: This shot uses a lens with a long focal length that acts like a telescope to magnify distant objects. Its narrow angle of view flattens depth perception.

Slow motion: The raw footage is shot at faster speed (more frames per second than the usual 24) so that when it is projected at a normal rate, the action appears slowed down. This shot is particularly effective in conveying dream states or fantasy or illusion or simply to create a lyrical effect.

Fast motion: The opposite of slow motion, it gives a comic effect, making humans seem to move like robots.

Time lapse: Extreme fast motion created by shooting 1 frame every 30 minutes, for example, so that 24 hours of real time is compressed into less than one minute of film time. Its use makes possible the study of changes too slow for the eye to see, like the blossoming of a flower. The opposite of time lapse is extreme slow motion, which makes it possible to study movements that occur too fast to see, like viewing the impact of a bullet.

Freeze frame: A still shot which is created by printing a single frame several times in succession to give the illusion of a still photograph when projected onto the screen.

MISE EN SCÈNE

Mise en scène is the French term which relates to the visual design and movements within the frame. It encompasses both the staging of the action and the way it's photographed.

MONTAGE (EDITING)

In the United States, the word for putting together the shots of a film is EDITING or CUTTING, while in Europe the term is **montage,** which suggests a building action, working up from the raw material. These two words betray two different attitudes toward the filmmaking process. U.S. filmmakers focus perhaps more on dissection and analysis, while European montage focuses more on the process of synthesis: a film is seen as being constructed (built) rather than edited (cut). **Montage** also has the related meaning of a number of short shots woven together in order to communicate a great deal of information or to create an unusual rhythmical effect (like *accelerando* in music).

EFFECTIVE USE OF SOUND

Natural sounds or even no sound at all can often be more gripping or moving than music. Also, music can be used incongruously or satirically for special effects.

EFFECTIVE USE OF COLOR

Black and white can often be more strikingly dramatic than color. Some filmmakers now jump back and forth between the two or make one merge into the other. Sepia (brownish tint) is sometimes used to create an antique effect, like the **freeze frame** at the end of *Butch Cassidy and the Sundance Kid* (1969).

JUDGMENT

INTRODUCTION

In the process of becoming familiar with the legs of the cinematic pedestal, and being able to recognize the major techniques and their effects, you will start to gravitate toward better films, partly because you will become more critically sensitive to flaws in the script, acting, plot, etc., but also more discriminating. You'll simply expect more and be unwilling to settle for less. The following is a very tentative list of general distinctions between what we might call "commercial" films and "art" films. Don't take these as iron-clad rules, but as generally recognized differences in both motive and effect.

ART VS. COMMERCIAL

When a film is considered an art film, what is it that makes it such? Above all, the art considerations come first. Indeed, it may be a commercial failure because its actors are not "stars." It may fail commercially because of its heavy theme or subtle symbolism or its somewhat literary screenplay, since many movies are aimed at the intelligence of a *fourth grader* (shocking, but true); and it may fail at the box office because its photography or background score or structure is too experimental and, therefore, unfamiliar to a viewer accustomed to the predictable and the conventional. It will, nevertheless, stand up to analysis and repeated viewings and discussions (the way a commercial movie will not) and will, like all great works of art, offer the viewer more each time it is viewed. But also, like all great art, it takes more effort to get in and to get something out of great films, just as it takes more effort to read Tolstoy's *War and Peace* than to read a harlequin romance.

Art films, then, often feature unknown actors, while commercial films feature popular stars; art films often have convoluted plots (it takes a second look to figure them out) or focus on deeper human issues that don't always lend themselves to easy solutions within a two-hour time span; commercial films, on the other hand, frequently go with simple, predictable formulas; art films are usually high on atmosphere (moods created by memorable images), while commercial films go for shock effects; art films often use natural sounds, or even no sound, for dramatic effects, while commercial films often exploit "manipulative music" or theme songs to create predictably sentimental reactions. Art films often fail at the box office because they are difficult to decipher the first time around—they often have unexpected endings, leaving us with unresolved tensions or unanswered questions. And they often move slowly in comparison to the action-packed pace of so many Hollywood blockbusters. Finally, art films are art because they are self-contained, they are "of a piece," a slice of life that haunts us forever after. Many commercial films, on the other hand, seem to have "to be continued" at the end. They continue with usually inferior sequels, not because there is so much more to say, but because the producers have found a formula to pack them in.

SUMMARY

It has been said that commercial films are made for money's sake, art films for art's sake. This does not mean that art films never make money, or that some commercially successful films are not artistic. Some commercial films are very good and, luckily, more and more seem to be artistically sound as well as good investments for the producers. Nevertheless, the huge cost of making movies can adversely effect the corporate decisions that determine quality and longevity.

CONCLUSION

The famous Swedish filmmaker Ingmar Bergman explained why his first movie projector exercised such a riveting appeal on his youthful imagination:

> This little rickety machine was my first conjuring set. And even today I remind myself with childish excitement that I am really a conjurer, since cinematography is based on deception of the human eye. When I show a film I am guilty of deceit. I use an apparatus which is constructed to take advantage of a certain human weakness, an apparatus with which I can sway my audience in a highly emotional manner—make them laugh, scream with fright, smile, believe in fairy stories, become indignant, feel shocked, charmed, deeply moved or perhaps yawn with boredom. Thus I am either an imposter or, when the audience is willing to be taken in, a conjurer. I perform conjuring tricks with [an] apparatus so expensive and so wonderful that any entertainer in history would have given anything to have it. (*Four Screenplays of Ingmar Bergman* 15)

FILM'S PERCEPTUAL IMPACT

Even more dramatically than Bergman himself could foresee, film, together with all of its manifestations (movies, television, videos, DVDs), is in the process of performing a conjuring trick of its own, transforming the world into an image of itself. Its pervasive influence reaches around the globe into nearly every household on earth. The immediate availability of its light-speed messages has transformed the earth into a global village, because the access time of any news has been reduced from months to minutes within the last century. "Whether we like it or not," Panofsky said in 1935, "it is the movies that mold, more than any other single force, the opinions, the taste, the language, the dress, the behavior, and even the physical appearance of a public comprising more than [90%] of the population of the earth (357). This statement is even truer today than it was then.

MOLDER OF VALUES

Surely one would want to know how such a powerful medium molds our perceptions of the world and ourselves! For until we become aware of how the medium works, we will be particularly vulnerable to its manipulative power. We have all been brought up short, realizing after reacting to some segment in a movie or TV program, that we wouldn't react that way in real life: we laugh at suggestive scenes or cheer for the villain. Of course, one of the basic laws of any theatrical involvement is audience collaboration in what Coleridge called the "willing suspension of disbelief." But because film is potentially more gripping than the other arts, it is also more difficult to control our reactions to the actions in any conscious manner. In a very real sense, film, more than any other single art medium, can force an unwilling suspension of disbelief onto its audiences. On a social plane, therefore, films have an even greater power to alter the world we live in. In *Star Wars* George Lucas created a modern myth shot through with epic struggles between good (Obi Wan Kenobi) and evil (Darth Vader). "Fairy Tales," he says, "are how people learn about good and evil, about how to conduct themselves in society" (qtd. in Harmetz 36). Nevertheless, he laments the loss of a moral base in most contemporary films. Whereas earlier in history, religion and myth provided the ethical framework for individual and social behavior, now film, in an unprecedented move, has usurped that role. Says Lucas:

> People in the film industry don't want to accept the responsibility that they had a hand in the way the world is loused up. But, for better or worse, the influence of the church, which used to be all-powerful, has been usurped by film. Films and television tell us the way we conduct our lives, what is right and wrong. When Burt Reynolds is drunk on beer in *Hooper* and racing cops in his rocket car, that reinforces the recklessness of the kids who've been drawn to the movie in the first place and are probably sitting in the theater drinking beer. (Qtd. in Harmetz 36)

ANTIRELIGION

Sneak Previews film critic, Michael Medved, levels an even more serious indictment at the film industry, claiming that Hollywood moguls are overtly hostile to religious values and practices, so much so that they continue to fund financial fiascos like *The Last Temptation of Christ,* not to mention scores of flops about villainous priests, murderous nuns, and greedy evangelists. He concludes in his book, *Hollywood vs. America,* that we are involved in a "cultural battle," a "war against standards . . . a war against judgment" (285).

WE DECIDE

As informed critics, we owe it to ourselves to be artistically and morally discriminating when choosing what to view from among the large offerings available in movie theaters, video outlets, and television programs. Luckily, we are not locked into seeing every outrageous thing the entertainment industry throws out, or throws up. There are many fine films, both here and abroad, waiting to be deciphered, savored, and digested.

SUMMARY AND RECENT DEVELOPMENTS

Film has defined the twentieth century for us, but it is no longer the same medium as we enter a new millennium. The languages of the media (print, film, music, radio, television) are merging into a synthesis called "multimedia." The engineer at IBM who first thought to connect a television CRT (cathode ray tube) screen to a computer may well be considered the godfather of multimedia (Monaco 520). The computer technology that drives this revolution has dramatically transformed the way movies are made, but it took considerable time before the technology was commercially feasible due to the enormous demands moving images and sound placed on processor speed, storage capacity, and communication bandwidth. For example, the memory needed to store 150,000 words of text would only permit one full-screen black and white image on a standard computer screen in the mid-nineties, when multimedia came of age. It is obviously no longer true that a picture is worth a thousand words (Monaco 525).

Film director Michael Ritchie, in an old documentary film made in the early 70s called *Film: The Art of the Impossible,* claimed that "the director forces you to believe things on his own terms, things that couldn't happen in real life at all." He proved his point by drawing lines on the screen of an old Movieola (an editing device from the days of celluloid film strips) to prove that it would have been impossible in a real ski race for Robert Redford to overtake his competitor on the turn in *Downhill Racer* (1969). This trick photography appears almost ludicrous in comparison to the more recent technological wizardry of such films as *Star Wars: Episode II* or *The Lord of the Rings.* Even Robert Zemekis's integration of Toons with real people in *Who Framed Roger Rabbit* (1988) is light years ahead of *Downhill Racer,* even though they are separated by a mere nineteen years of film history. Or consider his more recent classic, *Forrest Gump* (1994), where Forrest is placed into a 60s newsreel shaking hands with President Kennedy. Cinema is approaching virtual reality in its capacity to create incredibly credible fantasy worlds on the screen.

COMMENTARY ON THE ARTS

BERGMAN DISCUSSES FILM-MAKING FROM *FOUR SCREENPLAYS OF INGMAR BERGMAN*

My association with film goes back to the world of childhood.

My grandmother had a very large old apartment in Uppsala. I used to sit under the dining-room table there, "listening" to the sunshine which came in through the gigantic windows. The cathedral bells went ding-dong, and the sunlight moved about and "sounded" in a special way. One day, when winter was giving way to spring and I was five years old, a piano was being played in the next apartment. It played waltzes, nothing but waltzes. On the wall hung a large picture of Venice. As the sunlight moved across the picture the water in the canal began to flow, the pigeons flew up from the square, people talked and gesticulated. Bells sounded, not those of Uppsala Cathedral but from the picture itself. And the piano music also came from that remarkable picture of Venice.

A child who is born and brought up in a vicarage acquires an early familiarity with life and death behind the scenes. Father performed funerals, marriages, baptisms, gave advice and prepared sermons. The devil was an early acquaintance, and in the child's mind there was a need to personify him. This is where my magic lantern came in. It consisted of a small metal box with a carbide lamp—I can still remember the smell of the hot metal—and colored glass slides: Red Riding Hood and the Wolf, and all the others. And the Wolf was the Devil, without horns but with a tail and a gaping red mouth, strangely real yet incomprehensible, a picture of wickedness and temptation on the flowered wall of the nursery.

When I was ten years old I received my first, rattling film projector, with its chimney and lamp. I found it both mystifying and fascinating. The first film I had was nine feet long and brown in color. It showed a girl lying asleep in a meadow, who woke up and stretched out her arms, then disappeared to the right. That was all there was to it. The film was a great success and was projected every night until it broke and could not be mended any more.

This little rickety machine was my first conjuring set. And even today I remind myself with childish excitement that I am really a conjurer, since cinematography is based on deception of the human eye. I have worked it out that if I see a film which has a running time of one hour, I sit through twenty-seven minutes of complete darkness—the blankness between frames. When I show a film I am guilty of deceit. I use an apparatus which is constructed to take advantage of a certain human weakness, an apparatus with which I can sway my audience in a highly emotional manner—make them laugh, scream with fright, smile, believe in fairy stories, become indignant, feel shocked, charmed, deeply moved or perhaps yawn with boredom. Thus I am either an impostor or, when the audience is willing to be taken in, a conjurer. I perform conjuring tricks with apparatus so expensive and so wonderful that any entertainer in history would have given anything to have it.

A film for me begins with something very vague—a chance remark or a bit of conversation, a hazy but agreeable event unrelated to any particular situation. It can be a few bars of music, a shaft of light across the street. Sometimes in my work at the theater I have envisioned actors made up for yet unplayed roles.

These are split-second impressions that disappear as quickly as they come, yet leave behind a mood—like pleasant dreams. It is a mental state, not an actual story, but one abounding in fertile associations and images. Most of all, it is a brightly colored thread sticking out of the dark sack of the unconscious. If I begin to wind up this thread, and do it carefully, a complete film will emerge.

This primitive nucleus strives to achieve definite form, moving in a way that may be lazy and half asleep at first. Its stirring is accompanied by vibrations and rhythms which are very special and unique to each film. The picture sequences then assume a pattern in accordance with these rhythms, obeying laws born out of and conditioned by my original stimulus.

If that embryonic substance seems to have enough strength to be made into a film, I decide to materialize it. Then comes something very complicated and difficult: the transformation of rhythms, moods, atmosphere, tensions, sequences, tones and scents into words and sentences, into an understandable screenplay.

This is an almost impossible task.

The only thing that can be satisfactorily transferred from that original complex of rhythms and moods is the dialogue, and even dialogue is a sensitive substance which may offer resistance. Written dialogue is like a musical score, almost incomprehensible to the average person. Its interpretation demands a technical knack plus a certain kind of imagination and feeling qualities which are so often lacking, even among actors. One can write dialogue, but how it should be delivered, its rhythm and tempo, what is to take place between lines—all this must be omitted for practical reasons. Such a detailed script would be unreadable. I try to squeeze instructions as to location, characterization and atmosphere into my screenplays in understandable terms, but the success of this depends on my writing ability and the perceptiveness of the reader, which are not always predictable.

Now we come to essentials, by which I mean montage, rhythm and the relation of one picture to another—the vital third dimension without which the film is merely a dead product from a factory. Here I cannot clearly give a key, as in a musical score, nor a specific idea of the tempo which determines the relationship of the elements involved. It is quite impossible for me to indicate the way in which the film "breathes" and pulsates.

I have often wished for a kind of notation which would enable me to put on paper all the shades and tones of my vision, to record distinctly the inner structure of a film. For when I stand in the artistically devastating atmosphere of the studio, my hands and head full of all the trivial and irritating details that go with motion-picture production, it often takes a tremendous effort to remember how I originally saw and thought out this or that sequence, or what was the relation between the scene of four weeks ago and that of today. If I could express myself clearly, in explicit symbols, then this problem would be almost eliminated and I could work with absolute confidence that whenever I liked I could prove the relationship between the part and the whole and put my finger on the rhythm, the continuity of the film.

Thus the script is a very imperfect technical basis for a film. And there is another important point in this connection which I should like to mention. Film has nothing to do with literature; the character and substance of the two art forms are usually in conflict. This probably has something to do with the receptive process of the mind. The written word is read and assimilated by a conscious act of the will in alliance with the intellect; little by little it affects the imagination and the emotions. The process is different with a motion picture. When we experience a film, we consciously prime ourselves for illusion. Putting aside will and intellect, we make way for it in our imagination. The sequence of pictures plays directly on our feelings.

Music works in the same fashion; I would say that there is no art form that has so much in common with film as music. Both affect our emotions directly, not via the intellect. And film is mainly rhythm; it is inhalation and exhalation in continuous sequence. Ever since childhood, music has been my great source of recreation and stimulation, and I often experience a film or play musically.

It is mainly because of this difference between film and literature that we should avoid making films out of books. The irrational dimension of a literary work, the germ of its existence, is often untranslatable into visual terms—and it, in turn, destroys the special, irrational dimension of the film. If, despite this, we wish to translate something literary into film terms, we must make an infinite number of complicated adjustments which often bear little or no fruit in proportion to the effort expended.

I myself have never had any ambition to be an author. I do not want to write novels, short stories, essays, biographies, or even plays for the theater. I only want to make films—films about conditions, tensions, pictures, rhythms and characters which are in one way or another important to me. The motion picture, with its complicated process of birth, is my method of saying what I want to my fellowmen. I am a filmmaker, not an author.

Thus the writing of the script is a difficult period but a useful one, for it compels me to prove logically the validity of my ideas. In doing this, I am caught in a conflict—a conflict between my need to transmit a complicated situation through visual images, and my desire for absolute clarity. I do not intend my work to be solely for the benefit of myself or the few, but for the entertainment of the general public. The wishes of the public are imperative. But sometimes I risk following my own impulse, and it has been shown that the public can respond with surprising sensitivity to the most unconventional line of development.

When shooting begins, the most important thing is that those who work with me feel a definite contact, that all of us somehow cancel out our conflicts through working together. We must pull in one direction for the sake of the work at hand. Sometimes this leads to dispute, but the more definite and clear the "marching orders," the easier it is to reach the goal which has been set. This is the basis for my conduct as director, and perhaps the explanation of much of the nonsense that has been written about me.

While I cannot let myself be concerned with what people think and say about me personally, I believe that reviewers and critics have every right to interpret my films as they like. I refuse to interpret my work to others, and I cannot tell the critic what to think; each person has the right to understand a film as he sees it. Either he is attracted or repelled. A film is made to create reaction. If the audience does not react one way or another, it is an indifferent work and worthless.

I do not mean by this that I believe in being "different" at any price. A lot has been said about the value of originality, and I find this foolish. Either you are original or you are not. It is completely natural for artists to take from and give to each other, to borrow from and experience one another. In my own life, my great literary experience was Strindberg. There are works of his which can still make my hair stand on end—*The People of Hemso*, for example. And it is my dream to produce *Dream Play* some day. Olof Molander's production of it in 1934 was for me a fundamental dramatic experience.

On a personal level, there are many people who have meant a great deal to me. My father and mother were certainly of vital importance, not only in themselves but because they created a world for me to revolt against. In my family there was an atmosphere of hearty wholesomeness which I, a sensitive young plant, scorned and rebelled against. But that strict middle-class home gave me a wall to pound on, something to sharpen myself against. At the same time they taught me a number of values—efficiency, punctuality, a sense of financial responsibility—which may be "bourgeois" but are nevertheless important to the artist. They are part of the process of setting oneself severe standards.

Today as a film-maker I am conscientious, hardworking and extremely careful; my films involve good craftsmanship, and my pride is the pride of a good craftsman.

Among the people who have meant something in my professional development is Torsten Hammaren of Gothenburg. I went there from Halsingborg, where I had been head of the municipal theater for two years. I had no conception of what theater was; Hammaren taught me during the four years I stayed in Gothenburg. Then, when I made my first attempts at film, Alf Sjoberg—who directed *Torment*—taught me a great deal. And there was Lorens Marmstedt, who really taught me film-making from scratch after my first unsuccessful movie. Among other things I learned from Marmstedt is the one unbreakable rule: you must look at your own work very coldly and clearly; you must be a devil to yourself in the screening room when watching the day's rushes. Then there is Herbert Grevenius, one of the few who believed in me as a writer. I had trouble with script-writing, and was reaching out more and more to the drama, to dialogue, as a means of expression. He gave me great encouragement.

Finally, there is Carl Anders Dymling, my producer. He is crazy enough to place more faith in the sense of responsibility of a creative artist than in calculations of profit and loss. I am thus able to work with an integrity that has become the very air I breathe, and one of the main reasons I do not want to work outside of Sweden. The moment I lose this freedom I will cease to be a film-maker, because I have no skill in the art of compromise.

My only significance in the world of film lies in the freedom of my creativity.

Today, the ambitious film-maker is obliged to walk a tightrope without a net. He may be a conjurer, but no one conjures the producer, the bank director or the theater owners when the public refuses to go see a film and lay down the money by which producer, bank director, theater owner and conjurer can live. The conjurer may then be deprived of his magic wand; I would like to be able to measure the amount of talent, initiative and creative ability which has been destroyed by the film industry in its ruthlessly efficient sausage machine. What was play to me once has now become a struggle. Failure, criticism, public indifference all hurt more today than yesterday. The brutality of the industry is undisguised—yet that can be an advantage.

So much for people and the film business. I have been asked, as a clergyman's son, about the role of religion in my thinking and film-making. To me, religious problems are continuously alive. I never cease to concern myself with them; it goes on every hour of every day. Yet this does not take place on the emotional level, but on an intellectual one. Religious emotion, religious sentimentality, is something I got rid of long ago—I hope. The religious problem is an intellectual one to me: the relationship of my mind to my intuition. The result of this conflict is usually some kind of tower of Babel.

Philosophically, there is a book which was a tremendous experience for me: Mono Kaila's *Psychology of the Personality*. His thesis that man lives strictly according to his needs—negative and positive—was shattering to me, but terribly true. And I built on this ground.

People ask what are my intentions with my films—my aims. It is a difficult and dangerous question, and I usually give an evasive answer: I try to tell the truth about the human condition, the truth as I see it. This answer seems to satisfy everyone, but it is not quite correct. I prefer to describe what I would like my aim to be.

There is an old story of how the cathedral of Chartres was struck by lightning and burned to the ground. Then thousands of people came from all points of the compass, like a giant procession of ants, and together they began to rebuild the cathedral on its old site. They worked until the building was completed—master builders, artists, laborers, clowns, noblemen, priests, burghers. But they all remained anonymous, and no one knows to this day who built the cathedral of Chartres.

Regardless of my own beliefs and my own doubts, which are unimportant in this connection, it is my opinion that art lost its basic creative drive the moment it was separated from worship. It severed an umbilical cord and now lives its own sterile life, generating and degenerating itself. In former days the artist remained unknown and his work was to the glory of God. He lived and died without being more or less important than other artisans; "eternal values," "immortality" and "masterpiece" were terms not applicable in his case. The ability to create was a gift. In such a world flourished invulnerable assurance and natural humility

Today the individual has become the highest form and the greatest bane of artistic creation. The smallest wound or pain of the ego is examined under a microscope as if it were of eternal importance. The artist considers his isolation, his subjectivity, his individualism almost holy. Thus we finally gather in one large pen, where we stand and bleat about our loneliness without listening to each other and without realizing that we are smothering each other to death. The individualists stare into each other's eyes and yet deny the existence of each other. We walk in circles, so limited by our own anxieties that we can no longer distinguish between true and false, between the gangster's whim and the purest ideal.

Thus if I am asked what I would like the general purpose of my films to be, I would reply that I want to be one of the artists in the cathedral on the great plain. I want to make a dragon's head, an angel, a devil—or perhaps a saint—out of stone. It does not matter which; it is the sense of satisfaction that counts. Regardless of whether I believe or not, whether I am a Christian or not, I would play my part in the collective building of the cathedral.

DISCUSSION QUESTIONS

1. One of the central issues underlying the recent controversy over excessive media sex and violence is whether individuals are personally affected by vicarious identification, indeed, whether we can blame the media for the dramatic increase in social violence and sexual promiscuity. Spend a few minutes reading the following contrastive positions on this issue and then come up with what you think is a personally acceptable position. Give specific examples from your own experience.

   A. Whenever you read a book or have a conversation, the experience causes physical changes in your brain. In a matter of seconds, new circuits are formed, memories that can change forever the way you think about the world. . . . It's a little frightening to think that every time you walk away from an encounter, your brain has been altered, sometimes permanently. The obvious but disturbing truth is that people can impose these changes against your will. Someone can say something—an insult, a humiliation—and you carry it with you as long as you live. The memory is physically lodged inside you like a shard of glass healed inside a wound. . . . As science continues to make the case that memories cause physical changes, the distinction between mental violence, which is protected by law, and physical violence, which is illegal, is harder to understand. (Johnson xi–xii)

   B. People do not mechanically become what they watch. Nor do they watch nothing but slash-and-burn movies. There are demographic, spiritual, technological, economic, and other forces that certainly help explain the causal, nihilistic violence that slaughters more Americans *each year* than the fifty-eight thousand who died in Vietnam. (Gitlin 304)

   C. Give *your* position regarding the impact (positive and/or negative) of the media on society,

A SAMPLER OF GREAT FILMS

I. AMERICAN FILMS

   * *The African Queen* (1951)
   All Quiet on the Western Front (1930)
   Amadeus (1984)
   **An American in Paris* (1951)
   Annie Hall (1977)
   **Babe* (1995)
   **Beauty and the Beast* (1991)
   **Ben-Hur* (1959)
   The Birth of a Nation (1915)
   The Blue Angel (1930)
   Bonnie and Clyde (1967)
   **Carousel* (1956)
   Casablanca (1942)
   **Chariots of Fire* (1981)
   Citizen Kane (1941)
   **City Lights* (1931)
   The Crucible (1996)
   Dances with Wolves (1990)
   The Dead (1987)
   **Decoration Day* (1991)

*These films are not only superbly crafted—they're also feel good movies.

Dr. Strangelove (1964)
*Driving Miss Daisy (1989)
*E. T.—The Extra-terrestrial (1982)
*Fantasia (1940, 2000)
Forrest Gump (1994)
The French Connection (1971)
From Here to Eternity (1953)
Gallipoli (1981)
The General (1927)
The Godfather (1972, 1974)
*The Gods Must Be Crazy (1980)
*The Gold Rush (1925)
Gone with the Wind (1939)
The Grapes of Wrath (1940)
The Great Train Robbery (1903)
Hamlet (1948, 1990, 1996)
High Noon (1952)
How Green Was My Valley (1941)
Howard's End (1992)
The Hustler (1961)
It Happened One Night (1934)
*It's a Wonderful Life (1946)
King Kong (1933)
Lawrence of Arabia (1962)
*The Little Mermaid (1989)
*A Little Princess (1995)
The Magic Flute (1974)
The Maltese Falcon (1941)
*Marty (1955)
*Mary Poppins (1964)
*Miracle on 34th Street (1941)
Moulin Rouge (2001)
*Mr. Smith Goes to Washington (1939)
Nanook of the North (1922)
North By Northwest (1959)
On the Waterfront (1954)
Otello (1987)
The Oxbow Incident (1943)
Patton (1970)
The Pawnbroker (1965)
Psycho (1960)
The Quiet Man (1952)
The Red Balloon (1953)
Romeo and Juliet (1963)
Schindler's List (1993)
*Sense and Sensibility (1995)
*Seven Brides for Seven Brothers (1954)
*Shane (1953)
*Singin' in the Rain (1952)
Some Like It Hot (1959)
*Sounder (1972)

Stagecoach (1939)
Star Wars (1977)
The Sting (1974)
*The Ten Commandments (1956)
They Shoot Horses, Don't They? (1969)
To Kill a Mockingbird (1963)
Tootsie (1983)
Treasure of the Sierra Madre (1948)
*The Trip to Bountiful (1986)
2001: A Space Odyssey (1968)
*The Wizard of Oz (1939)
*The Yearling (1946)

II. FOREIGN FILMS

A. Historical

The Battleship Potemkin (1925)
The Bicycle Thief (1949)
The Blue Angel (1930)
The Cabinet of Dr. Caligari (1919)
The 400 Blows (1959)
Grand Illusion (1937)
Greed (1924)
Jules and Jim (1961)
La Strada (1954)
Pather Panchali (1954)
Rashomon (1951)
The Seven Samurai (1954)
The Seventh Seal (1956)
Stalker (1979)
The Umbrellas of Cherbourg (1964)

B. Contemporary

Au Revoir, Les Enfants (1987)
Babette's Feast (1987)
Cinema Paradiso (1989)
Cross My Heart (1991)
Forbidden Games (1951)
Il Postino (1994)
Jean de Florette (1987)
Life Is Beautiful (1998)
Manon of the Spring (1987)
My Father's Glory (1991)
My Life as a Dog (1987)
My Mother's Castle (1991)
Ponette (1996)
Raise the Red Lantern (1991)
The Tree of the Wooden Clogs (1978)
Un Couer en Hiver (1993)

WORKS CITED

Bergman, Ingmar. "Film Has Nothing to Do with Literature." *Modern Culture and the Arts*. Ed. J. B. Hall and Barry Ulanov. 2nd ed. New York: McGraw-Hill, 1972.

————. *Four Screenplays of Ingmar Bergman*. Trans. Lars Malmstrom and David Kushner. New York: Simon & Schuster, 1960.

Bobker, Lee R. *Elements of Film*. New York: Harcourt, Brace & World, 1969.

Gitlin, Todd. "By Hollywood Obsessed." *The World and I* (December 1992): 301–305.

Harmetz, Aljean. "Burden of Dreams: George Lucas." *American Film* (June 1983): 30–39.

Johnson, George. *In the Palaces of Memory: How We Build the Worlds inside Our Heads*. New York: Vintage Books, 1992.

Katz, Ephraim. *The Film Encyclopedia*. New York: HarperPerennial, 1994.

Mast, Gerald, and Marshall Cohen. *Film Theory and Criticism*. New York: Oxford University Press, 1979.

Medved, Michael. *Hollywood vs. America*. Rpt. in *The World and I* (December 1992): 281–299.

Monaco, James. *How to Read a Film*. New York: Oxford University Press, 2000.

Panofsky, Erwin. "Style and Medium in the Motion Pictures." *Modern Culture and the Arts*. Ed. J. B. Hall and Barry Ulanov. 2nd ed. New York: McGraw-Hill, 1972.

Ritchie, Michael. *Film: Art of the Impossible*. Learning Corporation of America, 1972.

WEBSITES OF INTEREST

American film and society since 1945 — http://books.google.com/books?id=SKPmB5ToawQC&printsec=frontcover&source=gbs_navlinks_s

Scene-by-scene synopsis of the Great Train Robbery — http://www.filmsite.org/grea.html

Video of GTR in 3 parts — http://memory.loc.gov/cgi-bin/query/r?ammem/papr:@filreq(@field(NUMBER+@band(edmp+2443s3))+@field(COLLID+edison))

Howard Suber on the Power of Film — http://www.youtube.com/watch?v=8obFRm8jeCU

Interview with George Lucas on his interest in film — http://www.slashfilm.com/2009/06/23/votd-interview-with-27-year-old-george-lucas/

THE VISUAL ARTS

Unit IV

Cave painting, 15,000–13,000 B.C.
Lascaux, France

INTRODUCTION TO THE VISUAL ARTS

Chapter *14*

INTRODUCTION

We learned in Chapter 2 that Coach "Digger" Phelps's life changed significantly as a result of his discovery of van Gogh's art. Vincent painted with great energy and honesty. His art is accessible to virtually everybody because it speaks directly of dilemmas we all face at one time or another. So we begin our discussion of the visual arts with a noble soul who has gradually become our trusted friend and guide into the strange and wonderful world of artistic creation. Ingmar Bergman has already taken us on a guided tour of his internal life as a filmmaker. Van Gogh can do the same because he left a legacy of letters from which we can see into his tormented mind and out at the world through his steel blue eyes. Consider his description in this letter to his brother, Theo, of the turning point when he decided to give his life to art:

> You must know, Theo, that Mauve has sent me a paint box with paint, brushes, palette, palette knife, oil, turpentine—in short, everything necessary. So it is now settled that I shall begin to paint, and I am glad things have gone so far. Well, I have been drawing a good deal recently, especially studies of the figures. . . . I am now longing to hear what Mauve will have to say. The other day I made some drawings of children, too, and liked it very much. These are days of great beauty in tone and color; after I have made some progress in painting, I will succeed in expressing a little of it. But we must stick to the point, and now that I have begun drawing the figure, I will continue it until I am more advanced; and when I work in the open air, it is to make studies of trees, viewing the trees like real figures. . . . But, Theo, I am so very happy with my paint box, and I think my getting it now,

after having drawn almost exclusively for at least a year, better than if I had started with it immediately. I think you will agree with me in this. . . . For, Theo, with painting my real career begins. Don't you think I am right to consider it so? (Qtd. in Hammacher 69).

WHAT DOES ART REVEAL?

VINCENT AS "EXHIBIT A"

In his short, unhappy life VAN GOGH (1857–1890) wrote nearly a thousand letters, often several a day, and many accompanied with illustrative drawings. Seldom in the history of art has an artist revealed his artistic inner life with such honesty and humanity as Vincent in letters to his older brother Theo. From these letters we see his beginning love affair with painting as well as his earnest ambition to touch others' lives with his art. While his letters reveal his motives for painting, it is the paintings which document the inner nature of the man himself. Van Gogh's paintings are, quite literally, windows into his soul. They are also the petrified remains of the world as he saw it in late nineteenth-century southern Europe.

ART AS WINDOW & MIRROR

Earlier we discussed the idea that the arts place a frame around **reality** and then take some captivating part of the world out of context in order that we might more readily contemplate and savor it. In the case of paintings, the framed canvas provides the window into the special world the artist sees. In every case, the artist leaves out parts, includes other parts, or alters the way the world looks to us, in order to conform to his or her inner vision and unique perception of reality. In fact, every person has an original prism with which to view the world. One of the great values of art is its capacity to allow us access to these alternative views of reality. Imagine each painting you view as both a *mirror* reflecting the artist's soul and a *window* opening onto the landscape of his or her times, coloring the artist's personal style as by a refracting glass.

VINCENT'S INSANITY

Van Gogh's tenuous hold on reality began to loosen in the late months of 1888. His mental condition worsened as a result of some violent quarrels with his companion, Paul Gauguin. One evening in a fit of anger Vincent cut off his left ear lobe with a razor and delivered it to a local prostitute. Theo rushed to Arles in southern France to help, but saw his brother's condition as hopeless. He wrote to his fiancée in Amsterdam on how matters stood:

> It was deeply saddening to witness all this, for from time to time he became conscious of his illness and in those moments he tried to cry—yet no tears came. Poor fighter and poor, poor sufferer. For the time being nobody can do anything to alleviate his suffering, though he himself feels it deeply and strongly. If he had been able to find somebody to whom he could have opened his heart, maybe it would never have come to all this. (Qtd. in Wallace 137)

WHAT IS REAL?

Vincent spent several months, off and on, in a mental institution at St. Remy, France. He eventually attempted suicide on July 27, 1890. He died two days later. Theo died of grief and insanity six months after that. Insanity is sometimes defined as, a mind out of sync with the way things really are. Technically, we are all mildly insane, because each person processes reality somewhat differently, especially artists. As Arthur Koestler once wrote:

> Perception is a part-innate, part-acquired skill of transforming the raw material of vision into the 'finished product.' . . . The ordinary mortal thinks most of the time in clichés—and sees most of the time in clichés. His visual schemata are prefabricated for him; he looks at the world through contact lenses without being aware of it. (376–377)

AN INDIAN PARABLE

The old Indian tale of the "Six Blind Men and the Elephant" dramatizes the fact that each person perceives reality differently. Each blind man attached himself to a different part of the elephant—the side, the trunk, the tusk, the leg, the ear, the tail—and concluded vastly different things about the nature of the elephant. Each argued for his own position: "The elephant is like a wall!" "No, it's like a snake!" "No, a spear!" "No, a tree!" "No, a fan!" "No, a rope!" The wise Rajah helped them realize that each was right in his own way. The blind men concluded: "The Rajah is right. Each one of us knows only a part. To find out the whole truth we must put all the parts together" (21). Can the arts help us assemble the puzzle of reality? If they can, how? If they cannot, why?

A painting is the tip of an iceberg hiding the deep levels of an artist's personality, as well as his or her attitudes about life. Our sensitivity to artistic style is an avenue to those deeper reaches of meaning. Just as one's own style is often imperceptible—how often do we think about how we hold a fork or tie our shoes?—so the artist's choices are often unconscious and instinctive. For that reason it is possible that a perceptive viewer can see things in a painting of which the artist is unaware, like observing the subtle visual cues in someone's body language after having read a book on the subject. So it is with style in the visual arts. Because artistic choices (conscious or otherwise) determine style, our understanding of these choices, such as medium, technique, subject matter, color, **texture,** formal organization, etc., will help in the decoding process necessary to fully "seeing into" the artist's life and times. As you read the next sections, notice how many choices an artist must make and begin to evaluate them as indexes of meaning. Understanding these artistic choices will show you the artist's style, and ultimately reveal the whole artist.

WHAT IS IT?

DEFINITIONS

It would seem that the easiest task before us is to determine what's there. With most works of visual art, this is not a problem: we recognize a painting as a two-dimensional painted canvas enclosed by a frame hanging on a wall. But, as seen with Constantine Brancusi's *Bird in Space,* the task may not be so simple:

> In 1926, [Brancusi's *Bird in Space*] was one of twenty-six sculptures Brancusi shipped from France for exhibition at the Brummer Gallery in New York. The U.S. Customs officials, who examined the objects for duty-free entry as works of art, took one look at *Bird in Space* and saw the similarities it bore to a propeller blade or some other industrial object. They insisted on imposing a commercial import tax on the work, refusing to believe that it was sculpture. (Krauss 99)

Plate 1:
Pietà, 1498–1499,
by Michelangelo.
St. Peter's Basilica, Vatican State

Plate 2:
Pietà Rondanini, 1564,
by Michelangelo.
Castello Sforzesco, Milan

Plate 3:
David, 1501–1504,
by Michelangelo,
Galleria dell' Academia, Florence

Plate 4:
David, 1623,
by Bernini.
Galleria Borghese, Rome

Plate 5:
Creation of Adam, 1511, by Michelangelo.
Vatican Palace, Vatican State

Plate 6:
Mona Lisa, 1503–1505,
by Leonardo da Vinci.
Louvre, Paris

Plate 8:
The Nightwatch, 1642,
by Rembrandt.
Rikjsmuseum,
Amsterdam

Plate 9:
The Swing, 1766,
by Jean Honoré Fragonard.
The Wallace Collection, London

Plate 11:
Liberty Leading the People, 1830,
by Eugene Delacroix.
Louvre, Paris

Plate 12:
Nymphéas (*Waterlilies*), 1920–26,
Claude Monet.
Musée de L'Orangerie, Paris

Plate 13:
The Stone Breakers, 1849,
by Gustave Courbet.
Destroyed during World War II.
Gemaeldegalerie, Dresden, Germany

Plate 14:
Mont Sainte-Victoire, 1904,
by Paul Cezanne.
Museum of Art, Philadelphia

Plate 15:
Starry Night, 1889, by Vincent van Gogh. The Museum of Modern Art, New York

Plate 16:
Guernica, 1937, by Pablo Picasso. Centro de Arte Reina Sofia, Madrid

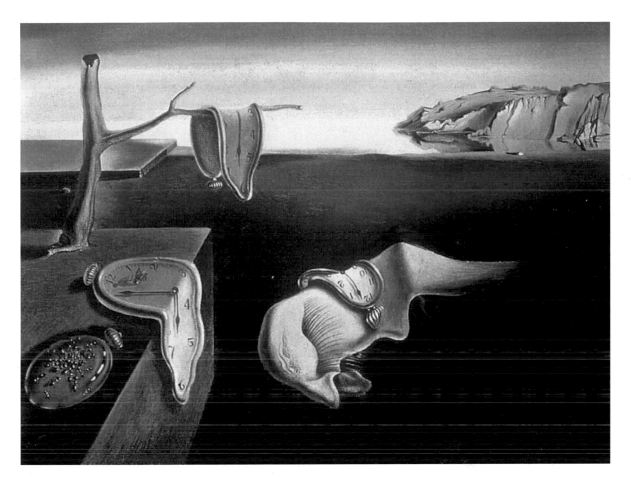

Plate 17:
The Persistence of Time, 1931,
by Salvador Dali.
The Museum of Modern Art,
New York

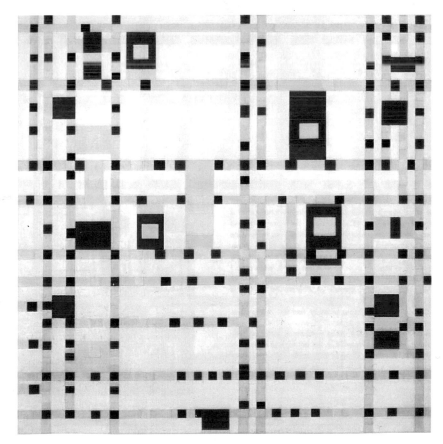

Plate 18:
Broadway Boogie Woogie, 1942–1943,
by Pier Mondrian.
The Museum of Modern Art,
New York

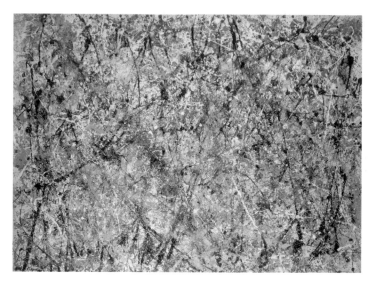

Plate 19:
Lavender Mist, 1950,
by Jackson Pollock.
National Gallery of Art, Washington D.C.

Plate 20:
The Judgment of Paris, 1632–1635,
by Peter Paul Reubens.
The National Gallery, London

Plate 23:
Christ Healing the Sick at Bethesda, 1883, Carl Heinrich Bloch. BYU Museum of Art, Provo, Utah

Plate 24:
Fallen Mounds, 1886, by W. B. Baker. BYU Museum of Art, Provo, Utah

Plate 25:
Grain Fields, 1890, by E. S. Evans. BYU Museum of Art, Provo, Utah

Plate 26:
Forgotten Man, 1934,
by Maynard Dixon.
BYU Museum of Art,
Provo, Utah

Plate 27:
Marilyn Monroe, 1967,
by Andy Warhol.
BYU Museum of Art, Provo, Utah

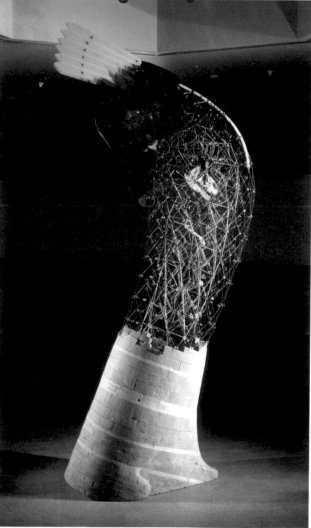

Plate 28:
Seer, 1994,
by Brower Hatcher.
BYU Museum of Art, Provo, Utah

Plate 29:
School of Athens, 1509–1511, by Raphael. Stanza della Segnatura, Vatican Palace, Rome

Plate 30:
The Night Café, 1888,
by Vincent van Gogh.
Yale University Art Gallery

Plate 31:
Miss van Buren, ca. 1891,
by Thomas Eakins.
The Phillips Gallery, Washington D.C.

Plate 32:
La Premier Chagrin (The First Grief), 1892,
by Daniel Ridgeway Knight.
BYU Museum of Art, Provo, Utah

ART = "ANYTHING OUT OF CONTEXT"

The customs people were unable to identify the lump of bronze as a work of art partly because it appeared out of context—in a shipping yard rather than a museum—so they got the wrong cue (Reality really is relative!). The same thing happened to a piece of junk sculpture that had been left near a dumpster behind a museum of modern art, with more disastrous results. The junk man was just doing his duty. It was never recovered. While these definitional mistakes may seem ludicrous to us, many people still wonder, "What is it?" This happens especially with modern sculpture and painting, because the line separating art from life has become so thin. Many California farmers wondered what Cristo's yellow vinyl "Running Fence" was doing stretched across 24 1/2 miles of rolling hills in Sonoma and Marin counties when there was no livestock to corral. But that's the difference between the practical and the artistic mind.

OBJECT/SUBJECT

Thus, there are two answers to the question, "What is it?": What is the OBJECT? (a painting, a piece of sculpture, etc.); and "What is the SUBJECT?" (what does it represent, if anything?). Since the advent of photography, artists have many subjects from which to choose. Again, their choice reflects their value system, preferences, and experience. A sculptor may create a large muscular figure or a small delicate sprite. He or she might do a portrait bust which looks just like the person or make a smooth twisting form which doesn't look like anything in particular, as Brancusi did with his *Bird in Space*. A painter could paint a landscape, seascape, cityscape, or simply chart the figments of the imagination, as the surrealists did. To simplify, subject matter is often categorized into types or *genres*.

GENRES

The most common classifications of subject in paintings are PORTRAIT, STILL LIFE, and LANDSCAPE (the term "genre painting" is also applied to works that depict commonplace situations realistically). Each category elicits different questions. For example, if the picture is a portrait, what are the effects of the posture, position (frontal, three-quarter, profile), facial expression (eye direction), attire (social class), surroundings in revealing the artist's attitudes about the subject? It has been said that every portrait is a self-portrait and that portrait likenesses are connected to the artist's own appearance. If the picture is a still life, what does it reveal about the tenor of the time

(opulence or domesticity)? Are the objects perishable (fruit, flowers) or permanent (jewels, pottery)? Do the objects have symbolic significance (transience, permanence)? If the painting is a landscape, what is the relationship between humans and their natural surroundings, or are there no humans at all? Is nature threatening or inviting? This difference is readily evident in contrasting the landscapes of two Dutch artists: van Gogh and Ruisdael.

WHAT IS IT MADE OF?

The following excerpt taken from the journals of WASSILY KANDINSKY (1866–1944), an early twentieth-century Russian painter, reveals the magical power medium has on the artist's imagination. Kandinsky's fascination with colors, endowing them with personality undoubtedly fueled his efforts to paint the first abstraction in history around 1910, in which a whole painting relies for its expressive effects on line, color, and form alone.

> As a thirteen or fourteen-year-old boy, I gradually saved up enough money to buy myself a paint box containing oil paints. I can still feel today the sensation I experienced then—or, to put it better, the experience I underwent then—of the paints emerging from the tube. One squeeze of the fingers, and out came these strange beings, one after the other, which one calls colors—exultant, solemn, brooding, dreamy, self-absorbed, deeply serious, with roguish exuberance, with a sigh of release, with a deep sound of mourning, with defiant power and resistance, with submissive, suppleness and devotion, with obstinate self-control, with sensitive, precarious balance. Living an independent life of their own, with all the necessary qualities for further, autonomous existence, prepared to make way readily, in an instant, for new combinations, to mingle with one another and create an infinite succession of new worlds. . . . Praise be to the palette for the delights it offers; formed from the elements defined above, it is itself a "work," more beautiful indeed than many a work. It sometimes seemed to me as if the brush, as it tore pieces with inexorable will from this living being that is color, conjured up in the process a musical sound. Sometimes I could hear the hiss of the colors as they mingled. It was an experience such as one might hear in the mysterious kitchens of the arcane alchemists. (371–372)

MEDIUM

Medium is the material basis of any art. There is no art without medium, because "messages" must travel through some material substance, whether it be a moving body in dance, a sounding body in music, or a tactile material of some kind (pigments, stone, clay, etc.) in the visual arts. In painting, medium refers to the various vehicles used to bind and disperse color pigments. Marshall McLuhan coined the phrase, "The medium is the message," by which he meant that media packaging profoundly affects the nature of the message conveyed. But his phrase also underscores an important point in the visual arts: that the artist's choice of medium greatly influences what the work communicates. In other words, the medium is not an inert element, but an active ingredient in the creative process, because it imposes its "material will" on the idea or feeling the artist is attempting to communicate. In fact, some subject matter is beyond the limitations of some mediums. A sculptor can't sculpt a sunset; a painter can't paint an idea. It could even be claimed that the artist "thinks" in terms of his chosen medium. Michelangelo, for example, thought of himself primarily as a sculptor, even though he was highly gifted in other mediums, such as painting, poetry, and architecture. The fact that he conceived his painting subjects three-dimensionally (as sculptures in the round) is clearly evident in his "sculpturesque" **fresco** figures on the Sistine Chapel Ceiling in Rome. Comparing his sculptures to his paintings, there is no doubt about his life-long love affair with sculpture.

THE HISTORICAL EVOLUTION OF VISUAL MEDIUMS

MEDIUM AS MESSAGE

Kandinsky's personal attachment to colors reveals an essential truth about the creative process: artists have an instinctive and joyful urge to mold the material world, to shape matter into pleasing forms, an activity that clearly defines what it means to create. In creating, artists share in the activity of the gods: they give shape to unformed matter. As we have seen, every age refashions its world to fit some pre-conceived pattern of perception. But because medium resists complete control, the material used leaves its indelible mark on the finished product. Mediums expand with the advancements of technology. An artist's first challenge is to push the medium to its expressive limits. Each age exploits and refines at least one medium above all others. The medium of our century is film in its myriad manifestations.

PALEOLITHIC CAVE PAINTINGS

The "artist-priest" worked by mixing water with earth pigments and charcoal. It is conjectured that the images were painted by rubbing natural oxides onto the surface of the stone walls. The artist's imagination seems often inspired by the irregular bulges on the cave walls to create animal portraits which conform to these natural blemishes on the wall surface.

EGYPTIAN WALL PAINTINGS

The 5000 to 10,000 years of experimentation from prehistoric times to Egyptian art didn't mark much progress in the development of the visual mediums per se: the Egyptian tombs are covered with a bewildering variety of different pictures of people and objects, but they were still painted with water and earth pigments. However, the forms had become tighter and more spatially organized on the flat surface, a change some art historians attribute to man's transition from food gatherer to farmer (certainly the landscape changed with the advent of fenced farms full of plowed fields and domesticated animals).

GRAECO-ROMAN ENCAUSTIC

Although ENCAUSTIC was used in late Egyptian times to paint the dead person's portrait on the mummy case, this medium came into its own in classical Greece and Rome. It involves combining pigments in some way with hot wax and burning them into a wood surface with hot irons. Encaustic portraits are very durable and typically quite realistic, although the encaustic is difficult to handle.

EARLY CHRISTIAN MOSAIC

Although not often classified as a major art, MOSAIC was extremely popular as a people's art in the early centuries of the Christian era, particularly in the East (**Byzantine** style). This medium was widely used among the wealthier Romans, who decorated their floors with often outlandish, even pornographic, and sometimes more whimsical designs, like crumbs or small animals. The tradition carried over into the early Christian era as the craftsmen lifted the medium off the floor and placed it high on the walls of the early Christian **basilicas**. The realistic, sometimes trivial, Roman images gave way to flat, bejeweled holy personages, like Jesus, Mary, and processions of martyrs and saints. The design was made of small bits (**tesserae**) of stone, glass, ceramic, or metal set into a ground of mortar. Its flat, jewel-like, surface lent itself to dimly lit interiors where the other-worldly rituals of the early church were performed. The mosaic masters controlled the light reflections by pressing the *tesserae* at certain angles to catch the light when seen from different directions.

ILLUMINATED MANUSCRIPTS

Another important medium in the early Middle Ages was **manuscript illumination**, the handwritten embellishments gracing the margins of medieval books. This art begins early in the Middle Ages with the founding of monasteries in the early sixth century and was rendered obsolete by the invention of printing in the middle of the fifteenth century (1450s). Initially, the blank spaces in the borders of the expensive pages of these early "books" were filled with fanciful little pen drawings or elaborations of the initial letter at the beginning of a paragraph. Gradually, this "monkish graffiti" grew into elaborate miniature paintings (done by the *miniator*) and the initial letters became highly complex designs (done by the *rubricator*). Creating illuminated manuscripts seems to have been the one aesthetic compensation for the austerity of a monk's life. These miniature images later became models for the figures depicted in the larger mediums of medieval churches: the wall murals, the sculpture around the portals, and the stained glass windows.

ROMANESQUE TAPESTRY

TAPESTRY, or the skill of rug-making raised to a fine art (and reminiscent of mosaic's "rise" in status from Roman floors to Early Christian walls), emerged sometime in the Middle Ages as an attempt to add beauty if not warmth to the cold austerity of a medieval castle. The process involves weaving a design with a spindle and colored or metallic threads (the woof) onto the plain, upright threads (the warp). What results is a sort of glorified rug made up of amazingly intricate and sometimes breathtakingly realistic designs painstakingly done over long periods of time. Usually only the very rich (in times past as well as today) could afford them. At their best, they are clear instances of a domestic craft raised to a fine art by consummate artisan skills. One of the most remarkable tapestries in the world, the Unicorn Tapestry, resides at The Cloisters of the Metropolitan Museum of Art in New York City.

GOTHIC STAINED GLASS

As the later medieval masons began to solve the architectural problems of building higher with less masonry, the thick, fortress-like walls of Romanesque churches gradually gave way to the skeletal framework of the Gothic **cathedral**. As a fortunate consequence, the walls were no longer needed to bear the weight and thus opened up space for STAINED GLASS windows, those kaleidoscopic prisms which transformed the worldly sunlight of the French countryside into the celestial radiance of heaven. Because direct sunlight passes through the stained glass, it achieves a greater luminosity than is possible in any other visual medium. The religious implications are clear. Abbot Suger, builder of the earliest **Gothic** structure (St. Denis outside Paris), wrote of the religious ecstasy generated by these windows of heaven:

> Thus, when . . . the loveliness of the many-colored gems has called me away from eternal cares, and worthy meditation has induced me to reflect . . . on the diversity of the sacred virtues: then it seems to me that I see myself dwelling, as it were, in some strange region of the universe which neither exists entirely in the slime of the earth nor entirely in the purity of Heaven; and that, by the grace of God, I can be transported from this inferior to that higher world in an anagogical manner. (Qtd. Panofsky 63–65)

It is clear from Abbot Suger's rhapsodic commentary that the Gothic passion for light had a profound theological significance. Early Christian scholastics like St. Thomas Aquinas conceived of light as the most direct corporeal manifestation of the Divine. As Wim Swaan explains: "Light, which could pass through glass without breaking it, was likened to 'the word of God, Light of the Father, that had passed through the body of the Virgin' and became a symbol of the Immaculate Conception" (48). Stained glass is made by melting silicon sand in a mixture of ashes and metallic oxides to create the different colors. The molten mass is then flattened, cooled, cut to the pattern of a cartoon and joined with wax into lead strips. The details are then painted in black enamel before the glass is raised into the window spaces and anchored in the wall.

RENAISSANCE FRESCO

FRESCO painting was devised as a means of painting directly on walls, ensuring that the picture would survive the ravages of time; when the water-base pigments are applied to the wet lime plaster surface, the colors become a part of the plaster, protected by a waterproof film of crystalline carbonate of lime. The fresco artist usually completed a preliminary sketch (*sinopia*) on the wall before the final fresh plaster surface (*intonaco*) was applied. The artist then transferred the images of a cartoon to the wall and marked the extremities of the figures before painting. Artists had to be unerring and rapid, because the wet plaster dried quickly. If a portion of the final *intonaco* coat remained unpainted at the end of the working period, it was scraped away before it dried, since true fresco must be painted on fresh plaster (*fresco* is Italian for fresh). A large fresco, like Michelangelo's Sistine Chapel Ceiling, was completed in small sections at a time at a cost of great physical labor: he completed the ceiling after almost four years of backbreaking work, its 5,800 square feet of surface peopled by a race of giants—more than three hundred larger-than-life figures in all. He admitted in the midst of his labors: "I strain more than any man who ever lived." When completed, he admitted that "the Pope is very well pleased (Michelangelo 215).

TEMPERA

True TEMPERA, as used for the luminous paintings of the fourteenth and fifteenth centuries in Italy, was made from pigment ground in water and mixed with egg. This surface also dries very rapidly. Tempera is usually applied to a wooden surface prepared with a layer of *gesso* (a mixture of chalk, whiting, plaster, and glue) which is then sanded and polished. The colors are then applied and built up with care to a smooth transparency. Andrew Wyeth, a contemporary American artist, has used this medium extensively. His *Christina's World* is a fine example of the detailed surfaces possible in this medium.

OIL PAINTING

Oil Painting, or painting with pigments mixed with linseed oil and applied to a wooden or canvas surface, began among a select group of great Flemish masters of the Northern Renaissance and has since become the most important visual art medium in the Western world (except now artists use a synthetic material, acrylic, which dries faster). Chief among these innovators was Jan van Eyck, whose famous painting *Giovanni Arnolfini and His Bride* (1434) (see Color Plate 21), represents one of the most stunning instances of rendering reality with photographic precision. From the Renaissance onward, major artists adopted this medium because of its malleability, the richness of its colors, and the expressive range of its effects—it can create jewel-like effects, highly glazed surfaces, or allow a bold build-up of the pigments (*impasto*) in the manner of van Gogh's expressionism. It is fascinating to read Vincent's letter to Theo documenting the moment when he discovered his most characteristic style trait. It was while he was trying to paint some young birch trees in the Dutch autumn. The problem he faced was how to render the depth of color, "the enormous force and solidity of that ground while still retaining the light of dusk":

It struck me how sturdily those little stems were rooted in the ground. I began painting them with a brush, but because the surface was already so heavily covered, a brush stroke was lost in it—then I squeezed the roots and trunks in from the tube, and modelled it a little with the brush. Yes—now they stand there rising from the ground, strongly rooted in it. In a certain way I am glad I have not learned painting, because then I might have *learned* to pass by such effects as this. (Letter 228, Sept. 1882, qtd. in Hammacher 76)

WATERCOLOR

Probably the oldest medium of all, **WATERCOLOR** has only come into its own in more recent times. Transparent water color is made from very finely ground pigment with a binder usually of gum arabic or glue. It gains its brilliance from the application of transparent washes over a white ground (the white paper). Opaque water colors are much the same as transparent water colors in structure but depend on white pigment rather than on the reflection of the white paper for high values. It allows for more controlled handling than transparent water color, but loses somewhat in brilliance and spontaneity. The most commonly used opaque water color is **gouache** (pronounced "gwash").

THE GRAPHIC ARTS

INTRODUCTION

There is a whole series of mediums which grew out of the invention of printing in the middle of the fifteenth century (1450s). These mediums can be reproduced from a "master." There are four basic types of printing processes: relief, intaglio, stencil, and lithograph, based on the manner in which the master image is made.

RELIEF

The most widely used relief process is WOODCUT. The surface of a block of close-grained wood, cut with the grain running parallel to its surface (plankwise), is inked and a design is cut into the surface. The surface is then inked again, a clean paper is applied and the raised portions are pressed onto the paper. The result is a mirror image of the design. The stiffness of the wood creates a bold, powerful, flat effect as can be seen in Leonard Baskin's *The American Indian*. Color prints from wood blocks usually require a separate block for every color to be printed. Sometimes the color areas are superimposed to create additional color mixtures.

The American Indian, *Leonard Baskin.*
Copyright © Brigham Young University, used with
permission of the BYU Museum of Art.

Tomb of the Savior, *Albrecht Dürer*

INTAGLIO

INTAGLIO (pronounced "intalyo," it means "to cut in" in Italian) differs radically from relief. Instead of printing the raised surface (as in woodcut), intaglio prints the indented areas. There are several ways to create this indented surface:

Engraving

Using a sharp stylus (graver or burin), the engraver cuts lines of varying depth and width into the surface of a copper plate, removing a thread-like curl of metal. The lines grow wider as the engraver gouges more deeply into the plate and thinner as he releases pressure or changes the angle of the tool to produce a shallower line. Thus, it is characteristic of the engraved line to swell and shrink in width. Engraved lines are characteristically clear with sharp edges, with the lines often very close together to create the effects of shading. Albrecht Dürer (1471–1528) was one of the early masters of this medium. Notice the intricate linear pattern and subtle shading he created in *Tomb of the Savior.* Our paper currency graphically illustrates the linear precision of this medium.

Etching

Because the design is created by drawing through a resin surface applied to a metal plate and immersing the plate in an acid bath, the lines of an etching, in contrast to engraving, are somewhat fuzzier and freer, like the fluid lines of a pencil drawing. Also the unexposed surfaces are often slightly pocked, due to the acid treatment. One of the great masters of this medium was the Dutch Baroque artist Rembrandt (1606–1669). His *Medea or the Marriage of Jason and Creusa* creates a sense of vast spaciousness framed by dark silhouettes beneath the arches, dramatizing the murderous fury of the scorned Medea lurking in the shadows at bottom right.

Drypoint

This print is made by drawing directly onto a copper or zinc plate with a sharp steel point, i.e., the "dry" *point* from which the process takes its name. Because of the effort needed to "scratch" the surface of the metal plate,

Medea, or the Marriage of Jason and Creusa, *Rembrandt*

the lines of drypoint are stiff, rather straight, and fairly short.

STENCIL

Prints may be made from STENCILS, i.e., pieces of thin metal, parchment paper, or other material resistant to ink or pigment, which are cut and perforated with the desired design. The most popular of these is silkscreen, sometimes called **serigraph.** Originally a cut stencil was attached to a silk-screen and color forced through the unmasked areas onto the paper beneath by means of a squeegee. More recently the areas to be printed are painted on a fine-meshed screen of silk cloth which has been stretched on a wooden frame and treated with a water-resistant medium (opaque glue or varnish). Then the pigment is worked through the parts of the screen not covered by the design. In our century, the modern pop artist, Andy Warhol (1930–1987), made Marilyn Monroe (see Color Plate 27) and

Campbell's Soup famous using this medium. Warhol's repeated silk screening of Marilyn Monroe's stereotypical face reduced her to the inert sameness of a mass product and changed us from interested viewers into unengaged spectators. Warhol's silkscreens want to be "glanced at like a TV screen, not scanned like a painting" (Hughes 348).

LITHOGRAPH

Invented in 1798 by Aloys Senefelder, a Bavarian playwright, this process is based on the principle that oil and water don't mix. The artist draws directly on a specially prepared limestone with a greasy ink or crayon, which is then treated with certain chemical solutions so that the drawing is fixed. When water is applied, the moisture is repelled by the greasy lines, but readily accepted by the porous surface of the stone, which is then inked and printed. LITHOGRAPH is the only graphic medium in which the artist can approximate actual shading. The finished product looks much like a crayon drawing, with the grainy surface derived from the waxy crayon being applied to the porous stone. Honoré Daumier (1808–1879), a French master of caricature, made his reputation by publishing satirical lithographs in *La Caricature* on themes of government corruption and human vanity. His *Aspect du Salon le Jour de l'Ouverture* depicts the caustic reactions of uninformed museum visitors.

Aspect du Salon le Jour de l'Ouverture, *Honoré Daumier*

HOW IS IT PUT TOGETHER? THE ELEMENTS

THE CHALLENGE: BLANK SPACE

Every practicing artist, whether poet, painter, or composer, faces, with each new work, the intimidation of the void: this can be a piece of paper, a blank canvas, or a large piece of lined manuscript paper. In every case, the creator must fill the vacuum with significant form. The opening words that Georges Seurat speaks in Stephen Sondheim's hit musical, *Sunday in the Park with George* (1984), clearly describes every painter's initial challenge: "White. A blank page or canvas. The challenge: bring order to the whole through design, composition, tension, balance, light, and harmony"; not so different from a writer facing a blank sheet of paper. In spite of the difference in medium (visual forms instead of words), the ordering process is quite similar. It involves manipulating the "elements of design," brought together through the balanced tension of lines, colors, and forms, into a harmonious whole.

LEARNING TO LOOK

Becoming visually sensitive to these elements of design marks the threshold over which we must pass to the inside track of understanding what makes paintings great. Ideally, the "inside track" to deciphering the visual language of painting comes from the actual process of painting. This is so because artists, before they can fully exercise their craft, must acquire the special perceptual skill of "seeing artistically." Most people don't understand this unless they have developed some artistic skill, like drawing or painting. Betty Edwards in her popular book *Drawing on the Right Side of the Brain* has reduced the complexity of this process to a shift from the logical linear left hemisphere of the brain to the intuitive spatial right mode. The drawing exercises in her book not only facilitate the mental shift from left to right mode, but also dramatically increase a person's capacity to see as the artist sees. Jewish author Chaim Potok has imaginatively re-created the discovery of this new way of seeing in his novel *My Name is Asher Lev.* When Asher suddenly discovers his eyes can feel as well as see, he says:

> That was the night I began to realize that something was happening to my eyes. I looked at my father and saw lines and planes I had never seen before. I could feel with my eyes. I could feel my eyes moving across the lines around his eyes and into and over the deep furrows on his forehead. . . . I felt myself flooded with the shapes and textures of the world around me. I closed my eyes. But I could

still see that way inside my head. I was seeing with another pair of eyes that had suddenly come awake. (105–106)

MAKING YOU SEE

Reading Potok makes it is easy to realize what Joseph Conrad must have meant when he admitted that his primary task as a writer was "to make you *see*" (225). Words and images belong to a shared heritage of aesthetic expression. Their common genealogy goes back over 2,000 years to the ancient belief that literature and painting were "sister arts" in the family of the arts presided over by the nine muses (daughters of Zeus and Mnemosyne, goddess of memory).

THE VISUAL ELEMENTS

While few of us are willing to take the time to develop these visual skills, just being aware of the elements of art—line, color, texture, form—can begin to open up the visually complex worlds created by the artist's special eye and hand. As we learn to "read" a painting, we will begin to realize that the picture frame is really a window frame opening outward onto the landscape of the past (the artist's present) and inward into the very mind of its creator. This is why the "book of art" has been called the most reliable index of an age.

LINE

The simplest visual element is a point ("Dot" is the name of Seurat's wife in Sondheim's musical). LINE is the extension of a point. Line is, therefore, also a record of action and, as such, endows any visual experience with a certain dynamism by virtue of what the eye does in the presence of line—it moves. In fact, it instinctively travels the "track" of lines to the important places in a painting. A good artist can manipulate this "journey" of our eyes very well. Thus line in the visual arts is the approximate equivalent of verbs in the literary arts: both breathe life into the forms and, in a significant way, create the forms. A predominant interest in line usually categorizes an artist's style as "classical."

There are, basically, three types of line:

1. *Horizontal:* a line of repose, producing a feeling of stasis and tranquility. This effect results from experience: our bodies are horizontal when we are at rest.

2. *Vertical:* a line of potential action, nobility, and upward-striving. Again, we impute to vertical lines such qualities, because these accompany our kinetic

responses to vertical objects in life: trees, telephone poles, church steeples, skyscrapers, etc.

3. *Diagonal:* the line of action, movement, and energy. Diagonal lines trace the abstract patterns of any moving body. Notice the lines formed by a boxer's body preparing to deliver a left hook,

COLOR

If line creates form, color intensifies the expressive content of a painting. In a rather simplistic way we could say that line engages our minds while color engages our emotions. Colors can also create movement, except their movement is almost always oblique (toward or away from us), while lines create lateral movement on the picture plane (although linear perspective draws the eye into an illusory space). For example, some colors tend to *advance* toward the viewer (the warm colors, for example) while other colors tend to *recede* from the viewer (the cool colors). Color has even been given sound properties: some have referred to fluorescent pink as a loud color, for example. In order to understand the function of color in art, it is useful to "dissect" it into its fundamental properties or "attributes." It is generally agreed that there are three:

1. *Hue:* HUE refers simply to the name of the color-blue, red, green, etc. Neither white, black, nor gray have the property of hue because white is the total reflection of all potential hues, while black, in theory at least, reflects none at all (put another way, black absorbs all colors, while white reflects all colors). To clarify their relationships, colors can be arranged on a "color wheel." The PRIMARY HUES (red, yellow, and blue) occupy the first three positions because, as a group, they reflect all elements of the color spectrum, and from them all other colors can be derived. They are basic colors in the sense that none of them can be mixed from any other colors, and no one primary hue contains elements of another. However, when they are mixed, we get the SECONDARY HUES (orange, green, and violet) in their adjacent positions between their two "parent" primary hues. TERTIARY HUES are mixtures of contiguous primaries and secondaries.

2. *Value:* Colors vary, not only according to hue, but within one hue. Red, for example, can be light or dark. A light value of red is pink. The lightness or darkness of a hue is controlled by the amount of white or black mixed with it. When the hues of a whole painting are predominantly dark, we say this painting is "low key." When the overall hues have a lot of white mixed in, we call it "high key," a distinction loosely analogous to the major and minor modes in music. Low key paintings evoke dark, ominous feelings, as in Ryder's *Death on a Pale Horse* (ca. 1910), while prevailing light hues conjure up brighter, more positive feelings toward the subject. Differences in VALUE can create three-dimensional form by contrasts of highlighted and shaded areas, like looking at an object underneath a spotlight. When the contrasts are bold, a dramatic effect is produced, as can be seen in many of the works of the Italian Baroque painter Caravaggio, or the Dutch Baroque painter Rembrandt, or, more recently, Carl Bloch's *Christ Healing the Sick at Bethesda* (see Color Plate 23). We call this kind of exaggerated value contrasts **chiaroscuro,** an Italian term which means literally "light-dark." On the other hand, subtle gradations of value in a painting can create delicate nuances of feeling, even mysterious states of mind, as can be seen in Leonardo's *Mona Lisa* (see Color Plate 6), the most famous face in the world. Her enigmatic smile and the supremely graceful softness of her hands results from a special technique Leonardo developed, called **sfumato** (Italian for "smoky").

3. *Intensity:* INTENSITY refers to the brightness or dullness of a color and can be controlled by manipulating the relationships between complementary hues. Two hues are "complementary" if, between them, they comprise the three primary colors. Thus green is the complement of red because it contains both blue and yellow. **Complementary colors** (situated opposite one another on the color wheel) will dull one another if mixed together (equal parts of each will result in a neutral gray), but will "intensify each other if placed side by side, That is the reason why redheads often wear green—the green makes their red hair even redder. Van Gogh frequently used complementary colors for expressive effect, as in his *Night Café,* 1888 (see Color Plate 30). Of his artistic intentions he wrote to his brother Theo: "[In my picture of the *Night Café*] I have tried to express the terrible passions of humanity by means of red and green" (qtd. in Wallace 113).

SPACE

There are three ways by which an artist can render the illusion of three-dimensional space on a two-dimensional surface: by manipulating value contrasts (noted above), or by making use of linear or aerial perspective. The latter two devices are functions of line and color respectively: lines converging on a vanishing point create the effect of space where there is none, as in E. S. Evans's *Grain Fields* (see Color Plate 25); distant landscapes permeated by a blue haze also suggest distance, reminding us of the effects of the atmosphere on distant objects as in Cezanne's *Mont Sainte-Victoire* (see Color Plate 14). The French have a general term for this visual deception—*trompe l'oeil*, literally "trick of the eye." A major part of our initial fascination with any highly representational painting is the illusion of the "real thing" the artist can bring off. Our awe at the artist's "conjuring" tricks ally us quite closely to some of the earliest art enthusiasts of ancient times.

FORM

Of all the elements an artist draws upon to create a masterpiece, perhaps the most critical is form or organization. Rembrandt was so concerned about the position of one of the figures in his *Syndics of the Clothiers Guild* (1662) that he repainted it several times. Whistler chose to name the famous portrait of his mother *Arrangement in Gray and Black,* even though it is now known almost universally as *Whistler's Mother.* The overall structure of a painting is set early on in the creative process. Some artists even claim that if the first few minutes of laying the groundwork do not work, the result will be flawed. One of our challenges is to see through the surface details to the simpler plan beneath, somewhat like seeing the blueprint behind the finished house, or the skeleton beneath the skin.

TYPES

There are basically two kinds of visual organization: symmetrical and asymmetrical.

1. *Symmetrical:* Symmetrical arrangements in a painting create visual layouts that are generally balanced (left to right; top to bottom). The linear patterns of the forms create different types of symmetry. For example, Raphael's *The School of Athens* exhibits a central focus converging on the horizon point between the two figures under the middle arch. The central objects in Monet's *Impression Sunrise,* the rising sun and the boat, while positioned slightly off center each direction, balance each other by being approximately equidistant from the center. Artists rarely position important objects directly in the center—it creates a static effect. A favorite Renaissance form is the pyramid, especially with portraits (single or group), as seen in Leonardo's *Mona Lisa.* Jan van Eyck's *Arnolfini and His Wife* positions the wedding pair almost exactly within two invisible panels, their heads exactly fitting into a circle that extends outward from the central convex mirror on the wall. Check it with a compass and you'll see how meticulously artists create the geometric "scaffoldings" for their paintings.

2. *Asymmetrical:* There are as many varieties of asymmetrical patterns as symmetrical, although the major difference has to do with off-center focus. Off-center paintings place most of the weight on the right or left of the canvas. For example in Maynard Dixon's *Forgotten Man* (see Color Plate 26), the man is placed to the left, next to a fire hydrant. To keep the design from becoming left heavy, the artist has the curb line slope right and the pedestrians all moving right. These subtle touches not only stabilize the painting visually, but showcase the main subject, the lonely man, ignored and isolated, a mere object like the hydrant on the sidewalk as life passes him by.

DISCUSSION QUESTIONS

1. Briefly explore your own perceptions of reality. How do you see the world? In terms of the sophic/mantic split, are you more analytical or more intuitive? Or a little of both? What has made you that way? Consider the following factors: race, gender, age, nationality, home, parents, friends, religion, education, etc. If you were an artist, what style would you paint in? If you painted a self-portrait, what would it look like? Would it look more like a van Gogh (expressionistic) or da Vinci (classical)?

2. Compare two paintings you like in terms of treatment of similar subject matter (portraiture, landscape, still life, etc.) and then briefly note the major differences. Explain which you prefer and why.

3. On two 8-and-a half-by-11-inch sheets of paper, (1) create a realistic drawing (preferably in pencil) of some recognizable object in your environment, (2) draw a colored abstraction of a feeling (be sure to indicate which feeling on the back of the sheet), (3) draw a "vase-face" by drawing a profile of a person's head on one side of the paper and then try to duplicate all the intricacies of the line on the other side. You will end up with an interesting profile of a vase, (4) create a copy of some interesting line drawing (a Picasso pencil portrait is ideal) by turning it upside down and drawing it that way. Don't turn it right-side-up until you're finished. You will be surprised to see how accurately you have executed the copy. (5)

shade in the negative space around an object (not the chair, but the air around it. This will teach you a few things:

a. It will help you understand the difficulty of the creative process.

b. It will help you understand how abstract designs can evoke emotions and meanings.

c. It may make you want to go out and develop your native artistic talents.

The ultimate goal to these seeing/drawing exercises is to begin to see spatially (acutely) rather than passively (practically). If you take this exercise seriously, you will begin to understand what Asher Lev experienced in Potok's novel: "I could feel my eyes moving across the lines around his eyes. . . . I felt myself flooded with the shapes and textures of the world around me. . . . *I was seeing with another pair of eyes*" (emphasis added).

WORKS CITED

Conrad, Joseph. "The Preface." *Nigger of the "Narcissus."* In *Heart of Darkness.* Ed. Robert Kimbrough. 3rd ed. New York: Norton, 1988.

Edwards, Betty. *Drawing on the Right Side of the Brain.* New York: St. Martin's, 1979.

Hammacher, A. M., and Renilde. *Van Gogh: A Documentary Biography.* London: Thames and Hudson, 1982.

Hughes, Robert. *The Shock of the New.* New York: Alfred A. Knopf, 1981.

Kandinsky, Wassily. *Kandinsky: Complete Writings on Art.* Vol. I. Boston: G. K. Hall, 1982.

Koestler, Arthur. *The Act of Creation.* London: Hutchinson, 1976.

Krauss, Rosalind E. *Passages in Modern Sculpture.* New York: Viking, 1977.

Michelangelo. *Michelangelo: The Sistine Chapel Ceiling.* Ed. Charles Seymour, Jr. New York: Norton, 1972.

Panofsky, Erwin, ed. *Abbott Suger.* Princeton, NJ: Princeton University Press, 1946, 1979.

Potok, Chaim. *My Name Is Asher Lev.* New York: Knopf, 1972.

Quigley, Lillian. *The Blind Men and the Elephant.* New York: Charles Scribner's Sons, 1959.

Swaan, Wim. *The Gothic Cathedral.* 1969. London: Omega Books, 1988.

Wallace, Robert. *The World of Van Gogh.* New York: Time-Life Books, 1969.

WEBSITES OF INTEREST

Case of Louis Wain: how our brain affects how we see — http://www.cerebromente.org.br/gallery/gall_leonardo/fig1-a.htm

Basic Psychology of Perception — http://allpsych.com/psychology101/perception.html

Cognitive Psychology: Sensation and Perception — http://psy.rin.ru/eng/article/8-101.html

Process of Stained glass — http://www.allthingsukrainian.com/Glass/StainedGlass1.htm

Process of Lithography — http://gould.australianmuseum.net.au/lithography/lithography_process.htm

Process of Silkscreen — http://www.reuels.com/reuels/Silk_Screen_Printing_Instructions.html

Art Sites by Mark Burns — http://www.getty.edu/art/gettyguide/

http://www.artlex.com/

http://www.metmuseum.org/toah/

http://www.learner.org/resources/series1.html

http://www.pbs.org/art21/

4/30   Canyon   J. Roman Andrus

Canyon. *J. Roman Andrus, Copyright © Brigham Young University, courtesy BYU Museum of Art.*

FORM, CONTENT, AND STYLE IN PAINTING
■Chapter 15

I. WHAT DOES IT MEAN?

Is a chair for seeing or for sitting? It depends upon whether you're an artist or whether you're tired. Alfred North Whitehead, the great English mathematician and philosopher, made an important point about visual meaning that has little to do with the practical considerations of knowing that a chair is something to sit on:

> We look up and see a coloured shape in front of us and we say—there is a chair. But what we have seen is the mere coloured shape. Perhaps an artist might not have jumped to the notion of a chair. He might have stopped at the mere contemplation of a beautiful color and a beautiful shape. But those of us who are not artists are very prone, especially if we are tired, to pass straight from the perception of the colored shape to the enjoyment of the chair. (Whitehead, qtd. in Read 11)

VISUAL MEANINGS

Meaning in any but the verbal arts (poetry and prose) is problematical, because we normally associate "meaning" with that which can be explained with words: "Is that what you *mean?*" But every art has meaning (purpose or intent): pure musical meaning resides in its tonal relationships and formal properties (when not accompanied by words); meaning in dance comes from the artistic elaboration and refinement of basic gestures; architectural meaning lies in the tension between form and function; the meaning in a painting derives from the interplay of the visual elements, the title, and all the biographical and cultural connections the artist has built into his work.

POLAR CONTRASTS

Since the basic visual elements are the "tool box" of all visual communication, it is useful to begin with a search for contrasts between them: DOT, the minimal visual unit, functions as the pointer and marker of space; LINE is the fluid articulator of forms found in endless variations of circles, squares, triangles, planar and three-dimensional; COLOR is the coordinate of tone (light/dark) and intensity (bright/dull) and maker of temperature, sound, and space, the most emotional and expressive visual element; and FORM is the articulator of visual unity (Dondis 15).

VISUAL LITERACY

Whitehead's quote argues for a formalistic approach to an object, to see a red chair as an interesting color and form *before* we jump to an enjoyment of its function. In our daily lives, this aesthetic stance is not very natural, nor very useful. But in the world of art, it is essential, because artistic value and meaning reside primarily in the configurations (patterns) of the visual elements (line, color, and form), just as meaning in verbal discourse depends upon the way you "place your words." Perhaps this is why many people don't enjoy visiting museums. It takes effort to see things this way. Whitehead concludes that the artist has "acquired this facility of ignoring the chair at the cost of great labour" (qtd. in Read 12).

In our society at large, there has been a growing effort to enlarge the definition of literacy. Rudolf Arnheim's pioneering efforts in fostering visual literacy in *Art and Visual Perception*, E. D. Hirsch's recent controversial study of *Cultural Literacy*, and John Allen Paulos's book on mathematical illiteracy, *Innumeracy*, represent some notable examples of the trend toward a broader definition of literacy, reflecting an awareness of broader definitions of human intelligence. For some reason, acute visual awareness is considered either beyond the control of the untalented or immediately obtainable. Both assumptions are wrong. According to Donis A. Dondis, the process of learning to make sense of the visual elements takes as much time as learning the ABCs, perhaps longer, because "visual information is more complicated and broader in its definitions and associative in its meanings" (183). And yet, words and images are closer kin than we might suppose, since they shared equal billing in the emergence of language itself. Arthur Koestler observed in *The Act of Creation:* "Thinking in concepts emerged from thinking in images through the slow development of the powers of abstraction and symbolization, just as the phonetic script emerged by similar processes out of pictorial symbols and hieroglyphics" (quoted in Dondis 8).

FORMALISM & CONTEXTUALISM

To simplify a very complex and intuitive process, it may be helpful to approach visual meaning from two different critical stances: **FORMALISM** and **CONTEXTUALISM.** These terms represent two quite distinct ways of looking at something and relate generally to critical approaches in the other arts as well, particularly literary criticism: the New Critics are rigorous formalists (they scrutinize only what is in the text itself); the Freudians are contextualists (they focus on psychological connections outside the text). We shift back and forth between these two visual orientations every day. For example, you probably don't remember the color or shape of your toothbrush. You're only interested in its use (contextualism). But if you lose it and get another of a different color and shape, each time you brush your teeth, you're aware of the differences (formalism). The practical and mundane has been supplanted by the aesthetic, at least until you get used to it. This also happens with letters of the alphabet in commercial logos: the shape, size, color, and form of the letters of the company name are virtually invisible until they are modified by the commercial artist into some unique arrangement that catches the eye and makes us remember to buy the product or service. In a more complex way, you do the same thing when viewing a painting. At first you are aware of the subject, say a landscape, because of the title and because it has rolling hills, sky, clouds, etc. (contextualism). But repeated scrutiny can lead to a growing awareness of how the colors and forms of the earth and sky interact to create a pleasing visual unity (formalism).

Formalism

In addition to what you learned to this point about the function and effect of the visual elements of art (line, color, and form), certain basic principles of design govern their formal unity and create their visual meaning. All meaning (visual, verbal, experiential) exists in the context of polarities. How could we understand hot without cold, light without dark, sweet without bitter? Similarly in the visual domain, "unity in diversity," as the ancients formulated it, or "harmony and contrast" as Dondis prefers, provide the paired opposites upon which visual meaning is built. As in music, where the last few bars provide "closure" or the completion of the harmonic tensions in the preceding phrases, so in ferreting out meaning in a painting. Contrast is the vital force leading to a comprehension of the whole. "Gestalt" psychology has helped us visualize wholes from the parts (*Gestalt* is German for form). As von Ehrenfels points out, "if each of twelve observers listened to one of the twelve tones of a melody, the sum of their experience would not correspond to what would be perceived if someone listened to the whole melody" [qtd. in Dondis, 151. Our objective in formalist criticism is to find the unity in the diversity of the elements strewn throughout the canvas.

Contextualism

Two invaluable sources of meaning outside the work itself come from the Bible and Greek mythology. Many people hate opera partly because they can't understand the sung text or are unable to follow the plot. A similar frustration occurs when going to a museum for the first time and being unable to make sense of the titles under each painting, as, for example: *The Judgment of Paris,* or *Execution of the Third of May, 1808,* or *Judith and Holofernes* or, heaven forbid, *Saturn Eating His Children.* Most people's education is deficient in the very ground from which artists, writers and composers have mined their richest veins of ore: Greek myth, biblical narrative, and world history. It won't be possible in the short space provided below to fully resolve these deficiencies, but we can begin to chart the territory, learn some basic terms, and become familiar with two main sources of art: classical myth and biblical symbols.

THE POWER & NECESSITY OF MYTH

MYTHOLOGY

When someone says that something is "mythical," he is probably implying that it is incredible (untrue).

However, in its original usage, the word *myth* (from the Greek *mythos*) meant simply "anything delivered by word of mouth." Later it came to denote a story or spoken narrative and was related to the Latin *fabula*, legend, or MYTH that included moral tales like Aesop's *Fables* as well as narratives explaining the origins of the earth, the heavens, and man. In an even broader sense, myth can be viewed as the "pattern of belief" of a people, a poetic record of communal relationships that cements them to each other and to their cultural heritage. Thus, according to Robert Graves, myth has two main functions: (1) to answer fundamental questions about our relationship with the universe, the kinds of questions children often ask, like "Who made the world? Who was the first person? Where do we go after death?" etc.; and (2) to justify an existing social system and account for its rites and customs (Graves v). Thus, myths, while usually not literally true, often contain seeds of deeper truths about the people who created them than any modern sociological or anthropological study could uncover. Herein lies a paradox about myths in particular, and about the arts in general.

MYTHICAL "TRUTH"

In comparing poetry to history in his *Poetics,* Aristotle favored poetry as a "higher thing . . . for poetry tends to express the universal, history the particular" (68). In other words, poetry, by drawing upon the universalizing power of the imagination, brings us closer to the way things really are than merely recounting the "facts." Applied to art, Picasso once said: "Art is not truth. Art is a lie that makes us realize truth" (qtd. in Ashton 21). So it is with myth. The Western world has given its allegiance to scientific evidence. Where this evidence conflicts with older mythic explanations, the latter is often thrown out. A telling example is the debate over what to teach in the public schools, creationism or evolution. The loss of mythic explanations, what Joseph Campbell calls "symbolic forms," poses a "serious danger" to society, for it leads to uncertainty, disequilibrium, and finally moral disintegration. To what should one be loyal, he asks, to the "supporting myths of our civilization or to the 'factualized' truths of . . . science?" (9) His answer: we need both traditions working in tandem to gain a complete picture of our outer and inner worlds. But of the two, the mythical is more vital to our wholeness. Science does not and cannot pretend to be "true" in any absolute sense. It is by definition tentative ("true" until more "facts" come in), while myth nourishes our psyches and helps us to integrate our lives.

By conducting a dialogue with these inward forces (personal dreams and social myths), we can come to terms with our own wiser, inward selves. Analogously, the society that cherishes and keeps its myths alive will be nourished from the richest strata of the human spirit (Campbell 13). To recognize some of the more important Greek myths, see Appendix II: *Sources of Art.*

THE IMPORTANCE OF SYMBOLS

DEFINITION

The paradoxical nature of myth provides an indirect parallel to the meaning and use of symbols in art. On a literal level, a SYMBOL is something that is itself and yet stands for something else, as the letters a-p-p-1-e form a word that stands for a round red thing you eat, or a flag as a piece of colored cloth that stands for a nation. All language is symbolic in this sense. But when language attempts to go beyond the literal meaning of everyday communication, symbols, like myths, take on an added figurative significance, thereby becoming more universal. Poetry tends to draw more heavily on figures of speech to suggest meaning that goes beyond the obvious. In the same way, symbols provide access to the deeper, richer, truer meanings in visual art, and this is especially true of religious art. To recognize some of the more important biblical symbols in art, see Appendix II: *Sources of Art.*

FORMALISM & CONTEXTUALISM APPLIED

FORMALISM

In the FORMALIST way of seeing, the viewer attends to line, color, and form alone by looking for artistic qualities separate from the larger context of the outside world. Such a viewer responds to the sensuous qualities of the work as object, rather than considering its history, the artist's life and moral values, etc. The following is a formalist analysis of van Gogh's *The Night Café* (see Color Plate 30) by Jerry Coulter, who argues that "all that is necessary is that we look at the work of art. Knowing who did it or where it came from might be interesting, but it is not necessary to our responding to the work" (qtd. in Bersson 10):

> The most powerful element in this small painting is color. The color is acidic. It has a strength and intensity that's unpleasant. The light and color that emanate from the room convey tension and unease. One doesn't have to know about van Gogh's personal life or his artistic intentions to feel these emotions. They are embodied in the

color relationships. The value [light/dark] contrasts in *The Night Café*—light yellows to dark reds and blue-greens—are very strong although it's not a value-oriented painting in the traditional sense. Then there are the discordant contrasts of the reds against the greens. All of these contrasts create a tension and excitement.

When one looks at the material itself—the way the paint is put on in rough, heavy textures—there's a kind of anxiety in it. There's a scratching, almost flailing in some places as opposed to a fluid, tender touching of brush to canvas. And although there is control, there seems to be a psychotic intensity behind it. It's all put down so excitably, scratched into or thrust onto the picture surface.

Animated by the intense, unpleasant color, the space in the painting feels almost claustrophobic. The perspective of the interior leads the eye to a little yellow opening in the back of the room which appears to be electrically hot. It's not the kind of place one would enter to calm down. It has an electric anxiety [and] is the brightest, hottest spot in the entire picture. It moves toward the eye although . . . it's supposed to be the area most distant from us. Yet another incompatibility and source of tension.

In keeping with these distortions of space and color, the lines in the back of the painting are as thick and strong as the lines in the foreground. That doesn't make sense. So again one gets the feeling that the space is not right. There's something wrong with the space, and although the discrepancies are relatively subtle from a realistic point of view, one feels a tension in it. . . .

The painting's overall composition, characterized as it is by contrast, variety, and a dynamic asymmetrical balance, strengthens the feeling generated by the individual elements [line, color, and form].

What is really interesting about *The Night Café* is that it is so small [28 1/2 by 36 1/2 inches] and yet so powerful. I think that's one of the charms of van Gogh's paintings. They're so small and intimate, yet when one is drawn into them, their intensity sends you reeling. That's the kind of tension and psychological power that characterizes van Gogh's art. (Bersson 10–14)

CONTEXTUALISM

A CONTEXTUALIST, on the other hand, would be more interested in the circumstances out of which *The Night Café* emerged. We have already learned of the sad conditions of van Gogh's personal life, thwarted on every side in his attempts to develop loving relationships with others or to express his pent-up emotions in socially acceptable ways. In the following excerpt from his letters to his brother Theo, he reveals some of his expressive intentions:

Then to the great joy of the landlord, of the postman whom I had already painted, of the visiting night prowlers and of myself, for three nights running I sat up to paint and went to bed during the day. I often think that the night is more alive and more richly colored than the day.

Now as for getting back the money I have paid to the landlord by means of my painting, I do not dwell on that, for the picture is one of the ugliest I have done. It is the equivalent, though different, of the "Potato Eaters."

I have tried to express the terrible passions of humanity by means of red and green. The room is blood red and dark yellow with a green billiard table in the middle; there are four citron-yellow lamps with a glow of orange and green. Everywhere there is the clash and contrast of the most disparate reds and greens in the figures of little sleeping hooligans, in the empty, dreary room, in violet and blue. The blood-red and the yellow-green of the billiard table, for instance, contrast with the soft tender Louis XV green of the counter, on which there is a pink nosegay. The white coat of the landlord, awake in a corner of that furnace, turns citron-yellow, or pale luminous green. (Qtd. in Bersson 14)

Van Gogh's explanation sheds invaluable light on his expressive purposes in this painting, while at the same time carefully delineating the nature and function of the visual elements, color in particular. This leads us to the inescapable conclusion that neither approach is self-sufficient, that formalism and contextualism are best seen as *complementary critical strategies* and should be used together in any critical analysis of a painting.

A UNIFIED APPROACH

The following excerpt from Rudolf Arnheim's *Art and Visual Perception* illustrates the insight possible from combining the two approaches. Michelangelo's *The Creation of Adam* (see Color Plate 5) from the Sistine Chapel Ceiling fresco expresses the act of creation on both levels of meaning with great power: the contextual (biblical) and the formal, where the lines create both contrast and continuity in the figures of God and Adam; they both help us see the relationships and experience the pattern of the creative process itself.

The "story" of Michelangelo's *Creation of Adam,* on the ceiling of the Sistine Chapel in Rome, is understood by every reader of the book of Genesis. But even the story is modified in a way that makes it more comprehensible and impressive to the eye. The Creator, instead of breathing a living soul into the body of clay—a motif not easily translatable into an expressive pattern—reaches out toward the arm of Adam as though an animating spark, leaping from fingertip to fingertip, were transmitted from the maker to the creature. The bridge of the arm visually connects two separate worlds: the self-contained compactness of the mantle that encloses God and is given forward motion by the diagonal of his body; and the incomplete, flat slice of

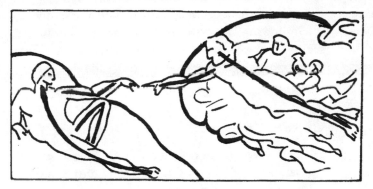

the earth, whose passivity is expressed in the backward slant of its contour. There is passivity also in the concave curve over which the body of Adam is molded. It is lying on the ground and enabled partly to rise by the attractive power of the approaching creator. The desire and potential capacity to get up and walk are indicated as a subordinate theme in the left leg, which also serves as a support of Adam's arm, unable to maintain itself freely like the energy-charged arm of God.

Our analysis shows the ultimate theme of the image, the idea of creation, is conveyed by what strikes the eye first and continues to organize the composition as we examine its details. The structural skeleton reveals the dynamic theme of the story. And since the pattern of transmitted, life-giving energy is not simply recorded by the sense of vision but presumably arouses in the mind a corresponding configuration of forces, the observer's reaction is more than a mere taking cognizance of an external object. The forces that characterize the meaning of the story come alive in the observer and produce the kind of stirring participation that distinguishes artistic experience from the detached acceptance of information. (458–460)

Just as art historians employ x-ray photographs to plumb beneath the surface of famous paintings to detect the inner workings of the creative process, so we as viewers must be adept at detecting the "scaffolding" of a painting, for it often provides clues, not only about how the parts of the work fit together, but about its meaning and ultimate significance. In this we are a bit like the archeologist who digs out ancient foundations and sifts through pottery shards to reconstruct a whole **civilization.**

II. HOW DOES IT MEAN? STYLE

WHAT IS STYLE?

Comte Georges Louis Leclerc de Buffon, an eighteenth-century French naturalist, penned a very famous dictum about style: *"Le style est l'homme même"* ("Style is the man himself"), by which he meant that style is made up of the outward signs of what's inside a person—his or her thoughts, feelings, values, etc. When applied to art in general we can say that style reflects who the artist really is, the unique imprint that personality exerts on a person's creative efforts. Style also mirrors an artist's skill and depth of character, a vital source of a great artist's universal appeal.

THE ARTIST AS OBSERVER

The layered onion provides another useful metaphor for defining an artist's style. The surface level reflects the artist's interpretation of reality. Not only will the artist's style gravitate toward one of the artistic expressions of human duality—classic or romantic—but it will manifest itself as a kind of "handwriting," for it is primarily instinctive and unconscious. The word *style* derives from the Latin *stilus,* an instrument for writing on wax tablets in ancient times. Notice how the characteristic "signatures" of Renoir, Seurat, and Picasso embody in miniature the overall linear expression and patterning of their paintings.

THE SENSUOUS   *Renoir*

THE INTELLECTUAL   *Seurat*

THE EMOTIONAL   *Picasso*

THE ARTIST AS COMMENTATOR

Here the artist reveals his or her conscious response to the conditions of the world by finding new ways of presenting his or her chosen subject. On this level, style differences exist on a continuum between the extremes of Realism and Abstractionism, between attempts to imitate the world as precisely as possible and creating a unique world of one's own. Moving from left to right on this continuum marks degrees of progressive distortion of the natural image one sees in the real world.

THREE STYLES

This level introduces us to three new style terms—REALISM, EXPRESSIONISM, and ABSTRACTIONISM. The term **realism** generally refers to paintings which look like windows onto the real world of appearances. This style appeals to the eye; it transfixes our gaze by offering an artificial semblance of reality. We sometimes have a difficult time believing that an artist could bring off such a credible representation with oil-based pigments on a flat surface. But if photographic realism were the sole criterion of artistic greatness, great art would be a stunt, more at home in the circus than in a museum. As artists expand their expressive capabilities, they often find it necessary to distort for expressive effect.

SUBJECT MATTER VS. EXPRESSIVE CONTENT

Here we must distinguish between two terms: "subject matter" and "expressive content." The former defines *what* is depicted; the latter, *how* the artist treats the subject. William Harnett's *The Old Violin* (1886) fascinates us by its photographic accuracy, situated on an antique door surrounded by a newspaper clipping, a letter, and a sheet of music. But the feeling for the high-pitched sounds and rapid cadenzas of a violin virtuoso are better captured in Raoul Duty's *The Yellow Violin* (1949), with its loose, linear filigree patterns corresponding to the sketchy sixteenth-note notation on the music sheet. Moving farther to the right on our distortion scale, we come to Georges Braque's *Musical Forms* (1913), a late Cubist painting that employs COLLAGE ("gluing" extraneous materials on the canvas surface) to create a nearly abstract design from the straight and curved lines of the violin, but reassembled at will by the painter's imagination. This kind of abstracting from reality tends to appeal more to the mind than to the eye (**realism**) or the emotions (**expressionism**).

All of the style terms we have used so far are what we might call "generic." They refer to general stylistic tendencies of artists throughout history, approaches to the world of appearances that recur time and again in different eras. But some of these terms are also attached to specific time periods. In this case, they define a discrete style and are, for that reason, usually capitalized to help us distinguish them from the more generic use above.

THE ARTIST AS INTERPRETER

As the artist interprets his world through his own original lens, his or her work reflects the views and values of the era in which they lived. On this deeper level, particular stylistic designations (isms) have historical meaning and can be fully understood only within that context. "The time a work of art was made has everything to do with the way it looks—with, in one key term, its *style*. In other words, the style of a work of art is a function of its historical period. . . . It is a fundamental working hypothesis of art history that works produced at the same time will generally have common stylistic traits." (Gardner 3). The following list outlines the most commonly used sequence of historical styles, with their dates, a brief description, and a work that illustrates the traits of each style:

CLASSICAL

Hellenic Greek: (fifth century B.C. Athens): idealized, rational; emphasis on beauty, form, order, and perfection; clean, simple lines.

Hellenistic Greek: (fourth and third centuries B.C., Pergamon, Turkey): realistic to the point of exaggeration; emotional; turbulent; overly dramatic and decorative.

Roman: (second century B.C. to third century A.D., Rome): realistic, down-to-earth, yet monumental; unoriginal, practical and utilitarian.

MEDIEVAL

Early Roman Christian: (Early fifth to eighth centuries, A.D. western Europe): simple, plain, stylized, flat; its architecture unadorned except for occasional mosaics borrowed from the Byzantine style.

Byzantine: (Late fifth and sixth centuries A.D., Byzantium, Constantinople, or Istanbul, Turkey): otherworldly, shimmering and jewel-like, flat and highly symbolic; its domed architecture and intricate, nonhuman sculptural designs recall the Arabic Middle East,

Romanesque: (eleventh and twelfth centuries, western Europe): "Roman-like" in its weightiness and use of the *rounded* arch; the sculpture is crude, yet playfully charming in its distorted, often child-like figures.

Gothic: (twelfth and thirteenth centuries, western and southern Europe): mystical, upward-striving; characterized by the *pointed* arch; severe, yet ornate, moving toward realism.

MODERN

Renaissance: (fourteenth and fifteenth centuries, western Europe): classical, humanistic, optimistic; a synthesis of Greek symmetry and idealism with Roman realism and worldliness.

Baroque: (sixteenth and seventeenth centuries, western Europe): grand, theatrical, emotional; dramatic with often swirling lines, emphasizing contrast and emotional extremes.

Rococo: (Early eighteenth century, mostly French): delicate, feminine, pastel, excessively ornamental with shell motifs and a fixation on love trysts.

Neoclassicism: (Late eighteenth century, Europe and America): exquisitely controlled lines, but often with overly faithful copying of classical formulas; typically static and unoriginal.

Romanticism: (nineteenth century, Europe and America): colorful, exotic, dynamic, nostalgic; longing for nature, the medieval, and the unattainable. Its motto: "Anywhere but here; anytime but now."

Realism: (Mid-nineteenth century, western Europe, mainly France): focus on minute description of the world; subject matter drawn from common life; in Naturalism, infected with a certain seaminess.

Impressionism: (last quarter of the nineteenth century, beginning in 1874, mainly in France): focusing on immediate, fleeting sensations in nature; obsessed with the transitory effects of color and light on soft surfaces.

Post-Impressionism: (late nineteenth century, France): rejection of the fleeting surface art of the Impressionists in favor of bolder colors, forms, and subjective expressions; i.e., from Impressions to Expressions. *Note:* the distinctive works of Cézanne and van Gogh continue the "Classic-Romantic" split in art and lay the foundations for the perpetuation of that split into the twentieth century.

Modernism: (twentieth century): in general, an explosion of "isms" in the direction of the extreme and the psychological, moving away from physical nature and human nature toward abstraction and subjective expressions of the psyche or social problems. *Note:* Mondrian and Pollack continue the "Classic-Romantic" split into the twentieth century as prime examples of the staying power of this stylistic polarity.

The Artist as CREATOR

The core of the onion reveals the enigma of the creative process itself. As we have already discovered, the deepest level of art is the most creative. In pursuing the creative act we arrive at the threshold of a mystery neither creator nor critic can fully fathom, but which gives substance and excitement to this whole endeavor.

WRITING ABOUT A PAINTING

INTRODUCTION

To recall the earlier discussion on "Writing about the Arts," WRITING is the avenue to LEARNING and THINKING, and good writing is learned by READING good writers. Your primary challenge is to write about a visual work of art in such a way that your reader will see and feel what couldn't otherwise be experienced without your verbal assistance. As you can readily see, art criticism requires a certain creative flair. And yet, "a picture is worth a thousand words," as the saying goes, so a pure verbal description of a painting would be very ponderous to read because the words are so inadequate in describing the actual visual experience. This is where the rubber hits the road, so to speak, in writing about the visual arts: the challenge of making words express that which is, at heart, a purely sensuous experience. Your task is to reconstruct verbally your aesthetic insights so vividly that your reader will relive as much of that experience as possible. Here is how you do it.

READING

Writers are like children; they learn by imitation. Reading what informed writers have to say about art provides the best apprenticeship for a fledgling art critic, because good writing sets the stage for developing a personal style. If we are physically what we eat, then we are mentally what we read and think. The best art critics engage our senses as well as our intellects and make us care about their subject. One of William Zinsser's favorites is George Nelson. Here is an instructive passage from Nelson's book *How to See:*

> Visual decoding takes place at a great variety of levels, and in this sense it is not basically different from the use of any language. When the Lone Ranger and his faithful Tonto stop at some scuff marks in the desert and conclude that a band of outlaws has passed that way, carrying a ravishing blond captive on a strawberry roan, and that the leader's horse had recently thrown a shoe, we marvel at their skill in getting so much information out of some disturbed earth. What these two would do if confronted by Picasso's *Guernica* is another question. Reading a painting takes another set of skills. . . .
>
> In visual reading, like verbal reading, the completeness of the reading relates directly to the quality of the reader's stored information. A cat may look at a king, as the old saying goes, but the visual message is more interesting if the onlooker also knows what a king is. Visual communication, therefore, is not unlike other kinds of communication in that it is broadcast and received and in that it

uses a code of language which has to be intelligible to the receiver. (Qtd. in Zinsser 104–105)

GOOD CRITICAL WRITING

Nelson's analogies are simple and yet full of graphically familiar insights. He practices what William James preached: to teach a person something, you must begin where he is and take him to where you want him to be. Not only does everyone know about the Lone Ranger, but the association is fraught with high adventure, a connection quite incompatible with most people's notions of a museum visit. Nelson cleverly tricks us into transferring our native enthusiasm for pop culture to his love of art, no small feat. His reference to the cat is, as Zinsser points out, "like a well-constructed joke": it takes us by surprise by making its point at the end, in the punch line. Humor and humanity are indispensable qualities in the writings of a good art critic. In addition, such a writer unexpectedly connects reading words with reading images, which suddenly raises the critical act of seeing to the level of intellectual validity, an indispensable premise to good art criticism, but a fact rarely acknowledged by the general public.

THINKING & LEARNING

Robert Hughes is one of the most intellectually engaging of recent writers on art. He writes with the shock of recognition appropriate to his best-known art book, *The Shock of the New*. Notice how deftly he sets Picasso's *Guernica* in the time stream of other great protest paintings of the past while simultaneously acknowledging its waning impact in an age of modern technology:

> [Picasso's *Guernica*] is the last of the line of formal images of battle and suffering that runs from Uccello's *Rout of San Romano* through Tintoretto to Rubens, and thence to Goya's *Third of May* and Delacroix's *Massacre of Chios*. . . . By the end of World War II, the role of the "war artist" had been rendered negligible by war photography. What did you believe, a drawing of an emaciated corpse in a pit that looked like bad, late German Expressionism, or the incontrovertible photographs from Belsen, Maidenek, and Auschwitz? . . . We still have political art, but we have no *effective* political art. (109–110, 111)

Good art critics create contexts in which we can understand both how art affected its contemporaries and how it relates to our own time. The great implied irony of Hughes's commentary on *Guernica* is this: great art stands beyond time, and yet the political impact of this greatest painting of the twentieth century has been undermined by the very technology and bestiality it foresaw.

WRITING PREPARATION

To have something to write requires "experience time." This is nowhere more true than in analyzing a painting. The huge number of paintings hanging in major art galleries and the limited time one usually sets aside for a museum visit work against this bottom-line requirement. It takes as much time to "read" a painting adequately as it does to read a short story, if not longer. It takes time for the eye to find formal connections, to consider color relationships and linear patterns, not to mention the time it takes to identify the figures and determine the meaning of any symbols. In addition, it is easy to become intimidated by the task of writing about something so seemingly simple and obvious as a single painting.

WRITER'S BLOCK

Robert Pirsig described a special kind of writer's block in his book *Zen and the Art of Motorcycle Maintenance*. As an English teacher, the persona in the story was having trouble with students who had nothing to say. One girl with strong-lensed glasses had decided to write a five-hundred-word essay about the United States. He persuaded her to narrow it to Bozeman, Montana, but she couldn't think of anything to say, so he said to narrow her topic to the *main street* of the town. But she still couldn't think of anything to say, and didn't know why. He was furious. "You're not *looking*" he said. . . ." Narrow it down to the *front* of *one* building on the main street of Bozeman. The Opera House. Start with the upper left-hand brick" (170, 171). She returned the next class period and handed him a five-thousand word essay. "I sat in the hamburger stand across the street," she said, "and started writing about the first brick, and the second brick, and then by the third brick it all started to come and I couldn't stop. They thought I was crazy, and they kept kidding me, but here it all is. I don't understand it" (171). The teacher forced her to "divide and conquer," to engage in what we might call "visual focusing," attending to details and gradually working your way to the "big picture." Clarity, one of the greatest virtues of good writing, comes from focusing on specific details and then expanding to significant generalities.

THE "STAGES OF ACCESS"

In summary, after you have chosen an *actual* painting to analyze (book illustrations, even when in color, are too small to get the impact of the original, and large posters are seldom "color-credible"), allow time for your PERSONAL RESPONSES to percolate. Spend a few minutes sorting out the painting's impact in a state of relaxed concentration, noticing how the smaller patterns begin to coalesce into larger patterns (squint your eyes if you can't see them). Write freely for ten minutes or so about your immediate responses to the work, attending to anything that strikes you as unusual or interesting. If you can think of nothing to write, just write, "I can think of nothing to write," until you start to write something interesting. Gradually let your mind probe beyond the obvious. Then begin to answer the six questions first posed in the section on "Aesthetic Judgment:"

1. *What is it?* In every art form, there are types or genres which make up the possibilities of the medium. In paintings, there are landscapes, still lifes, portraits, history paintings, abstractions, etc.

2. *What is it made of?* The answer to this question has to do with medium, the material from which the work is made: stone, wood, oil on canvas, etc.

3. *How is it put together?* Analyze the work by considering the impact of the following: the medium (what is it made of?); the ELEMENTS (how is it organized in terms of line, color, texture, etc.); and the OVERALL EFFECT (the organizational patterns).

4. *What does it mean?* The answer to this question has to do with the SUBJECT MATTER (What is it about? Look at the title for clues) and the EXPRESSIVE CONTENT (What is communicated by the subject matter?).

5. *How does it mean?* This question relates to matters of STYLE, not what is communicated, but how? For example, there are innumerable depictions of the crucifixion, but each artist renders it with a different intent and effect: Rubens's is heroic; El Greco's is ethereal; Dali's is bizarre.

6. *What difference does it make?* Conclude with your own reactions, in a carefully organized and interesting final critique of the work, a kind of grand synthesis of your explorations.

A TEST CASE FOR VISUAL ANALYSIS: PICASSO'S *GUERNICA* (1937)

INTRODUCTION

Let us carefully scrutinize one of the most powerful visual invectives against war in modern art, indeed one of the most shocking and significant paintings of the twentieth century. In the process, we will generally follow the pattern set up in the introduction to the visual arts, treating in order aspects of medium, line, color, style, and meaning.

CRITICAL LIMITATIONS

In beginning an analysis of a painting, it is important to acknowledge that any interpretation, except one based on the most obvious and mundane issues, is open to conjecture and modification. This does not mean that reliable conclusions regarding meaning and effect in art cannot be reached. But aesthetic interpretation is a very subjective thing, even among major art critics, who often disagree on issues that may seem self-evident to the general populace. And while art critics aren't as vociferous or as public as television film critics, it is important to realize that, as with perceptions of reality discussed earlier, each individual brings different expectations and gleans different meanings from the same work. This should not be seen as something frustrating or futile, but something inevitable and positive, that can only solidify one's critical stance by reinforcing the validity of any informed, caring response. Therefore, this is only one person's attempt at deciphering the meaning of a very complex work. Ellen C. Oppler, an expert on Picasso's *Guernica* (see Color Plate 16), admitted that, in spite of the fact that *Guernica* is Picasso's best-known painting and one of the masterpieces of our time, "Yet it is a problematic work, stylistically complex, with images difficult to decipher, whose meaning is unclear" (47). It also might be comforting to quote an appropriately off-handed disclaimer by the artist himself, who didn't have much good to say about professional art critics and who felt much closer to lay viewers and even children in regard to aesthetic interpretations:

> A picture is not thought out and settled beforehand. While it is being done it changes as one's thoughts change. And when it is finished, it still goes on changing, according to the state of mind of whoever is looking at it. A picture lives a life like a living creature, undergoing the changes imposed on us by our life from day to day. This is natural enough, as the picture lives only through the man who is looking at it. (Qtd. in Chipp 44)

HISTORICAL BACKGROUND

On Monday, April 26, 1937, at approximately 4:30 p.m. in the middle of a busy market day, waves of Nazi aircraft began devastating the tiny Basque town of Guernica in Northern Spain in what was to be the first instance of saturation bombing in history. Within three and a quarter hours the city was totally destroyed. World reaction was immediate outrage. Picasso, though he had spent most of his creative years in Paris, was an ardent Republican and loathed the fascist Franco. In January Picasso had been asked to contribute a major work for the Spanish Pavilion of the upcoming summer World's Fair in Paris. This inhumane episode in the Spanish Civil War gave Picasso his creative pretext. He began work on May 1, 1937, with six quick sketches, the first of which includes all the final protagonists: the woman with the lamp, a wounded horse, fallen victims, and the bull with a winged creature on its back. The painting's final basic form, including the main horizontals and verticals, was established almost instantly, just as Picasso had observed in 1935: "basically a picture doesn't change, . . . the first 'vision' remains almost intact" (qtd. in Oppler 76). He is said to have finished the work on June 4, in a little over a month of intense and agonizing creative activity.

MEDIUM

Understandably, Picasso chose to create his *magnum opus* in oil on canvas; the major works of visual art since the early Renaissance have been done in this medium. Few if any previous oil paintings have been this large, however: (11' 6" x 25' 8"). In fact, its nearly 12-foot height made it necessary to tilt the canvas slightly in the large beamed room he used as a studio in Paris. He moved his numerous sketches onto the large stretched canvas on May 11. In two separate later stages (IV and VI), Picasso experimented with COLLAGE, pasting colored cloth and wallpaper covering onto certain of the figures, but later thought better of this and had them removed. Thus, the work remains remarkably simple in terms of the materials used, in spite of its extremely complex organization and profound meanings.

LINE

This brings us to the basic visual elements of art: line and color. The whole organization of the canvas provides an interesting interplay, not only of straight and curved lines, but of rounded and pointed forms. As we have learned earlier, straight lines are inorganic and curved lines are organic (life lines). Similarly, straight lines are hard; curved lines suggest softness. Straight lines coming together at sharp points tend to create life-threatening images, whether primitive knives and spears, or modern nose cones for rockets and bombs. In fact, both primitive and modern tools of destruction are clearly depicted in central parts of the canvas (sword and bomb), which lends to the work a vast time framework. This is likely both conscious and instinctive, since Picasso's Cubism

reduced natural forms to angular, fractured shapes, especially appropriate to the harsh subject matter of *Guernica.*

COLOR

The swatches of colored, patterned cloth and wallpaper add a color dimension to the otherwise bleak white, gray, and black design. For a brief time Picasso even added red tears to the running woman. At a private unveiling witnessed only by close friends, he removed the wallpaper swatches and the red tears, probably because color implies life (especially red), and this is a painting of death. Thus, the monochromatic color scheme ended up providing a vivid symbol for the basic theme of the painting: the gray ash of death, the incinerated remains of a town, and the colorless, bleak future of a whole civilization. We must remember that the first atomic bomb was detonated over Hiroshima just eight years later (1945). In this sense, *Guernica* is a frighteningly prophetic painting, standing as it does on the threshold of the holocaust and modern atomic warfare, which even today threatens to destroy the world.

FORM

Very early on, in the first photographed state (May 11), Picasso divided the canvas with verticals on either side of exact center: the edge of the house on the right and the vertical line between the bull's head and the warrior's head on the left. In between these two small rectangular frames on either side is a clearly demarcated triangular shape in the center of the canvas. Its apex is the oil lamp, extending its axis downward to the right through the body of the running woman and to the left through the body of the horse toward the hand of the warrior. Frank D. Russell suggests that the structural organization of Guernica combines in uneasy tension the competing values of classical restraint and romantic fervor (102). Could it be that Picasso wanted to pay homage to these basic human tendencies and the two art styles that grow out of humanity's basic duality by creating two interlocking forms that abstractly represent the legacies of classicism and romanticism? The triangle was a favored form in both Greek classicism (think of the Greek temple **pediment)** and the Italian Renaissance (notice how many Renaissance paintings are built on pyramidal patterns). The three-part altar design, derived from the medieval **triptych,** alludes to the Christian notion of the trinity, with the half-figures on either side acting as hinges.

SYMBOLIC MEANINGS

Once we begin to detect the overall formal layout of the painting and what its forms might mean beyond their interlocking geometry, we are prepared to fit the remaining forms into the symbolic framework. The oil lamp, held aloft by the classicized nude reaching her arm through the window, is an obvious symbol for freedom (most familiar to Americans in the Statue of Liberty) and, perhaps, truth, since it illuminates the whole scene of carnage so fully. The broken sword of the plaster warrior is an almost too obvious reference to the "broken resistance," and yet the fragile flower growing from the warrior's clenched fist adds a tentative note of hope. Significantly, it is located directly below the other symbol of hope, the lamp.

The three animals depicted are also highly symbolic. The bird, barely visible between the heads of the horse and bull, traditionally symbolizes peace. In this position, it bespeaks a kind of mediating function between the victim (the horse) and the victimizer (the bull). Picasso, being Spanish, drew heavily on the images of the *corrida* (bullfight), Spain's national ritual. But there is little in Picasso's writings or interviews to help us much in determining symbolic meanings, except for the bull and horse. The bull, he once admitted, represented "brutality and darkness"; the horse, "the people" (in Jerome Seckler, "Picasso Explains," qtd. in Oppler 94, 145ff.). But in a Christian context, the horse seems to represent Christ, particularly since the threatening electric light above the horse's head suggests as much: an eye (God's all-seeing eye?); a missile (which we also see repeated in the mouths of the horse, the bull, and the screaming woman); a halo; even a crown of thorns (with its spiky rays). The spear piercing the horse's side is an additional visual connection to the Crucifixion.

The headlong sweep of falling figures from right to left across the canvas in progressive stages of approaching death recalls the falling pattern of another favorite medieval motif, the Deposition (where Christ is removed from the cross). he visual analogy is significant here, for the Deposition was designed to amplify the believer's sorrow over the suffering and death of Christ. Here, Picasso expands the theme to embrace all suffering humanity, framed on each end by the two women of the side panels who represent two extremes of human suffering: physical agony (death by fire) on the right and bereavement (suffering for a loved one) on the left. The heads, alike as those on two coins, conduct a tragic dialogue with heaven. The howling mother figure on the left is perhaps the more touching because her scream and bearing suggest that her agony reaches an elemental creature level beyond human

endurance, for what could be more painful than to witness the unmerited suffering and death of an innocent child (your own)? And this mother-child pairing recalls many related images in the history of art, in particular, the Madonna and Child, as well as Michelangelo's *Pietà* (see Color Plate 1).

CONCLUSION

PAST VALUES

Learning to be conversant about visual mediums, elements or modes of interpretation (contextual, formal and stylistic) marks an important stage on the road to cultural literacy although such information is only a key to the door. To gain access to what is inside the house of art requires much more than rote learning. The sensuous appeal of the fine arts, part of what we are calling the "aesthetic experience," comes gradually with a growing awareness of significant form wedded to profound content: to apply the principles of design to discovering meaning in visual forms and contexts. The Roman poet Horace argued that good art both delights (by its form) and instructs (with its content). This rather academic point teaches us something important about the moral core of great art: it gives us a vision of the grandeur of humanity's creative imagination within a system of ennobling values, a vision that is sadly lacking in modern Western society.

DILEMMAS

Barbara Tuchman, the noted American historian, was dismayed at a Smithsonian conference on "heroes" celebrating the fiftieth anniversary of the birth of Superman. They ended up discussing pop culture heroes like Elvis Presley, a little girl who had fallen down a well, and, of all people, the Mayflower Madame, a woman who ran a brothel in New York City. Tuchman's view of a hero, which is the traditional one, required at the very least that the hero have some "nobility of purpose" (Moyers 7). In this light, her example of a true hero was George Washington, "a remarkable man in every aspect of his character, in his courage, in his persistence, and in his amazing belief that he was right and that he would prevail in spite of enormous frustrations and difficulties" (8). We desperately need more real heroes to pattern our lives after, for the hero's business, according to John Gardner in *On Moral Fiction* is to provide "a noble image for men to be inspired and guided by in their own actions." The artist's business is "to celebrate the work of the hero, pass the image on, keep the heroic model of behavior fresh, generation on generation. . . ."Thus, "the gods set ideals, heroes enact them, and artists or artist-historians preserve the image as a guide for man" (29). Many media heroes of today's youth (in fact, the vast majority of "stars" in sports, music, television and film) provide decadent, spiritually bankrupt models of behavior, sabotaging the delicate process of emotional attachments to what is good, what Allan Bloom in *The Closing of the American Mind* called the "passionate relationship to the art and thought that are the substance of liberal education" (79). Lessing's description of Greek sculpture encapsulates for Bloom the fundamental principle of aesthetic education: "beautiful men made beautiful statues, and the city had beautiful statues in part to thank for beautiful citizens" (80). One hesitates to imagine what contemporary parallel might be raised to compare with Lessing's. Our popular arts have tended to appeal to the lowest common denominator, leaving us awash in a sea of trivia at best and exposed to dangerously perverted values at worst.

FUTURE PROMISE

Jamake Highwater rightly links aesthetic response to cultural literacy and social responsibility: "The attainment of a capacity for aesthetic response is infinitely more subtle than learning the mechanics of reading and writing a language. Despite such difficulties, until we discover methods to awaken a capacity for feeling in all our communities, we will continue to be in danger of losing ourselves, even if we win the entire world" (17).

SUMMARY & RECENT DEVELOPMENTS

Ever since modern art was first displayed in a public place in America at the Armory Show in New York in 1913, modern art has precipitated the greatest public outcry of any of the other arts. Why this is so is not clear, but it seems to be so. Detractors of modern art are legion, made up of otherwise sensitive, intelligent people from every professional persuasion. But for some reason, not entirely understood by any art historian, people generally experience visual disorientation and visceral frustration when confronted with many modern works, with reactions oscillating between caustic ridicule and deep-seated loathing (few are indifferent). This may have something to do with the fact that one almost universal expectation among viewers of paintings is realism; they expect a painting to look like something recognizable. Unfortunately, most works we tag as 'modern' are anything but realistic. They run the gamut from Picasso's fractured cubist por-

traits like *Les Damoiselles d'Avignon* (1907), to Salvador Dali's surrealistic nightmares *Persistence of Memory* (1931), to Piet Mondrian's jazzy and geometric *Broadway Boogie Woogie* (1942–43), to Jackson Pollock's abstractly expressionistic *Lavender Mist* (1950), to Mark Rothko's mystical *Centre Triptych* (1966), moving gradually through time from greater degrees of visual distortion to flat, non-representational fields of pure color. This move toward abstraction is punctuated along the way by visually interesting aberrations, like Marcel Duchamp's notorious *Fountain* (1917), an upside down urinal signed 'R. Mutt,' or Roy Lichtenstein's parodies of comic book illustrations, or Andy Warhol's multiple silkscreen images of Marilyn Monroe and Campbell's Soup can labels, or Robert Rauschenberg's notorious "combines" (mixed media conglomerations like *Monogram* (1955–1959), consisting of a stuffed angora goat with a tire around its middle on a painted base. When one artist saw this work he said: "If this is art, I quit!"

The 60s saw an abrupt, unexpected and essentially inexplicable shift from Pop Art and visual abstractions to Superrealism in sculpture and painting. Chuck Close, Richard Estes and Philip Pearlstein paint large canvases with a photographic detail that boggles both mind and eye, but Duane Hanson goes one step further by transferring this mania for realism to three-dimensional objects, mostly common folk of any typical American community. It's hard to resist wanting to talk to his life-size *Supermarket Shopper* (1970) made of polyester resin and fiberglass, supplemented with real accessories like blouse, skirt, scarf, shopping cart and assorted groceries.

The 80s and 90s have made it ever more difficult to take modern art seriously. In fact, it has prompted some to dismiss it entirely. Contemporary artists and social critics are embroiled in art controversies reaching to the highest levels of government over exhibitions of socially offensive art, such as Mapplethorpe's homoerotic and graphically homosexual photographs and André Serrano's blasphemous sculptures, one of which depicts a small cross immersed in a beaker of the artist's own urine. In such a climate of disdain, it becomes increasingly difficult for a caring public to be drawn into a dialogue about aesthetic values.

WRITING EXERCISES

Assuming that Buffon is correct in saying that "the style is the man," and assuming that the writer is correct in defining style as "the outward manifestation of the inner man," explore the style of a creative person you know well (a poet, painter, musician, performer, etc.) in terms of the following three suggestions:

1. Do a "stylistic analysis" of that person. Look for visible cues to personality, values, etc. For example, notice dress and hair styles; note gestures, body stance, language (vocabulary and inflections); have the person sign his/her name and notice any patterns that fit the other visual cues you have listed.

2. Then, analyze the style of a work by this person, using the layered "onion" metaphor in the discussion on style. Look for individualized treatment of the elements (words, colors, etc.) and anything else about choice of medium or formal organization that bespeaks the originality of this person's style and vision.

3. Finally, see what connections you can find between the personal style (dress, behavior, etc.) and his or her artistic style.

ANALYSIS EXPERIMENT

1. Take a friend to a gallery (or any place where actual paintings are on display) and discuss the work in terms of the critical questions you have learned. Do a "dry run" analysis together, using the format of HISTORICAL BACKGROUND, MEDIUM, LINE, COLOR, FORM, and MEANING. Explore the possibilities, of both FORMALIST and CONTEXTUALIST criticism by each taking a different critical stance.

WORKS CITED

Aristotle. *Poetics* Trans. S. H. Butcher. New York: Hill and Wang, 1961.

Arnheim, Rudolf. *Art and Visual Perception*. Berkeley: University of California Press, 1974.

Ashton, Dore. *Picasso on Art: A Selection of Views*. New York: Viking, 1972.

Bersson, Robert. *Worlds of Art*. Mountain View, CA.: Mayfield, 1991.

Bloom, Allan. *The Closing of the American Mind*. New York: Simon & Schuster, 1987.

Campbell, Joseph. *Myths to Live By*. New York: Bantam Books, 1973.

Chipp, Herschel B. *Theories of Modern Art*. Berkeley: University of California Press, 1971.

Dondis, Donis A. *A Primer of Visual Literacy*. Cambridge, MA.: MIT Press, 1973.

Gardner, John. *On Moral Fiction*. New York: Basic Books, 1978.

Gardner, Helen. *Art through the Ages*. 6th ed. New York: Harcourt Brace Jovanovich, 1975.

Graves, Robert. *New Larouse Encyclopedia of Mythology*. London: Batchworth, 1959.

Hammacher, Abraham Marie. *Van Gogh: A Documentary Biography*. London: Thames & Hudson, 1982.

Highwater, Jamake. "Imagination: The Key That Unlocks Art's Secret Language." *Christian Science Monitor* 28 June 1989, 16–17.

Hughes, Robert. *The Shock of the New*. New York: Knopf, 1981.

Lindsay, Kenneth C., and Peter Vergo, eds. *Kandinsky: Complete Writings on Art*. Vol. I (1901–1921) of *The Documents of Twentieth Century Art*. Boston: G. K. Hall & Co., 1982.

Moyers, Bill. *A World of Ideas*. New York: Doubleday, 1989.

Oppler, Ellen, ed. *Picasso's "Guernica."* New York: Norton, 1988.

Pirsig, Robert. *Zen and the Art of Motorcycle Maintenance*. New York: Bantam, 1975.

Potok, Chaim. *My Name Is Asher Lev*. New York: Knopf, 1972.

Read, Herbert. *The Philosophy of Modern Art*. New York: Meridian, 1961.

Russell, Frank D. *Picasso's "Guernica": The Labyrinth of Narrative Vision*. Montclair, NJ: Allanheld, Osmun, 1980.

Zinsser, William. *Writing to Learn*. New York: Harper & Row, 1988.

WEBSITES OF INTEREST

Slideshow of basic art elements —
http://www.slideshare.net/a01138028/
art-elements-presentation

Meaning/Interpretation of Guernica —
http://www.pbs.org/treasuresoftheworld/guernica/
glevel_1/5_meaning.html

Michelangelo's Moses

INTRODUCTION TO SCULPTURE

Chapter *16*

Sculpture, because of its durability and mostly human subject matter, represents one of the most accurate and compelling records of man's changing attitudes about himself and the world around him. Much of the great sculpture of the past has been used to ornament its sister art, architecture. Indeed, it is unclear in some of the most ancient monuments of art whether they are to be viewed as architecture or sculpture. Stonehenge and the great Pyramids at Giza are two cases in point. During the classical age, however, the two arts were clearly conceived as separate. Some of the greatest freestanding sculptures of all time were created in Athenian workshops of the fifth century B.C. And yet sculpture and architecture were intimately interconnected in both classical temples (like the Parthenon) and gothic **cathedrals** (like Chartres). It wasn't until the Italian Renaissance that the two arts parted company for good, and **virtuoso** sculptors emerged, like Ghiberti, Donatello, and Michelangelo, and the later greats like Bernini in the Baroque Era, Rodin in the nineteenth century, and Henry Moore in the twentieth.

SCULPTURE & THE HUMAN DIMENSION

INTRODUCTION

As a record of man's ability to represent the beauty of the human body in monumental ways, freestanding sculpture offered artists a great opportunity to explore the expressive potential of the human form. In fact, one could say that the growing realism of sculpture from the stiff frontality of late Egyptian sculpture to the marvelous realism of fifth-century **Hellenic** Greek statuary marked the discovery of the human body for the first time in history. The formal perfection of Greek statuary has rarely, if ever, been surpassed. Nevertheless, for some it is embarrassing or arousing to view a nude figure, even though it is only chiseled stone. Sir Kenneth Clark provides a useful distinction between the naked and the nude which might help maintain an aesthetic distance in such matters:

> To be naked is to be deprived of our clothes and the word implies some of the embarrassment which most of us feel in that condition. The word *nude,* on the other hand, carries, in educated usage, no uncomfortable overtone. The vague image it projects into the mind is not of a huddled and defenseless body, but of a balanced, prosperous and confident body: the body re-formed. (23)

THE PROCESS OF MAKING SCULPTURE

CARVING, MODELING, CONSTRUCTION

Sculptors employ one of three basic **sculptural processes** in creating their works: CARVING, which is a subtractive method (cutting the figure from stone, wood, etc.); MODELLING, an additive method (building up forms around armatures with malleable substances like clay)—if the clay form is fired we call the result TERRA COTTA; if it is covered with a thin wax surface, enclosed in another plaster form, fired, and then filled with molten bronze, it is BRONZE CASTING; and, finally, CONSTRUCTION, which involves connecting together previously formed pieces of material into an original work. The latter method emerged in more recent times, as modern sculptors began to assemble wood or metal fragments into what some people call "junk art," but which can be quite original, even beautiful. Modern technology offers sculptors a wide range of different materials to manipulate, compared to earlier artists, who were limited primarily to wood, stone, and clay.

MEDIUM LIMITATIONS

A good sculptor is both a designer and a workman, a dreamer and a digger, taking into account both the physical and sensory properties of his chosen materials and the limitations and possibilities of the available methods for working with them. Each material has a life of its own and thus imposes its own unique material quality on the finished work. A good sculptor is sensitive to these differences and will be true to the material. Some sculptors, however, will push the medium to its limits and even try to extend the medium beyond its conventional expressive limits. BERNINI (1598–1680), the great Italian Baroque sculptor of the seventeenth century, created the illusion of soft flesh or silken cloth in solid marble with breathtaking credibility, like Pluto's hand pressing into Persephone's soft thigh in his *Pluto and Persephone* (1621–1622).

HOW TO EXPERIENCE SCULPTURE

ADVANTAGES

Sculpture is rather unique among the visual arts in that its physical reality is so apparent and immediate. Paintings exist in an illusory space, created by the *trompe l'oeil* (trick of the eye) techniques of linear perspective, aerial perspective, shading, and illusionistic textures. But a piece of sculpture, has a presence in real space, like a human being, or a tree or cloud. HENRY MOORE (1898–1986), the great twentieth-century English sculptor once said: "Painting has lots of advantages over sculpture. I mean, you can't represent the sky in sculpture; you can't represent a piece of liver on a plate, the color, the *wetness*. You can't do it." And yet, "The big advantage that sculpture has over painting is that it can have innumerable, unending numbers of points of view. You stand dead in front of the middle of a painting; you don't go around to the side and the back to see" (qtd. in Hall 25).

TACTILE PRESENCE

The first step in experiencing sculpture, then, is to recognize it as a "thing that has a separate and independent existence," as the photographer David Finn suggests. "Although it may be modeled after a living subject, it is a being unto itself. It is not human. It is not alive. It is still and silent, frozen in an instant of time. Yet there is something eternal about it" (41). Think of Michelangelo's *Pietà*.

TEXTURE & LIGHT

Because sculpture is the most tactile (tangible) of the visual arts, it is important to develop the sense of touch, both with the eye and with the hand. As you begin to look for sustained periods of time, the mystery and beauty of the surface textures and forms will become more evident. You will begin to "relate" to the work in a special kind of two-way interaction. And since sculpture exists in real light (direct or indirect), look for the way light and shadow play on the surfaces. Sunlight shining on outdoor sculptures transforms the forms of sculpture from hour to hour; this is especially true of relief sculpture (forms still attached to their background). In a curious way, a blind man can "see" more in sculpture than the sighted, because he "sees" with a greatly enhanced tactile sense. We are like the blind man who has to learn to see with his hands. "We have to train our eyes," Finn observes, "to feel the sculpture in all its parts and from every conceivable vantage point, as if we were actually touching it" (20). His description of the deeper level of seeing recalls the quotation from Chaim Potok's *My Name Is Asher Lev*—"I could feel the lines with my eyes. . . . I was seeing with another pair of eyes that had suddenly come awake" (105–106).

> Walking around the sculpture, with your eyes peeled for lights and shadows and forms of flesh and hair and cloth, all making abstract patterns of unspeakable beauty, you are in effect touching all its parts with your eyes rather than with your hand. You have a sense of physical contact with the three-dimensional creation standing before you. When your eyes are doing the feeling, you have a very special kind of experience. It is not the touch of the material that provides the critical impression; it is as if your eyes have fingers that are able to explore the work from all sides. (Finn 22)

THE FEEL OF STONE

In spite of the vicarious visual identification with the real forms and real textures of sculptures, there is no substitute for actually touching the real thing. Unfortunately, this is rarely allowed in major museums, for obvious reasons. But whenever it is permitted, the experience can greatly enhance the appreciation of sculptural form. Photographing Michelangelo's *David and Slaves* one afternoon in the Academia in Florence provided Finn one of the peak experiences of his life. With "indescribable rapture" he touched "the breathtaking texture of the stone, the sweeping forms flowing up and in and round, the ridges and bumps and smoothed out parts that made up the surfaces of the sculpture." He concludes with this celebration of the sense of touch:

> There must have been a heavenly spirit in Michelangelo's fingers as they guided his tools, and I felt that spirit now transmitted like electric impulses through my fingers into my heart. I ran my hand again and again over those surfaces I could reach. It took only moments, but it was a timeless experience. (18)

THREE GIANTS OF THE MEDIUM

The works of three of history's greatest sculptors—Michelangelo, Rodin, and Henry Moore—represent the quintessence of this art form.

MICHELANGELO BUONAROTTI (1475–1564)

Historical Background

Even though he is equally famous in history as a painter (he executed the Sistine Chapel frescoes in just under four years), Michelangelo saw himself primarily as a sculptor. He always signed his letters, "Michelangelo Buonarotti, *scultore*." He was in love with Carrara marble from the rugged mountains of his native Tuscany and once claimed that the love of marble was in his blood. He once acknowledged that he absorbed the life of a sculptor "with my nurse's milk." As a child he was obsessed with drawing, but when he was thirteen he was taken into the Medici household in Florence and trained as a sculptor. Five years later he went to Rome and carved his sublime *Pietà* (see Color Plate 1). He solved the challenge of sculpting a grown man on a woman's lap by organizing the whole into a pyramidal shape, a favorite form of Italian Renaissance artists. This amazing work made his reputation for his own time and thereafter. His other most noted work, *David* (see Color Plate 3), was carved in 1504 for the city of Florence from a damaged and rejected seventeen-foot high piece of pure Carrara marble. With this monumental figure, Michelangelo surpassed all the aims of the sculptors of ancient Greece and became the most famous artist in Italy, a giant among giants.

"Terribilatà"

As he grew older his works were increasingly given the description *terribilità*, an untranslatable word meaning

something like "awesome mightiness." There was something alarming about the desperate energy of his creations, an unease increased by their sexual ambiguity. The musculature of some of the female figures and the rounded shapes of many of the male nudes generate a tension that is a significant source of their power. Michelangelo lived to be eighty-nine years old. The *Rondanini Pietà* (see Color plate 2), the sculpture he was working on the week he died, betrays all the anguish and genius of this great artist's last years and expresses a nobility and poignant depth not possible in his earlier, more polished works. In his deathbed confession he said, "I am dying just as I am beginning to learn the alphabet of my profession" (qtd. in Coughlin 192).

"il Divino"

They called him "The Divine Michelangelo." By the time he died, the apotheosis was complete. Benedetto Varchi, an eminent Florentine historian, delivered the funeral oration. After describing Michelangelo's achievements, he seems to have been staggered by his own recital, explaining: "This is a phenomenon so new, so unusual, so unheard of in all times, in all countries, in all history that . . . I am not only full of admiration, not only amazed, not only astonished and startled and like one reborn—but my pulse flutters, my blood runs cold, my mind reels, and my hair stands on end, so moved am I by . . . trepidations" (qtd. in Coughlin 10).

AUGUST RODIN (1840–1917)

Historical Background

As a child Rodin had been a poor scholar. His only wish had been to draw until one day at the *Petit École* in Paris, where he was studying design. He chanced to enter a room where pupils were modeling in clay, constructing molds, and making plaster casts. Of his introduction to clay he later wrote: "I felt as though I had landed in heaven" (qtd. in Hale 40). It was a revelation to him, but many years were to pass before he would be in a position to produce the work he wanted. For twenty years he labored at menial tasks for fashionable sculptors, and not until he was thirty-five could he afford a visit to Italy. In Florence he was overwhelmed by Michelangelo's statues, in particular those of the nude males *Day* and *Dusk* in the Medici Chapel, figures partly submerged in their rough-hewn marble. He saw himself as the purveyor of Michelangelo's monumental style into the modern age.

Age of Bronze

On his return from Italy he completed a statue of a young soldier called *The Age of Bronze* and submitted it to the Paris Salon in 1877. It was his first accepted work, but due to its startling realism, rumors spread that he had it cast from a living model. He was eventually vindicated by recasting a larger-than-life version, but due to the scandal his name became famous.

Gates of Hell

His first ideas for his *Gates of Hell* were inspired by Ghiberti's *Gates of Paradise* (a fifteenth-century Florentine work that had also inspired Michelangelo). Rodin decided to cover his gates with figures writhing with a despair inspired by Dante's graphic depictions of the sufferings of the damned in the *Inferno*. One of Rodin's achievements was to bring back into sculpture a sensitivity to mass, volume, and the interplay of hollows and bulges. Some of the figures he cast separately. One, *The Thinker,* achieved separate world acclaim. It was originally inspired by Michelangelo's "Jeremiah" on the Sistine Chapel Ceiling.

The Kiss

His greatest works were group pieces. *The Kiss* (1886), originally conceived as Paolo and Francesca (from Dante's *Inferno*) for the *Gates of Hell,* is the most sensuous of the many passionate couples that make up a large part of his output.

Burghers of Calais

One of his masterpieces is the *Burghers of Calais,* a monument to commemorate the self-sacrifice of five French citizens who offered themselves as hostages to King Edward II of England in 1347 to end the year-long siege of their famine-ravaged city. Rodin imagined the emotional state of each doomed man, their feelings of uncertainty and despair and, in the process, infused each with a supreme dignity and pathos.

Isadora Duncan

Rodin met Isadora Duncan, the American pioneer of modern dance, in Paris in 1900. She recounted her first encounter with the master in her own inimitable way: "He showed his works with the simplicity of the very great. Sometimes he murmured the names for his statues. . . . He ran his hand over them and caressed them. . . . Finally he took a small quantity of clay and pressed it between his palms. He breathed hard as he did so. The

heat steamed from him like a radiant furnace. In a few moments he had formed a woman's breast that palpitated beneath his fingers" (qtd in Hale 10–1 1).

The Last Realist

Rodin was one of the last sculptors of greatness in an artistic tradition that stretches back three thousand years. Already by the time of his death during World War I, most sculptors were marching to different drummers; the human figure was no longer the prime subject and index of art, except for the works of Henry Moore in the twentieth century.

HENRY MOORE (1898–1982)

Human Landscape

The human being as landscape—breasts and knees as mountain peaks and hips as cliffs—these are the images that come to mind when looking at the reclining figures of Henry Moore. He developed other forms in his long, productive life, but with these reclining figures he achieved his first major successes and for years they identified him in the eyes of the public.

Historical Background

Born in Yorkshire in 1898, the seventh of eight children of a coal miner, Moore first studied art in Leeds after army service in World War I. Later he went as an art student to London and was struck by the formal power of Aztec sculpture in the British Museum. But a visit to Italy in 1925, which introduced him to the undeniable richness of early Renaissance art, brought his own work virtually to a standstill. He could no longer believe that vitality was to be found only in primitive art, yet his creative powers were unable to reconcile the qualities of European and non-European sculpture. He was eventually to find his solution in the reclining female figure, a motif common to both. His first *Reclining Figure* is dated 1929. He returned to this very fertile subject time and again over the next fifty years.

Naturalism & Primitivism

Henry Moore was once asked by his good friend, the famous Shakespearian actor Charles Laughton, why he made holes in his large abstract sculptures. He replied: "I was carving one day and I discovered the sky on the other side." This anecdote reveals Moore's instinctive attraction to natural forms and simple methods. Although he sometimes created huge bronze abstractions, his primary focus was on the reduction of natural forms to their elemental essences, but executed in statues of often monumental proportions. Because he was enamored with both primitive and naturalistic (Renaissance) styles, his own style was a life-long attempt to merge these two seemingly contradictory tendencies in sculpture.

Stonehenge

In the late 50s Moore separated his figures into two parts and later (perhaps less successfully) into three. The *Two-piece Reclining Figures* of this period are like great outcrops of rock, broken and weathered. Some of his huge works (20–30 feet high) have an architectural dimension. He admitted once that "I was influenced by Stonehenge from the *beginning*. I was fascinated by it, *obsessed*. "Stonehenge," he claimed, "is *really* sculpture, because each of these blocks is a man-made, man-handled thing — a carving. Stonehenge is not a building, it is a *carving* (qtd. in Hall 28, emphasis added).

The Great Eclectic

Vitality, the life spirit, is what Moore cared about in sculpture. He felt this spirit had been lacking in English sculpture since the end of the Middle Ages; his inspiration came from early Gothic and Romanesque statues, from Sumerian sculpture, and above all from the images of gods carved by the peoples of Mexico. And yet, it was the late sculpture of Michelangelo that moved him most, in particular the *Rondanini Pietà*. Originally, Michelangelo created a smooth work, but was dissatisfied with it. Moore observed: "He knocked the head off . . . and he carved, re-carved it, the body with the head, the new top with the old legs. This gives it a strange effect . . . for me it's one of the most moving . . . even a superman like that had these frustrations. . . . The [great] artists stop caring about beauty and such abstract ideas, and yet their works get greater" (qtd. in Hall 93).

CONCLUSION

Thus, we can detect in the works of the great sculptors in history an unbroken link in the chain of great works from the past, each one drawing on the impact of its sublime predecessors to reinvest each succeeding generation's creations with a new vitality and monumental possibility. The miracle of all great sculpture, and indeed of all great realist work in the visual arts, is the artist's capacity to bring off the semblance of the real in a medium physically incompatible with the thing depicted. This miracle

is part and parcel of one of the earliest aesthetic judgments in history: Homer's description of one part of Achilles' shield in the *Iliad*. Describing some farmers plowing a fertile field, Homer says: "The field, though it was made of gold, grew black behind them, as a field does when it is being ploughed. The artist had achieved a miracle" (351). The miracle consists in investing the presence of one thing in the material of another.

SUMMARY & RECENT DEVELOPMENTS

The quotation at the end of Chapter 1 by the Lithuanian-born American painter Ben Shahn conveys the importance of art in defining a **culture**: "I have always believed that the character of a society is largely shaped and unified by its great creative works, that a society is molded upon its epics, and that it imagines in terms of its created things—its cathedrals, its works of art, its musical treasures, its literary and philosophical works" (39). Our National Cathedral in Washingmon, D.C. is a beautiful reminder of the European legacy (religious and cultural) that we owe to the past. Frederick E. Hart, the sculptor of the statuary on the West Facade, has created a maelstrom of nude figures rising out of primordial soup entitled *Ex Nihilo*, strikingly like the figures in Rodin's *Gates of Hell* in Paris. Even though the subjects are biblical and the context medieval gothic, the sculptor's later experiments with a new medium, cast acrylic resin, is cutting-edge modern. He also sculpted *Three Soldiers* near the entrance to the Vietnam War Memorial, but it was a young Yale art student, twenty one-year-old Maya Lin, who designed the Vietnam Wall, now Washington's most visited memorial. She also designed the Civil Rights Memorial in Montgomery, Alabama. Both memorials are known for their power to evoke deep emotional responses to tragic incidents in our recent history. Lin's design for the wall was a radical departure from traditional public war memorials: a long wall cut into the earth and etched with the names of more than 58,000 dead American soldiers. It ignited a firestorm of opposition when it was announced in 1981 but has since proved appropriate for our time. After completing the Civil Rights Memorial in 1989, Lin said she wanted to retire from designing memorials, but today that attitude seems to have softened. "My pet dream is the environmental issue," she says. "I like to do things in trilogies. I would love to explore one last memorial. This one might deal with extinction. It will deal with the environment" (qtd. by Jim Sexton 5).

Over the centuries, sculpted monuments have served our cultural needs well, from the Parthenon friezes of ancient Athens to the Statue of Liberty in the New York harbor. However, September 11th has changed parts of our society forever. The complete destruction of New York's World Trade Towers, themselves magnificent monuments to the success of American commerce, has left a huge hole in our collective hearts and in the center of lower Manhattan. One of the earliest proposals for this huge vacuum was for the world's tallest buildings in place of the other two. Some civic leaders, including former New York Mayor Ted Koch, support a plan to replace the buildings and erect a monument as well, while others angrily oppose it, on both aesthetic and moral grounds. The controversy only proves Shahn's claims. I will give Anna Quindlen the last word:

> The tragic cavern in lower Manhattan is not a design or a development problem but a test of the spiritual and emotional depth of an entire nation. The demands of democracy should not be confused with those of capitalism. To honor a tragedy of this magnitude requires a response of comparable magnitude. Maybe Maya Lin could suggest how best that could be done. But, maybe, looking at the flattened plain where once so many worked and where so many died, the answer is to honor the emptiness by leaving it as a mute memorial. Are we a people so pinched of heart that we would trade memory for real estate? If so, the terrorists really have won. (68)

CRITICAL EXERCISES

1. Review the art analysis above as your teacher might critique your own writing. Comment on how well the writer engaged the reader, whether the arguments were convincing, whether sound principles of judgments were used, how much insight was brought to the work, whether the allusions to related, non-artistic ideas were valid, etc.

2. Find an illustration of a representative piece of sculpture by each of these "Three Giants" and compare their styles. How are they alike? How are they different? In particular, how is Rodin's work like Michelangelo's (Rodin viewed Michelangelo as his artistic godfather), and how is Moore's like Michelangelo's and like Stonehenge (one of his primary architectural inspirations as a sculptor)?

3. Locate an accessible piece of sculpture in your own environment. Spend some time looking at it. Engage in some free writing about what you see: comment on the color, the forms, the size, the textures, the subject, and the siting (how it fits its location). Then explore its surfaces with your hands and explain what you discovered with your hands that was inaccessible to your eyes. Be as specific as you can. What did you learn about the tactile qualities of sculpture? About your own sensitivity to texture and form?

WORKS CITED

Bowness, Alan. "Picasso's Sculpture." In *Picasso 1880–1973.* London: Paul Elek, 1973.

Chipp, Herschel B. *Theories of Modern Art.* Berkeley: University of California Press, 1971.

Clark, Kenneth. *The Nude.* Garden City, NY: Doubleday, 1956.

Coughlin, Robert. *The World of Michelangelo.* Alexandria, VA: Time-Life, 1966.

Finn, David. *How to Look at Sculpture.* New York: Abrams, 1989.

Hale, William Harlan. *The World of Rodin.* New York: Time-Life, 1969.

Hall, Donald. "Portrait of the Artist as an Undiminished Man." *Quest* (November 1978): 22–92.

Homer. *The Iliad.* 1950; rpt. Baltimore, MD: Penguin Books, 1964.

Kay, Helen. *Picasso's World of Children.* New York: Doubleday, n.d.

Potok, Chaim. *My Name Is Asher Lev.* New York: Knopf, 1972.

Quindlen, Anna. "Look at What They've Done." *Newsweek* (3 June 2002).

Rothenberg, Albert. "Visual Art: Homospatial Thinking in the Creative Process." *Leonardo* 3, no. 1 (Winter 1980): 18.

Sexton, Jim. "Making Art That Heals." USA *Weekend* 1–3 November 1996.

Ben Shahn. *The Shape of Content.* Cambridge, MA: Harvard University Press, 1957.

WEBSITES OF INTEREST

http://www.knowitall.org/artopia/sculpture/movie/index.html

http://www.getty.edu/art/gettyguide/videoDetails?cat=2&segid=437

Stone/Marble carving process — http://www.nicknorris.com/stone_carving_process.htm

Example of Different types of Sculpture — http://www.knowitall.org/artopia/sculpture/studio/index.html

Process and Sculptures of Michelangelo — http://entertainment.howstuffworks.com/michelangelo-sculptures.htm

Parthenon, fifth century B.C., *Athens, Greece*

INTRODUCTION TO ARCHITECTURE
Chapter 17

If the need for shelter produced the first building, once that building existed it soon became a magic place for ritual: in primitive huts the tribal fathers sat in the place of honor; in larger buildings the authorities sat at the head of the conference table; even in suburban homes it is not unusual for each family member to sit at the same seat for meals. However, the buildings we will study as art works are usually monumental, built for communal or civic purposes and last for centuries (architecture is one of the oldest of the arts). Not only do some great edifices, like the pyramids at Giza, rival nature in their sublimity and size, but their very materials are closest to the world of nature: wood and stone. John Dewey wrote that architecture best expresses the great forces of nature:

> No other [artistic] products exhibit stresses and strains, thrusts and counterthrusts, gravity, light, cohesion, on a scale at all comparable to the architectural. . . . It expresses the structural constitution of nature itself. . . . For this reason, buildings, among all art objects, come the nearest to expressing the stability and endurance of existence itself. They are to mountains what music is to the sea (230).

WHAT IS ARCHITECTURE?
FORM & FUNCTION

The word architecture comes from the Greek *architekton,* which means chief (*archi*) plus builder (*tekton*), so it is useful to distinguish architecture from mere construction, as one would distinguish a furniture designer from a carpenter. Of all the arts, architecture is the one with which everyone has had most to do, because we experience it every day of our lives: we live in it, we work in it,

we attend church in it, we experience the arts in it (concert halls, opera houses, museums, etc.); some people are even buried in it, Of all the other fine arts, architecture is unique in that function plays the primary role in its purpose and effect. Before buildings can be beautiful, they must be functional. For that reason, judging architecture requires three criteria: form, function, and the relation between form and function.

THE "BADGE" OF CIVILIZATION

If **culture** emerges from man's refashioning of nature, then architecture embodies the values of the civilization that produced it. One of the primary measures of **civilization** is its architecture, for architecture requires large groups of organized people with the financial and human means to build great monuments to their kings and gods. "According to prevailing historical viewpoints in recent centuries [architecture is the badge of civilization], the certain credential without which a society cannot be called civilized (Jacobs 10). This may be overstating the case for architecture at the expense of less enduring human artifacts. Nevertheless, even though the nomadic tribes had laws, language, a social structure, and decorative arts, some would consider them barbarians until they learned how to build with stone. Jacobs argues:

> Architecture not only proclaims the existence of a civilization; it is a cultural phenomenon that reveals information about the society that built it with unequivocal directness. Unlike painting, sculpture, literature, the dramatic arts, theology, politics, and historical discourse, archi-

tecture almost never minces words. . . . It defines . . . the main source of power in a society. (14)

As Kenneth Clark wrote in *Civilisation:* "If I had to say which was telling the truth about society, a speech by a minister of Housing or the actual buildings put up in his time, I should believe the buildings" (1).

STONES SPEAK

Our focus in this section will be directed toward architecture as cultural landmark defining pivotal stages along the course of Western history. We will pay particular attention to its changing styles, because, of all the other arts, buildings exist in public space as a persistent visual presence, serving as perpetual models for succeeding styles. Not only do they proclaim "who's in charge here?" they exhibit in their varied forms and functions the central civilizing tendencies of a whole people. The stones of the Parthenon speak volumes about the Greek desire for excellence and their love of beautiful proportions; the Colosseum reveals the Roman genius for engineering; the French cathedral bespeaks medieval piety and sacrifice; and the modern skyscraper embodies the stunning achievements of modern technology. The last comparison (cathedral and skyscraper) especially dramatizes the importance of architecture as a gauge of cultural values: even though both were enormously expensive and provided a locus for the creative energies of the community, the Gothic cathedral was built to the glory of God, the modern skyscraper to the glory of Mammon, according to Kenneth Clark.

ARCHITECTURAL "GENEALOGIES"

As you learn to recognize the individual parts of various major architectural monuments throughout history,

pay particular attention to the evolution of styles, how one style forms the basis for each succeeding style, and how earlier styles (Graeco-Roman, especially) are revived and altered by later generations. You might even think of the progression of architectural styles as generational, like the family tree where one branch emerges later in altered but recognizable form in some tributary line. One of the pleasures of discovering "family resemblances" comes from recognizing the lineaments of the forefathers in the faces (facades) of the descendants. There are many distant relatives residing in the older sections of every medium-sized American city.

ARCHITECTURE THROUGH TIME & SPACE

SACRED SHELTERS

Ancient monuments are puzzles to the modern mind. In the first place, we cannot imagine how primitive peoples (beginning around 3000 B.C.), devoid of modern machine technology, could have erected such megalithic monuments as the pyramids or Stonehenge, for example. Raised between 2600 and 2400 B.C., the pyramids at Giza outside Cairo were part of a large burial complex for the Egyptian pharaohs. The Great Pyramid of Khufu consists of more than two million granite blocks, each weighing 2½ tons, rising to its present height of 450 feet. Stonehenge (ca. 2000 B.C.) is constructed of sarsen stones weighing upwards of fifty tons.

MATHEMATICAL RATIOS

We are also puzzled by the mathematical precision and cosmological orientation of these ancient edifices. In the nineteenth century, scholars (pyramidologists) began study-

Stonehenge, Salisbury Plain, England (ca. 2000 B.C.)

ing the proportions and geographical orientation of the Pyramid of Khufu. They discovered some remarkable qualities: its four sides face the four points of the compass, and, almost exactly at latitude 30 degrees north, "right on the line between the earth's two poles which crosses more land and less water than any other, and at the apex of a quadrant of a circle neatly containing the curve of the Nile Delta, thus perfectly sited to serve as a primary benchmark for a survey of the earth" (Michell 137). John Taylor recognized that the Pyramid's original height (480 ft.) represented the radius of a circle of which the perimeter of the base represented the circumference. Other mathematical subtleties convinced him and his successors that the monument recorded the ancient's knowledge of the dimensions of the earth (Michell 137–138).

THE EARTH AS ORGANISM

To better understand these seeming mysteries, it helps to realize that ancient builders viewed the world as a living creature in a living universe. Therefore, the monuments they constructed represented a microcosm of the macrocosm, a man-made link between humans and their gods. Religious monuments were designed to attract the gods or forces of nature to which they were dedicated by means of "sympathetic resonance" (Michell 124). This was accomplished by symbolic references to the appropriate deities, an orientation to the appropriate celestial body (usually the sun), and according to number patterns designed to invoke universal energy. Again, it seems almost preposterous to imagine that ancient peoples could conceive of "geodetic fractions," creating in the dimen-

sions of their temples mathematical fractions of the earth's true dimensions. The lintel (horizontal) stones of Stonehenge, for example, measure 1 sacred rod (3.4757485 ft.), or a six-millionth part of the earth's polar radius, a measure that Newton recognized corresponded to the Jewish "sacred cubit." Newton was "one of the last of the scholars of the old tradition, who accepted that the standards of ancient science were higher than the modern" (Michell 125). Thus we come to the humbling realization that modern conceptions of "progress" are often presumptuous and misleading, particularly when discussing the arts. The remarkable precision of ancient monuments and the advanced drafting skill and perceptual awareness revealed in Paleolithic **cave paintings** reveal the notable artistic achievements of even the earliest and seemingly most primitive of cultures. Therefore, if progress seems misplaced as a concept to account for change in the arts, it is perhaps safer to claim that Western architecture represents "a record of continuous evolution" from ancient Egyptian and Mesopotamian through the classical, medieval, and modern eras (Fletcher 5).

PRE-GREEK ARCHITECTURE

MESOPOTAMIAN & EGYPTIAN

The forms and orientation of Egyptian and Mesopotamian architecture were dictated primarily by religion, inspiring the monumental dimensions found in their **pyramids,** history's first major architectural form (Jacobs 19). The size, form, and function of ancient pyramids were due, in part, to the relatively flat river valleys of the Nile in Egypt and the land separating the Tigris and Euphrates

Gizeh pyramids (Kheops), Egypt (2520–2494 B.C.)

rivers in Mesopotamia (lit. between the rivers). To compete with the vast deserts and to construct man-made mountains that could reach to the heavens (physical intimacy with heaven promised spiritual intimacy with the gods), the Egyptians and Mesopotamians built pyramids, surrogate mountains to enhance man's upward reach. The Mesopotamians built stepped pyramids (called *zigurats*), which were really vertical elaborations of the primitive *mastabas* (elongated brick tombs with sloping sides and a flat top) made of baked brick, which explains why so few remain. The Egyptians had river access to stone quarries, so their granite and marble pyramids have survived intact for centuries.

EGYPTIAN

The Egyptians also built enormous temples and palaces, which contained some of the earliest types of supporting columns. The column surely ranks with the **dome** as one of the most dramatic forms ever perfected by the architects of antiquity. The stone columns in these ancient temples derive their form and function from tree trunks, the original supporting structures. Architectural columns can be identified by their **capitals** (the top part). The most common types in Egyptian architecture were modeled after papyrus, lotus, and palm motifs, closed or open bud or flower (shown at right).

TEMPLE AS COSMIC SYMBOL

The grandest of all Egyptian temples was the Great Temple of Ammon at Karnak, Thebes, measuring 1200 ft. by 360 ft. in an immense enclosure along with other temples and a sacred lake. Our word *temple* comes from the Greek *temenos,* which means a sacred space cut off from the world. The word is also related to the Latin

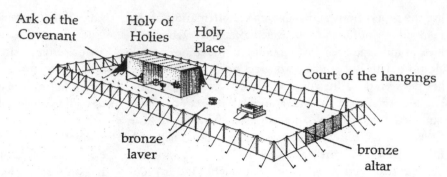

A. The Tabernacle of Moses, the Tent of the Congregation

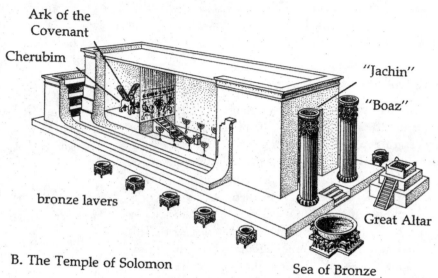

B. The Temple of Solomon

Courtesy of Deseret Book Company, Salt Lake City, Utah, and The Foundation for Ancient Research and Mormon Studies, Provo, Utah.

tempus, connected to TIME (as in musical tempo). In addition, *temple* is related etymologically to the Latin *templum,* the CUTTING POINT (as in template) between the *cardo* (NS line) and the *decumanus* (EW line) of the Roman city quadrants and from which the ancient observer of the heavens took his bearings. Thus, ancient temples represented a clear demarcation point connecting time and space, or, as Nibley noted, "a sort of halfway-house between heaven and earth" (47). That this cosmic view of ancient holy houses was widely recognized can easily be seen by comparing temple floor plans: virtually all of them, from ancient Egyptian and Greek temples to medieval Gothic cathedrals are sited on compass points and mark out a rectangular enclosure inside of which can be found a vestibule for cleansing and sacrifice, preparing for a Holy Place that leads to an inner Holy of Holies. The pattern seems clearest in the Israelitish models: the Tabernacle of Moses and the Temple of Solomon (see illustrations above).

The Acropolis in Athens, Greece, with the Parthenon on its summit.

THE CLASSICAL AGE: GREECE

INTRODUCTION

With the architecture of ancient Greece we come to the first early style which has exerted a profound impact on the styles of succeeding generations of buildings in Western civilization. In contrast to their Aegean and Egyptian predecessors, who were interested in private dwellings, the Greeks built primarily public buildings of a religious character—temples, altars, treasuries, and theaters.

THE PARTHENON

The most famous of all Greek temples is the Parthenon, the temple dedicated to the Goddess Athena Parthenos, protectress of Athens. It is situated on top of the **Acropolis,** the "city on a hill" in the center of Athens which was reserved for its holiest monuments (shown above; also see the photo at the start of the chapter).

ITS IMPORTANCE

Built between 447 and 438 B.C., the Parthenon is the high point of Doric architecture. Seen in its present partly ruined state, however, it may appear little more than a scaffolding of damaged pillars. What marks it as the forefather of all great classical buildings? One reason has to do with the happy coincidence that the most powerful statesman of Athens (Pericles) worked with the greatest architects (Ictinis and Callicrates) and the greatest sculptor (Phidias) at the moment (fifth century B.C.) when classical art had reached a high point in its long development.

ITS UNIQUENESS

Here are some things that make the Parthenon not only unique, but, in a larger sense, unprecedented and unexcelled in the history of architecture. In the first place, it embodies Protagoras' famous dictum: "Man is the measure of all things." The most vital factor, according to Donis A. Dondis (58–59) in the establishment of scale, is the measurement of man himself. In size, the Parthenon is neither so large as to dwarf man, nor so small as to diminish its stature as a temple to a god, thus conforming to the Greek desire for balanced harmony between extremes (Aristotle's "Golden Mean"). The mathematical formula of the **Golden Section** links human proportions to the mathematical ratios of the Parthenon (approximately 3 to 5). This is arrived at by bisecting a square and using the diagonal of one half of the square as a radius to extend the dimensions of the square to become a "Golden Rectangle."

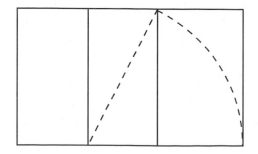

THE GREEK "GOLDEN AGE"

No wonder historians refer to fifth century B.C. Athenian civilization as the Greek "Golden Age." Fractions and multiples of this ratio found throughout the parts of the Parthenon help to account for its remarkable visual harmony. Since the eye (a sphere) bends a straight line seen from a distance into a concavity (bowed inward), the architects designed the columns with a slight convexity (bowed outward) to compensate (*entasis*). The foundation (*stylobate*) also bends upward slightly on each side and end. Thus, the axis of each column deviates from the perpendicular by 3 inches, so that if a line were drawn upwards from each column into the air, they would all meet about a mile above the Parthenon. These subtle deviations from the plumb create an organic effect of life and beauty (like the human body), because curved lines are life lines (straight lines don't exist in living things).

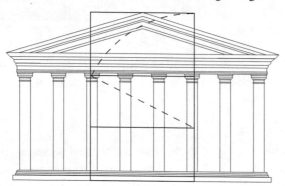

PARTHENON SCULPTURE

Three types of sculpture are integrated into the architectural framework of the Parthenon: the continuous low relief **frieze** extending around the entire inner building beneath the ceiling (depicting the Panathenaic procession); the high relief frieze beneath the **overhanging cornice** outside (depicting the battles between the Lapiths and centaurs); and the free-standing figures nestled in the pediments on each end (the eastern pediment, appropriately, depicts the birth of Athena out of the head of Zeus, while the western pediment shows Athena and Poseidon battling for the patronage of Athens). Known now as the Elgin Marbles, the damaged remnants of these elegant statues from the pediments can still be viewed in the British Museum (London). In some ways, the breathtaking perfection of the Parthenon sculptures, a rare blend of realism and idealism, has never been surpassed.

THE GREEK "ORDERS"

In order to make sense of classical architecture and to recognize its later manifestations in revival styles, it is nec-

essary to learn the related vocabulary. The illustration below indicates some of the more important parts of a Greek temple facade. These parts are not arbitrary arrangements. They are organically derived and aesthetically designed. Notice, for example, how the vertical effect of the fluted (grooved) columns (originally tree trunks) is subtly repeated in the **triglyphs** (originally the end beams of the roof) along the horizontal frieze above. Even the slight bulge of the columns (*entasis*) gives an effect of weight pressing down from above, like a muscle bearing weight.

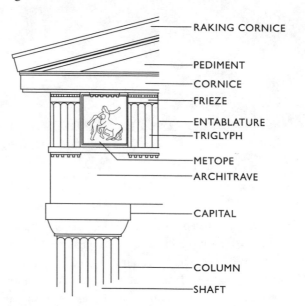

DORIC, IONIC, CORINTHIAN

There are three styles, or orders, of Greek architecture that have also been "anthropomorphized" by ancient Greek theorists. The **Doric,** which the Greeks thought of as bold and masculine, has a simple capital and no base, as seen in the Parthenon. The **Ionic,** which the Greeks viewed as more graceful and feminine, was characterized by taller, more slender fluted columns than the Doric, and by volutes (scroll-like ornaments) on the capital, as in the Erectheum (directly across from the Parthenon on the Acropolis). The flutes (grooves) on the columns reminded the Greeks of the folds in a woman's gown, the

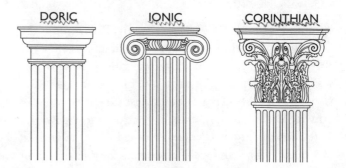

volutes of a woman's curled hair. The Greeks associated the **Corinthian** style with a wanton woman. It was distinguished from the Ionic by still greater height and by its acanthus-leaf capitals.

To round out their interest in organic motifs in their architecture, the Greeks incorporated various ornaments to dress up the borders of their buildings. The bead and reel, the egg and dart, and the tongue and dart are the more common moldings used in ancient Greek architecture, derived from the Erecthion on the Acropolis. They have been used repeatedly in classical revivals for over two thousand years.

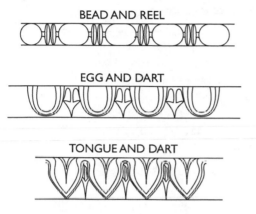

BEAD AND REEL

EGG AND DART

TONGUE AND DART

THE CLASSICAL AGE: ROME

The Romans absorbed the greatness of Greek culture as their own, calling it *humanitas* (humanity). They carved their own copies of the best of Greek portrait statues and built many of their temples after the manner of the rectangular Greek **megaron.** The "Maison Carée" in Nimes, France, was modeled loosely after the Parthenon, although it is perched on a podium, has engaged, instead of free-standing, columns, and an embellished vine frieze the Greeks would have considered extravagant. But no less an architect than Thomas Jefferson used it as a model for his design of the state capitol in Richmond, Virginia.

THE ROMAN ARCH

The **post-lintel** Greek temple design is atypical of Roman architectural practices, however. Their architects were more engineers than artists, their buildings more civic than religious. As the Greeks brought the ancient post-lintel design of Stonehenge and Egyptian temples to a peak of mathematical refinement, the Romans developed new ways of exploiting the arch, which originated in Mesopotamian cultures. Structurally, an arch makes more equitable use of the weight-bearing members by redistributing the stress among the wedge-shaped stones (*voissoirs*) that make up a simple arch. The stone lintel (b) is heavy and brittle. There are two forces at work: COMPRESSION (pressing together) on the top and TENSION (pulling apart) on the bottom, the point of highest stress. That is why stone columns are placed so close together. Since brittle material like stone works best in compression (being pressed together), the arch represents an ideal form for creating stable stone monuments.

The arch lends itself to a variety of forms (see illustrations below): it can stand alone (b); it can be extended laterally, leap-frog fashion, as in an aqueduct; it can be pushed backward along its horizontal axis into a barrel or tunnel **vault** (c); it can intersect at right angles with another barrel vault to form a groined vault (d); or it can be turned on its vertical axis to form a **dome** (e).

THE PANTHEON

One of the great Roman monuments from antiquity is the PANTHEON, whose name reveals its function as a temple to all the gods, a perfect symbol for Roman religious tolerance (notwithstanding the brutality of the Christian persecutions). The geometry of its parts marks a rare synthesis of previous architectural styles: the circular floor plan derives from ancient Greek and Roman circular temples (like the one at Delphi); the exterior portico pays homage to the Greek temple and all previous

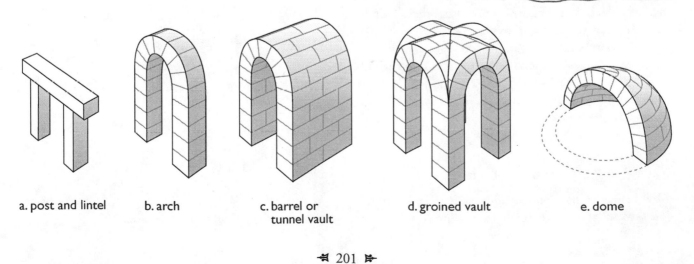

a. post and lintel   b. arch   c. barrel or tunnel vault   d. groined vault   e. dome

Pantheon, Rome, Italy (ca. 120 A.D.)

columned edifices; the coffered cement dome bears witness of Roman engineering ingenuity, a cylinder capped by a perfect hemisphere, both with a diameter of approximately 140 feet, thus making the interior correspond to an enormous sphere of unsupported space. In a significant way, the "palpable presence of space" (Gardner 222) in the Pantheon, first created by the Emperor Hadrian, its designer, anticipates the symbolic use of interior space in later Christian cathedrals.

THE EARLY MIDDLE AGES: EARLY CHRISTIAN/BYZANTINE

In a curious way, the Greek *megaron,* the columned rectangular prototype of the Greek temple, and the *stoa,* the columned courtyard in the marketplace at Athens, formed the nucleus of the Christian church, but modified in form and function as it passed through Roman hands. The Roman *basilica* (public hall) evolved from the columned courtyard and temple of the Greeks, but turned the Greek temple inside out by placing the columns on the inside and the walls on the outside. Its basic rectangular form with central **nave** and side aisles recalls the Greek temple, except that the Romans extended the ends into semicircular apses to provide space for the judges when law courts were in session. When the Christian religion received imperial sanction under Constantine in 313 A.D., the Roman basilica became the model for early Christian church architecture in the West; the model for eastern (**Byzantine**) Christian architecture was the circular temple, like the Pantheon.

EARLY WESTERN CHRISTIAN

By the early Christian era, all the architectural ingredients were present to form the foundation of the

Christian style in architecture: the **atrium** from the old Roman private dwelling (open area in the center of the house), the Roman basilica, and the Roman triumphal arch. In a real sense, the Christians simply expanded on the classical precedents and redefined the forms to fit their new religious symbolism. By extending part of the side walls near the apse into transepts, the floor plan turns into the likeness of the **cross** and the church becomes the surrogate body of Christ. The atrium, originally housing a pool of water, now serves as

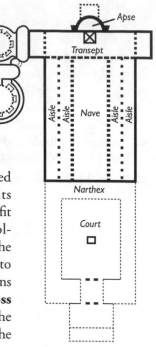

Floor plan of Old. St. Peter's

a cleansing area before entering the church proper. The **nave** (from Latin *navis* = ship) serves to "harbor" the faithful in the arms of the Church, protecting them from worldliness in the likeness of the ark, the "ship of the faithful," except now it is a spiritual protection from evil rather than physical protection from drowning. There are numerous nautical associations in Christian symbolism: the fish (whose Greek word *Icthys* creates an acronym for the phrase "Jesus Christ, Son of God, Savior") was a secret symbol in early Christianity with topical connections to the professions of some of the early Apostles (Peter and Andrew) and, by analogy, associated with their new spiritual professions as "fishers of men" as they were commissioned to throw the "gospel net" over all the world. Thus, a simple part, the nave, recalls a rich array of associated early Christian symbols. The ARCH framing the apse

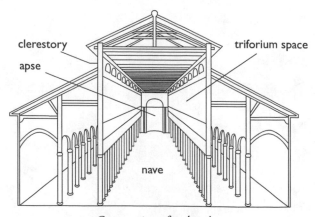

Cross section of a church.

recalls the ancient Roman triumphal arch, except now the victory is over sin and worldliness rather than the enemies of the empire. The APSE was the holy place where the emblems of Christ's body and blood were dispensed and where the altar stood. The mosaic decorations depicting heavenly scenes were appropriate to the divine destination of the believer's spiritual journey. The **clerestory,** containing windows placed high in the sidewalls beneath the ceiling, opened onto the sky beyond, inviting the faithful to lift their eyes to heaven. Thus, in their reworking of ancient forms the early Christians have given them different functions, putting new wine (their own symbolism) into old bottles (the ancient architectural forms) to create the foundation of one of Western Europe's richest and longest-lasting artistic traditions: medieval church architecture.

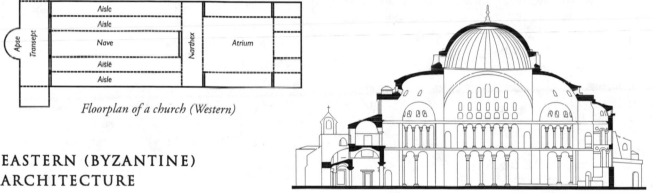

Floorplan of a church (Western)

EASTERN (BYZANTINE) ARCHITECTURE

EASTERN/WESTERN

The **Byzantine** style of early Christian architecture differs from its Western counterpart in a couple of ways. In the first place, the floor plans differ. As already noted, the Early Western Christian church is oriented on a longitudinal axis based on the Latin cross (long upright, short crosspiece), whereas, Byzantine churches generally have a central (vertical) axis built around a central dome over the Greek cross (arms of equal length) or some comparably centralized arrangement (square, circle, octagon, etc.)

HAGIA SOPHIA

All the elements of Early Western Christian architecture are in place in Byzantine structures; they are simply arranged differently. The aisles surround the nave, for example, instead of being placed beside it. Thus, the classical temples and the Roman domes combined with the Eastern (Greek) cross to create a unique style that persisted in Eastern Europe and the Middle East virtually up to the present. Interestingly, the largest and most imposing of Byzantine churches is also one of the oldest, the Church of Holy Wisdom (Hagia Sophia) in Istanbul (formerly Constantinople), built by the Eastern Emperor Justinian between A.D. 532 and 537. The floor plan reveals its debt to both early architectural traditions: an enormous central dome spanning a longitudinal nave. The link posed a difficult engineering problem: how to fit a round dome on a square base. The architects, Anthemius

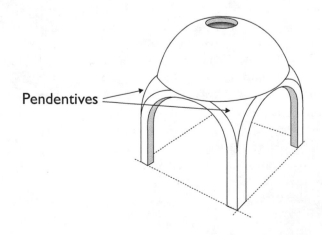

Section of Hagia Sophia, A.D. 532–537

of Tralles and Isidorus of Miletus, came up with an ingenious solution, considered by some to be one of the major innovations in the early history of architecture. They constructed a concave triangular section of masonry called a **pendentive** to navigate the transition from the square to the circle.

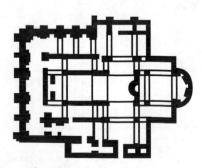

Floorplan of a church (Eastern)

Pendentives

THE RISE OF THE WEST

While the styles of Eastern Christian architecture and art remained relatively static over the next thousand years or so, the architecture of the West underwent marked changes from the early Middle Ages on. It took Western architects over five hundred years to approach the vast interior space of Hagia Sophia in their own cathedrals. Its size even rivaled the great monuments of Rome. Its dome stood 40 feet higher than the Pantheon's. The increasing sizes of Western churches can be partly attributed to their attempts to compete with Hagia Sophia's formidable dimensions. Word of its grandeur traveled the trade routes and the paths of the Crusaders. A comparison of the floor plans of the Early Christian church with its Romanesque and Gothic successors will reveal how inexorably the basilicas grew from their rather humble beginnings. In the Romanesque and Gothic ages, the increased size often resulted from civic rivalry, not unlike the intense sports competitions found among small-town teams in America. Raoul Glaber, an eleventh-century monk wrote: " . . . each Christian people strove against the others to erect nobler [churches]. It was as if the whole earth, having cast off the old . . . were clothing itself everywhere in the white robe of the church" (Holt **3,** qtd. in H. Gardner 329).

THE LATE MIDDLE AGES: ROMANESQUE/GOTHIC

ROMANESQUE

The impulse to build new churches and to compete with their neighbors in a newly emerging sense of national identity contributed to the rise of the **Romanesque** style and determined the great variety of national styles. Its emergence as a distinct style also had a lot to do with the need for strong fortifications from the ninth through the eleventh centuries. As a result, Romanesque architecture takes on two functions, the religious and the defensive, but both partake of similar stylistic elements: heavy rounded arches, thick walls with CORBELS topped by BATTLEMENTS and punctuated by TURRETS with CONICAL TOWERS. The term "Romanesque" was first used in the nineteenth century to designate the heavy castles of the mid-eleventh to the mid-twelfth centuries, characterized by the massive, round-arched look of Roman architecture.

ENGINEERING INNOVATIONS

The increasing size of the medieval church, however, brought with it new engineering challenges. In spite of the structural superiority of the arch in building with stone, the increased weight of the larger vaulted stone ceilings in Romanesque churches made it necessary to build thicker and thicker supporting walls to support the lateral thrust of the rounded arch. Eventually, the stone masons hit upon an ingenious solution: make the arch pointed and redistribute the downward and outward thrust of the arched vaults into supporting bridges (**flying buttresses**) outside the building (see illustration). Within a relatively short time, beginning in the middle of the twelfth century, the emerging **Gothic** style radiated outward from an area near Paris to fill most of Western Europe in the greatest building spree in history. More stone was quarried for cathedrals in France during the twelfth and thirteenth centuries than for all the great edifices of antiquity combined.

GOTHIC

What is a **cathedral?** Most simply put, it is the sacred building which houses the **cathedra** or bishop's throne in the central town of his diocese. When the bishop speaks for the Church, he speaks "ex cathedra," i.e., from his throne or seat. Chartres is the bishop's seat of the region of La Beauce in south central France. Its great Romanesque church burned down in 1194. By 1260 a new cathedral in the Gothic style had been erected in its

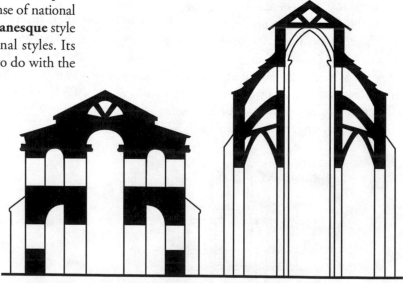

The rounded arches in Romanesque buildings required thick walls that limited their size. Gothic buildings used pointed arches and exterior bracing called flying buttresses that allowed thinner walls and larger buildings.

place, built around the old Romanesque western portal of the earlier church. Then in the early sixteenth century the north spire burned down and a replacement was built in the late gothic style. Thus, this magnificent edifice, sometimes called the "Queen of Cathedrals," reveals three great eras of medieval architecture in its stylistic variety (Romanesque, mature Gothic, and late Gothic). Like the Parthenon, it integrates a plethora of sculptural decoration with an engineering feat made more remarkable by the primitive building techniques available to the nameless masons who, through trial and error, managed to construct these enormous mountains of stone in honor of their god.

THE SCULPTURAL "TEXT"

Learning to read the sculpted images clustered around and inside a cathedral is like learning a new language. The symbolic details were carefully worked out by the intellectuals of the church. Their iconographic program forged links between Old Testament prefigurations of Christ and the New Testament fulfillment of Old Testament prophecies. As the Parthenon was dedicated to Athena, the cathedrals were dedicated to the Virgin Mary, Athena's medieval counterpart as patroness of the arts and protector of the city and its inhabitants. Most cathedrals are technically referred to as **Notre Dame de . . .** followed by the name of the town (Chartres, Rheims, Amiens, etc.). Mary presided over the seven liberal arts (grammar, logic, rhetoric, geometry, astronomy, arithmetic, and music), the central curriculum of the medieval cathedral schools and the basis for the foundation disciplines in today's "liberal arts education."

THE MEDIEVAL "SUMMAS"

As one of the great medieval "Summas" (summations of all knowledge), along with Dante's *Divine Comedy* in literature and St. Thomas Aquinas' *Summa Theologica* in theology, Chartres Cathedral stands as a perfect visual synthesis of medieval culture. It served both civic and sacred functions as well as providing an image-laden biblical "text" for the illiterate. Beside the sculptures of saints, apostles, and the ancestors of Christ one finds signs of the Zodiac and common people involved in typical labors, like harvesting wheat or pruning fruit trees. And due to the "ribbed cage" effect made possible by the pointed arch and flying buttresses, the thick wall space of the Romanesque church gave way to magnificent stained glass, which not only depicted holy personages to amplify the visual program of the exterior statuary, but filtered the interior space to approximate a celestial realm on earth. But, the most important symbolic element of the cathedral was the vast, otherworldly space, the space we first became fully aware of in the Pantheon in Rome. But now it represents the divine presence of God himself: like air, the ultimate reality as well as the ultimate mystery.

THE MYSTERY OF CHARTRES

One mystery remains that binds the anonymous builders of the cathedrals like Chartres to the Druid priests of the ancient megaliths like Stonehenge. Louis Charpentier in his book *The Mysteries of Chartres Cathedral* writes of the remarkable collaboration between stone mason and glazier. Every year on the 21st of June (the summer solstice) at approximately a quarter to five minutes before 1 p.m. a ray of sun casts a spot of light through a hole in the stained glass window onto a tenon (metal projection) which has been inserted into a particular flagstone. As Charpentier observes:

A concerted intention was at the bottom of this. Stonemason and glazier obeyed an order. And this order was given with a view to a specific time: the only moment in the year when a ray of the sun can fall on the flagstone is the summer solstice, when the sun reaches the climax of its northern journey. It was given them by an astronomer. . . . The place was chosen by a geometer. . . . When this little game of 'the sun on the slab' is played in one of the most venerated cathedrals of the West, in one of the places of highest fame in France, the idea takes hold of you that there is a mystery. It took hold of me. . . . The cathedral took on a life of its own, a life that puzzled me without, for all that, being alien. Everything seemed at the same time strange and familiar. (10)

Chartres Cathedral, Chartres, France (1194–1260)

THE RENAISSANCE

The **Renaissance** style, beginning in Italy in the early fifteenth century with the dedication of the great *Duomo* in Florence in 1436, by FILIPPO BRUNELLESCHI (1377–1446), marks the advent of one of the most self-conscious efforts to revive earlier styles in the history of architecture. We have already discovered that the history of architectural styles follows a dialectical process; that is, each succeeding style alters the preceding models, yet retains some essential characteristics of the parent style. For example, the Greeks drew inspiration from the columned temples of the Egyptians but changed the style of the capitals; the Romans built temples modeled directly after the Parthenon (like the "Maison Carée") but placed them on podiums and replaced the alternating **triglyph/metope** frieze with an elaborate vine motif; the early Christians copied the Roman basilica floor plan and used the Roman triumphal arch as a model for the tripartite (Trinity) windows on the exterior and to frame the apse on the interior but added transepts that gave it a cruciform floor plan; the Romanesque and Gothic styles expanded and altered the early Christian basilica to create the crowning achievement of late medieval architecture, the cathedral. In fact, the word *Renaissance* means rebirth of classical culture, so it was natural for them to draw on earlier precedents, not only Graeco-Roman, but even medieval, which they generally dismissed as barbaric (the word *gothic* suggests "barbarian"). The Renaissance, coming at the end of almost 2,000 years of classical and medieval architecture, had many stylistic options to choose from. Notice below the evolution of floor plans from Greek through Renaissance.

THE *DUOMO*

Brunelleschi's magnificent *Duomo* (Ital. for dome) sets the pattern for all high-pitched domed buildings. It num-bers among its descendants St. Peter's in Rome, St. Paul's in London, *Karlskirche* in Vienna, and our own national and state capitals in America. It would be difficult to overestimate its impact on succeeding generations of western European public buildings, but, seen individually, its parts can be traced to earlier precedents. Brunelleschi discovered these firsthand by a trip to Rome in 1401 with the sculptor, Donatello. Brunelleschi's genius fit them all together in a grand synthesis, thereby creating a new form from older parts. Consider the rich variety of his enlightened borrowings: a cut-away profile of the dome itself mirrors the shape of a gothic arch; the oculus beneath the lantern tower recalls the domed ceiling of the Pantheon; the octagonal base comes from the early Byzantine floor plans; the dome bound to a longitudinal nave combines the two essential forms of the Eastern and Western Christian styles; the half-domes buttressing the exterior walls of the octagon are reminiscent in form and function of a Byzantine church, like Hagia Sophia. Brunelleschi avoided relying on flying buttresses to shore up the enormous supporting walls because they were too gaudy and too "gothic." His solution was as ingenious as the Byzantine invention of pendentives. He built a smaller dome within the outer dome to reinforce it, thereby eliminating the need to break up the clean exterior elevation.

Duomo Santa Maria del Fiore

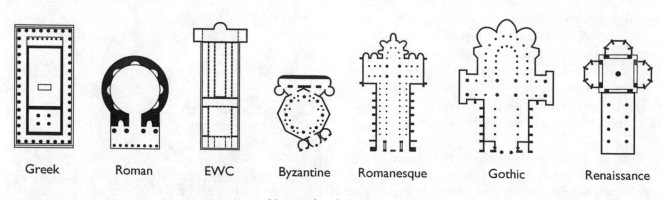

| Greek | Roman | EWC | Byzantine | Romanesque | Gothic | Renaissance |

Various church floor plans

PALLADIO

Thus, revival styles work best when they expand on previous material and adapt them to new cultural contexts; otherwise, they tend to be mere copies and have limited aesthetic merit. As we shall see, the eighteenth and nineteenth centuries spawned numerous offspring of both kinds. One particularly successful late Renaissance architect, Andrea Palladio (1508–1580), restructured the classical Greek temple facade to fit onto the vertical interior spaces of the Christian basilica, as seen in his Church of San Giorgio Maggiore (1565) in Venice. A more widely known contribution was his **"Palladian Window,"** an ingenious yet simple integration of the two classical modes of construction, Greek post-lintel and the Roman arch. Postmodern architects of the late twentieth century have been particularly fond of this window.

We would expect to find the following in Renaissance architecture: HIGH-PITCHED DOMES topped by a lantern tower; classical elements used mostly as decoration, like Greek **capitals** (doric, ionic, corinthian) and **ornamental pediments** (miniature pediments placed as decorative elements over the doors and windows), and Roman **pilasters** (flat columns built into the walls or facades) originally found in the Colosseum and Pantheon; **overhanging cornices**, often with ornamental bracket supports; **balustrades** (fencelike motifs along the roof line); and **stringcourses** (lines of masonry separating the building into horizontal sections). In general, the Renaissance style reveals a horizontal, rectilinear orientation in the elevation with geometrically balanced floor plans.

Overhanging cornice   Balustrade   Ornamental pediment

Pilaster   Stringcourse

Palace of the Senate, by Michelangelo (ca. 1537)

THE BAROQUE

You will often find the above elements in **Baroque** architecture. But, in contrast to the Renaissance styles, Baroque architecture tends toward a more vertical orientation and to a much more ornamented and curvilinear exterior and interior. And because the development of nation-states, begun in the Romanesque period, had by the seventeenth century become a pan-European phenomenon, the Baroque styles are species-specific to the countries that produced them. At the risk of being simplistic, we can make the following generalizations about the major national variants. Italian Baroque, because its home base contains so many classical monuments, tends to retain the classical vocabulary, although in curved contexts. One of the finest examples is the Church of the Four Fountains (1638–1641) in Rome (shown on p. 208) by Francesco Barromini (1599–1667). Comparing his church to Brunelleschi's Pazzi chapel (ca. 1440) reveals some telling differences between the two styles: the Baroque edifice rises in a vertical stacking of two sets of engaged columns, separated by three-dimensional ornamentation and oval medallions, within a context of undulating surfaces, while the Pazzi Chapel, in comparison, is severely geometrical and self-contained. A comparison of

Palladian window in the Gordon B. Hinckley Alumni Building, Brigham Young University, Provo, UT.

Borromini's Church of the Four Fountains (San Carlo alle Qattro Fontane) (Italian Baroque), Rome 1635–1667.

Filippo Brunelleschi, Pazzi Chapel (Renaissance), west Façade. Begun ca. 1440, Santa Croce, Florence.

the two floor plans indicates similar differences between rigorously geometrical shapes (circles, squares, and rectangles) in a system of modular relationships and a freely designed series of irregular oval patterns, the interior reversing the undulating lines of the facade. Spanish Baroque moves even farther toward ornamental excess in the hands of architects like Jose de Benito Churriguera (1665–1725), whose altarpiece for San Esteban in Salamanca is "an architectural-sculptural-pictorial extravaganza" (Fleming 337). The more florid aspects of the Spanish Baroque are even called "churrigueresque" after him. The FRENCH BAROQUE adopted a more classical stance toward baroque embellishments by retaining the classical decorative elements, but giving in to exaggerations in size, as seen in the vast dimensions and grounds of Versailles. The details of Louis XIV's grandiose palace outside Paris reveal a classical restraint, even if the interiors give way to ornamental excess. The **Mansard roof** is a unique feature of the French baroque, a steeply sloping roof punctuated by **dormer** windows (see illustration). For some reason, this particular roof shape has become very popular in twentieth-century apartment complexes. The English Baroque is even more unique, in that one of its most typical manifestations is an unlikely hybrid of a Greek temple base topped by a steep, gothic-like tower above the pediment, as seen in James Gibbs's St. Martin-in-the-Fields in London (1721–1726). Early English settlers in New England brought this style to America where it has become the standard of early American church architecture.

Versailles Palace (French Baroque), France (1661–1688).

St. Martin's-in-the-Fields (English Baroque), London, England (1721–1726).

TRADITIONAL STYLE REVIEW

Below are illustrations of the styles we have learned about up to the nineteenth century:

Greek (600–100 B.C.)

1. Rectangular floor plan of marble

2. Simple post-lintel construction with Doric, Ionic, Corinthian capitals on fluted (grooved) columns holding up the **entablature**

3. Ideal proportions; mathematical symmetry

4. Refinements of proportion to create optical illusions

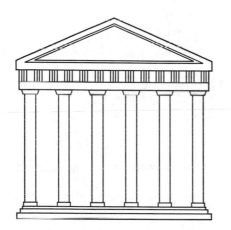

Roman (100 B.C.–A.D. 500)

1. Rectangular and circular floor plans

2. Ingenious use of the arch rather than strictly post-lintel

3. Fluted freestanding and engaged columns

4. Coffered (decorative sunken panels) ceilings over large spaces

5. Decorative use of medallions and keystones

Early Western Christian (300–A.D. 700)

1. Roman basilica floor plan of a center aisle, one or even two side aisles and an apse and transept at the east end

2. Plain facade with three-part (trinity) windows

3. Bell tower disengaged from facade

4. Ceiling coffered in square panels

5. Triforium space decorated with mosaics

Byzantine (300–A.D. 1000)

1. Greek cross floor plan

2. Great dome on pendentives buttressed by half domes all around

3. Plain exterior

4. Interiors of colored, richly grained marble with shimmering mosaics in the upper vaults

5. Pillars decorated in lacy yet geometrical patterns

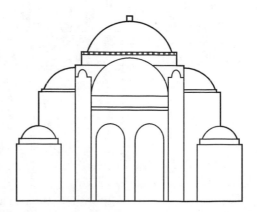

Romanesque (1000–1200)

1. Latin cross floor plan

2. Rounded arch with barrel and/or groined vaulting

3. Recessed doorways with multiple archivolts (arched bands)

4. Rose window sometimes appearing above entrance

5. Tower attached to main structure with conical roof and rounded-arch windows divided by slender columns

6. Hunched over, crouching figures carved on capitals of pillars

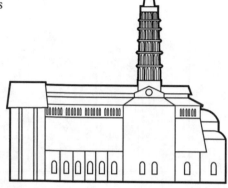

Gothic (1200–1400)

1. Latin cross floor plan

2. Soaring pointed arches, ribbed vaulting, flying buttresses, and gargoyles

3. High, pointed towers; decorated pinnacles with various modules and finials

4. Stained-glass rose and lancet (shaped like the point of an arrow) windows

5. Tall, recessed doorways (with pointed arches) decorated with elongated figures

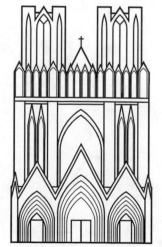

Renaissance (1400–1600)

1. Rectangular floor plan combining Greek post-lintel form and Roman arch form

2. Ribbed dome topped with lantern tower

3. Two or more stories of symmetrically balanced windows with alternating pediments

4. Decorative balustrade, pilasters, and ornamental pediments

5. Stringcourse accenting the horizontal emphasis

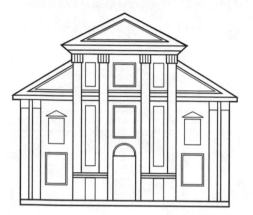

Baroque (1600–1800)

1. Circular floor plan with curved and swirling ornamentation

2. In-and-out movement of curved steps and balustrades (undulating facade)

3. Abundance of sculpture-especially in upper regions

4. Dramatic and exuberant use of light and dark patterns

5. Striking, illusory ceiling decoration

REVIVAL STYLES

One of the most satisfying aspects of learning to recognize traditional architectural styles is the chance to put your knowledge to work on buildings in your own community. The older sections of virtually every city in the United States contain many examples of eighteenth- and nineteenth-century architectural **revivals**. The following schema and list of elements for each revival will be of some use in orienting yourself to this delightful sleuthing experience. The largest and perhaps most authentic examples are located in the larger and older cities of America, like Washington D.C., Philadelphia, and New York City on the east coast, and in San Francisco, Sacramento, and San Diego on the west coast, but every larger city has its fair share.

Roman Revival (1800–1850)

1. More monumental than the Greek Revival

2. Rounded or angular pedimented windows

3. Projecting central pediment and classical portico

4. Symmetrical facade topped by a shallow dome

5. Embellished with Graeco-Roman ornamentation (triglyphs, corinthian capitals, etc.)

6. Roof balustrades with arched openings

7. In general, arch dome construction, which differentiates it from the Greek

Thomas Jefferson's Monticello in Virginia.

Greek Revival (1820–1850)

1. Gabled portions or temple facade (one or two stories)

2. Columns with Greek Doric or Ionic capitals

3. Emphasis on post-lintel (beam) construction

4. Greek ornamental motifs

Second Bank of the United States in Philadelphia, Pennsylvania.

5. Low or flat roofs

6. Decorative columns (either engaged columns or pilasters) often framing doors with heavy cornices

Romanesque (Richardsonian) Revival (1870–1890)

1. Heavy rusticated exterior stone or brick work

2. Turrets and conical roofs, occasionally with battlements and machicolations

3. Fortress-like facades with massive stone arches

4. Exterior sculptural decoration

5. Deeply set grouped windows (tripartite and often stained glass) with stone supports ("mullians")

6. Occasional **eyebrow dormers** built into roof

The City and County Building in Salt Lake City, Utah.

Gothic Revival (1830–1870)

1. Steep central gable flanked by smaller gables or **dormers** with pointed-area foliated windows

2. Asymmetrical facade

3. Overall aspect is vertical and highly picturesque, quaint ("gingerbread" house in domestic style)

Votivkirche in Vienna, Austria.

Renaissance (Italianate) Revival (1840–1880)

1. Low gabled roof with overhanging cornice and decorative brackets

2. Tall, arched windows with hood moldings, often Palladian windows

3. Elaborate entrances, often with balustrade

4. Often tall towers and corner quoins (interlocking stones to reinforce the corners where two walls meet)

5. Roofs occasionally topped with cupola

6. Flat facade or gated with projecting bay window

Victorian Eclectic (1830–1900)

This represents the catch-all mongrel type revival.

1. Unusual door and window shapes

2. Odd-shaped roof lines and dormers

3. Onion domes and mansard roof together

4. Turrets and balconies

5. Byzantine decoration, colored tiles and minarets

6. Palladian windows

The Carson Mansion in Eureka, California.

MODERN ARCHITECTURE: ORGANIC

FRANK LLOYD WRIGHT

All significant architecture manages to create a harmonious blend of form and function or it would not have survived, physically or aesthetically. But perhaps no time in history has one architect taken the challenge so seriously as Frank Lloyd Wright (1867–1959), whose mentor, Louis Sullivan (1856–1924), paved the way for the emergence of modern American architecture with his

Left: Louis Sullivan, Prudential Building, Buffalo, NY (1894–1895).

Below: Frank Lloyd Wright, "Falling Water" (Kaufmann House), Bear Run, PA (ca. 1937).

"skyscrapers." His student Frank Lloyd Wright was perhaps the most original and influential architect America has ever produced. His midwest perspective called for a great simplicity in design, an interdependence of man and nature that has given his style its name, "organic." For Wright, architecture is decidedly *not* the classical models, nor the "grandomania" of the Renaissance and Baroque. On the contrary, a building must express a sense of integration with the environment. Thus, for architecture to be truly organic, it must affirm that which is natural and humanizing. Its forms must conform to natural forms (the horizon, the configurations of the landscape), natural colors (greens, browns, blues), natural materials (stone, wood, glass), and natural forces (gravity countered by **cantilevering,** the extension of weight over unsupported space).

"Falling Water"

The supreme example of his new vision of organic living spaces resides in "Falling Water," the name given to the Edgar A. Kaufmann house in Bear Run, Pennsylvania, designed by Wright in 1936. Built as a second home for the family to escape to, the house was sited over a waterfall. Wright laid to rest the initial worries of local engineers who feared the weight would cause the rock foundation to collapse, by utilizing three kinds of canti-

levering: "extension from an anchorage (as in the iron arm suspending a kettle over the living room fire grate); counterbalancing (like simple scales); and loaded extension that permits limited anchorage (the way that a man squatting, with only the balls of his feet and toes touching the earth, extends his knees)" (Kaufmann 90). The fulcrum of these counter-forces centers on a large boulder that eventually became the natural stone seat in front of the fireplace. The stone for the flagstone floors and the outside rockwork was quarried from the adjacent site and polished to suggest the smooth surfaces of a stream bed. Wright even designed the exterior rockwork to correspond to the stratified forms of the natural rock formations by the waterfall. The expansive ribbon windows on all sides draw nature in and offer grand vistas onto the natural surroundings. All the furniture was specially designed in black American walnut, with long seats built along exterior walls, cantilevered just above the floor. Looking upward from downstream, the two cantilevered porches "echo" the ledge and the water passing over it. The home is situated on the north slope in order to take full advantage of the sunlight from the south. Its axis creates a quadrant connected to the four ancient elements: air (looking downstream from the porch); earth (toward the north anchor hill); fire (toward the fireplace); and water (descending the stairs to the stream below). Looking at its modern design, it is difficult to imagine that it was built over sixty years ago.

MODERN ARCHITECTURE: INTERNATIONAL

"Man-Made Nature"

The term **"International Style"** derives from a book by Henry Russell Hitchcock and Philip Johnson, *International Style: Architecture since 1922*, published in 1932 for a special exhibit of mostly European architects that same year at the Museum of Modern Art in New York. Influenced by Walter Gropius's Bauhaus in Germany, these architects (Richard Neutra, Ludwig Mies van der Rohe, Marcel Breuer, and Philip Johnson, among others) were interested in new materials and engineering principles that would enable them to construct tall urban structures capable of creating a man-made environment ideal for modern living. A good example is the Seagram Building in New York City. In contrast to Wright's "organic" philosophy, these architects preferred man-made "machines for living." Finnish-born architect Eero Saarinen (1910–1961) represents some of the best of the postwar International architects. His philosophy contrasts markedly with Wright's: "I think of architecture as the total of man's man-made physical surroundings. The only thing I leave out is nature. You might say it is man-made nature" ("Remarks" 164). Even though Saarinen's view seems to contradict Wright's, beneath their differences is a common belief that the best architecture enhances man's spiritual well-being. Wright defined his architecture as "that great living creative spirit which from generation to generation, from age to age, proceeds, persists, creates, according to the nature of man, and his circumstances as

Mies van der Rohe, Seagram Building, New York, (1956–1958).

they change. That is really architecture" ("An Organic Architecture" 156). Similarly, Saarinen argued that the primary purpose of architecture is "almost a religious one. . . . To shelter and enhance man's life on earth and to fulfill his belief in the nobility of his existence" ("Remarks" 165).

GATEWAY ARCH

One of Saarinen's most impressive monuments is the Gateway Arch in St. Louis (1967). In its form and function, it perfectly embodies Saarinen's three common principles of modern architecture: "function, structure, and being part of our time" ("Remarks" 165). It stands on the levee of the Mississippi at the beginning of Lewis and Clark's expedition to open the West after Thomas Jefferson's Louisiana Purchase in 1803. By means of a 630-foot inverted catenary arch (making it the tallest man-made monument in the land), it proclaims St. Louis's historic role as "Gateway to the West." Its simple arch construction allies it to the ancient Roman arch. Yet, beneath its stainless steel skin lie the resilient bonding materials of 25,000 tons of concrete and steel which far surpass anything Roman engineers could ever have dreamed possible. Night sightings on pre-determined anchor points enabled the engineers to achieve an accuracy of less than 1/64 of an inch error at the top. Due to its concrete and steel core and because the legs are sunk sixty feet into native bedrock, the top will deflect only 18 inches in a 150 mph wind. It joins a few other monuments, like the Golden Gate Bridge in San Francisco, as eloquent witnesses to the finest engineering feats of this century, in which there is a perfect blending of beauty and utility.

POSTMODERN ARCHITECTURE

Beginning in the 1970s, architects began to question the "less is more" aesthetic of the International school with the dehumanizing sterility of its large areas of unrelieved concrete and glass which made humans often feel like caged animals. Many architectural historians date the beginnings of post-modernism in architecture to the publication of Robert Venturi's book *Complexity and Contradiction in Architecture* (1966), in which he both summarizes the history of architecture and presents his critique of mainstream modernism's sterile glass and steel boxes. In the chapter "Nonstraightforward Architecture: A Gentle Manifesto," Venturi writes: "Architects can no longer afford to be intimidated by the puritanically moral language of orthodox modern architecture. I like elements which are hybrid rather than 'pure,' compromising rather than 'clean,' distorted rather than 'straightforward.' I am for messy vitality over obvious unity" (qtd. in Clendinning 122–123).

Eero Saarinen, Gateway Arch, St. Louis

As you can probably tell from Venturi's manifesto, post-modern architecture rejects modernism's clean lines and boxy spaces in favor of curvilinear patterns and ambiguous spaces, in short, a return to the past (eclecticism, combining styles) in a welcome relief from modernism's orthodoxy. Clendinning identifies four traits of the post-modern style in architecture: disunity, multiple meanings, playfulness, and surface decoration drawn from past styles. The recent works of architects like Philip Johnson, Michael Graves, and Frank Gehry exemplify these new goals in sometimes surprising, even shocking ways.

PHILIP JOHNSON

On the face of it, Philip Johnson seems an unlikely advocate for postmodernism since he collaborated with Mies van der Rohe in designing one of the flagships of the International style, the Seagram Building in New York (1958), but he clearly recognized in his later years that modernism's sterile, rectilinear spaces can detract from a humanizing environment. His revolutionary design for the AT&T Building in New York (1978–1983) shocked both critics and the public: he breaks up the rectilinear

Philip Johnson, AT&T Building (now the Sony Building), New York City, NY (1984)

facade with an arched Palladian portal at the base (harking back to late Renaissance architecture) and a Chip and Dale broken pediment at the apex, which prompted critics to call it a piece of glorified furniture (a "highboy"), while others saw it as a perfect headquarters for "Ma Bell"—"It had a pay phone coin slot at the top and a coin return at the bottom" (qtd. in Clendinning 125).

MICHAEL GRAVES

Michael Graves's Portland Public Service Building goes several steps farther in redefining a modern office building. The color combinations and eclectic details are totally unexpected: the base has three greenish-blue tiled, stepped stories, topped by a twelve-story cream-colored near-perfect cube, graced with pink fiberglass garlands like poster-board cutouts, and flattened columns (pilasters) six stories high with one-story-high protruding capitals. On paper it sounds like an impossible mixture of styles (Greek, Roman, Italian Mannerist, Pop Art, Art Deco), but it seems to work. At least it has gained acceptance as a monument to a new era of architecture, although the critics are still divided about its artistic merits. Arnason applauds its balanced eclecticism: "a truly civic building imbued with all the dignity of the human past made whole with a boldly asserted, living present" (quoted in Clendinning 126); but architect and architectural historian, Robert A. M. Stern disagrees: "But in reality, the building is more convincing as a billboard for an idea, rather than its embodiment" (quoted in Clendinning 127).

Michael Graves, Public Service Building, Portland, OR (1980).

FRANK GEHRY

The *Wunderkind* of Postmodernism is undoubtedly Frank Gehry, whose recent works seem to have been attacked by a blow torch and melted into amorphous sculptural formations. He obviously took the need to soften the hard contours of the international style quite literally. The warm public appeal of his architecture comes partly from his down-to-earth demeanor. He has few theories, even though his convoluted forms require very complex engineering methods to construct. But for the !general viewer, the *L. A. Times* suggests: "It is important to see all of Gehry's work from a perspective of blissful ignorance, to observe his structures from the childlike viewpoint of one who has no preconceptions about what architecture must be" (Dreyfuss 8). There is an exhilarating freedom and playfulness in his most famous works to date: his Nationale-Nederlanden Building (1992–1996) in Prague has been nicknamed "Fred and Ginger," because its rounded, leaning towers seem to dance together as Fred Astaire and Ginger Rogers; his Experience Music Project (1995–2000) in Seattle, which derives its name from the Jimi Hendrix Experience, is a "swoopy" building dedicated to the celebration of pop music. He drew his initial inspiration for the edifice by smashing two guitars and assembling the broken pieces. But perhaps his best-known work so far is the Guggenheim Museum (1991–1997) in Bilbao, Spain, which marked the first time Gehry systematically used CATIA computer software to design the curved surfaces of the museum, greatly simplifying design, construction, and controlling building costs by providing digital data that could be employed in the manufacturing process. As you might imagine, he is not universally appreciated. Some architects are angry with his seeming betrayal of traditional architecture; others are envious of his success. But, according to architectural historian, William J. Mitchell, both camps are wrong: "Gehry has, in fact, found a way of designing and building that is far more in

Frank Gehry, Nationale-Nederlander Building, Prague (1992–1996)

tune with the realities of our digitalizing, globalizing age than are the stale dogmas of machine-age Modernism" (353).

In recent years Gehry has done the seeming impossible: his outrageous designs equally please both critics and the public, creating a liberating reaction in general for the future of a style that may be the first ever to evoke an equal blend of humor and monumentality. This is close to Arnason's observation: "herein may lie the essence of Post-Modernism, which longs for the monumentality and symbolism of old but, lacking the faith originally embodied in those forms, must inevitably undermine them with ingenious puns and brilliant self-mockery" (qtd. in Clindinning 125–126).

SUMMARY & CURRENT DEVELOPMENTS

Where do we go from here? The 1990s marked the emergence of a rather unexpected but natural reaction to the energy and ecological crises of the past: "Green" architecture. Craig Kneeland, chief of the New York State Energy Research and Development Authority, has stated that the first replacement building at the World Trade Center site in New York will feature a green design: "The architects and the engineers made it clear they wanted a green building" (qtd. by McCall M1).

Frank Gehry, Guggenheim Museum, Bilbao, Spain (1991–1997).

What is a "green" building and where did the idea come from? The term *green* relates to ecological issues, of course. The movement began to take shape in the late 1970s with the oil embargo and growing public concern over rising energy costs. It became formally organized in Chicago in the summer of 1993 when thousands of architects, city planners, developers, builders, manufacturers, and suppliers met to discuss the issue of "sustainable development." In other words, how much urban development can the earth sustain? They concluded with a "Declaration of Interdependence for a Sustainable Future," agreeing to create a new ethic "as a multidisciplinary partnership" (Crosbie 5) to prevent us from destroying our common heritage. For the first time in human history we have the technology to monitor and document ecological problems as well as the technology to solve these problems, which are interconnected and interdependent. For example, "we now know that the chlorofluorocarbons we created to increase our comfort by improving insulation and coolants also deplete the protective ozone layer that, ironically, increases the need for energy, insulation and coolants" (Crosbie 4). The power driving this new movement is also economic. A study in 2001 by Portland State University estimated that "Oregon and Washington State alone could save $100 million a year by retrofitting older buildings and incorporating 'green' designs into new construction" (McCall M1). As an example, the Portland regional training office for American Honda Motor Co. "has floors made of recycled tires, a roof that funnels rainwater into an underground storage basin for landscape irrigation and toilets, even tables made from crushed sunflower shells" (McCall M2). Three U.S. cities (New York, Portland, and Austin) have become national leaders of the "green building" movement in an effort to improve energy efficiency and blend into nature in everything from skyscrapers to private homes. The success of this movement could provide a grand synthesis of the post-revival styles we have been discussing: international, organic, and **postmodern**.

CONCLUSION

Thus, we have come full circle in our journey through architectural history, a time framed on both ends by giant monuments that reach as far into the sky as man's technology and vision will allow, that unite significant form with indispensable function, that embrace vast spaces while commemorating pivotal events in a culture's history. The obvious difference lies in the gradual shift from sacred to secular motives, the same difference noted earlier between cathedrals and skyscrapers. As Luigi Barzini once said of our age: "We are great tech-

nicians, but small believers" (documentary film "Once Upon a Wall"). Our greatest architects still dream of a higher purpose:

> We cannot have an organic architecture unless we achieve an organic society! We may build some buildings for a few people knowing the significance or value of that sense of the whole which we are learning to call organic, but we cannot have an architecture for a society such as ours now is. We who love architecture and recognize it as the great sense of structure in whatever is—music, painting, sculpture, or life itself—we must somehow act as intermediaries—maybe missionaries. (Wright, *An Organic Architecture*)

WRITING EXERCISES

Take a closer look at a building in which you have spent some time. It could be your home, school, church, or some local public building like a theater or an assembly hall. Write down some brief observations about your feelings toward it, the appeal of its appearance (exterior, interior), the visual features of the facade (the "face" of the building) and the "human measure" of the interior (is it so large you feel diminished? or so small you feel cramped?). Does the interior enhance your need for beauty and comfort (convenience)? Does it have ample lighting? Are the colors inviting and harmonious? Finally, write a short paragraph explaining the particular relationship between its form (outer and inner) and its function as home, school, church, etc.

WORKS CITED

Barzini, Luigi. *Once Upon a Wall: The Great Age of Fresco.* Doc. film. Phoenix/BFA, 1969.

Charpentier, Louis. *The Mysteries of Chartres Cathedral.* London: Thorsons, 1972.

Clark, Kenneth. *Civilisation.* New York: Harper & Row, 1969.

Clendinning, Jane Piper. "Postmodern Architecture / Postmodern Music." *Postmodern Music / Postmodern Thought.* Ed. Judy Lochhead and Joseph Auner. New York and London: Routledge, 2002.

Crosbie, Michael J. *Green Architecture: A Guide to Sustainable Design.* Rockport, MA: Rockport Publishers, 1994.

Dewey, John. *Art as Experience.* New York: Capricorn, 1958.

Dondis, Donis A. *A Primer of Visual Literacy.* Boston: MIT, 1973.

Dreyfuss, John. "Gehry: The Architect as Artist." *Los Angeles Times* 7 November 1979, Part IV, 8.

Fleming, William. *Arts and Ideas.* 3rd ed. New York: Holt, Rinehart and Winston, n.d.

Fletcher, Sir Banister. *A History of Architecture on the Comparative Method.* New York: Scribner's, 1961.

Gardner, Helen. *Art through the Ages.* 6th ed. New York: Harcourt Brace Jovanovich, 1975.

Jacobs, David. *Architecture.* New York: Newsweek Books, 1974.

Kaufmann, Edgar, Jr. *Fallingwater.* New York: Abbeville, 1986.

McCall, William. "U.S. cities sprouting 'green' buildings." *Deseret News,* Sunday 16 June 2002, MI-2.

Michell, John. *The New View Over Atlantis.* New York: Harper & Row, 1969; rpt. 1986.

Mitchell, William J. "Roll over Euclid: How Frank Gehry Designs and Builds." *Frank Gehry, Architect.* Ed. J. Fiona Ragheb. New York. Solomon R. Guggenheim Museum, 2001.

Saarinen, Eero. "Remarks at Dickinson College, 1959." Qtd. In David Jacobs. *Architecture.* New York: Newsweck Books, 1974. 164–166.

Wright, Frank Lloyd. "An Organic Architecture 1939." Qtd. In David Jacobs. *Architecture.* New York: Newsweek Books, 1974. 154–157.

WEBSITES OF INTEREST

For the following, go to earth.google.com and click on the link for Gallery—
3D tour of Colosseum
3D tour of Cathedrals

Great Buildings online —
http://www.greatbuildings.com/

Virtual Tours of famous buildings —
http://ah.bfn.org/a/virtual/tc.html

Digital Archive of European Architecture —
http://www.bc.edu/bc_org/avp/cas/fnart/arch/contents_europe.html

Digital Images of Architecture —
http://www.bluffton.edu/~sullivanm/index/index2.html
http://www.pritzkerprize.com/
http://www.pbs.org/wgbh/nova/parthenon/
http://www.mcs.surrey.ac.uk/Personal/R.Knott/Fibonacci/fibInArt.html

AFTERWORD

After this long journey through a text about how to make sense of the fine arts, you deserve to know what good can result if you keep this cultural knowledge alive in your life. One of the painful truths I have come to understand after 35 years of teaching the humanities is the realization that, unless applied, most of what you have learned will be gone with the wind in a very short time. For this reason, I urge you to retain this text and to use it as a resource book for the rest of your life. Of all the G.E. classes offered at a university, few are as applicable to the ways you will spend your leisure time as this one is. When not at work, we entertain ourselves with reading books and magazines, listening to music, watching television and movies, going to concerts, visiting museums and famous monuments on vacation, traveling to exciting foreign places. On each occasion, you will experience some of these works of art and be able to employ some of the critical tools you have learned within the pages of this text.

Once you have succeeded in your studies here, you will enter the work force in a job that will provide sufficient income to support a family and allow you to enjoy the finer things of life in abundance. But the only way you can show that you have learned something of worth here is to have made it a part of your life when you leave here. And a good way you can show that it was worth the time and effort is to pass it on to those you love. Will your children learn to love the Good, the True, and the Beautiful from you? President Spencer W. Kimball once said, "Children may never recover from the ignorance of their mother." We have a solemn obligation as parents to pass on to our children the best that our cultural legacy has to offer. That means we must first make it our own. I hope some of what you were exposed to in this text will stay with you and enhance the way you see yourself and the world around you.

Whether we know it or not, each of us is a steward of the culture we inherited from the past. Like the rudder of a ship, this cultural legacy influences our present lives and helps us chart a favorable course into the future. Malachi 4:6 is a scripture we often use to define the bonds that link us to our genetic forefathers—"And he shall plant in the hearts of the children the promises made to the fathers, and the hearts of the children shall turn to their fathers" (Moroni's revised version in JSH 1:39). This scripture can also apply to our cultural forefathers, those who went before and prepared the way. My father-in-law, a noted chemist who taught for years at this institution, was once invited to give a speech at the 24th of July celebration in his home town in northern Arizona. His topic was drawn from the Old Testament account of Israel entering the Promised Land of Canaan, "a land flowing with milk and honey" (Exodus 3:8). Paraphrasing the situation recounted in the scriptures, he told his audience: "We are warmed by fires we did not light; we drink from wells we have not dug." This is even truer of Latter-day Israel. Every day of our lives we enjoy the bountiful harvest of the precious fruits of others' labors, even to the lights that illumine our nights and the clothes on our backs. But there are even more precious fruits, the artistic legacy from the past. The list is long, but it surely includes these cultural forebears whose creative efforts are waiting to instruct and ennoble us: Homer, Dante, Shakespeare, Michelangelo, Mozart, Beethoven,

Rembrandt, Rodin, Frank Lloyd Wright, Balanchine, Verdi, van Gogh, and Picasso. Let us turn our hearts and the hearts of our children to the works they have wrought.

Before you leave the university and commence the rest of your life's adventures, take a slow tour through the "Education in Zion" gallery located in the Joseph F. Smith Humanities Building. The texts, visuals, and videos chart a remarkable pattern of progress in educating the Saints for a Zion society that grew from the pioneering efforts of Karl G. Maeser. On the southernmost wall of the exhibit are two important quotes under the question: "How Will the Saints Educate Their Children?"

Although pioneer parents needed their children's help to clear land, construct shelters, and raise crops, the wisest of them also perceived the urgency of educating their children. Brigham Young reminded parents, "It is the duty of the Latter-day Saints, according to the revelations, to give their children the best education that can be pro-cured, both from the books of the world and the revelations of the Lord."

Elder Holland, then President of Brigham Young University, gave this solemn warning in 1981: "This church is always only one generation away from extinction. All we would have to do to destroy this work is to stop teaching our children for one generation."

President Hinckley, in a devotional address several years ago, admonished us: "Don't be a weak link in the family chain." He outlined the strong links in his own family, going back to his great grandfather. What Elder Holland says of the church applies equally well to the family, to your family. Resolve to share the jewels of our culture with your children, that they may live fulfilling lives, actively and instinctively seeking the virtuous, the lovely, the good and the praiseworthy. I invite you to turn your heart and the hearts of your children to these inestimable sources of instruction and inspiration that you may all live a more abundant life.

CRITICAL APPROACHES TO THE ARTS

APPENDIX 1

NOTES ON PREPARING FOR A PERFORMING ARTS EVENT

Critiquing the performing arts poses special problems for the critic. Because they are locked into a time frame, they require your undivided attention in order to catch the continuity as it passes by. And, because most people don't have very good visual memories, you may be tempted to take voluminous notes during the performance. This will obviously interrupt the continuity and hamper your "willing suspension of disbelief." In other words, two competing tasks face you in critiquing any performance: taking an objective critical stance while not losing track of the involving subjective aesthetic experience, or, conversely, maintaining an emotional immersion in the work while still taking objective mental notes of things that strike you as insights, strengths, weaknesses, etc. To bring off this delicate balancing act, we suggest the following:

1. Spend as much time as possible in advance preparation. Read any published reviews you can find on the performance. Usually the local newspapers will feature any new performance in their arts sections, often in the Sunday paper preceding the opening night. In short, GET ORIENTED BEFORE YOU GO.

2. For dramatic performances, the best preparation is to READ THE PLAY BEFORE YOU GO. This is always possible with canonical works like Shakespeare. In the case of opera (or any musical drama, for that matter, it would help immensely to have read the **libretto** or "little book" before the per-

formance. Most music lovers who don't like opera are frustrated by their inability to make sense of a performance where everything is sung, because they can't understand the words and, therefore, are unable to follow the action (plot). It would almost be like going to a foreign country and attending a play in a foreign language, except with opera, most of the emotional action is in the music. Reading the libretto beforehand will help solve this problem.

3. For music concerts (symphonic or choral or both), find out the pieces to be performed. This information is available at the concert hall or on posters. A quick phone call can help you gain access to the pieces to be performed. Then, go to a local library resource center and LISTEN TO THOSE PIECES BEFOREHAND. When you hear them in the concert hall, they will be familiar to you and you can spend your time concentrating on the performance itself. In fact, comparing a couple of different recordings of the same piece can give you a more finely tuned understanding of performance quality. It is sometimes striking how a familiar recording will condition you to expect the same tempo and dynamic ranges in an actual performance.

A CRITICAL APPROACH TO *Dance*

I. Preparation

A. First, you should review the points made in Chapter 6, *Aesthetic Judgment*, especially the six general questions to ask of any work of art.

B. You may choose either an actual performance or a recorded (television or film) version. The latter may be preferable in cases where you want to see the performance a second and third time. Ideally, dance should be experienced "live."

II. TWO HUMBLING REALITIES ABOUT DANCE CRITICISM

A. "In [dance], most of the aesthetic problems are as yet not only unsolved, but even unformulated" (Selma Jeanne Cohen, dance critic).

B. "Dancing leaves nothing else behind-no record, no text-and so the afterimage becomes the subject of dance criticism" (Arlene Croce, ix).

III. PREPARE FOR THE TYPE OF DANCE PERFORMED

A. Expectations play a large role in what we end up getting from a dance performance. Review the section of the text that discusses ballet, modern, folk, or ballroom before attending.

B. If possible, get an idea of the program before hand and bone up on the styles.

IV. WHAT TO LOOK FOR (AGAIN, CAREFULLY REVIEW THE RELEVANT SECTION IN THE TEXT ON THE TYPE PERFORMED)

A. *Gesture:* If, as Susanne K. Langer asserts, "Gesture is the basic abstraction whereby the dance illusion is made and organized" (174), then pay attention to how dance movements are expansions, elaborations, of the meaning of simple, human gestures (tenderness, attraction, repulsion, anger, joy, despair, etc.). Even in the modern of styles, you can capture "dance meaning" by attending to the gestural roots of the movements. What feelings are generated by these gestural exaggerations?

B. *Line:* We think of line more in terms of painting or sculpture, but dance exploits the expressive lines of the human body. Look for expressive moving body lines.

C. *Rhythm:* We think of **rhythm** more in terms of music, but dance would be dead without the breath of rhythmic movements. Apply your understanding of musical rhythms to dance movements (especially since dance is virtually always accompanied by music). Also look for "tempo" variations in the dance movements.

D. *Plot:* We think of plot more in terms of drama than dance, but since dance is a time art as drama, it "unfolds" in space and time. Be aware of what is happening in the sequence of dance movements to create a rising action leading to a climax and falling off again in a **dénouement.** But some modern dances have no literal story line.

E. *Space:* Be aware of the space "enlivened" by the dancers' movements. Think of one modern dancer's response: "The air around me seems to have the capacity to solidify or melt." It has something to do with what we refer to as **"negative space"** in a painting (the space behind the subject). Also note the impact of music, lighting and costumes.

F. *Coordinates:* Consider the dimensions created by the three dance coordinates: (1) PHYSICAL (the grace created by working against gravity); (2) PSYCHOLOGICAL (the expression created by expansion/contraction); and (3) INTERPERSONAL (the drama generated by two or more dancers interacting, as well as the dancers interacting with the live audience).

A CRITICAL APPROACH TO *Drama*

I. PREPARATION

A. First you should review the points made in Chapter 6, *Aesthetic Judgment,* especially the six general questions to ask of any work of art.

B. Choose a live performance, if possible, or a recorded performance (the latter will allow you to do a more thorough analysis by repeated viewing).

II. FIRST IMPRESSION

Ponder the initial impact of the performance: its immediate dramatic power and its thematic focus. What is the playwright communicating?

III. CONSCIOUS ANALYSIS

When we move from the first impression to a conscious analysis, two things occur: (1) the play changes, and (2) we change. On this level we discover the more complex meanings hidden behind the dialogue and action.

A. *The Given:* Do you have all the facts straight? Briefly paraphrase the plot, but *don't* recount the plot in your paper. Focus on the performance.

B. *The Elements:*

1. PLOT: analogous to the "spine" of the play, along which the action travels, gradually unfolding the meaning of the play and creating the "arch" of rising action, climax, and conclusion; look for the emerging "dramatic question" or "central conflict" which the following plot parts will help you chart.

   a. EXPOSITION: introducing characters and disseminating information.

   b. INCITING MOMENT: the point when the dramatic question emerges.

   c. COMPLICATION: the "thickening" of the plot and conflict.

   d. CRISIS: the "point of no return," when the outcome becomes set.

   e. CLIMAX: the high-point of the action where the "answer" emerges.

   f. DÉNOUEMENT: the emotional and intellectual resolution of the plot.

2. CHARACTERS: How credible, consistent, motivated are they? Who is the protagonist (hero) and antagonist (villain)? Are they fully developed or one-dimensional?

3. SETTING: What difference does the time and place of the play make?

4. MISE EN SCÈNE: Consider the impact of the visuals: sets, costumes, etc.

5. SYMBOLS: Look for symbolic meanings in objects, images, colors, ideas, and characters in the play.

IV. JUDGMENT

Your judgments rarely concern the play itself, although the works of amateur playwrights (students) are fair game. Your efforts will be mainly directed toward how effectively the director, actors, set designer, et al., "realized" the playwright's primary objectives. Reed McColm, student playwright and author of *Together Again for the First Time,* says it well: "If I were trying to get a message across, and I said it in such a way that people appreciated the message and then had the opportunity to accept it or reject it, I don't care whether they agree or disagree as long as they make a decision based on the evidence" (*Daily Universe* 16 Sept. 1986). NOTE: try to tie your various observations to a central image or idea.

A CRITICAL APPROACH TO *Music*

I. PREPARATION

A. Review the points made in Chapter 6, *Aesthetic Judgment.*

B. Choose to critique a live concert which features a piece familiar enough to have been recorded, if possible, so you can familiarize yourself with the music before the live concert and then return to the recording afterward for more careful scrutiny of the elements and forms.

II. WHAT TO LISTEN FOR (AARON COPLAND LISTED THREE LEVELS OF MUSICAL MEANING)

A. *The Sensuous Level:* Here you should attend to the sounds, their sensuous appeal, variety, and emotional effects (note the infinite variety possible within the family of symphonic instruments).

   Pay particular attention to featured soloists, their skill and expressiveness. Focus especially on the effects of timbre on this level.

B. *The Expressive Level:* Beginning listeners sometimes get into trouble if they emphasize this level too much, because it can lead to private rhapsodizing, letting the music become an accompaniment to one's personal reveries (like the soundtrack of a movie). This is the level where you seek for extramusical meanings, if appropriate, as in "program" music. Explain how the music imitates, describes, or narrates. This is also the level where you should feel free to articulate your own emotional responses to the music.

C. *The Sheerly Musical Level:* This is the level where you listen to music "on its own terms," probing what's happening with each of the elements:

   1. MELODY: This is usually the most memorable part of the piece. Consider its "profile" (shape) and mood (which scale or mode is it based on: major, minor, chromatic, pentatonic? etc.) Remember it is the melody (theme) that ties the piece together and creates our sense of its overall form.

   2. RHYTHM: Check the "pulse" of the piece by attending to the variations and regularities of the rhythm. Try to catch its "time signature" (beat pattern) and whether it speeds up or slows down (tempo). The "gut level" of music is often per-

ceived in terms of this element. What emotional response do the rhythms create?

3. HARMONY: This refers to the combination of tones in the piece, whether they be rich and full or thin and transparent. We also should listen for the liberating resolution of tonal tensions in the harmony, which usually comes at the end of phrases and, lastly, at the end of the piece (at the cadence, or coda, if it's symphonic music).

   Is the harmony more pleasant sounding (consonant) or harsh sounding (dissonant)? Is the harmonic "texture" more monophonic? (single line melody), polyphonic? (interweaving independent melodies, like rounds) or homophonic? (blocks of chords supporting the melody, like hymns).

4. FORM: Consider the form (pattern) of the piece: sectional or continuous? Identify it.

5. TEXT: In vocal music, there are usually words accompanying the music. What is the relationship between text and tune? How does the music amplify and emotionally deepen the meaning of the words?

NOTE: Always distinguish between the music and the performance in your writing.

A CRITICAL APPROACH TO *Music Drama*

I. PREPARATION

If possible, choose a music drama (opera, operetta, musical comedy) which has been recorded so you can "flesh out" your limited memory of the actual performance by repeated viewings. If a recording (sound and/or video) is not available, do as much background preparation as possible, like reading the libretto of the piece before attending a live performance, because sung dialogue is much more difficult to follow than spoken dialogue. In grand opera everything is sung, and often in a foreign language.

II. WHAT TO LOOK & LISTEN FOR

A. *Music:* When drama is paired with music, music usually takes over and predominates, so be fully aware of the expressive power of the music, in general (the orchestra), but pay particular attention to the quality of singing (solos and ensemble numbers). The musical bias will also be evident occasionally in the trade-off between good singing and good acting in live performances of music drama. Notice the kind and quality of the singing voices of the main characters and whether they can also act credibly. Again, how does the music match the dramatic context?

B. *Drama:* Music drama is almost always based on some literary or historical source. Find out what you can about the narrative backgrounds of the work. Briefly summarize the story (plot) by reading the libretto. In other words, apply some of what you learned from "A Critical Approach to Drama" in ferreting out the plot structure and rising action in the music drama, but don't expect its plot to compete in subtlety or power with spoken drama. Since it takes longer to sing a line than to say it, music drama is always short on drama and long on music.

C. *Spectacle:* Music dramas are sometimes referred to as "combined arts" because they bring together several art forms under one umbrella. Consider the related arts (besides music and drama) used to create the total effect of this kind of theater: dance, costumes, sets (often elaborate), etc. Are they related in a total scheme or design that creates a dramatic, musical, and visual unity?

III. JUDGMENT

Music drama is easy to make fun of because it is so complicated and inflated. Be willing to accept the conventions of opera (singing the whole time in grand opera, characters spontaneously breaking into song in operetta and musical comedy, in general, lavish sets, melodramatic plots, etc.) and you will enjoy this medium. You may want to approach writing about this medium by focusing on one element and discussing its relationship with the others.

A CRITICAL APPROACH TO *Film*

I. PREPARATION

A. First you should review the points made in Chapter 6, *Aesthetic Judgment,* especially the six general questions to ask of any work of art.

B. Choose a film to analyze that is clearly viewed as an "art film." This is not to say that some commercial films contain no art.

II. A CAUTION

Because film is a time art, a space art, and a combined art, the complex of appeals to our various senses moves by so rapidly that it is difficult to reflect at the time on what has produced our responses to it. It is important, therefore, that you see the film being reviewed at least twice (a video would be ideal, except the small television format detracts from the overall effect).

III. WHAT TO LOOK FOR

A. Film is built on a four-legged pedestal:

1. SCREENPLAY: It is unthinkable that a really first-rate film could be made from a second-rate script. Even though the visual image has greater impact in film than in live drama, the words spoken carry much of the dramatic power and intellectual content, so they must be "well-wrought." Nevertheless, the words alone are sterile without the visuals (ever try reading a screenplay?) and undergo many reworkings between the beginning and conclusion of the filming. Comment on the quality of the script (the credibility and power of the dialogue). Note whether it was commissioned or adapted from a literary source.

2. CINEMATOGRAPHY: Film is unique in that it can take us anywhere the camera can go in space. The mobile camera and the moving image create a remarkably fluid space. Be aware of how the camera manipulates your perspective and controls your reaction to what's happening on the screen. Consider the impact of the following camera techniques: the shots (high, low, close-up, long, master, pan, and track); the different camera speeds (fast, slow, freeze frame); the various lenses (normal, fish eye, wide angle, telephoto, zoom); the quality of the framing (view the framed image in a movie as you would analyze a painting); and consider the effects of supers (superimposed shots) as well as objective and subjective camera shots (reaction shots or POV's = point of view).

3. EDITING: The manipulation of time (establishing a rhythm, tempo, and controlling audience interpretation of the action) is the major factor in the art of film editing. If the camera work creates fluid space, editing creates fluid time, pregnant with meaning. Be aware of how the editing controls your reactions to the sequence of shots in a film. Consider the impact of the following editing techniques: transitions (straight cut, form cut, **cross cut** or parallel edit-ing, fade in/fade out, **dissolve**); montage (creating a build-up of meaning by successive shots or a highly stylized and accelerated form of editing); and other techniques such as repeat sequences, flashbacks, etc.

4. DIRECTING: "In every major film of the past twenty years, the artistic ideas, the philosophy, and the intellectual thrust have emanated from the director" (Bobker, 161). Of the army of technicians and creative people who collaborate on a major film, the general is the **director**. His touch is evident more than any other individual in the finished product. And every major director has a distinctive style. Consider the following categories in defining what that style is: choice of subject matter, script, mood or tone (epic, lyric, dramatic, tragic, comic, light, heavy, etc.), acting (controlled or spontaneous), composition of images, editing finesse, etc. To do justice to this category, you would have to have seen several films by the same director. Write a general but carefully argued description of the director's style.

B. Other things to look for and comment upon: acting, musical score, theme, social or political statement, particularly, how it has changed your way of looking at the world.

IV. JUDGMENT

Learn to evaluate your spontaneous reactions.

A. Emotions play a vital part in experiencing cinema. Allow the images to play on your emotions so they can be an avenue of access to the film's meaning and to your own self-discovery.

B. Probe for the underlying themes, motifs, and symbols in the film. A good art film will contain much beneath the surface of the images and the meaning of the text. The full meaning surfaces only after exploring the ramifications of the four pedestals described above. To do this requires more than one viewing. Like any drama, film action turns on conflict, interior and overt. Use your familiarity with the plot to tease out the deeper meanings.

C. One final point, you must be careful to identify who it is you are writing about—with film you can't just say "filmmaker" or "author," since so many professionals are involved.

A CRITICAL APPROACH TO *Painting*

I. PREPARATION

A. First you should review the points made in Chapter 6, *Aesthetic Judgment,* especially the six general questions to ask of any work of art.

B. Choose an *actual* painting to analyze, *not an illustration,* or even a large poster of the work you choose (the illustrations are too small and you can't see the textures and the illustrations and posters are seldom "color-credible").

II. THE FOUR "STAGES OF ACCESS"

A. *Internalizing personal responses*

1. Choose a work that intrigues you, either by its appeal or perplexity.

2. Spend some time sorting out its impact in a state of relaxed concentration.

3. Write down your immediate responses to the work, focusing on anything that interests you. Go beyond what seems self-evident. Write approximately one page.

B. *Exploring backgrounds*

1. Find out something about the artist if you can. If famous, rummage in the library, checking in art history books, encyclopedias, etc. If a local or lesser-known, try asking the owner, museum director, or, in special cases, try calling the artist himself.

2. Add any interesting notes to the previous free writing exercise.

C. *Analyzing the work*

1. What is the medium and the subject matter (see title)?

2. Where is the painting located?

3. How does the artist manipulate line, color, and texture to create a unified "aesthetic experience?" Does it have "integrity?"

   a. What are the dominant lines? What quality (angular? rounded?)?

   b. How do the colors relate to each other? What emotions do they evoke? Is the overall value (light/dark) high key or low?

c. What tactile effects do the textures evoke (rough? smooth? real? illusory?)?

4. What style designation is most appropriate (classic, romantic, realistic, impressionistic, expressionistic, surrealistic, abstract)?

5. What is the overall organizational pattern (supporting scaffolding)? Are there smaller "echoes" of larger patterns? Is there a significant relationship between shape and content?

D. *Synthesizing your explorations*

1. Organize your previous writings and notes into a carefully organized final critique of the work, drawing on your work in the previous stages. Conclude by discussing the content, how the artist achieved that expression (through medium, elements, organization, etc.) and how it affected you.

A CRITICAL APPROACH TO *Sculpture*

(NOTE: apply the guidelines already noted above for painting, except consider the following modifications under C. "Analyzing the Work")

C. *Analyzing the work*

1. Name of sculptor

2. Location of sculpture (is the setting appropriate to the subject?)

3. The subject matter (title)

4. The medium used (is it appropriate to the subject? What are the special limitations and challenges of this medium?)

5. How does the sculptor manipulate the visual elements of line, color, texture, and volume to create a unified expression?

   a. Do the lines create gestural expression? Do they vary significantly at different angles as you circle the work?

   b. Is the color consistent with the overall form and spatial environment?

   c. Does the sculptor work with or against the medium's natural textures?

   d. Does the texture (rough, smooth, etc.) fit the

intended expressive effect? Does it invite touching? How does it feel?

    e. What is the overall impact of the volume, the mass, and its place in space?

6. How would you define its style? Realistic? Abstract? Other?

A CRITICAL APPROACH TO *ARCHITECTURE*

I. PREPARATION

A. First you should review the points made in Chapter 6, *Aesthetic Judgment,* especially the six general questions to ask of any work of art.

B. You have one of two options here: (1) either choose a revival style or modern building to critique; or (2) choose one of each and compare the two. Your decision should be based on some definite (positive or negative) reaction. Preferably they should be buildings you have been in or can conveniently visit.

II. INDIVIDUAL ANALYSIS

A. *Revival style*

1. Where is the building located? Is the location appropriate to its style?

2. Around what time was the building constructed?

3. What is its purpose or function? Has it changed over time?

4. Identify as many revival elements as you can and then attempt to classify its predominant style (is it "Victorian Eclectic?")

5. Does the interior decor match the exterior facade? (should it?)

B. *Modern style*

1. Where is the building located? Is the location appropriate to its style?

2. Approximately when was the building constructed?

3. What is its purpose or function? How does its form relate to its function?

4. Discuss the modern technological techniques and new materials used in its construction.

5. What is the relationship between the interior and the exterior?

III. THE COMPARISON

Relate the impact of the two buildings in terms of

A. How their forms relate to their functions.

B. The overall feeling and appearance of the two buildings, i.e., how the visual elements combine to create an inviting environment, how well interior space is manipulated to fulfill their respective functions, what visual impact their forms and size make, etc.

IV. SYNTHESIS

Pull together all of the above materials into an interesting, insightful critique, including information about the architect(s) if possible. Feel free to add your own categories if your particular building choice so dictates. Above all, make it interesting to read!

WORKS CITED

Bobker, Lee R. *Elements of Film.* New York: Harcourt, Brace & World, 1969.

Croce, Arlene. *Afterimages.* New York: Alfred A. Knopf, 1978.

Langer, Susanne K. *Feeling and Form.* New York: Scribners, 1953.

SOURCES OF ART

Appendix 2

MYTHOLOGY AND THE BIBLE

SOURCES OF SUBJECT IN THE ARTS

THE GREEK DEITIES

In the beginning was Chaos (the abyss) until love and light created Cosmos (world order). Contrary to the creation story in Exodus, where God created the heavens and the earth, the Greeks believed that the universe created the gods; that is, "Father Heaven" (Uranus) and "Mother Earth" (Gaea) created the Titans, and the head Titan, Kronos (Roman name Saturn), and his wife-sister, Rhea (Roman name Ops), created the gods. Incest and patricide were evidently fairly common in the pre-mortal Greek heaven. When Kronos learned that one of his children would one day dethrone him, he systematically began eating his children to thwart the prophecy. Upon the birth of their sixth child, Zeus, Rhea spirited the child off to Crete and fed her husband a stone wrapped in a blanket. When Zeus grew to manhood, he secretly fed his father an emetic, which caused him to cough up Zeus's other brothers and sisters. The War in Heaven which ensued ended with Kronos's defeat and the accession of a new set of deities, the Olympians, named after Mount Olympus where they lived and were ruled over by Zeus (Jupiter) and his wife, Hera (Juno).

A word of caution: one should not judge the behavior of the Greek deities against any mortal moral code, since the Greeks viewed them as bigger than life in both their virtues and vices. The Greeks accepted them as superhuman and, for that reason, worthy of fear, if not reverence. Following is a description of the Olympian Family of Gods who ruled the Greek universe and man. (Their Roman names are given in parentheses):

ZEUS (Jupiter): The supreme god of the Greeks, Zeus was "Father of gods and men." He fathered Athena, Artemis, Apollo, Ares, Hermes, and Dionysus as well as innumerable other children by nymphs and mortals. His identifying symbols are the thunderbolt and the eagle.

HERA (Juno): The wife and sister of Zeus, protectress of marriage, married women, children and the home, Hera wanders over heaven and earth, the betrayed wife, always seeking out Zeus, who is invariably discovered in compromising circumstances. For this reason, her symbol is the peacock with a tail of a thousand eyes.

PALLAS ATHENA (Minerva): The daughter of Zeus alone, her birth full-grown and full-armored from the head of Zeus helps explain her attributes as goddess of wisdom and protectress in war of those who worshiped her, the Athenians. In fact, Athens is her city and the Parthenon is her temple (from her other name, Parthenos, the Maiden). In the contest with Poseidon (Neptune) for the patronage of Athens, she offered the olive tree. She can be recognized as armored, wearing a helmet and Zeus's breastplate (aegis), and carrying a shield and spear. Her bird, appropriately, is the owl.

PHOEBUS APOLLO: Son of Zeus and Leto, who also bore his twin sister, Artemis (Diana), Apollo is considered the most Greek of all the gods. He is foremost a god of light, both literally (a being of the sun without being the sungod himself, who was Helios) and figuratively (god of intelligence and prophecy). His name Phoebus means "brilliant." His holy place is at Delphi, where his oracle, the prophet of Delphi, foretells the future. He can be identified by his physical beauty, sometimes by a top-knot on his head, symbol of his great intelligence, by his lyre (he's also the god of music, in particular, and creativity in general) and by his bow and arrow. He was also known as the Healer, who first taught men the healing art. The laurel was his tree, made holy by his first love, Daphne, who was turned into a laurel tree by her father, the river god Peneus, when Apollo tried to force himself upon her.

ARTEMIS (Diana): Apollo's twin sister, virgin goddess of the hunt and protectress of forest animals, Artemis is associated with the light of the moon, thus sometimes called Phoebe and Selene (Luna in Latin).

APHRODITE (Venus): Goddess of love and the essence of feminine beauty, Aphrodite was born of the foam of the sea (her name in Greek derives from *aphros* = sea foam). Although she was married to Hephaestus (Vulcan), the lame and ugly god of the forge, she was really in love with Ares (Mars), god of war ("All's fair in love and war"). The myrtle was her tree; the dove, her bird. Her son, Eros (Cupid), conspired with his bow and arrow to smite people with love. He is often rendered blindfolded, suggesting that "love is blind."

HERMES (Mercury): The most familiar because of his frequent appearance in modern popular culture (Mercury automobiles and FTD florists), Hermes is the messenger god, son of Zeus and Maia (daughter of Atlas). He is also protector of flocks, thieves, merchants, and wayfarers. He can be recognized by his winged sandals, winged hat, and serpent-entwined staff (caduceus), which eventually became associated with healing (symbol of the American Medical Association).

HEPHAESTUS (Vulcan): The god of the forge, lame from birth and the only ugly god, was Hera's child, who bore him alone in retaliation for Zeus having brought forth Athena by himself. He was undesirable because of his smelly presence and frequently ridiculed for his twisted feet and stumbling gait, yet he was kind and peace-loving and greatly gifted as a skilled craftsman (he fashioned the great shield of Achilles during the Trojan War). Along with Athena, he was the Greek patron of handicrafts.

ARES (Mars): The god of war and Hephaestus's main competition for the favors of Aphrodite, Ares was hated by his parents, Zeus and Hera, although liked by Hades, the god of the Underworld, for Ares helped increase its population. He was embarrassing to the other gods when Hephaestus caught him and Aphrodite with a nearly invisible net while engaged in a secret rendezvous. Ironically, he didn't bear pain well. His symbol is the vulture.

POSEIDON (Neptune): The god of the sea, earthquakes and giver of horses, Poseidon is Zeus's brother and second only to him in eminence for the Greeks. His symbol is the trident, a three-pronged spear.

HADES (Pluto): The god of the Underworld and also of wealth (from his access to the earth's precious metals), Hades was also known as Dis by the Romans (Latin for rich). He was married to Persephone, daughter of Demeter (Ceres), whom he had abducted from Demeter. Demeter's grief caused the plants to die, bringing on autumn and winter. Persephone's annual return brings spring and summer. He is king of the Dead—not Death himself, whom the Greeks called Thanatos and the Romans, Orcus.

DIONYSUS (Bacchus): While most of the gods were a threat to mortals, the two great gods of the earth, Dionysus and Demeter, were generally beneficial. Dionysus was born in Thebes (Oedipus' hometown) to Zeus and a mortal woman, Semele. He was the only god whose parents were not both divine. He was the god of wine, which made him a dual god: wine could be beneficent, but could also drive men to violence. Thus the worship of this god involved two opposing ideas: ecstatic joy and savage brutality. He became the patron god of Greek drama and is frequently rendered drunk with grape fronds in his hair.

DEMETER (Ceres): The goddess of crops, giver of grain and fruit (her Latin name is the root of our word cereal), Demeter is the mother of Persephone, her only daughter, whose absence causes her grief and brings autumn and winter to the world.

HESTIA (Vesta): Hestia is Zeus's sister and, like Athena and Artemis, is a virgin goddess. She is the Goddess of the Hearth (Hestia is Greek for hearth), symbol of the home. Every meal began and ended with an offering to her. Each city had a public hearth sacred to Hestia, where the fire was never allowed to go out (source, perhaps, of our phrase, "Keep the home fires burning").

THE HEROES OF TROY

The story of the Trojan War begins at the wedding feast in honor of Achilles' parents, the sea nymph Thetis and Peleas. All the gods were invited, except Eris, the goddess of discord. To get revenge, she fashioned a golden apple with the inscription "To the Fairest" and threw it into the hall. Its presence prompted the three most beautiful goddesses, Hera, Aphrodite, and Athena, to vie for the prize. Zeus, realizing a no-win situation for himself, gave the judgment to Paris, a Trojan prince. Each goddess offered him a bribe. Hera promised to make him lord of Europe and Asia; Athena, that he would lead Troy to victory against the Greeks; and Aphrodite, that he could have the most beautiful woman in the world. Paris, a lady's man and something of a coward and weakling, chose the latter. His prize, Helen, the daughter of Zeus and Leda and sister of Castor and Pollux, was already married to Menelaus, King of Sparta and brother of the Greek general, Agamemnon. When Helen was abducted by Paris with Aphrodite's help, her father's earlier oath that they would all champion her husband's cause went into effect, and the Greek invasion of Troy began. This is the legendary cause of the Trojan War. The heroes who figure most prominently were ACHILLES, the greatest warrior of the Greeks, known for his wrath (the subject of Homer's great epic, the *Iliad*) and, later, his great compassion in allowing his defeated foe, Hector, a proper burial; HECTOR, a family man and the greatest warrior of the Trojans, but no match for Achilles on the battlefield, one-on-one; AGAMEMNON, commander of the Greek forces and Helen's brother-in-law, who was killed by his own wife, CLYTEMNESTRA "of the dark heart," for having sacrificed their daughter, IPHIGENIA, to Artemis to get his fleet of ships to Troy in the first place; ODYSSEUS (ULYSSES), King of Ithaca, and famed for his shrewdness, who invented the Trojan Horse that finally won victory for the Greeks, and then sailed home on a journey fraught with many dangers to find his wife, Penelope, beset with insistent suitors. He disposed of the suitors by locking all the doors to the palace and systematically killing them all with the aid of his son and father. His homeward "Odyssey" is recounted in Homer's other famous epic, the *Odyssey*.

BIBLICAL SYMBOLS

APOSTLES

The Twelve Apostles are messengers or witnesses of Christ in the New Testament. Traditionally they are represented clustered around or underneath Christ on his throne or standing at either side of Him, holding the symbols or instruments of their martyrdom with the exception of Peter, who holds the "keys of the kingdom."

Traditionally, the Twelve Apostles include Matthias and not Judas; conversely the Disciples include Judas but not Matthias.

BEASTS

The Bestiary was an ancient treatise on animals (based on the Greek PHYSIOLOGUS), giving a symbolic, moral, or religious interpretation to their traits, creating moralizing parallels between animals and their human counterparts. It actually rivaled the Bible in popularity during the Middle Ages and was frequently used by medieval artists in creating their visual allegories.

Butterfly: This represents the Resurrection because of its life cycle from chrysalis to mature butterfly, emerging from its cocoon as the body from the grave to fly upwards.

Dog: As the first domesticated animal, the dog symbolizes fidelity (for this reason, it's often named "Fido").

Dove: Symbol of the Holy Ghost, the dove appears at the baptism of Christ, the descent of the Holy Spirit on the Day of Pentecost, and at the Annunciation. It is also a peace symbol, with an olive branch in its mouth, from its role in the story of Noah's Ark. It is also a symbol of purity, when associated with Mary.

Dragon: With its lion's claws, eagle's wings, serpent's tail, and fiery breath, it is a symbol of Satan and evil. When placed underfoot, it is an attribute of Michael the Archangel, Margaret, Martha, St. George, and other dragonslayers.

Eagle: A symbol of the soaring spirit, the eagle symbolizes the Resurrection. It is also an attribute of St. John the Evangelist.

Fish: This stands for Christianity in general, the Disciples in particular—"I will make you fishers of men"—and Christ specifically: the five letters for the Greek word for fish (*Icthys*) creates an acronym of the phrase: "Jesus Christ, Son of God, Savior."

Goldfinch: Because it prefers thorny nests, the goldfinch suggests the Passion (Crown of Thorns). In the hand of the Infant Christ, it foreshadows the Savior's suffering.

Lamb: The most common animal symbol in Christian art, the lamb is sacred as the innocent and pure sacrificial animal, suggesting the Lamb of God as well as the Good Shepherd. A lamb holding a cross with blood pouring out of its side into a chalice is the

Agnus Dei (*Lamb of God*). A lamb holding a staff with a banner, decorated with a cross, represents the Resurrection. These lambs frequently have a cruciform halo. The lamb is also an attribute of John the Baptist.

Lion: Known as "King of Beasts" because of its lordly bearing and strength, the lion is the earthly counterpart of the eagle, lord of the skies. It also symbolizes the Resurrection, because legend says that cubs are born dead, only to be revived by their father's breath after three days.

Owl: The bird of night, the owl symbolizes solitude and death, but also represents wisdom.

Ox: Like the lamb, the ox is a sacrificial animal and metaphor for patience and humility. The winged ox is a symbol of St. Luke, the Evangelist.

Peacock: A symbol of immortality, it originated from the legend that its flesh won't decay. The "hundred eyes" of its tail are likened to the all-seeing Church.

Pelican: Because of its devotion to its offspring (legend has it that the young are killed by the father and then the mother pierces her own breast and revives them with her own blood), the pelican suggests the life-sustaining blood of the Eucharist.

Snake: Serpent: Traditional symbol of wisdom, the snake also represents evil (Satan, who tempted Eve in this form). A snake with a tail in its mouth symbolizes eternity (no beginning or end). When wound around a staff, it symbolizes Christ's healing power (derived from the Old Testament story of the Brazen Serpent in the wilderness).

Unicorn: Originally associated with the worship of a virgin mother goddess in remote antiquity, in Christian legend the unicorn becomes an ambiguous symbol of female chastity. Its horn had the power of purifying whatever it touched despite its phallic overtones, and, when enclosed within a fence or wall, symbolized Mary's virginity. The African rhino (the closest real animal to the legendary unicorn) is an endangered species today because the legend persists that the powdered remains of its horn has "aphrodisiac" potency.

Whale: The "great fish" of the Old Testament story of Jonah, the whale became a symbol of the Resurrection. It is also likened to the Devil, who draws unbelievers into the depths of Hell. Sometimes its gaping mouth represents the jaws of Hell.

COLORS

Color has been used symbolically by all civilizations. In Christian art, color operates on two basic levels: its inherent characteristics, for example, red as the color of fire; and its emotional connotations, i.e., red equals heat, therefore passion or suffering. Occasionally colors may have opposite symbolic meanings: love, as in the red cloak of St. John the Evangelist, a man of great love; or sin, as the red cloak worn by the Devil. Yellow can mean glory when worn by Peter or Joseph, but cowardice when worn by Judas.

Black: The emblem of mourning, penance, evil, and death.

Blue: This color symbolizes heaven, truth, and fidelity ("true blue"). Appropriately, blue is Mary's color.

Green: This color suggests hope, regeneration, and fertility. When attached to the palm or laurel, green symbolizes victory.

Purple: This color symbolizes sorrow and penitence. Purple may also signify love and truth. It is generally a royal color.

Red: Associated with passion, blood, and fire, red is the color of both love and hate, sin and suffering. When associated with black, it is the color of purgatory and the Devil.

White: White is symbolic of light, innocence, purity, joy, virginity; Christ always wears a white robe after the Resurrection. Mary often wears white at the Annunciation, just as the traditional bridal white is an allusion to the bride's purity (virginity).

Yellow or Gold: These two colors are symbolic of the sun and the color of Heaven, the color of "illuminated truth." In its negative connotations, yellow signifies deceit, jealousy, cowardice or treason; thus it is the color of heretics and nonbelievers (and Judas).

CROSS

The CROSS is the universal emblem of Christ but is also found in many pre-Christian contexts (Indian cave walls and Egyptian tombs), suggesting perhaps the fundamental combination of opposites in life (life/death; vertical/horizontal). In Christianity it symbolizes the Crucifixion and is connected to the Tree of Life, the wood of both suggesting both sin and redemption, death and rebirth. The following are the more common types of crosses:

Latin: The most common Christian cross, it symbolizes the Passion and is the universal attribute of most Christians. Variations are the Archiepiscopal (for archbishops, with two crossbars, the upper shorter) and the Papal (with three graduated, ascending bars). The Latin cross surmounting a globe is the cross of Church Triumphant, symbol of monarchs blessed with the authority of the Church (like the Holy Roman Emperors).

Greek: With arms of equal length, it serves as floor plan of many Byzantine Churches.

Tau: (Old Testament cross) is based on the Greek letter *tau,* or (T), which, according to legend, was used by the Israelites to mark their blood on the door posts during the Passover. It is also thought that Moses raised the brazen serpent on a pole shaped like a tau cross. A variation of this is the Egyptian *ankh* or *crux ansate,* a tau cross with a looped handle.

Chrismon: A widely used medieval monogram made up of the Greek letters *chi* (X) and *rho* (P) it makes up the first two letters of Christ's name in Greek. When superimposed, they form the abbreviation of two important aspects of Christ's Atonement: the "Good Shepherd and the "Crucified One." It is also called the "Chi-Rho Monogram."

EVANGELISTS

The four Evangelists—Matthew, Mark, Luke, and John—are the authors of the four Gospels in the New Testament which bear their names (the word *evangelist* means "bearer of good news"). The word *gospel* comes from the Anglo-Saxon "God-spell," meaning literally "good news." The Evangelists are associated with four "beasts" referred to in Ezekiel's vision (Ezekiel 1:5ff.) and linked by association to the content of each Gospel: the winged man represents Christ's Incarnation, the winged ox his Passion, the winged lion his Resurrection, and the eagle his Ascension.

Matthew: His symbol is the winged man or angel, since his Gospel traces the genealogy of Christ and emphasizes Christ's immortality. Matthew is also understandably the patron saint of bankers and tax collectors.

Mark: His Gospel begins with the words "the voice of one crying in the wilderness," which is likened to the lion's roar and emphasizes Christ's royal lineage; therefore, his symbol is a winged lion. He is the patron saint of Venice and its Byzantine basilica.

Luke: Trained in Antioch as a physician, Luke is represented as a winged ox, because his Gospel opens with the account of Zacharias's sacrifice (the ox is a traditional sacrificial beast) and because it emphasizes Christ's sacrifice and atonement. He is the patron saint of artists, physicians, and goldsmiths.

John: The author of the Gospel as well as three epistles and the Book of Revelation, John was the youngest Apostle, the brother of James the Great, both sons of Zebedee. He typically comforts Mary at the foot of the cross. His attribute is the eagle, reference to the soaring majesty of his writing of Christ's divinity and ascension.

FLOWERS AND FRUITS

The earth's flora suggest the seasonal cycle of life, death, and resurrection. Associated with colors, they take on those attributes. Botanical symbolism flourished during the Middle Ages: the Virgin Mary, for example, was described by St. Bernard of Clairvaux as "the violet of humility, the lily of chastity, and the rose of charity." Some flowers even have names that reveal their early connections with Mary—Lady's slipper, Lady's smock, etc.

Almond: In its Italian form (*mandorla*) it is the name given to the oval halo which encloses the body of Mary or Christ, symbolic of the aura of light that surrounds their whole beings, like a "body halo," but also refers to the seed or womb as prime sources of life. In Latin the mandorla is called the *vesica piscis,* or fish bladder, another oblique Christian connection to the traditional symbol of Christians, the fish.

Anemone: Emblem of death and mourning, This flower was supposed to have sprung miraculously out of the ground during the Crucifixion. Some botanists have concluded that the biblical "lilies of the field" were in fact a species of anemone that grows in the Holy Land.

Apple: Mainly associated with Adam and Eve in the Garden of Eden, the apple represents the traditional forbidden fruit from the Tree of Knowledge of Good and Evil. The Latin word *malum* means both apple and evil, which may be the origin of the apple symbol. In this context, it symbolizes disobedience and original sin, as well as willing indulgence in sensual pleasures. Notice how often Eve partakes of this fruit with her left hand, an allusion to the evil of left-handedness—the word in Latin for left is *sinister*—and connected to biblical notions of the sheep on His right and the goats on His left. It is still present in some of our colloquialisms—a man's "Adam's apple," for example.

Clover: Long viewed as a symbol of both good and evil, the four-leafed shamrock is good luck; the five-leafed clover is bad luck; and, like all trefoils, the three-leaf clover stands for the Trinity.

Columbine: This is another symbol of sorrow, because of its deep blue-purple color. In bunches of seven flowers the columbine refers to the Seven Sorrows of Mary. Its name comes from a word meaning dove-like, because of its wing-shaped flower, and so also becomes an emblem of the Holy Ghost.

Holly: Like all thorny plants, it is a symbol of the Passion, in particular, an allusion to the Crown of Thorns (the red berries remind us of the Savior's drops of blood); as evergreen, it also symbolizes eternity.

Iris: The iris is a symbol of Mary's sorrow, a prefiguration of the lance which pierced Christ's side on the cross (Iris leaves are blade-like), which causes Mary's grief over her Son's suffering. This symbol is derived from a biblical passage in Luke, when Jesus is brought to the temple as a baby and Simeon blesses him and says to Mary: "Yea, a spear shall pierce through him to the wounding of thine own soul also; that the thoughts of many hearts may be revealed" (Luke 2:35, Inspired Version). In addition, the blood and water which issued from Christ's side when pierced with the sword was thought to represent emblems of the Eucharist (Sacrament) and baptism. "Just as Eve was fashioned from the rib taken from Adam's side, so the two main Christian sacraments flowed from the side of Christ, the 'New Adam'; thus the Church, the "Bride of the Lord, was born, as it were, from the wound" (James Hall, *Dictionary of Subjects and Symbols*).

Laurel: As evergreen, it represents eternity; as classical borrowing, it suggests triumph: victors wore laurel wreaths on their heads.

Lily: The major botanical symbol of Mary's purity (Song of Solomon 2:1–2: "a lily among thorns"), it is virtually always associated with depictions of the Annunciation.

Pomegranate: A symbol of eternity and fertility because of its many seeds, the pomegranate has also long been considered a symbol of royalty, because of its crown-like terminal. It also refers to the Church, whose many parts (seeds) are contained within a single whole.

Rose: The white rose is a symbol of purity, the yellow rose of perfection, the red rose of martyrdom, but, in general, the rose is a symbol of the Virgin Mary, who is called a "rose without thorns" since she was free of original sin. The five petals of the wild rose are equated with the five joys of Mary and the five letters in her name "Maria." The "Rose of Sharon," mentioned in the *Canticles* 2:1, is associated with Christ.

Vine: This is a symbol of Christ, which he applied to himself—"I am the vine, and my Father is the husbandman" (John 15:1)—and of the Eucharist (wine).

Violet: This flower is associated with Christian humility ("shrinking violet") because it grows close to the ground and its blossoms droop.

FOUR HORSEMEN OF THE APOCALYPSE (SEE REVELATION 6:1–8)

After the Black Death (1348) had killed nearly half of Europe's population, the survivors and their descendants for generations dreaded the Last Things predicted in John's Apocalyptic vision of the end of the world, when the four terrible horsemen break the first four seals: "pestilence" symbolized by the Conqueror on a WHITE horse, holding a bow and arrow; "war" symbolized by a warrior on a RED horse, holding a sword; "famine" symbolized by a figure on a BLACK horse, holding a scales; and "death" symbolized by a cadaverous old man on a PALE horse, holding a scythe or trident and sometimes an hourglass.

INITIALS

Initials appear in Christian art, both as monograms and as abbreviations, decorative devices as well as identifying labels.

Alpha and Omega (A **Ω**): The first and last letters of the Greek alphabet suggest Christ's immortality as "the first and the last."

INRI: As the abbreviation for "Jesus of Nazareth King of the Jews" in Latin, they are usually inscribed on a scroll and nailed above Christ's head on the cross.

T: This letter stands for *theos,* the Greek word for God, often appearing on the shoulder of St. Anthony.

XP: These are the Greek letters *chi* and *rho,* the first two letters of the Greek word for Christ, also associated in reverse order with the Latin word for peace (*pax*).

NUMBERS

Numbers figure prominently in both Classical and Christian symbolism.

One: One symbolizes unity and divinity.

Two: This number suggests the dual nature, human and divine, of Christ and of man.

Three: This number represents supreme power to the Greeks (beginning, middle, end) and the Trinity for Christians (the mysterious unity of Three in One). Also the triangle.

Four: The number related to the earth: the four elements (air, earth, fire, water), the four "humors" of man (blood, phlegm, yellow bile, black bile), the four points of the compass, the four corners of the world, etc.

Five: This number represents the five wounds of Christ. It also represents man (a combination of four limbs governed by a head).

Six: This is the number of the Creation of the world in six days.

Seven: This is the sum of the divine number (3) and the earthly number (4) equals seven, which symbolizes man (his biblical age is seventy, three score and ten) and the seventh day the Gods rested.

Eight: This is the number of regeneration with its spiraling shape, eternally in motion. It represents Resurrection (on the eighth day after Christ's entry into Jerusalem).

Nine: This is the angelic number of the nine choirs of angels.

Ten: This was believed to be the number of perfection, the sum of three (the Trinity) and seven (man).

SAINTS

Saints are the heroes of the early Church, the intermediaries between man and God. Their lives form the fabric of church history and they figure prominently in Christian iconography.

St. Eustace: He was originally a Roman general (Placidas) under the Emperor Trajan. While hunting outside Rome, he found a stag with a lighted crucifix between its antlers and was immediately converted to Christianity and was subsequently martyred by being placed in a large brass bull and roasted to death. He is identified by antlers and is the patron saint of hunters.

St. George: He was a soldier of the Roman army in Asia Minor who converted to Christianity. According to legend, a dragon threatened the town of Silene in Libya, poisoning the air with its breath and eating the citizens' children. As the king's daughter was in danger, St. George approached the lair, crossed himself, and slew the dragon. According to another version, St. George first wounded the dragon and had the princess lead it back into town like a dog on a leash, only slaying it when the pagans of Silene agreed to be baptized. He was beheaded during the persecutions of Diocletian.

St. John, the Baptist: This famous figure is considered the last Prophet of the Old Testament and the first saint of the New Testament. He is often pictured as a hermit with "his raiment of camel's hair and a leathern girdle about his loins" (Matthew 3:4). He may also hold a lamb decorated with a scroll with the words *Ecce Agnus Dei* ("Behold the Lamb of God).

St. Michael: He was the greatest of the archangels, captain of the heavenly hosts whom he led against Satan's rebellious angels during the great War in Heaven (Revelations 12: 7–9). He often appears in full armor, frequently holding the scales of justice.

St. Sebastian: He was a member of the elite Praetorian guard under the Roman Emperor, Diocletian. When the emperor discovered Sebastian was a Christian, he ordered him to be shot through with arrows. The archers supposedly had orders to aim at the least vital parts, in order to prolong his death agony. A woman (St. Irene) found him and nursed him back to health. He went to Diocletian and declared his faith in Jesus Christ. This time he was taken to an arena and beaten to death and his body put into a sewer so it couldn't be found by his friends. But he was discovered and buried in the catacombs at the feet of St. Peter and St. Paul. In ancient times the plague was believed to have been brought about by Apollo's arrows. Therefore, St. Sebastian became one of the chief saints invoked against the dread disease in the Middle Ages. In art he is shown tied to a tree or column pierced through with arrows.

MISCELLANEOUS OBJECTS

The following objects which have symbolic significance are frequently encountered in Christian art.

Candle: The light of God. When held by St. Joseph, it represents the light which Christ's birth has given the world.

Flag or Banner: White with a red cross symbolizes victory; if held by the Lamb of God, it represents Christ's victory over death. Christ always carries this banner after the Resurrection and in the Descent into Hell.

Harp: Symbolizes all music which glorifies God. Attribute of King David.

Hourglass: Attribute of Time, signifying the brevity of life. The skeleton, symbol of Death, often holds an hourglass.

Keys: Symbolic of St. Peter, to whom God gave the "keys of the kingdom."

Mirror: Symbol of the Virgin's purity, but also suggests human vanity.

Moon: Anciently, it was a symbol of the virgin goddess, Artemis (Diana), and the moon goddess, Luna. In Christian symbolism it represents Mary's chastity (see Revelation 12:1).

Peacock: Suggests both vanity (strutting plumage) and immortality (it was thought that its flesh wouldn't decay). Because of its pristine beauty, it is often symbolic of Paradise. The design on its tail feathers signified the all-seeing eye of God.

Scales: Symbol of weighing virtues and vices in preparation for the Last Judgment.

Shell, Scallop: Symbol of St. James the Great (Santiago) in Spain; with drops of water it symbolizes baptism. John the Baptist often pours the water from a scallop shell over the head of Christ.

Ship: Symbol for the Church, according to St. Hippolytus's simile: "The world is a sea in which the Church, like a ship, is beaten by the waves, but not submerged" (qtd. in Sill 134). The image persists in parts of Christian architecture, like the "nave" (from Latin *navis* = ship) in a Christian basilica, which represents the Church as "ship of the faithful," harboring the devout from the storms of worldliness and alluding to the original "ship" (Noah's ark) which saved humankind from total destruction. The literal rescue combines with the figurative Christian meaning: Christ saves us from spiritual death.

Shoes: When discarded, shoes suggest holy ground, an allusion to God's command to Moses to remove his shoes "for the place whereon thou standest is holy ground" (Exodus 3:5).

Sword: This is a general symbol for martyrs who died by the sword. A flaming sword identifies Jophiel, guardian of the Tree of Knowledge, who drove Adam and Eve out of Paradise.

Towel: White and spotless, it suggests purity, but often combined with other articles of cleanliness, such as the pitcher and basin (frequent accessories of Flemish paintings of the Virgin Mary).

From: Gertrude Grace Sill, A *Handbook of Symbols in Christian Art* (New York: Macmillan, 1975).

CAN A HUMANIST GET TO HEAVEN?

━━━━━━━━━━━━━━━━━━━━ **Appendix** 3

ISSUES OF THE SACRED AND THE SECULAR IN THE HUMANITIES

by Jon D. Green

INTRODUCTION

First, we should be clear about definitions. A humanist, in the traditional definition derived from the Italian Renaissance, was simply a teacher of the humanities, what the Italians called the *studia humanitatis,* "a well-defined cycle of scholarly disciplines that included the study of grammar, rhetoric, poetry, history, and moral philosophy, i.e., a broad spectrum of secular learning independent of—but not necessarily irreconcilable with—other scholarly disciplines of the university curriculum such as theology metaphysics, natural philosophy, medicine, and mathematics."[1] However, in spite of the qualification that humanism is "not necessarily irreconcilable with . . . theology," most definitions and most people then and now have placed humanism outside of and sometimes at cross purposes with religion: it is seen as "an intellectual movement . . . characterized by . . . an emphasis on human interests rather than on religion or the world of nature."[2]

In twentieth-century American society, teachers of the humanities are occasionally labeled "secular humanists," which has a decidedly negative, antireligious connotation, especially inflammatory when used in closed meetings by members of local school boards, sitting in emergency sessions to work out compromises with school librarians over which books ought to be banned or burned. In this atmosphere of suspicion, humanists are sometimes seen as the enemy of home, school, and church. This perceived humanist threat to the priority of religious values over human values has found its way into the attitudes of many

Latter-day Saints and could be seen as one of the divisions between the so-called "Iron Rodders" and the "Liahonas," or, put more simply, the "faithful" and the "intellectuals," as if faith and intellect were innately incompatible. The underlying tone of suspicion and animosity toward humanists is perhaps best revealed in Orson Scott Card's dual definitions in *Saintspeak:*[3]

1. To a Mormon puritan, [a humanist is] a member of a godless conspiracy to supplant the truth of the scriptures with the obscene or atheistic teaching of men. Humanists believe in things like evolution, relativity, philosophy, and art—as if anything discovered or made by human beings could have any value in the eyes of God. If stamping out humanism means rejecting every work of science, philosophy, or art since Plato, we are well rid of them.

2. To a Mormon humanist, anyone who believes that God has created mankind with a godlike potential and that people should therefore try to discover truth through their God-given powers of reason, experiment, and observation, as well as through studying the scriptures and receiving revelation. Humanists accept as valuable things like evolution, relativity, philosophy, and art—for God is pleased when mankind discovers truth and creates beauty, even if many mistakes are made along the way.

In reality, Orson Scott Card's duality is somewhat misleading. There is a third category for those of us humanists who truly embrace the gospel of Jesus Christ, namely, Card's first definition of a humanist who really is an enemy to religion and, as one colleague puts it, "tries to sneak into the Church wearing the robes of the [good] humanists" I am attempting to describe. I don't identify myself with Calvin Grondahl's cartoon caricature that accompanies Card's definition. (Who would, even those who are sloppy secular humanists?) Still, my life seems to have gradually gravitated from the "puritan" to the "humanist" pole, but without leaving the puritan core behind, the very anchor some Mormon intellectuals seem to lose as their allegiance to worldly knowledge short-circuits and eventually destroys their simple faith. Indeed, it is more than that. The safety net requires not only the interaction and embrace of both, but the proper setting of priorities: "But seek ye first the kingdom of God and his righteousness; and all these things shall be added unto you" (Matthew 6:33).

The conditions of my employment as both humanities and religion teacher at this university over the past twenty-five years have almost forced me to come to terms with the tensions that humanism creates in an authoritarian and religious environment. Nevertheless, the results have been most gratifying and fulfilling. I am convinced that the humanities and religion are natural siblings, not sworn enemies as some would have us believe. In this brief space, I will demonstrate with some personal examples how gospel principles have reinforced the humanizing dimensions of the discipline, and how cultural facts and artifacts can be "theologized" and preserved by reference to gospel principles.

PHILOSOPHY AND/OR RELIGION

Several years ago I engaged in a troubling but brief discussion with a fellow humanities colleague over the question of whether the Department of Humanities is superfluous at the "Lord's University." Why do we need worldly philosophers telling us about the Good, the True, and the Beautiful when we have immediate access to revealed truth and continuous revelation? Why indeed? I experienced a sudden crisis of professional confidence and felt the seamless web of connections I had stitched together over the years between my chosen field and my inherited religion begin to come unraveled. I recalled an earlier exchange with a seminary teacher in my home town after my mission as I was poised to depart for the university. "Whatever you do," he said, "don't take any philosophy classes at the Y; they will destroy your testimony!" I took his advice for one semester. Then I enrolled in Chauncey Riddle's Philosophy 284 class and discovered the rigorous and intimidating world of the mind. I came out of that class armed with the rudiments of my own philosophy, but grounded in the firm footings of gospel truth. Not every LDS philosophy teacher could have brought that off so smoothly, of course, but on reflection it made me realize that, notwithstanding the unmistakable allusions to the antagonistic relationship that can exist between the scriptures and the "philosophies of men" voiced in our holy rituals, God is not pleased when we give allegiance to one at the expense of the other.

In the process of working out this personal dilemma, I came up with a lecture and a handout for my students, entitled "Gospel Values in the Arts," which has provided the vital impetus to articulate for myself the true embrace of the gospel of Jesus Christ in the life of a humanities teacher who also teaches religion. The evidence I have gathered forms a framework for inclusion rather than exclusion in my quest for knowledge and truth, using as a point of departure Brigham Young's expansive definition of our religion as "compris[ing] every glory, honor, excellency and truth there is in the heavens, on the earth or beneath the earth."[4]

Brother Brigham would not be comfortable with the position that religious truths are somehow incompatible with worldly knowledge. He would surely agree that there is a way by which the Holy Spirit can greatly enhance the process of reconciling both religious and secular truths. I will define these two broad sources of knowledge as "mantic" and "sophic" respectively. Mantic comes from the Greek *mantis,* meaning prophet or holy man (as in "praying mantis") and relates to our words "manic," "mania," and "maniac." Sophic derives from the Greek *sophos* meaning wise and relates to our words "philosophy" (love of wisdom) and "sophomore" (wise fool). In the course of my arguments and examples, I will take the Devil's Advocate point of view by altering our underlying assumptions: instead of focusing on what the world can learn from us, I will cite examples of where we can and must learn from the world if we are to bring the world to the revealed truths God has entrusted to our care. Instead of sentries standing guard at the door of knowledge, we must be solicitors, inviting in and sifting through the vast store of discoveries made by inspired men and women of the world. Sidney B. Sperry once wrote:

> Are the creative activities of men in the realms of music, art, mathematics, science, and the like to be regarded as revelation? I think they should be. . . . The art, sculpture, and literature of the ancient Greeks have scarcely ever been surpassed. The paintings of a Rembrandt, Raphael, or Rubens thrill us. The mathematics and physics of men like Newton, Leibnitz, Einstein, Heisenberg, Urey, Teller, and Fermi have brought tremendous physical advances into

our world. May we not regard these advances and works of beauty as Godgiven, with men acting as the instruments through whom His kindness is bestowed? In other words, God has given relationships to man in the form of sculpture, music, painting, literature, mathematics, and physics, not to mention other media through which the creative urge acts.[5]

BRIGHAM YOUNG'S VISION: THE "GATHERING"

I fully subscribe to President Benson's challenge to "first lay the groundwork of the gospel truth in every subject and then, if necessary, to show where the world may fall short of that standard." But we need to add two other stages to this sifting process: first, to acknowledge where we may fall short of understanding and appreciating the achievements of the world in our own disciplines; and secondly, to gather rigorously all discovered truths into our minds and hearts, that they may not be lost forever.

This is precisely the view taken by Brigham Young, whose name this university bears. He not only asserts that our religion "circumscribes all art, science, and literature pertaining to heaven, earth and hell," but also that "every art and science known and studied by the children of men is comprised within the Gospel."[6] He doesn't mean that everything is the gospel. He qualifies his statement by saying: "It matters not what the subject be, if it tends to improve the mind, exalt the feelings, and enlarge the capacity,"[7] in short, if it serves to educate the "whole man," which, in a larger sense, is to create a "holy man," for wholeness and holiness are paired virtues of Brigham's vision. Especially vital is what Hugh Nibley has called Brigham Young's "grandiose intellectual project, which was nothing less than the salvaging of world civilization!"[8]

The "Gathering" involved bringing not only the faithful into the gospel net but also the cultural treasures surviving in the earth from every age and culture: "All the knowledge, wisdom, power, and glory that have been bestowed upon the nations of the earth, from the days of Adam until now, must be gathered home to Zion"[9] President Young added, "My faith and my desire are that there should be people upon the earth prepared to receive this wisdom. It should not be forfeited as to be taken from the earth."[10] That is a direct charge to us. The question, then that I shall pose is this: "How can we prepare to receive and preserve these treasures?" For they exist in abundance in every discipline taught at this university.

There are ways we can impede this important "gathering" process: (1) by refusing to acknowledge the value of the word's contributions to our disciplines and (2) by neglecting to discover the fruitful connections that exist between our disciplines and our religion. Failing to do this puts Brother Brigham's inspired educational endeavor at risk and leads to a dangerous provincialism, which narrows our gaze so that even religious truths lose their power to edify. Even reading the scriptures, if not undertaken in the spirit of improving the mind, exalting the feelings, and enlarging the capacity, does not belong to our religion. Brother Brigham continues: "'Shall I sit down and read the Bible, the Book of Mormon, and the Book of Covenants all the time' says one. Yes, if you please, and when you have done you may be nothing but a sectarian after all. It is your duty to study everything upon the face of the earth, in addition to reading those books."[11] We have not yet gathered into our embrace all the scientific discoveries and creative achievements of the past; in fact, we have barely scratched the surface. The wife of a colleague has a perfect rejoinder to the question often asked those of us who teach the humanities and the arts: "When will we have our Bachs, Shakespeares and Michaelangelos in the church?" She answers simply: "When we have audiences and readers who can understand and appreciate Bach, Shakespeare, and Michelangelo!"

Brigham Young's three criteria mentioned above provide a useful framework for organizing my evidence for inclusion rather than exclusion as we try to bridge the mantic and the sophic in our culture.

"IF IT TENDS TO IMPROVE THE MIND."

Humans are called dual creatures because they are bifurcated beings, struggling to reconcile naturally competing impulses in a basic dualistic nature. These are often expressed as head vs. heart or spirit vs. flesh. But in reality, our minds are themselves bifurcated. The human brain is a bilateral organ, made up of the so-called left hemisphere—which oversees logical, linear modes of thought—and the right hemisphere—which controls symbolic, spatial, imaginative functions. The two hemispheres are connected by a fibrous tissue called the *corpus callosum*. In spite of this connector, most humans use their two brains in isolation most of the time, as though they didn't exist in the same head.

Most creative minds, however, shift easily from one hemisphere to another in the process of making illuminating connections between seemingly unlike things. Whether it is Archimedes discovering the solution to a complex mathematical problem while taking a bath or Shakespeare inventing a pregnant metaphor—"Juliet is the sun"—to capture the essence of Romeo's idolatrous love for his Juliet, the pleasure of improving the mind has much to do with the process of making connections. When Aristotle claimed that "to learn gives the liveliest pleasure,"[12] he was making a creative leap from biology to drama, for his Poetics is finally a "dissection" of tragedy into its six component parts and a careful analysis of each part. More specifically, Aristotle was referring to the "pleasure felt in things imitated,"[13] the pleasure, incidentally, the ancients derived from the mythic powers inherent in the arts. In contrasting poetry to history, he finds that poetry is a "higher thing . . . for poetry tends to express the universal, history the particular."[14] Myths, as the ancients recognized, created important connections between the cosmos and the human imagination.

The birth of metaphor, for example, is congruent with the birth of thought itself. I can imagine one of our ancient ancestors noticing the nourishing influence of rain on plants as they grow from the earth and imaginatively identifying Father Heaven with Mother Earth. Experiencing something of the way plants grow and humans are made, it would be unthinkable to reverse the traditional genders of heaven and earth. All poets, from our mythic metaphor-making ancestors to Shakespeare and Eliot, have drawn on the power of inventing creative connections between things. In this context, it is virtually impossible to separate the pleasure of learning from the pleasure of creating.

Nevertheless, Aristotle devoted his immensely influential philosophy primarily to matters of the intellect. His impact on later thinkers from medieval to modern centered on the persuasive power of logic. One medieval theologian, St. Thomas Aquinas, even tried to prove the doctrines and dogmas of the Christian church by means of carefully reasoned arguments in an amazing intellectual monument, the *Summa Theologica,* which purports to rationalize the irrational. An earlier Church Father, St. Augustine, came perhaps closer to effecting a reconciliation of the two, but, in the end, he capitulated to reason. As his biographer Combes concludes, "the protests of his heart [were] silenced before the implacable dictates of his intellect."[15] It wasn't until the Renaissance Humanists came on the scene in late fifteenth century Italy that any successful attempt at fusing (instead of merely reconciling) Greek philosophy and Christian dogma occurred. Marsilio Ficino, in his major work, *Theologia Platonica,* attempted to prove that all revelation was essentially one. He attempted to prove that the life of the universe and humankind was controlled and dominated by a continuous "spiritual circuit" that led from God to the world and from the world to God. For him, Plato was both a Moses talking Attic Greek and an heir to the wisdom of Orpheus, Zoraster, and the Egyptian sages. Still, Ficino's fusion of philosophy and theology really demystifies religion by philosophizing it. The Christian Humanist of northern Europe, in particular Erasmus of Rotterdam and Sir Thomas More of England, came as close as anyone to setting the two traditions in a proper relationship. For them, the study of Christian writings went hand in hand with research in the Graeco-Roman classics, and their scholarship was simply meant to further the cause of ecclesiastical reform. "As a Humanist, Erasmus believed in education in the *humanitas* sense advocated by Cicero, emphasizing study of the classics and honoring the dignity of the individual. As a believing Christian, he promoted the 'philosophy of Christ' as expressed in the Sermon on the Mount and in Jesus' example of a humble and virtuous life."[16]

Wherever faithful Latter-day Saints become seriously engaged in improving the mind, the ancient contradictions between reason and religion easily arise. Augustine, Aquinas, and Ficino have shown us the impossibility of reconciling the two if we give reason priority or if we try to give equal allegiance to both. The union only works when the sacred takes precedence, yet embraces the secular, much as a successful marriage between a man and a woman. Quoting Pascal, Lowell S. Bennion says as much (although I may be putting words in his mouth), when he joins the two in "a marriage that has all the tension, adjustments, frustrations, joys and ecstasy one finds in a marriage between man and woman. . . . If one subjects everything to reason our religion will lose its mystery and its supernatural character. If one offends the principles of reason our religion will be absurd and ridiculous. . . . These are two equally dangerous extremes—to shut out reason and to let nothing else in."[17] Studying philosophers who have struggled with this dichotomy, even unsuccessfully, can keep us from making that mistake ourselves, for we have much less excuse, given the "intelligent" core of our theology. And yet, among many LDS there is a deep-seated mistrust of the intellect in matters of religion, not to mention our failure to develop our minds to the level of our spiritual understanding. The Prophet Joseph Smith said: "We consider that God has created man with a mind capable of instruction, and a faculty which may be enlarged in proportion to the heed and diligence given to the light communicated from heaven to the intellect."[18] "Note well," Hugh Nibley admonishes, "that the Prophet makes no distinction between things of the spirit and things of the intellect."[19] At the highest state of spiritual illumination, faith and intellect are one. The force that raises us up the ladder of knowledge is obedience. Forgetting this simple truth is the stumbling block of many an intellectual apostate. To be learned is to know a lot. To be wise is to act on what we know. Alma teaches that obedience controls both the direction and the speed at which we learn truth: "And he that will not harden his heart, to him is given the greater portion of the word, until it is given unto him to know the mysteries of God until he know them in full. And they that will harden their hearts, to them is given the lesser portion of the word until they know nothing concerning his mysteries; and then they are taken captive by the devil, and led by his will down to destruction. Now this is what is meant by the chains of hell" (Alma 12:10–11). Thus, we can conclude this section with a simple but true chiasmus: The more we do of what we know is right, the more we will know of what is right to do. Balancing knowing and doing provides a vital key to the eternal improvement of the mind.

"IF IT TENDS TO EXALT THE FEELINGS."

The humanities act as a kind of bridge between the intellectual disciplines of the liberal arts (grammar, logic, rhetoric) and the emotional domains of the fine arts. St. Augustine teaches us a profound truth about man's divided nature in his *Confessions* when he pleads with God: "'Give me chastity and continency, only not yet.' For I feared lest Thou shouldst hear me soon, and soon cure me of the disease of concupiscence, which I wished to have satisfied, rather than extinguished."[20] Whenever we are torn between intellectual commitments and emotional involvements, the latter will eventually prevail over time, because feelings are more powerful motivators to action than ideas. Aristotle's contemporary, Plato, severely censored the arts in his utopian view of society, *The Republic,* because he realized the power of the arts, especially music, to sway the emotions. Musical training, he wrote, "is a more potent instrument than any other, because rhythm and harmony find their way into the inward places of the soul, on which they mightily fasten, imparting grace, and making the soul of him who is rightly educated graceful, or of him who is ill-educated ungraceful."[21]

The Prophet Joseph said virtually the same thing, but tied music's refining power to the Holy Spirit when he "recommended the Saints to cultivate as high a state of perfection in their musical harmonies as the standard of the faith he had brought was superior to sectarian religion."[22] On the other hand, "music can [also], by its tempo, by its beat, by its intensity, dull the spiritual sensitivity of men."[23]

In similar ways, all of the fine arts have the potential power to "refine" a person's soul, if that soul has already made its peace with itself and with God. Otherwise, the arts merely provide a substitute for a spiritual high. And if art lovers are monsters at heart, like the Gestapo opera enthusiasts of Nazi Germany, they simply end up more refined monsters. And yet, under the right circumstances,

it is often difficult to distinguish aesthetic from spiritual experiences. They both work on the human heart in very similar ways and lead, ultimately, to similar ends: a deepening sensitivity to and desire for the Good, the True, and the Beautiful. For the ancient Greeks, these three human values were prized most highly. They belonged together, in a way similar to our own Articles of Faith: "If there is anything virtuous, lovely, or of good report or praiseworthy, we seek after these things" (Thirteenth Article of Faith).

"IF IT TENDS TO ENLARGE THE CAPACITY [TO BECOME ONE]."

The ultimate aim of a holistic education is the creation of the "whole man," which is, incidentally, the chief motto of this institution, and which is also designed to create a "holy man," one with true integrity (the word itself implies unity, as in "integer," a whole number). Studying the visual arts gives a new twist to the traditional concept of integrity. Successful paintings, like successful people, hang together well. A painting has integrity, for example, when its parts combine in harmony with the whole, and when the form matches and enhances the expressive content. One of the most successful examples of this kind of aesthetic unity is Michelangelo's *Creation of Adam* on the Sistine Chapel ceiling. In addition to its own amazing harmony of forms and meanings, it is part of a much larger space of interlocking shapes and themes which express a Neoplatonic synthesis of Greek philosophy and Hebrew–Christian theology, a marvelous visual integration of the mantic and the sophic.

But within its own centrally located rectangular panel one quickly becomes aware of repeated patterns that provide the scaffolding for a deeply theological interpretation. The reclining body of Adam generally matches the diagonal sweep of God, suggesting that Adam was made in God's image. The dynamic line that runs from Adam's arm across their extended fingers through God's arms and ending at the figure of the Baby Jesus reminds us of Paul's statement to the Corinthians: "For as in Adam all die, even so in Christ shall all be made alive" (1 Corinthians 15:22). The huge vortex of God's retinue of figures framed in a swirling purple cloak gives visual expression to this creative life source and would fit neatly into the concave hollow of Adam's body, much like the matching coastlines of Africa and South America. This interlocking "structural skeleton," writes Rudolf Arnheim, "reveals the dynamic theme of the story . . . the pattern of transmitted, life-giving energy [which] arouses in the mind a corresponding configuration of forces" related to the act of creation.[24] A recent article in the *Journal of the American Medical Association* posits a further theory.[25] Since Adam is obviously already alive (his eyes are open, he is reaching to God for something), could the brain profile of God's domain suggest that Michelangelo had intended the transfer of intelligence, rather than life? We will probably never know, but it raises interesting theological questions concerning the renaissance conception of fetal life, the entrance of the spirit at birth, and the premortal source of intelligence.

In addition, the graphic for Spielberg's *E.T.* several years ago prompted me to write a paper on "*E.T.* and the Finger of God: The Religious Significance of an Iconological Allusion." I discovered that there is a long history of religious meaning in Egyptian, Jewish, and early Christian texts relating to the symbolic significance of the hand of God. On a panel of relief sculpture in the tombs of Tel-el-Amarnia, each ray of the sun terminates in a miniature hand, one of which is presenting the "Ankh," or symbol of life. In Jewish legend, God's right hand was the source of his higher powers. Charles Seymour, in attempting to explain the meaning of God's extended finger in Michelangelo's fresco panel, cities Augustine's *De Spiritu et Littera* as the Christian source for this visual metaphor of the "finger-spirit of God." Augustine writes: "That Holy Spirit, through whom charity which is the fullness of the law is shed abroad in our hearts, is also called in the Gospel the finger of God; in other words, the finger of God is God's spirit through whom we are sanctified."[26]

As Latter-day Saints, we could easily add our own associations to the history of God's power residing in his hand. The most obvious association arises in the laying on of hands when transmitting priesthood authority, healing the sick, or confirming the baptismal ordinance and dispensing the Gift of the Holy Ghost. We might also recall the obvious parallels in our temple ordinances, where God's hand also reaches through, teaches us, and draws us back through the veil into a surrogate celestial realm.

The great blessing to be living at the end of time (in the Dispensation of the Fulness of Times) is the opportunity to discover the common threads that bind us to our religious and cultural roots. As "sacred humanists" on the Lord's last errand before He reappears in all His glory, we have an obligation to exhume, preserve, and pass on the rich legacy we have inherited from our cultural ancestors and to integrate it into the canon of revealed truth so that both can be mutually illuminated. Even more so, we must build bridges between our theology and the world's philosophy, between our sophic and mantic traditions, and even between our divided selves, by resisting the temptation to be one-sided. Charles Darwin in his later years admitted that his sole pursuit of scientific knowledge left him only half a man. His poignant regret should be fair warning to us all:

> Poetry of many kinds . . . gave me great pleasure, and even as a schoolboy I took intense delight in Shakespeare, especially in the historical plays. I have also said that formerly pictures gave me considerable, and music very great, delight. But now for many years I cannot endure to read a line of poetry: I have tried lately to read Shakespeare and found it so intolerably dull that it nauseated me. I have also lost almost any taste for pictures or music . . . My mind seems to have become a kind of machine for grinding general laws out of large collections of fact, but why this should have caused the atrophy of that part of the brain alone, on which the higher tastes depend, I cannot conceive. . . . The loss of these tastes is a loss of happiness, and may possibly be injurious to the intellect, and more probably to the moral character, by enfeebling the emotional part of our nature.[27]

CONCLUSION

Due to an unfortunate shift in meaning, humanism in our society (even at this university) has been saddled with a negative connotation, but its etymological roots place it in very positive company indeed. It comes from the Latin *humus,* which means earth and is directly related to human (to be above the animals), humane (to be above the merely human), and humanity (to reach out and embrace all mankind). The word *humanity* is our translation of the Latin *humanitas,* the very term coined by Cicero to define the priceless cultural legacy the Romans inherited from the Greeks, and that the Renaissance humanists fleshed out with the overlay of Christianity. Indeed, the roots of the Christian ethic are also hidden in *humus,* which is the core of our word *humility* and points to the biblical explanation of our earth-bound origins and destiny: "for dust thou art, and unto dust shalt thou return" (Genesis 3:19). The aged Darwin teaches us of the personal risk involved in neglecting this humanizing heritage, the humility necessary to lay the proper moral foundation under that heritage, and the interdependency of each discipline on the other. Brother Brigham's university is the only place on earth that I know of where these are designed and intended to come together. When we are whole, then we will be holy. Only then will we truly qualify as the Lord's university.

NOTES

1. Philip P. Wiener, *Dictionary of the History of Ideas* (New York: Scribner's, 1968, 1973) 2: 515.

2. Funk and Wagnel's *Standard College Dictionary* (New York: Harcourt, Brace and World, 1963).

3. Orson Scott Card, *Saintspeak* (Salt Lake City: Orion Books, 1982).

4. Brigham Young, *Journal of Discourses* (Liverpool: Albert Carrington, 1869) 12: 257.

5. Joseph Smith, Jr., qtd. in *History of the Organization of the Seventies,* ed. Sidney B. Sperry (Appendix, 1878), *Doctrine and Covenants Compendium* (Salt Lake City: Bookcraft, 1960) 14–15, 22–23.

6. Brigham Young, qtd. by Hugh Nibley, "Educating the Saints—A Brigham Young Mosaic," *BYU Studies* 11 no. 1 (Autumn 1970): 62.

7. Brigham Young, *Journal of Discourses* (Liverpool: F. D. Richards, 1855) 1: 335.

8. Hugh Nibley, "Educating the Saints: A Brigham Young Mosaic," *BYU Studies,* 11 no. 1 (Autumn 1970): 68.

9. Brigham Young, *Journal of Discourses* (Liverpool: George Q. Cannon, 1861) 8: 297.

10. Ibid. 8: 319.

11. Young, *Journal of Discourses* (Liverpool: F. D. Richards, 1855), 2: 93.

12. Aristotle's *Poetics* IV, ed. Francis Fergusson (New York: Hill and Wang, 1968).

13. Ibid. 55.

14. Ibid. 68.

15. Combs, qtd. in Hugh Nibley, *The World and the Prophets,* ed. John W. Welch et al., *The Collected Works of Hugh Nibley* (Salt Lake City: Deseret Book Co.; Provo, UT: Foundations for Ancient Research and Mormon Studies, 1987) 3: 83.

16. Roy Matthews, and Dewitt Platt, "The Western Humanities," unpublished manuscript (Mountain View, CA: Mayfield Publishing) 356.

17. Lowell L. Bennion, "The Uses of the Mind in Religion," *BYU Studies* 14 no. 1 (1973): 47–48.

18. Joseph Fielding Smith, comp., *Teachings of the Prophet Joseph Smith* (Salt Lake City: Deseret Book Co., 1973) 51.

19. Hugh Nibley, "Zeal without Knowledge," in *Nibley on the Timely and the Timeless* (Provo, UT: Religious Studies Center, Brigham Young University, 1978) 268.

20. Saint Augustine, *The Confessions* VIII, ed. Robert M. Hutchins, *Great Books of the Western World* (Chicago: Encyclopaedia Britannica, 1952) 17.

21. Plato, *The Republic* III, trans. Benjamin Jowett, ed. Robert M. Hutchins, in *The Dialogues of Plato, Great Books of the Western World* (Chicago: Encyclopaedia Britannica, 1952) 40 1.

22. Smith, *Teachings of the Prophet Joseph Smith,* 14–15.

23. Boyd K. Packer, "Inspiring Music—Worthy Thoughts," *Ensign* 4 (January 1974): 25–28.

24. Rudolf Arnheim, *Art and Visual Perception: A Psychology of the Creative Eye* (Berkeley: University of California Press, 1974) 460.

25. Frank Lynn Meshberger, "An Interpretation of Michelangelo's Creation of Adam Based on Neuroanatomy," *Journal of the American Medical Association* 264 no. 4 (10 October 1990): 1837ff.

26. Augustine, *The Confessions* VIII, 94.

27. Charles Darwin, *The Life and Letters of Charles Darwin,* ed. Francis Darwin (New York: D. Appleton and Company, 1896) 81–82.

GLOSSARY

Note: This Glossary is not comprehensive, but targets the terms most frequently used in this text and in general discussions about the fine arts.

ABA. In music, a three-part structure that consists of an opening section, a second section, and return to the first section. Also called ternary form.

Acronym. A word formed by combining the initial letters or syllables of a series of words to form a name, as PAC for political action committee.

Acropolis. The "city on a hill" in the center of Athens reserved for its holiest temples.

Aesthetic. Relating to the senses in general and to beauty in art and nature in particular.

Aesthetics. That branch of philosophy relating to questions about the **fine arts**.

Aesthetic Experience. A sensory/emotional experience with the arts or nature.

Aesthetic Stance. "Aesthetic" relates to experiences with the senses, in general, and, more specifically, with a focused involvement with the arts (aesthetic experience). An aesthetic stance is the necessary prelude to such an experience, characterized by a "willing suspension of disbelief," as Samuel Taylor Coleridge defined it.

Aleatory. From *aleator* = gambler, this modern musical style consists of chance sounds chosen by the performer or left to chance, as John Cage's "Silent Sonata" (four minutes and thirty-three seconds of silence), which consists of whatever sounds happen to occur during that time.

Allegorical Interpretation. One of the Four Senses of Interpretation in literature relating to the double significance of objects and ideas, wherein a story represents meanings independent of the characters and actions, as in John Bunyon's *Pilgrims Progress*.

Alliteration. In poetry, the repetition of the initial consonant sounds for rhythmic effect, as in "The furrow followed free."

Anagogical Interpretation. The highest of the Four Senses of Interpretation in literature relating to the spiritual meaning behind events or characters, as when certain passages in Virgil's writings were interpreted in the Middle Ages as foretelling the coming of Christ.

Anapestic. A poetic foot with two weakly accented syllables followed by a strongly accented syllable, as in the word *disappear*.

Arabesque. A ballet position in which one arm and one leg is extended, making the longest possible line.

Architecture. The art of designing great edifices, as distinct from the mere construction of buildings for function only. From the Greek *architekton*, which means "chief builder."

Architrave. In post-lintel architecture, the lintel or lowest part of the entablature which rests directly on the capitals of the columns.

Aria. A solo song sung in an opera.

Art. In general, an aesthetically pleasing arrangement of elements in some medium. Etymologically (in terms of the derivation of the word), art refers to a technical skill and the product of that skill, a well-wrought work. In terms of modern art, it has been defined as "anything out of context."

Arts, Fine. The organization of modern arts categories, according to their different means of dissemination: literary arts (poetry, prose, etc.); performing arts (dance, music, drama, music drama, and film); and visual arts (painting, sculpture, and architecture).

Arts, Liberal. Originating in the medieval cathedral schools, the seven "liberal arts" comprised the curriculum of an educated person: the Trivium (grammar, rhetoric, and logic); and the Quadrivium (geometry, astronomy, arithmetic, and music).

Aside. A dramatic convention by which an actor addresses the audience directly but is not supposed to be heard by the other actors on the stage. Often used in comedies.

Atonality/Tonality. In music, tonality defines the presence of a "tonal center"; in other words, the piece is written in a particular key (C major, B♭ minor, etc.). Atonality is the absence of a key center, as in Arnold Schönberg's music (he obliterates the key center by creating a "twelve-tone system" whereby no tone of the chromatic scale is played more than any other).

Atrium. The central open court of an ancient Roman house. In early Christian architecture, the open colonnaded court before the entrance (**narthex**).

Attitude. A ballet position similar to the **arabesque** but with the extended leg bent.

Avant garde. A term used to designate artistic innovators, "the advanced guard," the group most daring in technique or ideas.

Ballad. A simple and enduring verse narrative of four lines of iambic verse alternating tetrameter and trimeter.

Ballerina. A female ballet dancer, the best of whom is referred to as a prima ballerina.

Ballet. From Italian *balo* (dance), ballet is a highly conventionalized theatrical dance form following a strict technique and formulistic body movements.

Balletomane. The word, which means "ballet enthusi-ast," was first used in Russia early in the nineteenth century.

Ballroom Dance. Originally a social dance form popular since the turn of the century in dance halls and social gatherings, since 1929 in England has become popular in international championships involving two basic styles of competition: Standard (Waltz, Tango, Foxtrot, Quickstep, Viennese Waltz) and Latin (Cha Cha, Samba, Rumba, Paso Doble, Jive).

Balustrade. A line of small pillars supported by a handrail; usually found on the roof line of classical (Renaissance) buildings.

Baroque. An art style of the seventeenth century characterized by grandiose expressions of emotion and elaborate decoration.

Basilica. A public hall in Rome that formed the model for the Early Christian Church, divided by columns into a nave and aisles with a rounded apse at one end and a clerestory beneath the ceiling.

Battlements. An indented parapet along the top of many medieval castles; also called **crenelations**.

Binary Form. In music, a form with only two parts, as in the **AB** song form.

Brass Choir. In music, the instruments in an orchestra made of brass (trumpet, French horn, trombone, tuba).

Buttress. In architecture, a structure built against a wall to shore it up, sometimes called **engaged buttress**, and **flying buttress** if it extends beyond the wall.

Byzantine. An art style originating in Byzantium (on the Bosporus), characterized by shallow domes, centralized floorplans, and lavish mosaics in architecture, and flat iconic images in art.

Cabaret. A nightclub providing short programs of live entertainment popular in the late nineteenth century that influenced the development of musical theatre.

Cabriole. A leap in ballet in which the dancer's working leg is followed by the other leg, which beats against it, sending it higher.

Cacophony. The opposite of **euphony** in poetry; a harsh, unpleasant combination of sounds using fricatives and plosives.

Canon. This term has two definitions: cultural and musical. The cultural definition relates to a standard principle, standard or criterion, as the books of the Bible, accepted as a moral standard (the "Standard Works"), or a group of literary works accepted as standards of excellence in a field (the masterworks of Western literature); musically, the term defines a motive (melody) that is exactly repeated in another voice (imitative counterpoint), a texture we experience every time we sing a round, like "Row, Row, Row Your Boat."

Cantata. A mostly sacred vocal form in music containing arias, recitatives, solo and ensemble parts.

Cantilever. A beam or slab in architecture extending horizontally over unsupported space.

Capital. The "cap" on the top of a column in classical architecture.

Catharsis. In Aristotle's theory of drama (in the *Poetics*), the purgation of the emotions of pity and fear when experiencing a tragedy.

Cathedra. The bishop's seat or throne in a **cathedral**.

Cathedral. The edifice designed to house the **cathedra**, the crowning glory of medieval architecture.

Cave Paintings. The art produced by prehistoric (Paleolithic) peoples in deep, dark caverns located mostly in Southern France (Lascaux) and Northern Spain (Altamira).

Chiaroscuro. The dramatic use of light and dark in painting or drawing to create three-dimensionality.

Chi-Rho Monogram. See **Chrismon**.

Choreographer. Literally, a designer of dance.

Chorus. In music, a group of singers, sometimes called a choir. In drama, the convention of having groups of individuals dance, chant, and sing; most typical of ancient Greek drama.

Chrismon. Also called the Chi-Rho Monogram, it represents the two overlapping letters of the Greek alphabet that begin Christ's name (X and P) which suggest two aspects of His nature: Christ the Crucified One and Christ the Good Shepherd.

Cinema. Refers to motion pictures in general and art films in particular; derived from the Greek word *kinema*, meaning to move.

Cinematography. The art of the moving image; what the cinematographer does with the motion picture camera, a key element in the making of a quality movie.

Civilization. A state of human society characterized by a high level of intellectual, social, and cultural development.

Clerestory. The window openings in Early Christian churches just below the ceiling, symbolic of the light of heaven.

Coda. From the Italian for "tail," a passage added to the end of a musical composition to produce a satisfactory conclusion; the last section of the **First Movement Form**.

Collage. From French for "pasting," an artwork made by pasting together various materials, such as newsprint, to create textures or to combine two-dimensional and three-dimensional reality.

Coloratura. A style of singing that exploits the color and virtuosity of the soprano voice, having a very high range and great vocal flexibility.

Comedy. Theatre celebrating life and less-than-perfect characters dealing with human folly in light and humorous ways; often used as comic relief to Greek tragedies.

Complementary Colors. Colors that exist opposite the color wheel from each and contain between them all three primary colors; green and red are complementary colors.

Connotation. As opposed to **denotation** (the dictionary meaning), connotation suggests related associations or words, as "spring *connotes* warmth, life, and love."

Consonance/Dissonance. In music, simultaneously sounding tones are consonant or dissonant depending on whether they produce pleasant or unpleasant effects. For example, a major triad is consonant (CEG); a minor second is dissonant (C C#).

Contextualism. A critical method in analyzing art whereby the critic establishes illuminating connections outside the work in the artist's biography, or sources in myth, bible, history.

Contrapposto. The positioning of the body in sculpture whereby one leg bears the weight, causing a "counterpoise" or S curve in the hip/shoulder axis.

Coordinates of Dance. The three mentioned in the text are (1) physical (tension between weight and weightlessness); (2) psychological (tension between breathing in and breathing out); (3)social (tension between attraction and repulsion).

Corbels. Overlapping brackets of stone or brick projecting from the face of a wall, in which each course extends farther out from the wall than the course below, generally used to support a cornice or an arch. A corbel arch is formed by a similar projection inward from each side.

Corinthian. One of the three styles of ancient Greek architecture (along with **Doric** and **Ionic**) characterized by elaborate fronds of acanthus leaves on the **capital**.

Cornice. The projecting feature on the crown of a building, commonly known as the eaves.

Counterpoint. In music, the simultaneously sounding of two or more different melodies, or the overlapping sounding of one melody; also known as polyphony.

Creative Process. The process usually followed by all significant creative acts: first insight, saturation, incubation, "Ah-Ha," and verification.

Creativity. A trait of all great innovators in the arts and sciences, characterized by independence, self-confidence, unconventionality, alertness, and ambition.

Critic. A word that comes from the Greek *kritikos,* which means one who judges according to some criterion or standard.

Critical Paradigm. A pattern of relationships that reveals the central questions asked about any work of art: artist, audience, work, nature.

Cross. A central symbol of Christianity; the two most frequently used crosses in Christian art are the Latin and Greek crosses.

Cross Cut. In film, an editing technique pioneered by D. W. Griffith which conveys two parallel actions happening simultaneously; also called **parallel editing**.

Culture. The happy result of conditions that favor human growth in a society, such as the training, development, and refinement of the mind, morals, and artistic sensibilities.

Cut. In a film, any joining of two shots with a splice, to create an instantaneous change from one frame to another.

Dactylic. A poetic foot characterized by a stressed syllable followed by two unstressed syllables, as in the word *yesterday.*

Dance. Body movements beyond spontaneous gestures that combine in a pleasing and significant way.

Danseur. A male ballet dancer.

Denotation. The dictionary meaning of a word, as opposed to the suggestion of **connotation**.

Dénouement. The "unraveling" of a dramatic plot, which comes at the end of the play.

Dialectical. Literally, to "speak between"; in other words, the art of argumentation or debate, or arriving at the truth by question and answer, especially associated with Hegel's critical process: establishing a *thesis* (argument), followed by an *antithesis* (counter-argument), leading to a *synthesis* (resolution).

Director. The major creative figure and decision maker behind the making of a film or the production of a play. He or she directs the efforts of the cast and the staff to achieve his or her creative vision.

Dissolve. A transition between shots during which the first image gradually disappears while the second image gradually appears.

Dissonance. *See* **Consonance/Dissonance**.

Dithyramb. A frenzied poem sung in honor of the god Dionysus to the accompaniment of singing and dancing, which ostensibly marked the ritual origins of Greek tragedy.

Dome. A major feature of Roman and Renaissance architecture, made by turning an arch on its vertical axis.

Doric. One of the three orders of Greek architecture (along with the **Ionic** and **Corinthian),** characterized by a simple cap on the top of a column.

Dramatic. Of or pertaining to drama or the theatre; expressive of the emotion associated with drama.

Drypoint. A print process in the graphic arts made by drawing directly onto a copper or zinc plate with a sharp steel stylus.

Duomo. Means "dome" in Italian, but refers specifically to Brunelleschi's great domed cathedral in Florence.

Dynamics. In music, the element related to changing volume (loud and soft).

Editor. The individual who edits together the raw footage in a film to create meaning and drama.

Encaustic. A pre-Christian visual arts medium which combines pigments with hot wax and burns them into a wood surface with hot irons.

Engraving. A graphic arts medium by which the design is made by cutting lines into a copper plate.

Entablature. In classical architecture, everything above the column capitals.

Entasis. The slight bulge in the vertical line of columns on a classical temple facade.

Epic. One of the three classical literary genres (along with **lyric** and **dramatic**); a long narrative poem in heightened style about the deeds of a hero.

Etching. A graphic arts medium by which the design is made by drawing through a resin surface on a copper plate and dipping the exposed surface into an acid bath.

Ethnic Dance. Dances that grow out of religious roots, like the Indian rain dance.

Euphony. In opposition to **cacophony,** pleasant-sounding words.

Exposition. In theatre, the first part of the play, which "exposes" the characters and dramatic situations; in music, the first part of the **First Movement Form,** which "exposes" the major themes.

Eyebrow dormers. Narrow window slits with curved upper line inserted into a sloped roof; popular in nineteenth-century Victorian mansions.

Fade. A transitional technique in film in which the image either fades into blank space (fade out) or the image gradually appears from a blank screen (fade in).

Fine Arts. *See* **Arts, Fine.**

Ferroconcrete. Concrete reinforced with rods or webs of steel and used in virtually all major modern building projects.

First Movement Form. See **Sonata Allegro Form.**

Flying Buttresses. An indispensable, outside supporting member of a Gothic cathedral, it presses inward on the vertical piers to keep the building from collapsing. It's called a "flying" buttress because it looks like a bridge built out from the roof line across open space and connected to outside piers.

Folk Dance. Dances that grow out of the social mores of a people (folk) and often later get codified and performed as spectacle dances on a stage.

Formalism. A critical approach to the analysis of the visual arts whereby the critic focuses on what exists within the frame (line, color, texture, etc.) and doesn't worry about extraneous matters, like the artist's life or sources, as a **contextualist** critic would do.

Forte. Loud in music, often abbreviated f, in contrast to **piano** (soft).

Four Senses of Interpretation. The levels traditionally used in interpreting scriptural and allegorical writings: the **literal**, the **allegorical**, the **moral**, and the **anagogical**.

Free Verse. In poetry, verse that does not follow any strict metrical or rhyme scheme.

Freeze Frame. In film, a still shot created by printing a single frame several times in succession to give the illusion of a still photograph.

Fresco. A painting method in which the pigments are painted directly on wet plaster, thereby becoming a permanent part of the wall or ceiling.

Frieze. A horizontal band of relief sculpture typically found in the **entablature** of a classical temple.

Genre. Types or categories of art forms, in particular literature, characterized by a particular style, form or content.

Gesamtkunstwerk. German for "total art work," it refers specifically to the grand operatic tradition of Wagner, in which music, drama, set design, and literature were unified by the mind of one genius.

Gesso. A white plaster material used during the Middle Ages and Renaissance as a ground to prepare a panel or canvas for painting.

Glaze. An old painting method, involving the build-up of transparent layers of thin paint over the surface to create an effect of depth and luminosity, in contrast to **impasto.**

Golden Section. The name given to the proportion derived from the division of a line into what Euclid called "extreme and mean ratio" and which has since become an ideal proportion in the visual arts. It can be expressed numerically as a progression 0.618, 1.618, 1,618, 4.623 . . . (the Fibonacci Sequence: 1 2 3 5 8 13 . . .) or algebraically as a/b = b/(a+b).

Gothic. The art style of the late Middle Ages, characterized by a pointed arch, **flying buttresses**, and **stained glass** windows in architecture and, generally, by verticality, elegance, and lightness, moving toward **realism**.

Gouache. Opaque watercolor, created by mixing regular watercolor pigments with glue, thus preventing the normal reflection of the ground (white paper surface beneath).

Gregorian Chant. The musical system used during the Middle Ages, characterized by a rigorously **monophonic** texture with little or no clear melody or rhythm.

Harmony. Created by playing two or more notes together, it creates texture and, together with **tonality** (a sense of a tonal center), generates emotional reactions in music.

Hellenic. The style of Greek art and architecture during the Golden Age of Greece (fifth century B.C.), characterized by beautiful proportions held in check by a formal rigor and simplicity.

Hellenistic. The "other" style of Greek art during the time of Alexander the Great (fourth century B.C.), characterized by exaggerations prompted by an overly dramatic and decorative sensibility.

Homophony. The third kind of musical texture (along with **monophony** and **polyphony**), in which chordal structures are built over a clearly defined bass line and underneath a clear melodic line.

Hue. The technical word for color, and one of its chief attributes.

Humanities. As defined by this text, the humanities are the bridge linking the **liberal arts** (the major tools of criticism) and the **fine arts** (the subject matter to which the criticism is applied).

Hyperbole. In poetry, the technical term for **overstatement**.

Iambic. The most common poetic foot, characterized by an unstressed syllable followed by a stressed syllable, as in the word *today*.

Imagery. In general, the mental duplication of a sense impression, used in poetry to evoke richly sensuous effects (visual, auditory, taste-smell, and touch-kinetic).

Impasto. The bold build-up of oil paints on a canvas, in the manner of van Gogh, in contrast to **glazes**.

Impressionism. A French art movement of the latter half of the nineteenth century, characterized by fleeting sensations of light and color on soft surfaces and a deep attraction to nature; received its name from a Renoir painting, *Impression Sunrise*, at the first exhibition in 1874.

Intaglio. A printmaking process in which ink is transferred from the grooves of a metal plate to paper under extreme pressure; it means to "cut in" in Italian, as contrasted, for example, with the **relief** process of printing the raised surfaces found in woodcut.

Intensity. One of the three attributes of color (along with **hue** and **value**), which is controlled either by mixing complementary colors together (to lower the intensity) or to place complements side by side (to raise the intensity).

International Style. The first truly modern style in architecture, spearheaded by Gropius's Bauhaus in Germany and by Mies van der Rohe and Philip Johnson in the U.S., characterized by tall urban structures designed to create an ideal man-made environment.

Intonaco. The final layer of plaster upon which the fresco artist paints his or her design.

Ionic. One of the three classical orders of architecture (along with **Doric** and **Corinthian**), characterized by a more slender shaft (column) and scroll designs (volutes) on the **capitals**.

Iris. A transition device in film in which a circle begins from a single point in the center of the screen and expands to fill the entire screen (iris out), or the opposite (iris in).

Irony. A broad term referring to the practice of "saying one thing but meaning another."

Jazz. A general term for the twentieth-century development of American popular music, growing out of black music traditions like ragtime, the blues, swing, live, and bebop.

Jeté. In ballet, a jump from one foot to another; a split executed in mid-air is called a *grand jeté*.

Jump Cut. In film, the instantaneous cut from one part of a scene to a subsequent part, creating a shock effect by deleting some of the footage within the shot.

Key Signature. The indication of the key, given in flats (♭) or sharps (♯).

Leitmotif. A musical fragment (motive) used in the operas of Wagner, to suggest extramusical meanings associated with ideas, objects, or feelings.

Liberal Arts. *See* **Arts, Liberal**.

Libretto. The words sung in an opera (Literally "little book").

Line. The visual element that gives a painting its structure (somewhat like melodic "line" in music).

Lyric. One of the three classical literary genres (along with **epic** and **dramatic**), characterized by a personal, introspective poetic expression; in ancient times, such poetry was performed to the accompaniment of a lyre.

Madrigal. A secular, unaccompanied song sung in parts (usually four or five).

Mansard Roof. A four-sided roof having a double slope on all sides, consisting of a nearly flat upper part with steeply pitched sides, the steep sides punctuated with inserted (dormer) windows; it was named after Francois Mansart (1598–1666), the greatest French architect of his day. The mansard roof is one of those good ideas (like Alfred Nobel's dynamite) that somehow turns into a disaster in the wrong hands.

Mantic. A traditional source of knowledge—experience gained through intuition or religion—as opposed to the **sophic** approach.

Manuscript Illumination. A medieval art form that grew out of the efforts of monastery copyists to decorate the borders of their manuscript pages.

Mass. The central ritual of the Catholic Church commemorating Christ's sacrifice by partaking of the Eucharist; organized into two major types (the Proper and the Ordinary).

Match Cut. A cut that connects two shots by means of matching images or movements.

Medium. The material ("stuff") out of which an art is made (wood, sound, words, etc.).

Megaron. A simple rectangular colonnaded building that formed the basis of ancient Greek temples.

Melody. The unique arrangement of musical tones that creates the "subject" of most musical pieces.

Metaphor. An analogy (direct comparison) of two seemingly unlike things, as in the poetic "Juliet is the sun."

Meter. In music, the way we measure **rhythm** (with time signatures); in poetry, the way we measure **rhythm** in a line (by means of poetic feet).

Metope. Relief sculptures on **friezes** in classical temples.

Minimalist Music. As a result of the controlled improvisation of the simpler musical styles of Asia (India and Indonesia), Western composers have simplified the complexity of serialism in a direction that has been called *minimalism,* whereby the composer, using a synthesizer, improvises over "canned" rhythms and melodic patterns. Such music can sound monotonous but actually be subtly complex.

Mise en scène. The complete visual environment in theater, dance, and film.

Monophony. One of the three musical textures (along with **polyphony** and **homophony),** characterized by a single melody line sung in solo or unison.

Montage. The working up of sequences of scenes in film which create a unified dramatic effect.

Mosaic. This medium involves creating a design by placing small pieces of colored glass or stone, called *tesserae,* onto a plaster surface. The reflected light creates a luminous effect in church interiors.

Motet. An unaccompanied polyphonic religious composition popular from the thirteenth through the eighteenth centuries.

Musical. A uniquely American form of musical theatre with light dramatic plots, popular songs, and belt vocal delivery.

Myth. A legendary story (sometimes based in fact) that explains natural phenomena or captures the belief system of a people.

Narthex. A porch or vestibule of a church, generally colonnaded or arcaded and preceding the nave.

Nave. The part of a church between the entrance and the **apse** and **transept.**

Negative Space. The area of a painting not taken up by the objects painted, and of which the artist is always very much aware.

Neoclassicism. A style in art during the early part of the nineteenth century, characterized by exquisitely controlled lines, but often rather static and unoriginal.

Notre Dame. Technically the name for most gothic cathedrals, dedicated to "our lady," namely Mary, the mother of Christ.

Ode. A long, elevated form of poetry dealing with one theme.

Oil Painting. A medium of the visual arts that rose during the early Renaissance in the northern countries, based on the use of linseed oil as a binder to the pigments, allowing stunningly realistic renderings of the world.

Onomatopoeia. A poetic sound device wherein a word sounds like what it symbolizes.

Op Art. A twentieth-century art movement that exploits optical effects for artistic purposes.

Opera. A musical theatre creation of the Baroque age, characterized by sung drama, lavish costumes and sets, and rather melodramatic plots; includes arias, ensembles, orchestra, recitatives, etc.

Opera Buffa. Literally comic opera, in which some of the delivery is spoken.

Opera Seria. Literally serious opera, in which all the dialogue is sung.

Opera Verismo. A nineteenth-century style of Italian opera typical of Verdi's works, especially his *La Traviata* (1853), in which natural settings and costumes set the backdrop for real situations.

Oratorio. A musical setting for solo voices, chorus, and orchestra of an extended story (religious or contemplative) performed in a concert hall or a church.

Organic Architecture. The style of Frank Lloyd Wright, which emphasizes the need for the building to be integrated into the site and to reflect links to nature (color, form, etc.).

Ornamental Pediments. Small pediments over the windows and doors of Renaissance palaces.

Overhanging Cornice. The extended eaves of a Renaissance building, often supported by ornamental brackets.

Overstatement. In poetry, saying more than is expected to make a point; also called **hyperbole**.

Oxymoron. A self-contradictory combination of words (meaning in Greek "sharp-dull"), as in "Parting is such sweet sorrow."

Palladian Window. A window designed originally by the late Renaissance architect Palladio, containing a concise union of Greek (post-lintel) and Roman (arch) styles.

Pan. In film, the movement of the camera from right to left, or left to right, on its vertical axis.

Pas de deux. A "duet" in ballet, usually between a **danseur** and **ballerina**, and typically having a rather set sequence of events (solos and duets).

Passion. Like a cantata or oratorio, it contains solos, choruses, recitatives, etc., but treats the story of the Crucifixion as told by one of the four Evangelists.

Pediment. The triangular frame at the end of the gabled roof of a classical temple.

Pendentive. The triangular transition in Byzantine domed churches from a square base to a round dome.

Percussion. One of the four groups of instruments in a symphony orchestra, which create sound by beating surfaces.

Personification. A poetic figure of speech that endows inanimate things with human qualities.

Piano. Both a keyboard instrument and a dynamic level (soft), as opposed to **forte** (loud).

Pilaster. A flat column built into a wall, originally Roman, but most often associated with Renaissance architecture.

Pirouette. One or more complete turns of the ballet dancer on point.

Plot. The pattern of the action in a play, which may have a different sequence than the story; Aristotle calls this the "soul" of the play.

Poetry. Highly condensed literary forms, as opposed to prose.

Polyphony. One of the three musical textures (along with **monophony** and **homophony**), characterized by two or more different melodies played together, or one melody played at different times.

Port de bras. In ballet, any movement of the arms.

Post-Impressionism. The movement following **Impressionism**, characterized by intense expressionism (van Gogh) or rigorously structural paintings (Cézanne).

Post-lintel Construction. The type of building principle used in most ancient architecture up to the Roman era, most typical of Greek classicism.

Postmodern. A contemporary style most connected to architecture, characterized by a return to decoration, in particular arched windows (**Palladian Windows**) and often unusual forms and colors schemes.

POV. In film, a "point of view" shot (subjective camera shot), in which we see the actor/actress looking and then see what is seen.

Pyramids. Ancient triangular monuments indigenous to Mesopotamian and Egyptian architecture.

Rack Focus. In film, the shift of focus from close to distant or distant to close.

Realism. An art style of the mid-nineteenth century, characterized by realistic renderings of a world that focuses on the actual conditions of life.

Reality. As defined in the text, the perceptions each individual has of the world, relative to his or her own attitude and knowledge; it is, therefore, relative to each individual.

Recapitulation. The last part of the **First Movement Form** in orchestral music, marking the return to the **Exposition**.

Recitative. In opera, the speech-song delivery that furthers the plot.

Renaissance. An art style that began in Italy during the early fifteenth century, characterized by a return to classical ideals, in particular a blend of Greek idealism and Roman realism.

Revivals. In architecture, the revival of earlier styles in various combinations during the eighteenth, nineteenth, and twentieth centuries.

Rhyme. Similar sounding words at the end of lines of poetry, based on the vowels and succeeding consonants of the accented syllables.

Rhythm. The "life blood" of music, the beat patterns that give the music its forward thrust and interest.

Rococo. An art style of the early eighteenth century, characterized by rather superficial, often erotic themes and situations, with mostly pastel colors and highly intricate details.

Romanesque. An art style of the eleventh and twelfth centuries, characterized by weightiness and use of the rounded arch; the sculpture is crude, yet playfully charming.

Romanticism. An early nineteenth-century movement in art, characterized by exotic, medieval themes, nostalgic longing, and love of nature.

Rubato. A term denoting a certain plasticity and freedom in musical tempos; it means "to rob."

Scales. The unique arrangement of musical tones in a certain order of intervals (as major and minor) from which melodies are created.

Sculptural Processes. The three basic ways sculpture is created: carving, modeling, and construction.

Serialism. The logical extension of Schönberg's Twelve-tone System (giving equal time to each tone of the chromatic scale in a piece of music), whereby the principle of equal time is applied to other musical elements, like **timbre** (tone color) and **texture**.

Serigraph. A stencil process, whereby the pigments are forced through the unmasked areas of a silk screen.

Sfumato. The unique style of Leonardo da Vinci's paintings, whereby he created soft textures by the subtle shading of light and dark areas; from Italian for "smoky."

Shot. One uninterrupted running of the movie camera.

Simile. A poetic comparison of two seemingly unlike things with "as" or "like."

Sinopia. The underdrawing of a **fresco** on the penultimate layer of plaster; a kind of "dry run."

Socratic Method. A way of teaching and learning originating with Socrates that requires more the questioning of answers than the answering of questions.

Soliloquy. A kind of "solo" delivery of a dramatic character, in which the audience learns what the hero is thinking and feeling.

Sonata Allegro Form (or **First Movement Form**). In symphonic music, a large **ABA** form that follows the pattern of **Exposition**, **Development**, **Recapitulation**, and **Coda**.

Sonnet. A fourteen-line poem in either three quatrains and a couplet (Shakespearean) or an octave and sestet (Petrarchan) that follows a strict metrical pattern and meter.

Sophic. A traditional source of knowledge—human knowledge attained through the intellect—as opposed to **mantic**.

Spondaic. A poetic foot that has two stressed syllables, as in the word _daybreak_.

Stained glass. Created by a patch work design of different colors of glass. The pieces of glass are held together by leading and often illustrate religious stories. It emerged in the Middle Ages as the crown jewel of **gothic** cathedrals.

String Choir. The group of string instruments in a symphony orchestra (violin, viola, cello, and bass viol), characterized by a sustained tone; the strings give an orchestra its "symphonic" sound.

Stringcourse. The line separating a building horizontally into a heavier lower part and a lighter higher part; typical of Renaissance architecture.

Strophe. Generally, a literary (poetic) term synonymous with stanza, a regular and usually rhymed subdivision of a poem; technically, strophes are defined as irregular, unrhymed subdivisions.

Tapestry. A woven ornamental fabric used for wall hangings, in which the woof is supplied by a spindle, the design being formed by stitches across the warp.

Tempera. Painting with pigment ground in water and mixed with egg.

Tempo. One of the elements of music that designates the speed of performance.

Ternary Forms. In music, forms that have an **ABA** pattern, returning to the beginning at the end.

Tesserae. Small pieces of ceramic, glass, or stone used to create the design in a **mosaic**.

Texture. In music, the single thread of **monophony**, the interweaving threads of **polyphony**, or the vertical texture of **homophony**. In the visual arts, the tactile **values** of the work, real or illusory.

Tilt. The movement of the camera on its horizontal axis, up or down.

Timbre. In music, the characteristic sound of any instrument; also called "tone color."

Time Signature. The guide to the rhythmic patterns in the music: measured by the kind of note and the number of beats in each measure (4/4, 6/8 etc.)

Tonality. *See* **Atonality/Tonality.**

Tracking Shot. A camera shot in which the camera travels along a track to capture the action in a film; also called a dolly or truck shot.

Tragedy. The most sublime of the dramatic forms; originated in Greece and focuses on the unmerited misfortune, suffering, and death of the tragic hero.

Triglyph. The linear grooves in a classical frieze, often separated by **metopes**.

Triptych. A three-part altarpiece popular during the Middle Ages and Renaissance, symbol of the Trinity.

Trochaic. A poetic foot with an accented syllable following by an unaccented syllable, as in <u>daily</u>.

Trompe l'oeil. Literally "trick of the eye," characterizing paintings with remarkable realism.

Understatement. In poetry, saying less than you mean for dramatic effect.

Value. The control of light and dark in a painting, by adding black or white to the pigments.

Vaudeville. Stage entertainment offering a variety of short acts such as song-and-dance routines and juggling performances, in short, variety shows that were popular in New York at the turn of the twentieth century, heralding the emergence of American musical comedy. The Ziegfield Follies represent a type of vaudeville.

Vault. A curved ceiling in architecture, either barrel (simple curve) or groin (intersecting barrel vaults at right angles).

Virtuoso. A performer with unusual skill, usually associated with music.

Voissoirs. Wedge-shaped stones that are cut to fit into the curvature of an arch.

Watercolor. The oldest and one of the most accessible of painting mediums.

Wipe. In film, a transition device whereby a line passes across the screen in any direction, eliminating the first image as it passes through the frame and replacing it with the next image.

Woodwind Choir. The orchestral instruments made mostly of wood, which create sound by blowing over a hole or through a mouthpiece made of reed.

Zoom. In film, a shot using a special lens to adjust the distance from near to far, or from far to near; sometimes used in place of tracking shots.

PERMISSIONS

COLOR PLATES

Plate 16: *Guernica,* by Pablo Picasso, 1937. Centre de Arte Reina Sofia, Madrid. Copyright (c) 2002 Estate of Pablo Picasso / Artists Rights Society (ARS), New York.

Plate 17: *The Persistence of Memory,* by Salvador Dali. The Museum of Modern Art, New York. Given anonymously. (c) 2002 Salvador Dali, Gala-Salvador Dali Foundation / Artists Rights Society (ARS), New York.

Plate 18: *Broadway Boogie Woogie,* by Piet Mondrian, 1942–1943. The Museum of Modern Art, New York, given anonymously. (c) 2002 Mondrian / Holtzman Trust, c/o/ Beeldrecht / Artists Rights Society (ARS), New York.

Plate 19: *Lavender Mist,* by Jackson Pollack. National Gallery of Art, Washington, D.C. Alisa Mellon Bruce Fund, (c) 2002 The Pollock-Krasner Foundation / Artists Rights Society (ARS), New York.

Plate 23: *Christ Healing the Sick at Bethesda,* by Carl Bloch, used courtesy of BYU Museum of Art.

Plate 24: *Fallen Monarchs,* by William Bliss Baker, used courtesy of BYU Museum of Art.

Plate 25: *Grain Fields,* by Edwin Evans, used courtesy of BYU Museum of Art.

Plate 26: *Forgotten Man,* by Maynard Dixon, used courtesy of BYU Museum of Art.

Plate 27: *Marilyn Monroe,* by Andy Warhol, used courtesy of BYU Museum of Art.

Plate 28: *The Seer,* by Brower Hatcher, used courtesy of Brower Hatcher.

OTHER ILLUSTRATIONS

The Wave, by McRae Magleby, courtesy of McRae Magleby. Drawing Hands, M. C. Escher, (c) 2002 Cordon Art B.V.—Baarn—Holland. All rights reserved.

PERMISSIONS

ARTICLES AND POEMS

"Because I Could Not Stop for Death," reprinted by permission of the Publishers and the Trustees of Amherst College from *The Poems of Emily Dickinson,* edited by Thomas H. Johnson, Cambridge, MA.: The Belknap Press of Harvard University Press, Copyright (c) 1951, 1955, 1979 by the President and Fellows of Harvard College.

"Freewriting," from *Writing Without Teachers* by Peter Elbow, copyright (c) 1973, 1998 by Peter Elbow. Used with permission of Oxford University Press.

"My Graduation Speech," from *Conscientious Objections* by Neil Postman, copyright (c) 1988 by Neil Postman. Used by permission of Alfred A. Knopf, a division of Random House.

"Upon Receiving the Nobel Prize for Literature, 1950, " copyright (c) by William Faulkner, from *Essays,*

INDEX